Epistemology for the Rest of the World

EPISTEMOLOGY FOR THE REST OF THE WORLD

Edited by
Masaharu Mizumoto
Stephen Stich
Eric McCready

OXFORD
UNIVERSITY PRESS

Oxford University Press is a department of the University of Oxford. It furthers
the University's objective of excellence in research, scholarship, and education
by publishing worldwide. Oxford is a registered trade mark of Oxford University
Press in the UK and certain other countries.

Published in the United States of America by Oxford University Press
198 Madison Avenue, New York, NY 10016, United States of America.

© Oxford University Press 2018

CIP data is on file at the Library of Congress
ISBN 978-0-19-086508-5

9 8 7 6 5 4 3 2 1

Printed by Sheridan Books, Inc., United States of America

CONTENTS

MANIFESTO

STEPHEN STICH AND MASAHARU MIZUMOTO

Anglophone scholars in the human sciences often unwittingly frame their research hypotheses in English-specific terms. For example, when evolutionary biologists postulate a "universal sense of right and wrong" or puzzle over the evolutionary origins of "animal altruism," there is little awareness of the problematical fact that their words "right," "wrong," and "altruism" are English-specific constructs that lack precise equivalents in many languages of the world, including many European languages (Goddard and Wierzbicka 2014, 251).

Philosophers who refuse to bother about semantics, on the grounds that they want to study the nonlinguistic world and not our talk about that world, resemble astronomers who refuse to bother about the theory of telescopes, on the grounds that they want to study the stars and not our observation of them. Such an attitude may be good enough for amateurs; applied to more advanced inquiries, it produces crude errors. Those metaphysicians who ignore language in order not to project it onto the world are the very ones most likely to fall for just that fallacy, because the validity of their reasoning depends on unexamined assumptions about the structure of the language in which they reason (Williamson 2006).

1. A BIT OF HISTORY

Throughout much of the history of Western philosophy, the central goals of epistemology have included giving an account of what knowledge is, explaining how knowledge is possible, and setting out and defending a normative account of belief revision that specifies the good and bad ways of forming and updating beliefs. Many methods were used in an effort to achieve these goals.

In the middle years of the twentieth century, a new method became enormously influential in many branches of philosophy. The analysis of philosophically important concepts came to be seen as the central project of philosophy, and the method to be used was the careful examination of the ordinary use of words. This philosophical movement became known as "The Linguistic Turn" (Rorty [1962]1992), and its method was embraced by many philosophers concerned with epistemological issues. For example, according to Norman Malcolm,

> If we want to examine the use of a word we must study the use of the sentences in which the word occurs. We investigate the *concept of knowledge* by studying the usage of sentences in which "know" and cognate words occur. (1951, 336; emphasis added)

More recently, epistemology has seen what Peter Ludlow has dubbed "the new linguistic turn," as philosophers debating the contextualist response to skepticism and related issues have "explored the possibility that there might be linguistic evidence for or against" contextualism. Ludlow (2005) goes on to note that though the new linguistic turn in epistemology "breaks with the original linguistic turn in a number of respects, [it] follows it in the idea that we can use features of our language of knowledge attribution to support or . . . refute certain positions in epistemology" (12). A great deal has been written about the historical and philosophical reasons for the "first" linguistic turn; it is widely agreed that Wittgenstein played an important role, and so did Logical Positivism.

However, many philosophers have argued that the linguistic turn led epistemology in the wrong direction. Quine (1969) urged that epistemology should be naturalized and treated as a branch of psychology. Kornblith (2002, 28) agrees that epistemology should be naturalized and argues that knowledge is a natural kind to be studied by cognitive ethology. Sosa (2007) argues that the claim that analytic philosophy in general, and epistemology in particular, is primarily concerned with conceptual analysis is "deplorably misleading" (100). And Allan Hazlett (2010) has argued that the marriage of epistemology and the linguistic analysis of ordinary language is an unhappy one and it is time for a divorce.

2. THE MOTIVATION FOR THIS VOLUME

The challenges to the linguistic turns in epistemology raised by these philosophers and others are interesting and important. They were the backdrop for the planning of this volume. But on center stage when we decided to assemble the volume was a feature of the linguistic turns in epistemology that has received much less attention. The linguistic turns did not merely claim that we can "use features of the language of knowledge attribution to support or refute certain positions in epistemology" (Ludlow). Rather, as the earlier quote from Ludlow makes clear, it claimed that we can use features of "our" language, and "our language" was almost always English. The new linguistic turn in epistemology attempts to use features of contemporary English knowledge attribution to support or refute certain positions in epistemology. In a similar way, the first linguistic turn in epistemology was actually aimed at analyzing the concept of knowledge used by contemporary speakers of English, by studying the usage of English sentences in which the English word "know" and cognate words occur.

The central question we want to pose in this volume is: *Is there any justification for this practice*? Another way to pose the question is: *What's so special about contemporary English*?

3. WHAT'S SO SPECIAL ABOUT ENGLISH?

Contemporary English is one of approximately 6,000 languages spoken in the world. It is the native language of less than 6% of the world's population. Moreover, when Western epistemology emerged, in Ancient Greece, English did not exist. So why should the usage of sentences in contemporary English in which "know" and cognate words occur, the concept of knowledge expressed by those words, or features of the language of knowledge attribution in contemporary English, play any special role in epistemology?

In addition to their theoretical importance, we suspect that these questions are of considerable *practical importance* for philosophers around the world. Though it is not often openly discussed, we think there is reason to believe that the dominant role of English usage and English locutions of knowledge attribution has a demoralizing effect on many philosophers outside the English-speaking world. Young philosophers who were initially interested in epistemology are, we believe, growing disillusioned with contemporary epistemology, where subtle facts about English usage are given great weight, and facts about Japanese or Chinese or Hindi or Korean usage are never mentioned. This may be part of the explanation for the relative lack of interest in and sympathy with analytic epistemology in Japan and elsewhere in Asia.

Is there any justification for this practice? One possible answer invokes what might be called the *universality thesis*, which claims that the properties of the English word "know," English sentences of the form "S knows that p," and related locutions that have been studied by Anglophone epistemologists are shared by the standard translations of these expressions in most or all languages. If this were true, then the focus on English would simply be a matter of convenience for the vast majority of analytic epistemologists who are native speakers of or fluent in English.

There are a number of different ways in which the universality thesis has been or might be defended. Some of them are quite general, making claims about all sentences in all natural languages. Others are specific to lexical terms like "know" or sentences involving them. We'll start with the general defenses.

According to Jerrold J. Katz (1976), what makes natural languages unique is what he calls the "effability thesis": "Every proposition is the sense of some sentence in each natural language" (37). And the effability thesis, Katz maintains, entails the "translatability thesis":

> For any pair of natural languages and for any sentence S in one and any sense σ of S, there is at least one sentence S' in the other language such that σ is a sense of S'. (39)

Similar claims have been made by Sapir (1949) and van Benthem (1991). Von Fintel and Matthewson (2008) maintain that "a weakened version of translatability [that allows differences in presuppositions, implicature, etc., but still] maintains that at the level of core truth-conditional content, what one language can express any other can express as well . . . is a position that is quite widespread among linguists, and it seems like a reasonable stance to us as well" (2008, 146).

However, it is far from clear that either effability or translatability would provide the kind of universality that would be needed to justify the practice of focusing on English terms and sentences in epistemology and elsewhere in philosophy. For Katz and other defenders of the translatability thesis concede that there may be lexical items in one language (say, English) that have no translation into some other languages. For example, there are no words in Pirahã for "neutrino" and "mass," and no (current) way to translate "Neutrinos have mass." But Katz (1976) views this as merely a "temporary vocabulary gap" (40). Von Fintel and Matthewson follow suit, quoting Sapir (1949) saying it is "purely and simply a matter of vocabulary and of no interest whatever from the standpoint of linguistic form" (154). But if there are no sentences in contemporary Japanese (or Mandarin or Hindi) that have the same truth-conditional content as English sentences of the form "S knowns that p," and no sentences in contemporary English that have the same truth-conditional content as Japanese sentences of the form "S shitte-iru *p*" or "S wakatte-iru *p*" (which are typically viewed as the standard translations of "S knows that *p*"), then it is hard to see how the practice of focusing on English usage in epistemology would be vindicated by the (alleged) fact that a new term which captures the concept expressed by the English term "knows" could be introduced into Japanese.

A more promising approach to defending the universality thesis puts general claims about the nature of language to one side and focuses on the contemporary English term "know," the concept it expresses, and the use of contemporary English sentences of the form "S knows that *p*." If the concept is expressed by an ordinary expression in all languages, then the practice of focusing on contemporary English terms, concepts, and sentences in epistemology is much less problematic (though *not* unproblematic, since one might have concerns about the "linguistic turns" themselves).

Perhaps the best known defenders of the claim that "know" is a lexical universal are Anna Wierzbicka and Cliff Goddard, the leaders of the Natural Semantic Metalanguage (NSM) program. According to Wierzbicka and Goddard, "know" is a *semantic prime* common to all languages (Goddard 2010, 462 and 474; Wierzbicka 2011, 382; Goddard and Wierzbicka 2014, 12). Though this is interesting and provocative work, we are not convinced that the evidence offered by researchers in the NSM tradition supports a version of the universality thesis that will vindicate the focus on contemporary English in epistemology. At the center of our concern is the criterion of concept identity and cross-linguistic meaning identity that is appropriate for an epistemological analysis of knowledge.

Frank Jackson (1998) maintains that if an English speaker's intuitions about Gettier cases are different from "ours" (i.e., his and those of most philosophers), and if it is clear that she is not confused about the cases being considered, then the right thing to conclude is that her concept of knowledge is different from "ours." But the evidence marshaled in the NSM tradition gives us no reason at all to think that speakers of all languages share "our" Gettier intuitions. Indeed, there is some evidence suggesting that not all English speakers share "our" Gettier intuitions (Starmans and Friedman 2012, 2014). Jackson's view on concept individuation (or something close to it) was shared by Fred Dretske (pers. comm. with Mizumoto). The sort of evidence about Gettier intuitions that Jackson and Dretske would require before concluding that many (or most or all) languages have a term expressing the same concept that "know" expresses in English was not available to Wierzbicka and Goddard. So if this, or something in this vicinity, is the appropriate notion of concept identity for epistemology—and we think it is—then Wierzbicka and Goddard have not come close to showing that "know" is a semantic universal.

Similarly, if "know" in English is factive, then, for epistemological purposes, a verb in another language does not have the same meaning if it is non-factive. But here again the evidence marshaled in the NSM tradition clearly does not establish that verbs standardly translated as "know" are factive. Indeed, in an influential paper, Allan Hazlett (2010) has argued that "know" in English is not factive! We take no stand on Hazlett's provocative claim. What makes his paper important for our purposes is that it shows how *hard* it is to establish whether a verb is factive. If it has not been done for "know" in contemporary English, it is clear that work in the NSM tradition has not shown whether the standard translations for "know" are factive in Japanese (or Mandarin or Hindi or Pirahã). This provides another reason for concluding that Wierzbicka, Goddard, and their colleagues have not made a persuasive case that "know" is the sort of semantic universal that would justify the practice of epistemologists focusing on the contemporary English term "know" and the concept it expresses.

Is the universality thesis true? The answer, we submit, is that at present, we really don't know. And since the universality thesis is the most obvious way to defend the prevailing practice of focusing on the epistemic language and epistemic concepts of contemporary English speakers, it is important to find out. Thus, the most important claim of our manifesto is that *epistemologists (and linguists, and psychologists and experimental philosophers) should pay much more attention to the epistemic language and epistemic concepts that prevail in cultures around the world.* Cross-linguistic and cross-cultural analysis of epistemic terms, sentences, and concepts has a crucial role to play in philosophical epistemology.

One possible outcome of the cross-linguistic and cross-cultural studies that we are urging is the discovery that "know" and its standard translations are indeed cross-cultural universals, expressing the same concept and exhibiting the same linguistic properties in all languages. This would be a remarkable discovery that would cry out for an explanation. It would open an important new area of interdisciplinary inquiry. The other possible outcome—and the one we suspect is more likely—is that the universality thesis is false, and that the epistemic concepts and locutions of contemporary English are culturally local and do not have close counterparts in many other languages and cultures. How should epistemologists deal with this outcome?

We think it important for epistemologists to explore and debate the options. In the remainder of this brief manifesto, we'll sketch three of those options, though we are under no illusion that they are the only options, or the best ones.

4. THREE WAYS OF DEALING WITH THE FALSEHOOD OF THE UNIVERSALITY THESIS

The first option we'll consider is suggested by Paul Grice (1989) in a passage in which he considers the possibility that other people may not use the philosophically important expressions he is analyzing in the same way he does.

> Even if my assumption that what goes for me goes for others is mistaken, it does not matter; my philosophical puzzles have arisen in connection with my use of E [some philosophically troubling expression], and my conceptual analysis will be of value to me (and to any others who may find that their use of E coincides with mine). (75)

In a recent article, Avner Baz (2012) expands on Grice's proposal, offering the following Grice-inspired response to the possibility of cross-cultural diversity in philosophical concepts:

> It seems eminently plausible that people who are sufficiently different from each other in their basic sensibilities, practices, and metaphysical commitments will also be different from each other, more or less significantly and more or less pervasively, in their concepts. . . . However, if the prevailing program can help us become clearer just with respect to our concepts—the ones we share only with those sufficiently like us . . . —this is enough to make it worth pursuing. The answer to [the] question of why we should care about what is merely our concept is accordingly simple: because it is ours, and to become clearer about it is to become clearer about those features and dimensions of ourselves and of our world to which this concept is responsive and of which it is therefore revelatory. (323)

Of course, people in other cultures can say exactly the same thing: "My conceptual analysis will be of value to me and to any others who may find that their use of

知っている (Japanese)
जानना　　　 (Hindi)
知道　　　　 (Chinese)
알고있다　　 (Korean)
ຮູ້ຈັກ　　　 (Lao)
دری　　　　 (Arabic)

coincides with mine." So, the Gricean reaction to linguistic and conceptual diversity suggests a fragmentation of epistemology into

English epistemology
Japanese epistemology
Hindi epistemology
Chinese epistemology
Korean epistemology
Lao epistemology
Arabic epistemology

And so on. Here, it might be argued that these language-linked "epistemologies" should not be considered part of epistemology at all. Rather, they might more plausibly be viewed as part of linguistics—perhaps a part of comparative lexical semantics. One might also ask whether when a Japanese-speaking philosopher says "S 知っている p" (which is standardly translated as "S knows that p") and an English-speaking philosopher says "S does not know that p," are they really disagreeing?

As we noted earlier, Hazlett (2010) has suggested that we "give up on the linguistic method" in epistemology, and has advocated "a divorce for the linguistic theory of knowledge attributions and traditional epistemology" (500). Though his reasons do not appeal to linguistic and conceptual diversity, a "Hazlett divorce" might be one tempting response to cross-cultural differences.

The final option we will mention is to integrate the findings about the epistemic language and epistemic concepts in many cultures to build a multicultural and multi-linguistic epistemology. This is an enticing idea. But it is far from clear—to us—how such a project could be carried out. One of our hopes in assembling this volume is that it will stimulate philosophical thought on what a multicultural and multi-linguistic epistemology might be.

REFERENCES

Baz, Avner. (2012). "Must Philosophers Rely On Intuitions?" *Journal of Philosophy* 109 (4): 316–337.

Goddard, Cliff. (2010). "The Natural Semantic Metalanguage Approach." In *The Oxford Handbook of Linguistic Analysis*, ed. Bernd Heine and Heiko Narrog, 459–484. Oxford: Oxford University Press.

Goddard, Cliff, and Anna Wierzbicka. (2014). *Words and Meanings.* Oxford: Oxford University Press.

Grice, Paul. (1989). *Studies in the Way of Words*. Cambridge, MA: Harvard University Press.

Hazlett, Allan. (2010). "The Myth of Factive Verbs." *Philosophy and Phenomenological Research* 80(3): 497–522.

Jackson, Frank. (1998). *From Metaphysics to Ethics: A Defense of Conceptual Analysis*. Oxford: Oxford University Press.

Katz, Jerrold J. (1976). "A Hypothesis About the Uniqueness of Natural Language." In *Origins and Evolution of Language and Speech*, ed. Stevan R. Harnad, Horst D. Steklis, and Jane Lancaster, 33–41. *Annals of the New York Academy of Sciences*, 280.

Kornblith, H. (2002). *Knowledge and Its Place in Nature*. Oxford: Clarendon Press.

Ludlow, Peter. (2005). "Contextualism and the New Linguistic Turn in Epistemology." 11–50. In *Contextualism in Philosophy: Knowledge, Meaning, and Truth*, ed. Gerhard Preyer and Georg Peter, New York: Oxford University Press.

Malcolm, N. (1951). Philosophy for philosophers. *The Philosophical Review*, 60(3), 329–340.

Quine. W. V. (1969). "Epistemology Naturalized." *Ontological Relativity and Other Essays*, 69–90. New York: Columbia University Press.

Rorty, Richard, ed. ([1962]1992). *The Linguistic Turn*. Chicago: Chicago University Press.

Sapir, E. (1949). The psychological reality of the phoneme. Reprinted in English translation in: DC Mandelbaum (ed.) Selected writings of Edward Sapir. Berkeley and Los Angeles.

Sosa, E. (2007). "Experimental Philosophy and Philosophical Intuition." *Philosophical Studies* 132: 99–107.

Starmans, C., and O. Friedman. (2012). "The Folk Conception of Knowledge." *Cognition* 124: 272–283.

Starmans, C., and O. Friedman. (2014). "No, No, KNOW! Academic Disciplines Disagree About the Nature of Knowledge." Paper presented at the Common-Sense Beliefs and Lay Theories Preconference at the Fifteenth Annual Society for Personality and Social Psychology, Austin, Texas.

Van Benthem, Johan. (1991). "Linguistic Universals in Logical Semantics." In *Semantic Universals and Universal Semantics*, ed. D. Zaefferer, 17–36. GRASS series. Berlin: Foris.

Von Fintel, K., and L. Matthewson. (2008). "Universals in Semantics." *Linguistic Review* 25(1–2): 139–201.

Wierzbicka, Anna. (2011). "Common Language of All People: The Innate Language of Thought." *Problems of Information Transmission* 47(4): 878–897.

Williamson, T. (2006). Must do better. *Truth and Realism*, 177–187.

CONTRIBUTORS

Alexander, Joshua (Philosophy Department, Siena College)

Arakawa, Kiyohide (Faculty of Regional Policy, Aichi University)

Chatterjee, Amita (Department of Philosophy, Jadavpur University)

Ganeri, Jonardon (College of Arts and Science, New York University)

Glougie, Jennifer (Department of Linguistics, The University of British Columbia)

Gonnerman, Chad (Philosophy Department, University of Southern Indiana)

Hashimoto, Takaaki (Department of Social Psychology, The University of Tokyo)

Hazlett, Allan (Department of Philosophy, Washington University in St. Louis)

Iida, Takashi (Department of Philosophy, College of Humanities and Sciences, Nihon University)

Karasawa, Kaori (Department of Social Psychology, Tokyo University)

Lien, Chinfa (Graduate Institute of Linguistics , National Tsing Hua University)

Machery, Edouard (History and Philosophy of Science, University of Pittsburgh)

Matthewson, Lisa (Department of Linguistics, University of British Columbia)

McCready, Eric (Department of English and American Literature, Aoyama Gakuin University)

Mi, Chienkuo (Philosophy Department, Soochow University, Taiwan; Philosophy School, Nankai University)

Mizumoto, Masaharu (School of Knowledge Science, Japan Advanced Institute of Science and Technology)

Rose, David (Philosophy, Neuroscience and Psychology Program, Washington University, St. Louis)

Ryan, Shane (Department of History, Philosophy, and Religious Studies, Nazarbayev University)

Sirker, Smita (Centre for Philosophy, School of Social Sciences, Jawaharlal Nehru University)

Stich, Stephen (Department of Philosophy & Center for Cognitive Science, Rutgers University)

Struchiner, Noel (Catholic University of Rio de Janeiro)

Tsai, Cheng-hung (Philosophy Department, Soochow University, Taiwan)

Turri, John (Philosophy Department and Cognitive Science Program, University of Waterloo)

Usui, Naoki (Faculty of Humanities, Law and Economics, Mie University)

Waterman, John (Department of History and Philosophy, University of New England)

Wierzbicka, Anna (Department of Linguistics, Australian National University)

Yan, Karen (Institute of Philosophy of Mind and Cognition, National Yang-Ming University)

Epistemology for the Rest of the World

Introduction

In the contemporary world, the use of English is becoming more and more dominant. Naturally, the same is true in philosophy. Thus, even philosophers in the "rest of the world" use English to discuss philosophy, and they even write papers in English. There is, however, nothing inherent in philosophy that requires the use of English. The use of English in philosophy is utterly a contingent consequence of political and economic history. Exactly the same philosophy could have been done using any language other than English. Or so we are supposed to think. But is this true? How about epistemology, in which the use of "know" (and other epistemic terms) plays a crucial role?

This kind of question was one of the main motivations for the conference "Epistemology for the Rest of the World," held in Tokyo in 2013, from which this volume has sprung. The volume consists of twelve chapters, some being papers originally presented at the conference, some newly invited. More than half the authors are philosophers, but the others are linguists. They discuss various issues surrounding what is called the "universality thesis" in this book's manifesto—the thesis that, roughly speaking, properties of the English word "know" are shared by counterparts in most or all other languages. Some argue directly against this thesis, some defend it, and others discuss methodological or metaphilosophical issues surrounding the debate.

The first several chapters focus on some non-English languages. Opening the volume is Jonardon Ganeri's "Epistemology from a Sanskritic Point of View" (chapter 1), which is literally an investigation of epistemology in Sanskrit literature. There, the author explicitly argues against the universality thesis. Ganeri starts with the neologisms like "true/false knowledge" and "valid/invalid knowledge" that the readers of the translations of Sanskrit philosophical texts typically encounter. They followed from the confusion of one Sanskrit noun (*jñāna*), which is not factive, with another (*pramā*), which is indeed factive. Naturally, we should use the latter to translate the English word "knowledge." He even suggests that if Pranab Sen and Allan Hazlett are right, in that the English "know" is not factive either, "*pramā* is actually a better term to capture the normative concept epistemologists are interested in than *knowledge* is." (14). In this sense, Ganeri admits the possibility that one natural language is *better suited to do epistemology* than other languages (so that other languages should better adopt the vocabulary of a "better" language to do epistemology). An interesting point of this noun (*pramā*) is that it refers to a "successful performance" of an "act of experiencing," like hitting the target. Thus, in Sanskrit intuition, "epistemology is to be pictured as a cognitive performance." (15). This is contrasted with the static nature (mainly expressing a state) of the English counterpart (*knowledge*), whose consequence is the notion of justification in anglophone epistemology. There is no counterpart of epistemic justification in Sanskrit, he argues, and even states that "justification is a parochial feature of a way of thinking rooted in English lexical quirks." (*ibid.*). Ganeri then proceeds to present four "Śrīharṣa cases," which are supposed to show that there can be accurate experience without epistemic success, or the twelfth-century Gettier cases. They are all highly relevant to contemporary epistemological discussions, but Śrīharṣa's aim is to show that the act of defining epistemic success is absurd, which contemporary epistemologists like Williamson would be delighted to hear (given his knowledge-first approach). But Ganeri also contrasts Śrīharṣa's own view about the cases with the view of another Sanskrit philosopher, Gaṅgeśa, who claims that such Śrīharṣa cases are still cases of epistemic success (*pramā*), only succeeding in a fragile (rather than robust) way. We may find the exact analogues of such a debate in contemporary epistemology.

Takashi Iida's "Knowledge and Belief Through the Mirror of Japanese" (chapter 2) discusses Japanese counterparts of the English "know" and "believe," with careful and informative grammatical details of the Japanese language in general. Such Japanese mental verbs are unique in their sensitivity to the difference in grammatical person. For example, the mental verbs in Japanese counterpart of "I think Taro went home" have, even though they are used in the basic form, a special grammatical person restriction such that they cannot be used in the corresponding third-person sentence in that form. Interestingly, there is no corresponding restriction in the case of the Japanese counterpart of "I know Taro went home." The

Japanese knowledge verb (here he assumes *shiru*) simply cannot be used in its basic form (radical *shi* + suffix *ru*) in any person (either the first, second, or third) to express a state of knowledge.[1] Iida tries to explain this kind of phenomenon in terms of the aspectual properties of these verbs. He then focus on the complements of Japanese mental verbs, and argues that such verbs take two kinds of sentential complement, one for their objects and the other for their contents, which are grammatically distinguished in Japanese. Based on this consideration, Iida explains the factivity of the Japanese knowledge verb. In conclusion, he suggests that the consideration of this grammatically encoded difference of complement structure "may lead us to discover some conceptual possibilities which we may not notice or have a difficulty to do so if we have only English as our clue."

Kiyohide Arakawa and Masaharu Mizumoto examine Chinese knowledge verbs, in contrast with their Japanese and English counterparts, in "Multiple Chinese Verbs Equivalent to the English Verb "Know" (chapter 3). They pick out three Chinese knowledge verbs (*renshi*, *zhidao*, and *liaojie*) and differentiate the syntactical and semantic characters of them. The interesting aspect of knowledge verbs that the authors focus on is the extent of activity implied by each one. On the one hand, "know" is basically a stative verb (expressing a state of affairs), but it also has a nonstative use. On the other hand, the Japanese knowledge verb (*shiru*) is a punctual (instantaneous or nondurative) verb, while it also has a progressive form (*shitteiru*) for expressing a state. However, Chinese verbs do not have a natural use as active verbs without auxiliary verbs or being in the past tense. In particular, in Japanese and English there are natural (though idiomatic) uses as an order (like "Know yourself"), or perfectly natural uses of "I decided to know" and its counterpart in Japanese, but there is no natural use of their counterparts using Chinese knowledge verbs. Through such observations, epistemologists may infer how significant the possible epistemological implications of such differences are.

Although Arakawa and Mizumoto focus on contemporary Chinese knowledge verbs, Shane Ryan and Chienkuo Mi discuss ancient Chinese knowledge verbs as used in the *Analects*, in their "The Contribution of Confucius to Virtue Epistemology" (chapter 4). Two such verbs (*zhi* and *shi*) roughly correspond to, they claim, Sosa's animal knowledge and reflective knowledge. Their topic then, naturally, is the relationship between Confucian philosophy and virtue epistemology. They present the case for regarding Confucius as an epistemological thinker, rather than (as

---

1. In order to do so, we need to add, typically what is usually taken as an aspect marker, *tei*, as in *shitteiru*.

generally considered) an ethical thinker. By extracting the epistemological significance of Confucian thought, they aim to make a contribution to contemporary epistemology, just as Ganeri does for Sanskrit. For example, the distinction of two Chinese verbs for reflection (省 and 思) may contribute to the debate over the epistemological significance of reflection, proposed by virtue epistemologists but criticized by Kornblith. They use the Fake Barn case to demonstrate the account using such a distinction. They then suggest a possible contribution to social epistemology by extracting a theory of "extended knowledge," drawing on another Confucian text, *The Great Learning*.

Even though, by emphasizing linguistic diversity these authors are apparently against the universality thesis, they nonetheless aim at a positive contribution to epistemology, and in doing so are not questioning the unity of the concept of knowledge. In contrast, Masaharu Mizumoto, in his "'Know' and Its Japanese Counterparts: *Shitte-iru* and *Wakatte-iru*" (chapter 5), maintains the true pluralism of the concepts of knowledge. He also discusses the Japanese knowledge verb *shiru* (as Iida and Arakawa & Mizumoto have also discussed), but claims that there is another verb for propositional knowledge in Japanese, *wakaru*. He first examines these two Japanese knowledge verbs first through the data of felicity judgment, and then through the data of questionnaire research with standard epistemological vignettes. Even though these verbs are mostly intersubstitutable, such data show significant differences of use in many epistemologically interesting cases (including the TrueTemp case), where one use is independent of practical concerns while another is sensitive to practical abilities. The comparison with English "know" suggests that, contrary to what almost all Japanese think, the standard translation of "know" into Japanese is not closer to the other Japanese knowledge verb. At the same time, the difference between these Japanese knowledge verbs actually corresponds with the opposition in many epistemological debates. This therefore raises a serious question of what anglophone epistemologists are disputing when they debate the notion of knowledge based on the English "know." Indeed, even if (though unlikely) their concept of knowledge (let alone their intuitions about it) is completely independent of English "know," the skepticism about a "right" view of knowledge lingers, since this is like asking which of two Japanese knowledge verbs is the "right" one. Mizumoto claims that, even though cross-linguistic study of this sort is usually plagued with worries of cultural difference, since this study is immune to such worry (with two verbs being used by the same speakers), it conclusively establishes that there are multiple, different concepts of knowledge (as long as these two Japanese verbs are knowledge verbs at all).

Unlike these first five chapters, in chapter 7, Lisa Matthewson and Jennifer Glougie focus on the notions of justification and truth in "Justification and Truth: Evidence from Languages of the World." They use data from many different languages, and investigate whether and how languages encode the epistemological concepts of justification and truth. According to the authors, many languages provide speakers with conventionalized ways to track their level of justification for what speakers assert, and to emphasize their commitment to its truth. In particular, they argue that a subset of evidential elements tracks whether speakers' evidence meets a certain threshold of reliability, based on the data of justification-based evidentials in Cuzco Quechua, Nivacle, St'át'imcets, Nɬeʔkepmxcín, and English. They show some universal aspect of the types of evidence that count as providing justification, which they argue is similar across these languages. Matthewson and Glougie also find universality in truth through their investigation of verum emphasis (or the speaker's emphasis on truth) in German, English, and Gitksan, an examination that shows striking cross-linguistic similarities in the properties of the construction. For these authors, "the linguistic evidence reveals some potentially important insights about how humans view truth." (165). They then point to the similarity of discourse conditions under which speakers encode the truth and those under which they encode justification. Both justification-based evidentials and verum emphasis appear when speakers need to defend their assertions against implied or explicit disagreement or skepticism. Thus "the cross-linguistic similarities in both justification encoding and verum behavior suggest that these phenomena reveal something about how humans view the concepts of justification, truth, and ultimately perhaps knowledge." (173–4)

John Waterman, Chad Gonnerman, Karen Yan, and Joshua Alexander address epistemic universalism, a variant of the universality thesis that epistemic intuitions are culturally universal, in their "Knowledge, Certainty, and Skepticism: A Cross-Cultural Study" (chapter 8). They investigate the relationships between cultural background, folk knowledge attribution, and "salience effects" (where making certain possibilities salient affects knowledge attribution), using participants from the United States, China, and India (using Mandarin for Chinese subjects, and both English and Hindi for Indians). While they suggest that epistemic universalism underwrites ordinary practice in contemporary epistemology, their data suggest that even though salience effects are culturally universal, their strength is not. In particular, what Waterman and colleagues found is that subjective certainty affects the relationship between salience and folk knowledge attribution, but its magnitude changes from one culture to another. They claim that, their findings suggest a new view of epistemic universalism, which allows for *both* similarity and difference of patterns in epistemic intuitions. Note also that although Waterman and colleagues take the relevant factor to be cultural rather than linguistic variance, the linguistic diversity is still relevant here, as they would admit, and their conclusion is still subject to revision by future discoveries about the speakers of other languages.

The rest of the chapters in this volume are concerned more with methodological and metaphilosophical issues, although most of them are also committed to their own views on the universality thesis. For example, chapter 6, "Gettier Was Framed," by Edouard Machery and colleagues, discusses data from Brazil, Japan, India, and the United States. What the authors found is an impressive similarity in the patterns of responses by people across cultures and languages. There was one anomaly in part of the Indian data, which they explain as a special feature of the knowledge verb in Bengali (and in Sanskrit; see also Ganeri, chapter 1, this volume). Their main emphasis, however, is on the validity of the method of cases in epistemology more than on the universality thesis. If there were significant differences in Gettier intuitions across cultures, the method of cases would have been questioned. However, they also found some differences owing to other factors, presumably shared by all cultures and languages—namely, framing effects (effects of variations in irrelevant narrative details) and order effects (effects of variations in the order in which cases are presented), which they call "presentation effects." Owing to such effects, they claim, it is not clear whether people's intuitions support the epistemologists' assumption about Gettier cases (that the protagonist does not know), and they recommend we suspend judgment about such cases. This, according to them, will cast doubt on the method of cases in philosophy in general.

In chapter 9, "I KNOW: A Human Universal," Anna Wierzbicka, who is the founder of the NSM (Natural Semantic Metalanguage) program, argues directly for the universality thesis, claiming that KNOW is "an indefinable and universal human concept." She cites examples not only from French, German, and (her native) Polish but also from Russian, Australian aboriginals (such as Warlpiri), and others, as well as from Old English. An interesting point is that even though Wierzbicka claims that all cultures have the same concept of "knowing" (she distinguishes it from the concept of "knowledge," claiming that the latter is not universally shared), she also says that we should not be comparing cultures in terms of "justified true belief" "because neither 'justified' nor 'belief' are universal human concepts" (225, whereas "true" is found in all languages and therefore can "serve as a tool for cross-cultural comparison"). Thus, given this observation, Wierzbicka claims that, "universal meanings such as KNOW, THINK, TRUE, and MAYBE give us better tools for investigating 'core folk epistemology' across cultures than language- and culture-specific ones like "believe," "justified belief," or "knowledge" (*ibid.*). It should be noted that her claim of the universality of a concept is based on the a few relevant "canonical sentences," which provide "specified and cross-translatable contexts" (223). In the case of "know," such canonical sentences (which she also calls "universal frames") are, "I know," "this someone knows it," "this someone knows something," and "this someone knows something about something." Interestingly, she opposes taking "know that" to be among such universal frames. She thinks that the view that the concept of knowledge is inherently linked with a that-clause is mistaken, and she analyzes "knowing that" in terms of the universal frame of "someone knows it" (section 9). Epistemologists may raise many questions about her main theses; even so, the virtue of this chapter partly lies in its details. For example, in discussing "knowing how" (she analyzes "knowing how" in terms of *knowing something*, rather than *knowing that*), she points out that the basic knowledge verb in Polish is used for "know how to open it" but not for "know how to swim" (241). This kind of fact seems very important for the contemporary epistemological debate of intellectualism versus anti-intellectualism. In a more general point also relevant to this volume, when in discussing the difficult questions of "indigenous knowledge," Wierzbicka argues that "[. . .] if the supposed 'indigenous' knowledge is described through English words which have no equivalents in indigenous languages, then the outcome does not represent authentic indigenous knowledge but an amalgam of indigenous knowledge and Anglo conceptualization (reflected in English-specific verbalization)" (232). She calls this "cultural opacity." It should be clear that this problem of opacity also exists in philosophy whenever epistemologists discuss knowledge, and may remain so even if they are careful enough to consider possible linguistic and cultural diversity.

However, Allan Hazlett, who is the proponent of "Divorce" in epistemology (see the manifesto, this volume), does not seem concerned about this issue in his "The Theory of Knowledge without (Comparative) Linguistics" (chapter 10). Even though Wierzbicka's claim was supposedly empirical, if it is an a priori assumption that every language must have a word that "knows" translates, as Hazlett claims, then it sounds like a "piece of chauvinism" (258). Moreover, he argues, even if it is empirically true (that every language has a counterpart of "know"), it does not follow that every language must have a word that is *synonymous* with "know," since, if he is right, it is a "mistake" to think that the best translation of a word requires it to be also synonymous with that word (*ibid.*). Thus, taking this to be a methodological concern in the theory of knowledge, Hazlett rejects the idea that linguistic evidence is relevant to the theory of knowledge, and instead proposes a project of theorizing knowledge in which linguistic evidence is irrelevant. Rather, he takes knowledge as an evaluative concept. This means, that it is even a "conceptual truth" that knowledge is *valuable* (259). While Hazlett admits that there are two aspects of knowledge—descriptive and evaluative—he thinks that the descriptive aspect should be settled merely by *stipulation* (*ibid.*). Instead, we should concentrate on the evaluative aspect of knowledge by investigating the value of various cognitive attitudes (that are candidates of knowledge)—which is, then, to ask what cognitive attitudes are valuable. He responds to the charge of cultural chauvinism by saying that we "can and often do engage in reasoned dialogue about evaluative matters with members of other cultures. Our evaluative judgments are not mere expressions of our parochial perspectives; they are claims that we hope to defend in a shared space of reasons, which we almost inevitably can discuss and debate with anyone who is willing" (263). Whether or not this answers the challenge in a satisfactory way, Hazlett's theory of knowledge is indeed open to the "reasoned dialogue," and to this extent, linguistic data of other languages are relevant, especially when speakers of one language think that a property of what their knowledge verb expresses is valuable, while speakers of another language do not because their own knowledge verb is insensitive to it. This volume is of course meant to provide the very first stage for such dialogue.

Cheng-hung Tsai and Chinfa Lien examine the universality thesis in their "On How to Defend or Disprove the Universality Thesis" (chapter 11). Using Stanley's intellectualism as a typical instance of the universality thesis, they claim that both its critics and its defenders presuppose a nonepistemic construal of the universality thesis. To spell out what the epistemic/nonepistemic construal is, Tsai and Lien distinguish three levels (linguistic-phenomenal/normative-phenomenal/meta-normative) of inquiries in the language of the epistemic. Thus, the rationale for the normative judgments (a third-level inquiry) may take the form, "It is correct to use this knowledge verb in this way *because* this is how the speakers of this language use it," which is not epistemic but merely conventional. It is this level (rationale) that they demand to be epistemic. Citing various claims that the Chinese model of knowledge differs significantly from the Western one, they ask whether the difference is epistemic or not. What philosophers count as the epistemic as a matter of fact (like knowledge, justification, evidence, reasoning, rationality, etc.), they claim, are all related to truth, although they themselves are not truth (276). So, for example, the rationale for the normative judgments of the form "This knowledge verb should be used in this way *because* this way of using it demotes a truth-conductive factor" *is* epistemic, according to the authors.

Tsai and Lien demand that, "if the study of cross-linguistic variation in epistemic terms intends to be significant in the *epistemological* research, the study must tell us how it defines the epistemic and how cross-linguistic variation relates to the epistemic it defines" (276–277, emphasis in original). Unfortunately, they claim, the participants of debates about the universality thesis (including Stanley and his opponents) presuppose only a nonepistemic construal of the universality thesis, which "distorts or neglects the crucial aspect of the universality thesis." That is, what should be claimed to be shared by epistemic verbs in all the languages is "the *epistemic* properties" (277). "If in the very beginning what motives human beings to study epistemology is the desire to figure out the particular relation between mind and world, then a study of the language of the epistemic, *if* it is an epistemological study, must tell us how linguistic properties of a particular language determines the particular relation between mind and world." (*ibid.*). Thus any alleged counterevidence to the universality thesis should, Tsai and Lien conclude, be "concerned with the metaphysical relation between mind and world, rather than a mere comparison of linguistic usages." (*ibid.*).

Finally, John Turri argues for the universality thesis from a very different perspective in his "Primate Social Cognition and the Core Human Knowledge Concept" (chapter 12). His question is whether humans possess a knowledge concept as part of universal "folk epistemology." Citing recent empirical results of cross-cultural and cross-linguistic studies, he hypothesizes that people do share some such universal concept of knowledge, but he criticizes armchair epistemologists who claim to the same effect, saying they mischaracterize ordinary knowledge judgments while acknowledging the plausibility of the motivations of their projects. Thus, he "blends" some such motivations from the armchair project and the cross-cultural empirical project (284). Rather than focusing on facts about specific languages, he thus turns to recent findings from comparative psychology and primatology (comparing humans with nonhuman primates), which he thinks establish that humans possess a species-typical knowledge concept. More specifically, these findings show that knowledge attributions are a central part of primate social cognition, used to predict others' behaviors and guide decision-making. The core human knowledge concept is that of truth detection (across different sensory modalities) and retention (through memory), and may also include rudimentary forms of indirect truth discovery through inference. In virtue of their evolutionary heritage, humans inherited the primate social-cognitive system and thus share this core knowledge concept. This seems, therefore, an instance of ethology-based naturalistic epistemology *à la* Kornblith. Turri concludes that "a knowledge concept is part of an ancient primate social-cognitive system" (286). which is a "species-typical knowledge concept whose essence cannot be fully understood by studying humans alone" (287). This is an approach very different from that taken by other authors in this volume, but certainly one convincing way of supporting the universality thesis. But whether this approach will succeed in effectively reducing (or dismissing) all the alleged conceptual differences presented in the earlier chapters of this volume, whether this "species-typical" concept is what contemporary epistemologists are really interested in, or even whether Turri's conclusion is really incompatible with the observations and data presented in the earlier chapters against the universality thesis should be left for future investigations.

Overall, the chapters by Ganeri, Iida, Ryan and Mi, and Mizumoto (and perhaps Arakawa and Mizumoto) claim the linguistic diversity of the (linguistic) concept of knowledge, while Wierzbicka and Turri explicitly (and Mathewson and Glougie indirectly through notions of truth and justification) argue for, and Machery and colleagues tentatively accept, the universality of it. Waterman and colleagues can also be taken to belong to the latter group. However, the first four authors (Ganeri, Iida, and Ryan and Mi) still assume the unity of the folk epistemological concept of knowledge that is independent of language-specific concepts, so that (by also assuming that such a folk concept is the epistemological concept of knowledge) the study of such linguistic diversity can directly *contribute to* epistemology. Mizumoto, alternatively, claims that there are multiple folk concepts of knowledge, and remains neutral or pessimistic about the reality of *the* epistemological concept of knowledge as long as it is a *folk* concept. In this sense, his position (suggesting information-theoretic approach as a possible alternative) is closer to Hazlett, who (while being neutral about the linguistic diversity of the concept of knowledge) is explicitly pessimistic about the direct route from linguistic concepts to an epistemological concept of knowledge. This is also a stance of Tsai and Lien, who are also cautious about the move from the folk to the epistemological. By questioning the method of cases, Machery and colleagues are nevertheless neutral or silent on this issue, while Turri is officially committed to the identification of the folk concept of knowledge with the epistemological concept of knowledge.

It is, of course, impossible to conclude the fate or prospect of the universality thesis here, which is the work to be done in further research by philosophers and linguists, but at the least we can say that it would be even *surprising* if all these linguistic considerations are *irrelevant* to epistemology. Also, the authors of the later chapters discussing the epistemological significances of possible cultural/linguistic diversity did not have access to chapters in the earlier part of this volume when they were writing. Some of these authors might change their minds after reading these chapters, while others might not. That is also the job of this volume's readers, as this is the first volume ever to investigate strictly this topic. The essays collected here will certainly play a significant role in future discussions of this important topic, or such is the hope of the editors of this volume.

Masaharu Mizumoto

CHAPTER 1

Epistemology from a Sanskritic Point of View

JONARDON GANERI

1. A CASE OF FALSE COGNATES

It is far from uncommon when reading translations of Sanskrit philosophical texts into English to encounter the neologisms "true knowledge,"
"false knowledge," "valid knowledge," and "invalid knowledge." At first
sight these phrases seem to indicate something amiss in the translator's
understanding of the concept of knowledge, for if knowledge is factive,
then surely phrases like "false knowledge" and "invalid knowledge" are
oxymorons (as in "faith unfaithful kept him falsely true")? If it is a conceptual truth about the English verb *know* that "S knows that *p*" entails
or presupposes that *p*, then the "true" in the phrase "true knowledge" is
redundant. In fact, these curious neologisms are very revealing about variations in the use of epistemic terminology between English and Sanskrit,
something that becomes clear when one looks to see which Sanskrit terms
are getting translated in this way. The key term being translated as "knowledge" is the Sanskrit noun *jñāna*, derived from the verb *jñā*. This noun is
cognate with Latin *cognosere*, with Greek *gnosis*, and so with English *knowledge*. In everyday Sanskrit usage, it is indeed often rightly translated as
"knowledge," and that is also the meaning one will find if one looks it up in
a Sanskrit–English dictionary. Yet, and this is where confusion comes in,
there is another meaning of *jñāna*, more common in the philosophical literature but also current in popular usage, where a better translation would

be *cognition*. Unlike *to know, to cognize* is not a factive verb, and when an event of cognition arises, there is a further question as to whether it is true or false. When used this way, the contrast being emphasized is with affective and conative states. A similar confusion has been noted with regard to the translation of Latin *cognitio* as used in early modern European works. Jonathan Bennett (1984) notes, for example, that the translation of *cognitio* as "knowledge" rather than as "cognition" "has negatively affected scholarship on Spinoza" (127). Thus, in philosophical Sanskrit, *jñāna* is a false cognate of English *knowledge*.

This fact is significant because the same term is inherited in many modern Indian languages including Hindi. So when experiments are conducted whose aim is to test the Gettier intuitions of Hindi speakers, and when the experimental questionnaire is translated from English into Hindi using *jñāna* as a translation for *knowledge*, the apparent discovery that Hindi speakers do not share anglophone intuitions about Gettier cases may be an aberration resulting from the use of a false cognate rather than constituting a genuine experimental finding about cross-cultural variation. There is an even greater risk of confusion when the test is performed in English on Indians speaking English as a second language. For what happens then is that the subject mentally translates the English word *knowledge* in the test scenario into Hindi *jñāna*, and is willing to say of a case that there is knowledge, but meaning only to assert thereby that there is cognition (see also Turri 2013, 9–13, and Seyedsayamdost 2015 for evidence that earlier reports of differences in Gettier intuitions among South Asians are not borne out by empirical study).

In philosophical Sanskrit, *jñāna* is distinguished from another epistemic term, *pramā*. The noun *pramā* is derived from the verb *pra+mā*, meaning "to measure." This noun, unlike *jñāna*, is indeed used factively; indeed, in standard works it is explicated as meaning an experience that represents things as they are (*yathārtha-anubhūti*). It is *pramā* which ends up being translated as "true knowledge" or "valid knowledge" by translators wishing to preserve this point and nevertheless regarding *knowledge* as a true cognate of *jñāna*. Matilal (2002) has summed up the whole situation rather well:

> The Sanskrit term *pramā* is usually translated by a careful translator today as "knowledge." This is certainly an improvement upon the older and wrong translation of *pramā* as "valid knowledge." It may be of some interest to see why such a mistaken phrase was offered by earlier (mostly Indian) scholars as a translation of *pramā*. A *pramā* is usually regarded as a special kind of *jñāna* whose truth is guaranteed. This is mostly, though not always, true in Sanskrit (classical) philosophical literature. The word *jñāna*, however, is sometimes used

for "knowledge" in ordinary Sanskrit. A knowledgeable person is called *jñānin*. Even in philosophical Sanskrit the distinction between *jñāna* (which can be better translated as a cognitive event or an awareness-episode) and *pramā* is not always maintained, and hence we see *jñāna* used indiscriminately for *pramā*; and it is left to us to gather from the context whether an ordinary cognitive event or a piece of knowledge is being referred to. This interchangeability of *jñāna* for *pramā* has apparently led modern interpreters of Indian philosophy to confuse the issue, and most of them have felt the need for some adjective like "valid" to qualify "knowledge" in order apparently to gain the full force of *pramā* which is distinct from ordinary awareness. This was at best misleading and at worst a blunder that perpetuated misunderstanding of Indian philosophical doctrines by English readers. (150)

2. PERFORMATIVE SANSKRIT *PRAMĀ* VERSUS STATIC ENGLISH *KNOWLEDGE*

I have noted that *pramā* is, unlike *jñāna*, factive. For Matilal, as we have seen, this brings the term closer to the English term *knowledge*. Recently, however, Pranab Sen has argued that English *know* is not factive (Sen 2000/2007; Hazlett 2012 has more recently also defended this claim, apparently without acquaintance with Sen's work). If he is right, then one possibility is that *pramā* is actually a better term to capture the normative concept epistemologists are interested in than *knowledge* is; *knowledge* in English would have parochial features that make it inappropriate or unsuitable for use in epistemology. If what we want to investigate is the epistemic credibility of our cognitive life, then perhaps the Sanskrit vocabulary of *pramā* is a better vehicle for doing so than the English vocabulary of knowledge. There is also an important difference in perspective encoded in the two vocabularies. This follows from the fact that both *pramā* and *jñāna* refer to cognitive episodes, while the English term *belief* normally denotes a dispositional state. Thus, *pramā* is to be analyzed not as true belief but as a true awareness episode. A consequence is that *pramā*, as a cognitive event, has a causal history, and when one asks if a given cognitive event is *pramā* or not (whether it has *pramātva*, *pramā*-ness), it is natural to seek an answer in the form of a causal explanation. One wonders whether the same causal factors that brought about the cognitive event also bring about its property of being true, for example. More generally, the term *pramā* refers to a successful performance of an act of experiencing, where success is a matter of experiencing things the way they are, hitting the truth, just as success for an archer is a matter of hitting the target with an arrow. In

Sanskrit intuition, epistemology is to be pictured as the study of cognitive performance.

The rather different picture that English vocabulary encourages is a static one in which there are standing dispositional states, somewhat like virtues, and the relevant question is not whether a performance is successful but whether a standing state is merited. Does the believer have the ability, if demanded to do so, to produce something that would count as evidence or justification for the claim that the belief is true? It would thus be wrong to translate *pramā* as *knowledge*, and then to wonder what counts as justification in the Sanskrit model. The answer is that nothing does, because justification is a parochial feature of a way of thinking rooted in English lexical quirks. A different question must be posed instead: Are there any important epistemic differences between different types of successful (truth-hitting) performances of experience?

3. RIVAL INTUITIONS ABOUT *PRAMĀ*

Contextualism is a claim about the semantics of epistemic attribution. As DeRose (1992) puts it, "The truth-conditions of 'S knows that *p*' vary depending on the context in which it is uttered" (914), context here including the interests, expectations, and so on of knowledge ascribers. As I will now show in some detail, two of the most important classical Indian epistemologists have strikingly divergent intuitions about the attribution-conditions of *pramā*. Śrīharṣa argues that truth alone does not suffice, and he presents a series of cases where a subject has a true awareness episode, but in which he claims no attribution of *pramā* is correct. Gaṅgeśa's opposing view is that truth is sufficient, even in these cases. What seems to be in question is whether Śrīharṣa's cases reveal something hidden about the truth-conditions of *pramā*—that more is in general called to ensure epistemic credibility than successful epistemic performance alone—or whether he is in fact manipulating our intuitions, that he is tutoring us into a new and more demanding way of using the term than is the case in ordinary speech.

I mentioned that for the ancients in India, epistemic success was a matter of cognizing nature (*tattva-jñāna*), experiencing things as they are (*yathārtha-anubhūti*). Outside of epistemic success lay not only inaccurate experience but also doubt, dream, hypothesis, assumption, and pretense. The value of epistemic success lay in the escape it afforded from the torments of a cognitive dystopia. It seemed to the ancients that the route to epistemic success was through the ability clearly to tell things apart, and so through clarification of concepts and formulation of definitions. This included clarity about the concept of epistemic success itself, and the varied provenance of epistemic success. For how could one inquire unless one knew the techniques and targets of inquiry; and only through inquiry can there be clarity, and so in the end peace of mind. The energies of the classical philosophers were therefore spent, and lavishly so, in the search for definitions.

Śrīharṣa, in the twelfth century, saw all this as the height of folly. Mastery of a concept does not require knowledge of a definition, and that is good because nothing anyway can be defined, not even knowledge. Śrīharṣa invents a practice of refutation to set against the practice of definition, but he is not against the things themselves: there is argument and there is philosophy, just as there is experience and there is language; what there is not are definitions. Śrīharṣa was no skeptic, therefore, nor was he a quietist of Nāgārjunian bent. He was perfectly happy to commit himself to large philosophical claims and to make use of the efficacy of argument. Śrīharṣa is not against philosophy but wants a more liberal philosophical method, using concepts but not fixing them. One need not have a definition of aesthetic greatness to appreciate a particular work of art as great. Śrīharṣa's argument that knowledge cannot be defined finds a more recent echo in the work of Timothy Williamson (2000; again, it is unfortunate that Williamson appears to be unacquainted with Śrīharṣa's earlier work).

Śrīharṣa's typical method of refutation was to tie the philosophers' definitions in so many dialectical knots that they eventually choked to death. He claimed to prefer this method because its very complexity discouraged abuse by the disingenuous. When it came to the definition of epistemic success, however, and only in this case, Śrīharṣa introduces a different approach (perhaps this is because Jayarāśi before him had tried the other approach without success). He tells miniature stories, the import of which is that there can be accurate experience which is not epistemic success. His stories serve to test—or perhaps to train—his readers' epistemic intuitions. Let me call such any such story a "Śrīharṣa case." His aim is not to show that the definition of epistemic success requires supplementation but, rather, that the act of defining epistemic success is absurd. This is why a Śrīharṣa case is different in ambition from a Gettier case in contemporary epistemology. A feature of the cases is that there is always an implied contrast scenario, and what is tested are the differential intuitions one has in the two scenarios. The first of four Śrīharṣa cases is the case of the Self-Confident Gambler. This gambler sees the closed fist of his opponent and is immediately convinced that the fist contains exactly five shells. His conviction is a pure guess, but Śrīharṣa is careful to point out that the fact that chance is involved does not allow us to respond that he does not really believe; for a farmer, too, is convinced that the scattered seeds will yield a crop, even knowing at the same time that chance events may intervene. And indeed there are five shells in the closed fist; the conviction is correct. The implied contrast scenario is one where all is the same except that there are four shells, not five, and the gambler's conviction is misplaced.

The second Śrīharṣa case is the case of the Deceived Deducer. A deduction is made to the effect that a fire is burning on the far-off mountain, based on the premise that a plume of smoke can be seen rising above it. What is seen, in fact, is a plume of mist in the crisp early morning air: the premise is false, but we are nevertheless to suppose that there is a fire and the deducer is accurate in his firmly inferred belief that this is so. Śrīharṣa says that the inferential belief that there is a fire on the mountain does not fall into the category of epistemic success (*pramā*), and it is not clear if he thinks he is simply reporting the intuition of any competent user of the Sanskrit word *pramā* or if he is actually tutoring those intuitions with the help of the story. It does not make any difference to the case that the deducer is not having a singular thought about a particular fire, and this case does in fact bear a structural resemblance to a standard Gettier case involving existentially quantified belief; and it was Matilal (1986, 135–140) who was the first to point this out—since then, other Indian examples have been found in the work of the Buddhist philosopher Dharmottara, and an extensive Tibetan discussion has also been found (Stoltz 2007). In Dharmottara's vivid example, a swarm of flies is taken as evidence that there is a piece of rotting meat: there is indeed meat there, but what looked like a swarm is in fact just black dust.

A third Śrīharṣa case is the case of the Misprimed Perceiver. A person spots a far-off creature and sees that it is a cow. The categorial perception is a result of the perceiver's exercise of an ability to distinguish cows from other four-legged creatures by the visual cue of having a dewlap. In this case, however, visual cuing is achieved by a piece of cloth that hangs under the cow's neck, not the dewlap; yet the perception is correct. Categorial perception is noninferential: the role of the visual cue is not to provide a premise in a deduction but, rather, to trigger categorization. Śrīharṣa claims that the miscuing undermines the perceiver's right to claim to know (and this example serves, by and by, to undermine Harman's "no false lemmas" strategy against Gettier).

A fourth and final Śrīharṣa case appears only later in the discussion, and for that reason is often overlooked. This is the case of the Lucky Listener. An entirely unreliable witness reports that there are five flowers on the bank of the river; and indeed there are. A second witness, this one wholly reliable, makes the same report. Here Śrīharṣa explicitly describes a pair of contrasting scenarios. In the first scenario, he seems to suggest, the listener has true belief but not epistemic success; in the second, the listener knows the reported fact. The point is that merely believing what one hears, even when true, is no way to know. Again, the Mādhyamika philosopher Candrakīrti had a similar example (and I wonder if Śrīharṣa knew of these Buddhist examples). Candrakīrti considers two people who testify to witnessing a crime, one actually having seen it happen and the other maliciously lying. Should the judge base a guilty verdict on the testimony of the second person, our intuition is that justice has not been done (Matilal 1986, 104). If fairness is to justice what truth is to epistemic success, then the point of the examples seems to be that conformity to a norm requires more than just getting it right.

One might be tempted initially to respond that in every case there is a fault in the functioning of the source of epistemic success, but Śrīharṣa argues that appeal to the origins of one's beliefs cannot solve the problem of definition. That is because there is no way to say what the fault is, in terms general enough to cover every case, other than that the fault is that the source of the belief has not yielded accuracy. The proposed definition is now that epistemic success is true belief produced by a source that produces a true belief, and the new condition clearly adds nothing to the original. To give an example, it is certainly useful to know what are the sources of clean water, but one cannot define clean water by saying it is such water as comes from a certain source.

4. GAṄGEŚA

For Śrīharṣa, the lesson to be learned is that the very attempt to define epistemic success is absurd. One response is that he has loaded the dice by asking for a context-free definition of a context-sensitive concept. The fourteenth-century Nyāya philosopher Gaṅgeśa, though, draws a different conclusion. The lesson to be learned is that the right response to the Śrīharṣa cases cannot be to go in search of additional conditions on epistemic success. In those cases, something has gone wrong, but Śrīharṣa is manipulating our intuitions when he says that they are cases where epistemic success comes apart from accuracy. The right response, according to Gaṅgeśa, is to reaffirm the original theory of epistemic success as accuracy, and at the same time to diagnose the epistemic problem in the Śrīharṣa cases as having different origins. In every case, there is epistemic success, but what we need to do is to draw a distinction between epistemic success that is robust and epistemic success that is fragile. Fragile epistemic success is intolerant of even small variation in the parameters of the situation. There could easily have been four, not five, shells in the closed fist, and then the gambler would not have known. Fragile epistemic success is easily broken. This fragility explains why we are reluctant to agree that the gambler has acquired anything epistemically valuable, but acquiring merely fragile epistemic success is nevertheless not the same as failing to acquire epistemic success at all. Every one of the Śrīharṣa cases is an illustration of fragile epistemic success, not an example of epistemic failure. Epistemic success really is nothing more than believing of something that it is what it is, and not believing of it that it is when it is not. The sources of epistemic success generally give rise to robustness, but even when they misfire, one may still be lucky enough to gain fragile epistemic success, although more often than not one will be led only to error or doubt. Epistemic success just is true belief, because when a belief is true its causal history necessarily constitutes evidence for it (truth necessitates evidential etiology; necessarily, when a belief is true, cause equals because). Doubt destabilizes epistemic success, and when doubts have arisen—for example, in contexts of inquiry—what is needed to resolve them is robustness (the Sanskrit term *niścaya* being sometimes used here). Śrīharṣa tries to game our intuitions in such a way that we start to think what we meant all along by "epistemic success" is robustness. Gaṅgeśa's view is that we ought not even play the game he invites us to play—the game of searching for an additional condition. Epistemic success is a matter of hitting the target, winning the prize (here, truth), so "knowledge-ness consists in truth-hitting character" (Matilal 1986, 141) and how one came to do it or whether one could repeat the feat does not change the fact that one has won.

Recently, a fascinating experiment was conducted. Various standard cases from contemporary epistemology, including Gettier cases and Goldman's famous "barn" example, were translated into Sanskrit and a very learned traditional Sanskrit philosopher, Paṇḍit Viśvabandhu Bhaṭṭācārya—someone with no training in Western philosophy and very little English—was asked for his reaction (see Bhaṭṭācārya 2000). In every case, he insists that if the awareness is true, then it is proper to attribute *pramā*. His linguistic intuitions concur with Gaṅgeśa against Śrīharṣa. This, however, does not prevent one from distinguishing two different kinds of epistemic performance, with two different standards of success. Viśvabandhu is, however, steeped in the philosophical tradition of Gaṅgeśa, and this may itself have colored his intuitions.

5. CONCLUSION: THE UNIVERSALITY THESIS DENIED

The universality thesis states that "the properties of the English word *know* and the English sentence 'S knows that *p*' that have been studied by epistemologists are shared by the translations of these expressions in most or all languages." I have argued not only that Sanskrit *prama*, the closest term to English *knowledge*, has different properties, but that *its* properties, rather than those of the English term, are the ones most closely related to what epistemologists are actually interested in investigating. English epistemic vocabulary brings with it a variety of parochial associations, including a static rather than a performative picture of epistemic agency, an emphasis on the "driving license" model of justification which skews discussion about the actual value of our epistemic practices, and even, if Sen is right, a nonfactive semantics quite at odds with the goals and aspirations of epistemology. What we are interested in as epistemologists is the nature of epistemic performance, the importance of epistemic agency, and the concept of epistemic success. The Project Statement that inspired this volume of essays asks "What should philosophers interested in epistemology make of all this?" I suggest that what they should learn is the need to take seriously how epistemology is done in languages other than English.

REFERENCES

Bennett, Jonathan. (1984). *A Study of Spinoza's Ethics*. : Hackett.

Bhaṭṭācārya, Viśvabandhu. (2000). "Valid Cognition (*prama*) and the Truth (*satyatā*) of its Object." In *Concepts of Knowledge: East and West*, trans. J. L. Shaw, 107–118. Kolkata: Ramakrishna Mission Institute of Culture.

DeRose, Keith. (1992). "Contextualism and Knowledge Attributions." *Philosophy and Phenomenological Research* 52(4): 913–929.

Hazlett, Allan. (2012). "Factive Presupposition and the Truth Condition on Knowledge." *Acta Analytica* 27(4): 461–478.

Matilal, Bimal Krishna. (1986). *Perception: An Essay on Classical Indian Theories of Knowledge*. Oxford: Oxford University Press.

Matilal, Bimal Krishna. (2002). "Knowledge, Truth and Pramātva." In *Mind, Language and World*, edited by Jonardon Ganeri, 149–161. Oxford: Oxford University Press.

Sen, Pranab K. (2000/2007). "Knowledge, Truth, and Scepticism." In J. L. Shaw (ed.) *Concepts of Knowledge: East and West*, 234–243. Kolkata: Ramakrishna Mission Institute of Culture. [Reprinted in his *Knowledge, Truth and Realism: Essays in Philosophical Analysis*. Delhi : Munshiram Manoharlal]

Seyedsayamdost, Hamid. (2015). "On Normativity and Epistemic Intuitions: Failures of Replication." *Episteme* 12(1): 95–116.

Stoltz, Jonathan. (2007). "Gettier and Factivity in Indo-Tibetan Epistemology." *Philosophical Quarterly* 57(228): 394–415.

Turri, John. (2013). "A Conspicuous Art: Putting Gettier to the Test." *Philosophers' Imprint* 13(10): 1–16.

Williamson, Timothy. (2000). *Knowledge and Its Limits*. Oxford: Oxford University Press.

CHAPTER 2
Knowledge and Belief Through the Mirror of Japanese

TAKASHI IIDA

1. NOUNS AND VERBS

The distinction between knowledge and belief has been such a familiar subject in Western philosophy since the time of Plato that it might as well be one of the first topics a student encounters in an introductory course in philosophy. This is also the case with a student taking a philosophy course in Japan, where Western philosophy arrived one and a half centuries ago. Like many philosophical terms in use now in Japan, the nouns for "knowledge" and "belief" were coined after or borrowed from some traditional texts in order to express the concepts that came from a different tradition.[1]

Although the terminology and the way of expressing the distinction in abstract terms came relatively late from elsewhere, we may find that the same distinction, or at least the one that is very close to it, is not alien to modern Japanese usage. This shows that such a distinction is not an artifact of the academic language of philosophy but, rather, is now rooted in the Japanese spoken by ordinary people.[2]

---

1. According to Tajima (1983), before the Meiji era, *chisiki* used to mean "Buddhist high priests," but it started to be used as a translation of "knowledge" in the 1860s.

2. It is an important and interesting question whether the introduction of Western philosophy had an influence in forming the distinction that is reflected in the present usage of Japanese. My present project is, however, to describe what this distinction is and see whether it is the same as the one that has been the main concern in Western epistemology.

The most widely used nouns in Japan today for "knowledge" and "belief" as used in philosophy are 知識 *chishiki* and 信念 *shin-nen*, the former for knowledge and the latter for belief. As you see, they both are written as combinations of two Chinese characters. In both of them, the first character is the important one and also is the first one in the written forms of corresponding verbs; that is, 知る *shiru* is the verb that corresponds to 知識 *chishiki*, and 信じる *shinjiru* is the verb that corresponds to 信念 *shin-nen*.

There are many things with this terminology that make us hesitate to identify them with the standard English terms in philosophy. First, unlike the English noun "knowledge," the Japanese noun *chishiki* can be modified by adjectives that indicate incorrectness, lack of grounds, or vagueness without making the resulting expression contradictory or incoherent. Thus, all of the following make sense:[3]

(1) *machigatta   chisiki*
     incorrect   knowledge

(2) *konkyo   no   nai   chisiki*
     grounds   GEN   without   knowledge

(3) *aimai-na   chishiki*
     vague   knowledge

These examples make us doubt that the Japanese *chisiki* can be a correct translation of English "knowledge." First, it seems more like a commonly held belief or a shared piece of information than knowledge.

Second, although it might be more or less true also with the English "belief," Japanese *shin-nen* cannot be applied to an ordinary belief about commonsensical things like a belief about tomorrow's weather without causing a sense of exaggeration or pomposity. When you talk about someone's *shin-nen*, it is typically about her life principles or convictions and never about your children's whereabouts or the time of next train. This applies also to the corresponding verb *shinjiru*, though to a less extent.

It may be from such a reason that nouns other than *shin-nen* have been proposed for the concept of belief. Some Japanese scholars of ancient Greek philosophy used 臆見 *okken* or 意見 *iken* as a translation of Greek *doxa*. An English word closest to them in meaning may be "opinion." Though 臆

3. The following is a list of abbreviations used in this chapter: ACC: accusative, COP: copula, GEN: genitive, LOC: locative, NOT: negation, NOM: nominative, NOMI: nominalizer, TOP: topic, PAST: past, POL: polite, PROG: progressive, QUO: quotation, RESU: resultative, TOP: topic.

見 *okken* may be too old-fashioned to be used now, 意見 *iken* is frequently heard in everyday conversation. A problem is that there do not exist any verbs corresponding to it. Hence, some proposed a newly coined noun 思念 *shinen*, which consists of the first character of the verb 思う *omou* and the second character of 信念 *shin-nen*. As the verb *omou* is used in relation to ordinary beliefs, there is no problem that *shinjiru* has. Its drawback is that it has no natural corresponding noun, and the word invented for remedying this defect, namely 思念 *shinen*, has never taken root in everyday Japanese.[4] Thus, 信念 *shin-nen* seems to be the term usually adopted now by a philosopher who has to talk about belief, though with some reluctance.

It is almost always a bad policy, however, to concentrate on abstract nouns that are supposed to refer to the concepts we wish to consider; if we want to see the concepts at work, we had better look at the relevant verbs and adjectives, which may be combined with other expressions in various ways, and hence can teach us how the concepts in question are related to other concepts. Accordingly, it is not a pair of the nouns "knowledge" and "belief" but, rather, that of the verbs "know" and "believe" that epistemologists have focused on. So let us try to do the same with Japanese.

If we consider the use of the verb *shiru* instead of the noun *chisiki*, then we will notice that it is much more similar to the use of English "know." Suppose that A uttered the following sentence:[5]

(4) Taro   ga   kaet-ta   koto   wa   shit-   te-iru.
        NOM   went home   NOMI   TOP   know   RESU
    'I know that Taro went home.'

Further suppose that B pointed out to A that Taro had not gone home and still was around. Then A should retract his assertion of (4).

Or, consider a question that is expressed by the following interrogative sentence.

(5) Taro   ga   kaet-ta   koto   wa   shit-
        NOM   went home   NOMI   TOP   know

    te-i-   masu   ka.
    RESU   POL   ?
    'Do you know that Taro went home.'

---

4. Another word that was proposed as a translation of *doxa*—namely, 思いなし *omoinashi*—had the same fate.

5. RESU is an abbreviation of "resultative," which will be explained in section 2.1. NOMI is for "nominalizer."

If A asks you this question, then A supposes that it can be answered by yes or no. If you think that Taro did not go home, then you will tell A that the question is not the right one. This means that A presupposes that Taro went home.

Or again, consider a negative sentence with *shiru*. If we just negate (4), then the resulting sentence

(6) ?Taro ga kaet-ta koto wa shira-nai.
       NOM went home NOMI TOP know-NEG
    Literally, 'I don't know that Taro went home.'

sounds strange.[6] That is because in uttering it, the speaker denies her knowledge about Taro's going home while she presupposes that he went home.[7] Such incoherence will disappear if we change (6) to past tense or into the third person. Here is what we have if we adopt the first option:

(7) Taro ga kaet-ta koto wa shira-nakat-ta.
       NOM went home NOMI TOP know-NEG-PAST
    'I did not know that Taro had gone home.'

If A utters this sentence and we agree to it, then we must recognize the truth of *Taro ga kaetta* (Taro went home).

In sum, if we assume that (4)–(6) have the form

S + *koto* + *wa* + Φ(*shiru*),

where Φ (V) indicates syntactical operations that form interrogative or negative forms of the verb V, then they have in common the presupposition that S is true. In the terminology of Karttunen (1970), *shiru* is a factive verb.

Another indication that Japanese *shiru* is similar to English "know" is the difference between the following two:

(8) Taro ga kuru koto o machigae-te shit-ta.
       NOM come NOMI ACC mistakenly knew
    'I knew by mistake that Taro was to come.'

---

6. Though the simple negative form of *shit-te-iru* should be *shit-te-i-nai, shira-nai* without *te-i* is used much more often. This is an interesting phenomenon that needs explaining, but it does not affect the point in question here. (6) sounds still strange, if *shira-nai* is replaced by *shit-te-i-nai*.

7. There is a way of disclaiming knowledge without presupposing that very knowledge. It is to replace *wa* with *nante* in (6). *Nante* is used in the form S + *koto* + *nante* + *shira-nai* and it cancels a presupposition that *koto* gives rise to.

(9) Taro ga   kuru to   machigae-te shinji-ta.
         NOM   come QUO   mistakenly   believed
     'I mistakenly believed that Taro was to come.'

You see from their translations into English that adverbial modification with *machigae-te* ("in a mistaken way") has different semantic effects on *shiru* and *shinjiru*, which is one of several verbs that may correspond to "believe"; if it is the latter that is modified by *machigae-te*, then what is mistaken is the believed content, whereas if it is *shiru*, then what is mistaken could not be the content but, instead, the very fact that I got that piece of information; there is no implication that it is wrong; on the contrary, (8) presupposes that it is true.[8]

This seems to corroborate that *shiru* is a factive verb like "know." However, an exchange like the following might be cited as a counterexample to such a claim:

(10) A: Taro ga   kuru -tte shit-teru?
              NOM   come (*)   know-RES

      B: Un.
          yes

      A: Demo, sore -tte uso   nandat-tte.
          but   that (*)   false COP-(*)
A: (Literally) 'Do you know that Taro is coming?'
         B: 'Yes.'
         A: 'But, they say it is false.'

This exchange seems to make it doubtful that *shiru* is a factive verb. For if it is so, then A's utterances should sound incoherent because A's second utterance denies the presupposition of her first utterance; but there does not seem to be an incoherence in what A says.

It is important to realize that the use of -*tte* in the first utterance of A is essential for this example; if you substitute -*tte* with a more formal *koto*, then the entire exchange will give an impression of incoherence. Why is there such a difference?

8. The adverb *machigaet-te* and the adjective *machigatta* (cf. example (1)) come from the same root and have the same meaning. It is worth noting that between *machigatta chisiki* ("incorrect knowledge") and *machigatta shin-nen* ("incorrect belief") there is no difference like the one between (8) and (9); they both refer to incorrect beliefs.

The particle -tte not only appears frequently in spoken Japanese but also has a wide variety of functions. Even in our small example (10), as indicated by the asterisk (*) it occurs three times and its function is different each time it occurs. In the second utterance of A, there are two occurrences of -tte, the first of which is working as a topic marker and the second as a particle indicating what comes before as a hearsay.[9] The function of -tte in the first utterance of A is different from either of them; it is most likely that it is an abbreviation of a more complex expression like:

(11)   to   iu   uwasa,
        QUO   say   rumor

or

(12)   to   iu   hanashi.
        QUO   say   news

Thus, the whole utterance might be translated as "Do you know the rumor (or news) that Taro is coming?"[10] and what is presupposed in its utterance is only the existence of such rumor or news, not its correctness.

This example teaches us at least two things. First, Japanese *shiru* takes a variety of objects, just as the English "know" does; they may be persons, places, things, stories, events, facts, and so on. Second, as there is a general tendency in Japanese to refrain from explicitly mentioning the things that are understood in the context, we must ask ourselves whether we are not missing any element that has only a virtual presence in what we hear or see before we derive some substantial conclusion from sample Japanese examples.

As for the verbs that are related to beliefs, 信じる *shinjiru* is the most frequently encountered one in the context of philosophy; obviously that is because it corresponds to the noun 信念 *shin-nen*, which is considered now the standard translation of "belief" in philosophy. It has, however, the same kinds of problems as the noun has—namely, *shinjiru* sounds strange when it is used in relation to ordinary beliefs expressed in the course of an everyday conversation. For such purposes, we may use 思う *omou*. (14)

9. See Maruyama (2002) for a classification of the various functions of -tte and their examples.
10. The expression *to iu*, which consists of a quotation particle *to* and a verb *iu* meaning "say," functions here as a phrase that connects a sentence S and a noun N; "S *to iu* N" corresponds to the English "N that S," as in "a rumor that Taro is coming."

must sound much more natural than (13) to a speaker of Japanese, but both can be translated as "I believe that Taro went home."

(13) Taro ga   kaet-ta   to   shinjiru.
           NOM went home   QUO   believe

(14) Taro ga   kaet-ta   to   omou.
           NOM went home   QUO   think

The verbs that were mentioned so far—namely, *shiru, shinjiru,* and *omou*—all belong to a class of Japanese verbs called "verbs of thinking." If we wish to know how the distinction between knowledge and belief is reflected in Japanese, we have to consider the general character of this class of expressions and look at the differences among them. This is what I do in the main part of this chapter.

A verb of thinking typically forms a mental predicate—that is, a predicate which expresses a mental phenomenon. A mental predicate in Japanese is very sensitive to the difference of person; in particular, its first-person uses and the non-first-person uses are clearly distinguished. As Japanese verbs and adjectives do not inflect according to person and as subject expressions are frequently dropped when they are understood in the context, how this is achieved may seem mysterious, but it is not so; or, at least I hope to show that it is not. The difference in person is also connected with aspectual phenomena in Japanese. In the next section, we will see aspectual properties of the verbs of thinking and how they are connected to the difference in grammatical person.

Later, I will try to classify verbs of thinking according to what kind of arguments they can take. It is a characteristic of Japanese that a sentence complement that a verb of thinking takes is clearly marked whether it is an object of a mental activity or it is its content. This will naturally explain the factivity of *shiru,* but it has also other interesting consequences. In particular, it might give an interesting viewpoint to reconsider the semantics of propositional attitudes.

2. ASPECT AND PERSON

2.1. Instantaneous and Continuous Verbs

An influential and still valuable classification of Japanese verbs was proposed by Kindaichi Haruhiko in an article published in 1950.[11] It has an interesting similarity with a well-known classification of English verbs

11. Kindaichi (1950).

made by Zeno Vendler,[12] but it is obviously independent of the latter, which was published in 1957.

Kindaichi's fourfold classification has an auxiliary verb *te-iru* as its center. First, there are a small number of verbs that cannot be used with *te-iru*; they are called "state verbs" and examples are *iru* (be located) and *dekiru* (be able to). Second, some verbs denote a progressive state of an action or event, when they are combined with *te-iru*; they are called "continuous verbs" and examples are *hashiru* (run) and *kaku* (write). Third, some verbs denote an existing state that has resulted from an action or event, when they are combined with *te-iru*; they are called "instantaneous verbs" and examples are *shinu* (die) and *taoreru* (fall down). Fourth, some verbs are always used with *te-iru* and never by themselves; Kindaichi called them "the verbs of the fourth kind" but more specific names like "property verbs" have been proposed by others; examples are *sobieru* ("rise"—said of mountains) and *togaru* ("pointed"—said of noses). While state verbs and the verbs of the fourth kind form predicates that denote states, instantaneous verbs and continuous ones form predicates that denote changes.[13]

Generally speaking, a change can be known in two ways.[14] Sometimes it can be known by perceiving the change itself, and sometimes it can be known by perceiving the result of the change. On the one hand, when we follow the motion of a rolling ball by our eyes, we perceive the change itself, which is the change in the locations of the ball. On the other hand, when we notice that a ball is not at the location we saw before, we know the change by perceiving its result.

Corresponding to two ways of perceiving a change, there are two ways of speaking about a change. One is to speak of a change as a progressing process, and another is to speak of it as an event that brings forth a certain result. The two ways are displayed in the following two sentences:

(15) Taro   ga   hashit-   te-iru
          NOM   run   PROG
     'Taro is running.'

(16) Ki   ga   taore   te-iru
     tree(s) NOM   fall down   RESU
     'A tree/trees are fallen.'[15]

---

12. Vendler (1957).
13. The following six paragraphs are derived from Iida (2001, 166ff).
14. See Galton (1984, 28–30).
15. This is not the only interpretation. *Ki* might as well refer to some definite tree or trees given in a context.

In (15), *hashit-te-iru* expresses the change in its progression, while *taore-te-iru* in (16) expresses the change in its result. Accordingly, an auxiliary verb *te-iru* indicates either a progressive state (PROG) or a resulting state (RESU).

Some changes can be known only by perceiving their results, because the changing processes themselves cannot be perceived. For example, we cannot perceive directly the process of a child's growing; we know that a child has grown only by a number of different perceptions of the same child over an extended time. This is because the change is too slow to be perceived. In contrast, if a change is very rapid, it can be perceived only by what has resulted from it. In particular, if a change takes place in an instant, then there is no way to know it other than by noticing its results.

This seems to be the usually cited reason why verbs like *taoreru* (fall down), which occurs in (16), should be called an "instantaneous verb." I suspect that this cannot be right, however. Is it really an instantaneous event for a tree to fall down? Can't we see the very process of a tree's falling down? There are also various ways of expressing such a process:

(17) Ki   ga   taore   te-iku.
     tree(s) NOM   fall down   go

(18) Ki   ga   taore   te-it-   te-iru.
     tree(s) NOM   fall down   go   PROG

Though *ki* (tree or trees) may be definite or indefinite, and singular or plural depending on the context, both sentences mean the same thing if the interpretation of *ki* is fixed; for example, it may mean that a tree is going down. In particular, the fact that the auxiliary verb *te-iru* in (18) should be interpreted as expressing a progressive aspect shows that the verb *taoreru*, which is usually classified as an instantaneous verb, now functions as a continuous one.

A better conception of the "instantaneousness" of an instantaneous verb is to consider it as expressing a change that a certain subject A undergoes. In the most general term, such a change is either A's acquiring a certain property P or A's losing P.[16] They can be regarded as changes between states.

Let H be A's having P, and –H be A's not having P, and let us say that H and –H are contrary to each other. In general, changes between a state to its

16. You may note that this is very similar to Aristotle's characterization of change in his *Physics*.

contrary must be instantaneous. The reason why this is so is purely logical. As long as we stick to classical two-valued logic, for every instant t, it is not possible that both H and its contrary –H hold at t, and either H or –H must hold at t.[17] Hence, there cannot be an extended period in which a change from H to –H (or vice versa) takes place.

Thus, the distinction between continuous verbs and instantaneous verbs consists in two different conceptions of changes. When we describe a change by a continuous verb, we describe it as a process that goes through different stages in an extended period. In contrast, when we describe a change by an instantaneous verb, we describe it as a change between holding and nonholding of a certain state. There are some events that can be described either way. An event of a tree's falling down may be described as an instantaneous change in the tree's state, as in (16), or as a process that takes time, as in (17) and (18). The verb *taoreru* ("fall down") occurs as an instantaneous verb in (16), while it occurs as a continuous verb in (17) and (18).

Now let us consider which kinds of verbs are those verbs of thinking that are most relevant to our present concern—namely, *shiru, shinjiru,* and *omou.* As they all take the auxiliary verb *te-iru,* they are not state verbs. They are not the fourth kind of verbs, either, because they can be used without *te-iru.* Hence, they are either continuous or instantaneous verbs. Of course, as we saw in the case of *taoreru,* it is possible that some of them can be used as either in their different occurrences.

One way of identifying a continuous verb is to see whether it can be a part of complex verb phrases "V + *hajimeru* /*hajimaru*" (to start V-ing), "V + *oeru* /*owaru* (to end V-ing), and "V + *te-iru* + *saichuu* + *da* (to be in the middle of V-ing).[18] As a continuous verb denotes a process that develops over an extended time, it is possible to distinguish its different stages; it should have a beginning, middle, and end.

Although our three verbs *shiru, shinjiru,* and *omou* can form complex verb phrases "V + *hajimeru,*" it is not possible to form other two sorts of complex verb phrases from them. This suggests that they are all instantaneous verbs. Then, a verb phrase consisting of any one of them and *te-iru* should refer not to a process that goes on for an extended period but, rather, to a

17. Of course, this will be no longer true if we adopt a logic that is different from a two-valued one. As a matter of fact, Landman argued that our talk of the instant of change calls for an adoption of a logic that is not two-valued. See Landman (1991, chap. 5).

18. *Hajimeru* and *oeru* are for transitive verbs, and *hajimaru* and *owaru* are for intransitive verbs.

state that results from some epistemic or doxastic event. This may well be true with respect to *shiru*. Consider this:

(19) Taro   ga   kaet-ta   koto   o   Hanako   wa
             NOM   went home   NOMI   ACC   TOP
     shit-   te-iru.
     know   RESU
     'Hanako knows that Taro went home.'

For (19) to be true, Hanako must have come to know that Taro went home at a certain time in the past. At that time, Hanako underwent a change in her states—namely, a change from a state of not knowing this fact to that of knowing it. The verb *shiru* denotes such a change, and unlike the English "know," it does not denote a mental state of knowing. Thus, *shiru* corresponds to "get to know" in English, and the Japanese counterpart of the stative "know" must be *shit-te-iru*.

The matter is not so clear with *omou* and *shinjiru*, however. First, let us consider the case of *omou*:

(20) Taro   ga   kaet-ta   to   Hanako   wa   omot-
             NOM   went home   QUO   TOP   think
     te-iru.
     RESU(?)
     'Hanako thinks/believes that Taro went home.'

Is (20) true because there was an event that is described by the following sentence?

(21) Taro   ga   kaet-ta   to   Hanako   wa   omot-
             NOM   went home   QUO   TOP   think
     ta.
     PAST
     'Hanako thought/believed that Taro went home.'

Just as with the English "think" and "believe," *omou* and *shinjiru* may mean either occurrent episodes or enduring dispositions. It seems reasonable to construe the states that *omot-te-iru* and *shinji-te-iru* refer to as dispositions. (21) is most naturally interpreted as talking about a past episode of Hanako's occurrent belief. On the one hand, it seems that the mere truth of (21) is not sufficient for (20) to be true; if (20) describes a dispositional state of Hanako, then more than one episode of thinking described by (21) is required for her to acquire that state. On the other hand, it does not seem to be right to classify *omou* as a continuous verb and regard *omot-te-iru* as referring to an ongoing mental process, because a disposition is a state and not an activity.

Such considerations make us suspect that *omou* does not fit into the scheme of verb classification we have been working within. It may be the case that the verbs of thinking form a special class that cannot be easily explained by the contrast between continuous and instantaneous verbs. Shortly, we will see that there is another reason to suggest this.

Lastly, *shinjiru* seems to offer an intermediate case between *shiru* and *omou*. Let us consider this:

(22) Taro   ga   kaet-ta   to   Hanako wa   shinji-
            NOM   went home QUO   TOP   believe
      te-iru.
      RESU(?)
      'Hanako believes that Taro went home.'

On the one hand, this can be interpreted as describing a state of Hanako that resulted from her coming to believe that Taro went home just as in the case of *shiru*. On the other hand, if that state is a disposition, the existence of just one episode in the past of her believing that does not seem to be enough to ascribe it to her.

Such a difference between *omou* and *shinjiru* may be a reflection of the fact that they have different implications as to how strongly a person adheres to her belief. We have already noted that *shinjiru* is usually employed for some important beliefs a person is convinced of. Thus, if a person is once convinced of a certain belief, then she will likely to believe it since then. This is a nuance *shinjiru* sometimes has. Compared to it, *omou* is used for a much wider variety of beliefs; it may be about casual ones and longstanding ones. Thus, if you wish to ascribe a belief held in this manner to a person for a certain extended period, you need some evidence to show that she keeps holding it during the period.

Let us review our discussion so far. We have considered which sorts of verbs *shiru, omou,* and *shinjiru*, which are thought to correspond to the English "know" and "believe," are in a scheme for classifying Japanese verbs by their aspectual properties. As this scheme is based on seeing how modifying a verb with an auxiliary verb *te-iru* affects it semantically, we tried to see what each of *shit-te-iru, omot-te-iru,* and *shinji-te-iru* means. Our findings can be summarized as follows:

First, the three verbs are all event verbs in original form, but become state predicates with *te-iru*. Hence, what corresponds to the English stative verbs "know" and "believe" are *shit-te-iru* and *omot-te-iru* or *shinji-te-iru*.

Second, although the three verbs are classified as instantaneous verbs, which denotes a change in a subject from a state to its contrary state, it is not clear whether such a change can be brought about by a single episode of the event that these verbs denote; at least it is not clear with *omou* and, to a less extent, with *shinjiru*, although there may not be a similar problem with *shiru*.

As mental predicates, verbs of thinking have a characteristic that their aspectual behavior is closely connected with the difference in grammatical person. Now we turn to this topic.

2.2. Personal Constraints

There are strict personal constraints on the uses of mental predicates in Japanese. Suppose we are asked to translate the following two sentences into a Japanese that is as natural as possible.

(23)   I am in pain.

(24)   She is in pain

Then, the most likely results we come up with will be these:

(25)   Itai.
       in pain

(26)   Ita   so-u   da.
       in pain   looks like COP

Even though (25) consists of just an adjective in its basic form, there is no danger of misunderstanding whose pain is in question; it can only mean that the speaker is in pain. This is because when a Japanese mental predicate is used in its basic form, it must be in the first person. In contrast, if you wish to use a mental predicate in the second or third person, you have to modify it in some way to show that the predication is based on some evidence; conversely, if a mental predicate is used with an expression like *so-u* or *yo-u*, which indicates indirectness, you will know that it is not predicated to the speaker.

In uttering (23) or (25), its utterer expresses her pain. This utterance is what some philosophers have called "avowals." An avowal has a special authority ("first-person authority"); it has no need to be backed by evidence, but there is a presumption that it is not mistaken.[19] In contrast, if you ascribe pain to others, you have to be able to cite evidence if you are asked to do so. This contrast between the first-person avowal and the second- or third-person report is shown much more clearly in (25) and (26) than in (23) and (24). If you compare Japanese examples with English ones, you will be struck by how sharply the personal constraints on the uses of mental predicates separate avowals from reports or descriptions in Japanese.

An adjective like *itai* constitutes a state predicate. One of the characteristics of a state predicate is that we can use it to describe a present state or a future one. This is also true in English.

(27)   He goes to Tokyo.

(28)   He lives in Tokyo.

While his going to Tokyo must be in the future at the time of the utterance of (27), his living in Tokyo can be a state that is contemporaneous with the utterance of (28). This is because "go to Tokyo" is an event predicate while "live in Tokyo" is a state one. The following examples show that the same contrast exists in Japanese.

(29)   Kare   wa   Toukyou   ni   iku.
       he   TOP   Tokyo   LOC   go
       'He goes to Tokyo.'

(30)   Kare   wa   Toukyou   ni   iru.
       he   TOP   Tokyo   LOC   is
       'He is in Tokyo.'

While (29) describes a future event, (30) may describe a contemporaneous state.[20] I have to use *iru* instead of *sumu*, which corresponds to "live," because *sumu* is an event verb. As matter of fact, there are only small number of state verbs in Japanese.

The three verbs of thinking we are concerned with—namely, *shiru* ("know"), *omou* ("think," "believe"), and *shinjiru* ("believe")—are all event verbs, as we saw earlier. However, *omou* and *shinjiru* are special in that they

19. See the first two essays in Davidson (2001). Also, see an entry on avowals in Glock (1996).
20. Example (30) is ambiguous and it may describe a future event as well.

can be used to express present states in their basic form. We have already seen examples of this in (13) and (14), which I repeat here in the polite form that is usual in more formal speech:

(13′)　Taro　ga　　kaet-ta　　　to　　shinji　masu.
　　　　　　　NOM　went home　QUO　believe　POL

(14′)　Taro　ga　　kaet-ta　　　to　　omoi　masu.
　　　　　　　NOM　went home　QUO　think　POL

Though in polite form, *shinjiru* and *omou* are used here in basic form; as they are mental predicates, they must be in the first person. They are event verbs and their tenses are non-past, but they express the present mental states of the speaker. Thus, both of them can be translated as "I believe that Taro went home" or "I think that Taro went home." This is a rather remarkable fact that has attracted the attention of a number of Japanese grammarians, and some of them have proposed that such verbs of thinking constitute a separate class that is different from both state predicates and event predicates.[21]

It must be noted, however, that the reason why a speaker can express her present mental state by using *shinjiru* or *omou* is entirely different from the reason why she can talk of the present state by using a stative verb like *iru*, as in (30). On the one hand, there is no restriction on person in the latter case; a stative verb like *iru* can be used to talk of a present state whether it is in the first person or not. On the other hand, the fact that (13) and (14) are in the first person is essential for them to be usable to express its utterer's present state. While (30) is a description of a present state, (13) and (14) are expressions of a speaker's attitudes.[22] In other words, it is the difference between a description and an avowal.

The matter is different with *shiru* ("know"). If we replace *shinjiru* or *omou* with *shiru* in (13) or (14), then the resulting sentence

(31)　Taro　ga　　kaet-ta　　　to　　shiri　masu
　　　　　　NOM　went home　QUO　know　POL

cannot be in the first person. Although (31) is a little strange as it is, if we add a particle like *ne* and *yo* at its end, it will be all right and mean either

21. See Kudo (1995).
22. In everyday conversation, *omou* in the first-person present is most frequently used as a quasi-modal expression to avoid giving an impression of a straightforward assertion. Such uses of *omou* are not incompatible with its use for expressing a speaker's present attitude. *Shinjiru* has no corresponding quasi-modal use.

that you will know that Taro went home or somebody understood in the context will know that.

When the basic forms of *omou* and *shinjiru* are used in the present tense, as in (13) and (14), they express a speaker's present attitudes. Just as a speaker expresses her pain in (25), a speaker of (13) or (14) expresses her belief. As an avowal, there is a presumption that her utterance is true. However, if she makes a claim to knowledge, she has no special authority with respect to it. The fact that there is no counterpart to (13) and (14) with *shiru* gives us another reason to think that Japanese *shiru* expresses the concept of knowledge.

The same kinds of personal constraints on mental predicates as in (25) and (26) are also in force with the past tense.

(32) Itakat-   ta.
      in pain   PAST

(33) Itakat-   ta   yo-u   da.
      in pain   PAST   looks like   COP

Again, (32) must be in the first person; it cannot be otherwise. And the presence of *yo-u* in (33) makes it clear that it must be in the second or third person.

Just as it was in the present-tense case, when we wish to report our past experience of pain, it is enough to use the adjective *itai* ("in pain") with the past tense marker *ta*. But, if we wish to talk about some other person's past experience, the predication must be modified with some expression indicating indirectness.

In this respect, there is no difference among *omou*, *shinjiru*, and *shiru*. If we turn (13), (14), and (31) into past-tense sentences, they all will be interpreted as the first-person utterances, provided they are not part of narratives like stories or novels.

When a speaker uses the basic forms of the three verbs in the past tense, she reports some past mental events of her own. Even when her utterance has *omou* or *shinjiru*, it will be no longer an avowal. Still, they report a mental event the occurrence of which is directly known only to the speaker, and hence, it cannot be reported by anyone other than her without some expression that signifies indirectness. This must be the source of the asymmetry between the first-person case and other cases.[23]

23. Exceptions to this are in the context of a story or a novel where there is a narrator who is supposed to know what the characters think and feel.

The case of *shiru* needs an explanation, however. Let us consider a sentence that is the past-tense version of (31):

(31P) Taro ga   kaet-ta   to   shiri   mashi ta.
           NOM went home QUO   know   POL   PAST

This contains a claim of knowledge, but it is primarily a report of a mental event in which a speaker comes to acquire that knowledge. If you think that a knowledge claim contained in (31P) is wrong—that is, you think that Taro did not go home—then you may criticize this utterance for that. But coming to know something is a mental event that can be known directly only by the person in question. Even though you think that the speaker of (31P) is wrong in having thought that Taro went home, you cannot deny without a particular reason that she thought that she came to know that. To this extent, there exists the same asymmetry as the one that existed in the past-tense uses of *shinjiru* and *omou*.

The personal constraints in Japanese reflect an epistemological gulf that exists between expressing beliefs or claiming knowledge and attributing them to others. While you can express your belief or claim your knowledge straight away, if you wish to attribute a belief or a piece of knowledge to others, you always have to indicate that you have some evidence or clue that is a basis for such an attribution.

The asymmetry between the first-person cases and other cases becomes less pronounced if we use these three verbs of thinking with the auxiliary verb *te-iru*. Consider these:

(34) Taro ga   kaet-ta   to   shinji   te-i   masu.
           NOM went home QUO   believe RESU(?)   POL

(35) Taro ga   kaet-ta   to   omot-   te-i   masu.
           NOM went home QUO   think   RESU(?)   POL

(36) Taro ga   kaet-ta   to   shit-   te-i   masu.
           NOM went home QUO   know   RESU   POL

They can all be employed for any person, whether it is first person or not. The same applies to the past-tense sentences that result from (34)–(36) when the occurrences of *masu* are replaced with those of *mashita*.

There are still differences between their first-person uses and non-first-person ones. If (34) and (35) are used in the first person, they are avowals, while they are descriptions—or more specifically, ascriptions of a belief—when they are used in the second or third person. (36) in the first person is a claim of knowledge, while it is an ascription of the same to others.[24] Moreover, the particles like *yo-u* and *so-u* that signify a conjecture can be added only in the non-first-person cases.

There needs to be an explanation why modifying the verbs by *te-iru* makes it possible to use them by themselves to describe mental states of others. A story commonly given by grammarians runs like this: Take one of the three verbs we are concerned with. Though it is an instantaneous verb, if it is modified by *te-iru*, it denotes a state that extends in time. This means that there is a chance to get evidence from the behavior of a person as to her mental state. This seems to show that Japanese is not so solipsistic as not to allow directly ascribing belief or knowledge to others.

Whether this explanation is convincing enough or not, we may regard sentences like (34)–(36) as providing us with the standard form of ascribing belief or knowledge to somebody. In order to present it in an appropriate way, some changes need to be made. First, to make it easier to compare with English sentences, let an epistemic or doxastic subject be explicitly represented in a sentence. Second, for simplicity's sake, don't require a sentence to be presented in polite form. Let S be a declarative sentence,[25] A a name of a person, and V an appropriate conjugated form of one of the three verbs of thinking, *shinjiru*, *omou*, and *shiru*. Then, the standard form of ascribing belief or knowledge that S to a person A is this:

(I)   S + *to* + A + *wa* + V + *te-i-ru*

If we suppose that Hanako is the person who is implicitly understood in certain utterances of (34)–(36), then they will be expressed in the standard form in this way.

(37) Taro ga   kaet-ta   to   Hanako wa
            NOM   went home   QUO   TOP

      shinji   te-iru.
      believe RESU(?)

---

24. The past-tense versions of (34)–(36) all function as ascriptions, including the first-person case, which ascribe a belief or knowledge to one's past self.

25. In fact, S might be an interrogative sentence as well. But, here we will be concerned only with declarative cases.

(38) Taro   ga   kaet-ta   to   Hanako wa
              NOM   went home   QUO   TOP

      omot-   te-iru.
      believe RESU(?)

(39) Taro   ga   kaet-ta   to   Hanako wa
              NOM   went home   QUO   TOP

      shit-   te-iru.
      Know   RESU(?)

You may notice that we have already encountered (37) and (38) as (22) and (20), respectively.

3. OBJECT AND CONTENT

3.1. *To* and *Koto*

Any Japanese speaker who is presented with the "standard form" for the ascription of belief or knowledge as earlier will notice that there is another construction that is similar to it. It is this:

(II)   S + *koto* + *o* + A + *wa* + V + *te-i-ru*

The sentences in this form corresponding to (37)–(39) are these. Note that we have already encountered (42) as (19).

(40) Taro ga   kaet-ta   koto   o   Hanako
            NOM   went home   NOMI   ACC

      wa   shinji te-iru.
      TOP   believe RESU(?)

(41) Taro ga   kaet-ta   koto   o   Hanako
            NOM   went home   NOMI   ACC

      wa   omot-   te-iru.
      TOP   think   PROG

(42) Taro ga   kaet-ta   koto   o   Hanako
            NOM   went home   NOMI   ACC

      wa   shit-   te-iru.
      TOP   know   RESU

Let us compare (40)–(42) with (37)–(39), and see whether there is any significant difference between them.

The first difference you may notice is how *omou* is translated into English in (38) and (41). In (41), it cannot be translated as "believe." Its meaning must be something like "Hanako is thinking about the fact that Taro went home." Moreover, here *omot-te-iru* clearly refers to a progressive state of thinking. All this shows that (41) has a different meaning from (38). As a matter of fact, we can argue that they are logically independent of each other. For believing that S does not necessarily involve thinking about the fact that S, and you may be actually thinking about the fact S without believing that S.

In contrast, there seems to be little difference between (39) and (42), which have *shiru* as their main verb; they are logically equivalent to each other. It might be true that (42) with *koto* sounds more natural than (39) with *to*, but it is undeniable that (39) is grammatically correct.

How are (37) and (40) related to each other? On the one hand, for a person who understands them, it is obvious that (40) implies (37). On the other hand, such a person would hesitate to say that (37) implies (40); it is because (40) presupposes that Taro went home but there is no such presupposition in (37).

Thus, interestingly, *shiru, shinjiru,* and *omou* show different logical behavior with constructions (I) and (II)—let us call them "*to*-construction" and "*koto*-construction," respectively. In order to understand what makes such a difference, we had better consider the functions of *to* and *koto*, which are sometimes called "sentential complement markers."[26]

To-construction and *koto*-construction are found not only with the verbs of thinking but also with those that express emotions or denote communicational activities, including linguistic ones. In (43), *to* is used with the verb *iu* ("say"), and *koto* appears with *yorokobu* ("be glad") in (44).

(43) Taro ga   kaet-ta   to   Hanako wa   it-ta.
          NOM   went home   QUO   TOP   said
     'Hanako said that Taro went home.

(44) Taro ga   kae-tta   koto   o   Hanako
          NOM   went home   NOMI   ACC
     wa   yorokon-   de-iru.
     TOP   be glad   RESU

'Hanako is glad that Taro went home.'

26. See Inoue (1976, 251–267). This is a discussion of our topic from the standpoint of early generative grammar.

Syntactically "S + *koto*" is a noun phrase and it must be followed by a case particle when it occurs in a sentence. For most of the cases, *koto* may be replaced with *no* without affecting the meaning; you can see that this is true with (40), (42), or (44). *Koto* and *no* can be regarded as a nominalizer that turns a sentence into a noun phrase.

In contrast, "S + *to*" works more like an adverbial; it does not need to be followed by a case particle in a sentence. *To* is the chief device for quoting linguistic expressions in Japanese, and it can be used not only with declarative sentences but also with other kinds of sentences and nonsentential expressions. Moreover, it can introduce a direct discourse and an indirect discourse.[27]

The most striking difference between *to* and *koto* can be seen in the difference between (37) and (40). As we noted earlier, (40) with *koto* presupposes that Taro went home, while (37) with *to* has no such presupposition. There are many cases like this, and Kuno tried to explain this phenomenon by proposing a hypothesis that *koto* indicates a speaker's presupposition—that is, in using a noun phrase "S + *koto*" in an utterance, a speaker presupposes that S is true.[28] Kuno's hypothesis about *koto* has given rise to a lively discussion among Japanese grammarians. The discussion has been centered mainly on two points.

First, as Kuno himself admitted, it is not true that *every* occurrence of "S + *koto*" gives rise to a presupposition. The following example shows that *koto* does not necessarily generate a presupposition, even in the context of "S + *koto* + *o* + *shinjiru*":

(45) Taro   ga   buji de-iru koto   o
              NOM   safe   COP   NOMI   ACC

      shinji-   te-iru
      believe   RESU(?)
      'I believe that Taro is safe.'

Hence, it is essential to find out exactly when an occurrence of "S + *koto*" gives rise to a presupposition and why it does.

Second, as (39) shows, when *shiru* ("know") is concerned, "S + *to*" also gives rise to a presupposition that S is true. Kuno treated this case as an exception, but since then several scholars have pointed out that there are

---

27. For a general discussion of quotation in Japanese, see Kamada (2000).
28. Kuno (1973).

a number of verbs like *shiru* with which "S + *to*" and "S + *koto*" generate a presupposition that S is true. Some examples are the following:

kizuku	notice, realize
satoru	see that, realize
omoi-dasu	recall, remember

Given the fact that *to* does not generally give rise to a presupposition, such a behavior of this class of verbs should be explained.

Of these two problems, the first seems to be the more important; not only that, but it must be the more difficult one to solve. It is almost certain that the noun phrases of the form "S + *koto*" are not uniform in their semantical properties. To have a systematic account of them, we need a wide-ranging survey of linguistic material. What I can do here is only to suggest a line of approach that seems promising to me. But before doing that, I present a proposal that may offer us an answer to the second problem.

3.2. Counter-Factive and Factive Verbs

With some verbs, *to*-construction and *koto*-construction can be combined within a single sentence. As they take two sentential complements, let us call such verbs "two-complement verbs." They give us a hint as to the different functions of *to* and *koto* in a sentence. *Setsumei-suru* ("explain") is one of such verbs.

(46)	Taro	ga		kae-tta	koto	o	Hanako
		NOM		went home	NOMI	ACC	
	wa	Jiro		Ga	kita	kara	da
	TOP			NOM	came	because	COP
	to	setsumei-shi-	te-iru.				
	QUO	explain	RESU				

This sentence has a structure

(I+II) S_1 + *koto* + *o* + A + *wa* + S_2 + *to* + V + *te-i-ru*.

Pietroski argued that the English verb "explain" can have two kinds of arguments. In his words, "the verb can combine with a Theme-specifier corresponding to the explanandum, or an Import-specifier (typically) corresponding to the explanans."[29] He gave the following sentences as examples of this:[30]

(a) Nora explained that Fido barked.
(b) Nora explained the fact that Fido barked.

The first gives us an explanans and the latter gives an explanandum. In English, it is impossible to combine (a) and (b) in one single clause sentence. (46) shows that it can be achieved in Japanese because the Japanese verb *setsumei-suru* can take two sentential complements in a single sentence. If we try to translate (46) into English, then we have to use "explain" twice, as in the following:

(46E)   Hanako explains the fact that Taro went home by explaining that Jiro came.

It must be clear that *koto* introduces "a Theme-specifier" and *to* "an Import- specifier." Here I use a different terminology. Just as an explanation has its object (explanandum) and its content (explanans), many activities that are denoted by the verbs we are concerned with here have both objects and contents. Take, for example, *ayamaru* ("apologize"); when you apologize, you apologize for something—probably some action of yours—which is an object of apologizing, and you apologize that so-and-so, which is a content of apologizing. Then, let us call a sentential complement which is introduced by *koto* "an object complement" and that which is introduced by *to* "a content complement." We also call the former simply a "*koto* complement" and the latter a "*to* complement."

Surprisingly, it has seldom been noticed of the verbs we are concerned with—namely, those relating to thinking, emotions, and communicational activities—that many of them can take both kinds of sentential complements within a single sentence, just as we saw with *setsumei-suru* ("explain") in (46).

Among the verbs that take both kinds of complements, there is a class of verbs that have been known as "counter-factive verbs." Examples in English that are usually given are "pretend" and "misremember." They are thought

29. Pietroski (2005, 226). He was also aware of the distinction between *koto* and *to* in Japanese. In this connection, see also Motomura (2003). Although I have sympathy with his general position for which he thinks the distinction offers a support, my concern here is different.
30. Pietroski (2005, 223).

to presuppose the falsity of their sentential complements. For example, an English sentence "John pretended that he was a good boy" and its negation "John did not pretend that he was a good boy" both imply the falsity of the complement "he was a good boy."

Japanese verbs that are usually given as examples of counter-factive verbs are these:

Omoi-chigai-suru misunderstand, misconstrue
Gokai-suru misunderstand, think wrongly
Itsuwaru pretend

Let us take as an example a sentence that has *gokai-suru* as its main verb:

(47) Hanako   wa   Taro ga   kaet-ta   to
                TOP   NOM   went home QUO

gokai-shi   te-iru.
misunderstand   RESU
'Hanako wrongly thinks that Taro went home.'

This sentence has only a content complement, which is

S: *Taro ga kaet-ta*. 'Taro went home.'

It must have also an object complement. What should it be? I suggest that it should be the negation of S, namely,

¬S: *Taro ga kaet-te-i-nai*. 'Taro has not gone home.'

Thus, I suppose that (47) is in fact a sentence that has both an object complement and a content complement—namely, this:

(47') Taro   ga   kaet-te-i   nai   no   o
                    NOM   went home   NOT   NOMI   ACC

Hanako   wa   Taro   ga   kaet-ta   to
              TOP   NOM   went home   QUO

gokai-shi   te-iru.
misunderstand   RESU
'Hanako mistakes Taro's not having gone home for his having gone home.'

Here, a nominalizer *koto* is replaced by *no* which sounds more natural in this context.

Generally speaking, my proposal is that, for a counter-factive verb V, a sentence of the form

(*)   A + *wa* + S + *to* + V + *te-i-ru*

should be construed as having the following form in fact:[31]

(**)   ¬S + *koto* /*no* + *o* + A + *wa* + S + *to* + V + *te-i-ru*

where ¬S is the negation of S.

Under this proposal, the counter-factivity can be easily explained, provided that the *koto* or *no* which occurs in (**) generates a presupposition that the preceding sentence is true. For, suppose that V is a counter-factive verb and that (*) is true; as (*) is in fact (**), it is a presupposition of its truth that ¬S should be true; hence, it is a presupposition of (*) that S should be false.

It should be noted that a mere equivalence between (*) and (**) might not be enough, because it may happen that two sentences are logically equivalent without having the same presuppositions.

A thought that naturally occurs at this point is to wonder whether the same strategy may not be applied to the case of factive verbs. Take, as an example, one of the verbs I listed before as factive ones—say, *satoru* ("see that," "realize")—and form a sentence similar to (47):

(48)   Hanako wa   Taro   ga   kaet-ta   to
                TOP   NOM   went home   QUO
         satot-   te-iru.
         realize   RESU
         'Hanako realizes that Taro went home.'

This sentence has only a content complement, but there can be a sentence having an object complement as well.

(48′)   Taro   ga   kaet-ta   no   o   Hanako
                NOM   went home   NOMI   ACC

---

31. Instead of ¬S, we may have any sentence that is incompatible with S and satisfies an additional condition C* as an object complement. I have to leave it for another occasion to find out what this additional condition should be.

	wa	Taro	ga		kaet-ta	to	satot-
	TOP		NOM		went home	QUO	realize

te-iru.

RESU

'Hanako realizes the fact that Taro went home in realizing that Taro went home.'

This looks and sounds extremely redundant, but if you rewrite it by using an anaphor *so-u*, then the result will be a perfectly natural sentence:

(48″)
Taro	ga	kaet-ta	no	o	Hanako
	NOM	went home	NOMI	ACC	

wa	so-u	to		satot-	te-iru.
TOP	SO	QUO		realize	RESU

'Hanako realizes the fact that Taro went home in realizing so.'

It must be obvious what our proposal will be for this case: namely, for a factive verb V, a sentence of the form

(+)   A + *wa* + S + *to* + V + *te-i-ru*

should be construed as having the following form in fact:[32]

(++)   S + *koto* /*no* + *o* + A + *wa* + S + *to* + V + *te-i-ru*.

An explanation of factivity is straightforward. As (+) is in fact (++) and (++) has the presupposition that S is true because of the presence of *koto* / *no* in it, (+) itself has a presupposition that S is true.

Thus, a sentence of the form

(i)
S	to	shit-	te-i-ru.
	QUO	know	RESU

has really a form

(ii)
S	koto/no	o	S	to	shit-	te-i-ru.
	NOMI	ACC		QUO	know	RESU

---

32. Just as the counter-factive case, we may have any sentence that is equivalent to S and satisfies an additional condition C^+ as an object complement. Again it has to be left for another occasion to investigate what C^+ should be.

and has a presuppostion that S, because it constitutes the object complement, although it occurs only implicitly.

The present proposal holds that a factive and counter-factive should always take an object complement. This might be unintuitive, but even for
factive verbs there seems to be some intuition that favors it. It is that a
sentence which has only a content complement like (i) gives an impression
of incompleteness compared to the one with only an object complement,
like the following:[33]

(iii)   S   koto   o   shit-   te-i-ru.
        NOMI ACC know RESU

At any rate, it is obvious that we need much more linguistic data in order
to decide whether the present proposal is a feasible one.[34] However, I would
like to point out one merit that my proposal has. In tracing back the source
of a presupposition that a sentence of the form (i) has to the one of the form
(ii), the present proposal makes it plausible that the presupposition involved
in factive and counter-factive verbs have a single origin—namely, a sentential
complement of the form "S + *koto*" or "S + *no*." Our last business in this chapter
is to consider how these expressions can be the origin of the presuppositions.

3.3. The Origin of Factivity

A noun phrase of the form "S + *koto*" or "S + *no*" gives rise to a presupposition even when it does not occur as an object complement of a factive or
counter-factive verb. We have seen its example in (40), which I repeat here:

(40)   Taro   ga   kaet-ta   koto   o   Hanako
              NOM   went home   NOMI   ACC

       wa   shinji   te-iru.
       TOP   believe   RESU(?)
       'Hanako believes the fact that Taro went home.'

33. Pietroski gives an interesting observation about the English "explain," which has
relevance to our subject. "There is an asymmetry, in that (60) [= Nora explained that
Fido barked.] feels somehow 'incomplete' if an explanandum/Theme is not determined
contextually; while (61) [= Nora explained the fact that Fido barked.] does not require,
at least not in the same way, that an explanans/Import be specified contextually"
(Pietroski 2005, 224).
34. Of course, the proposal in its present form must be much improved, as was
suggested in the footnotes 31 and 32.

On the one hand, that Taro went home is a presupposition of (40) is confirmed if you consider its negation.

(49) Taro ga   kaet-ta   koto o   Hanako
           NOM   went home   NOMI ACC

      wa   shinji te-i.   nai
      TOP   believe RESU(?)   NOT
      'Hanako does not believe the fact that Taro went home.'

(49) has the same presupposition as (40).

On the other hand, it is far from the truth that "S + *koto*" and "S + *no*" always generate a presupposition that S is true. There are no presupposition of this sort in the following sentences[35], which include the sentence (45) that we have already seen before.

(45) Taro   ga   buji de-iru koto   o
                  NOM   safe COP   NOMI   ACC

      shinji-   te-iru.
      believe   RESU(?)
      'I believe that Taro is safe.'

(50) Eigo   o   hanasu no   wa   muzukashii.
      English ACC   speak   NOMI   TOP   difficult
      (Speaking English is difficult.)

(51) Taro   wa   Hanako   to   atta   koto
             TOP   with   met   NOMI

      o   hiteishi- te-iru.
      ACC   Deny   RESU
      'Taro denies that he met Hanako.'

Hence, it has been an important question in Japanese grammar to find out exactly what makes the difference in the presuppositional behavior of noun phrases of the form "S + *koto*" or "S + *no*." I believe that one promising

---

35. The sentences (50) and (51) are taken from Sunagawa 1988. They are her examples (25b) and (33), respectively.

line of approach to this problem is to see whether the following hypothesis will be verified or not:

Hypothesis: An occurrence of a noun phrase of the form "S + *koto*" or "S + *no*" generates a presupposition that S is true if and only if it occurs as a definite noun phrase.

In order to understand this hypothesis, it is necessary to have some idea about the way the definite/indefinite distinction is realized in Japanese. Unlike English, Japanese has no articles, either definite or indefinite. Furthermore, there is no distinction among its noun phrases between singular and plural. There is a big difference, however, between the distinction of definite/indefinite and that of singular/plural. It is frequently impossible to judge whether a given occurrence of a noun phrase is supposed to denote a single thing or a number of things, even when the context is clear. And yet in most cases, there will be no difficulty in understanding what is said in a sentence where it occurs. However, in Japanese also, given a context, it is usually clear whether a given occurrence of a noun phrase is definite or indefinite; if you cannot determine which it is, you will not understand what is said in a sentence where it occurs. This suggests that there must be some way for a speaker of Japanese to know whether a given occurrence of a noun phrase is definite or not. [36]

For a relatively large class of noun phrases, there is a sort of test, which I described in Iida 2007, to determine whether a given occurrence of a noun phrase is definite or not. Unfortunately, this test is not general enough to cover all occurrences of noun phrases; in particular, it does not apply to the kind of noun phrases we are now dealing with.

Still, there exists strong intuitions that suggest the occurrences of noun phrases of this sort in (45), (50), and (51) do not denote particular events or facts but, rather, certain types of events or facts. In (45), what is believed to exist is not some particular situation in which Taro is safe but, instead, any state that counts as Taro's being safe. In (50), what is said to be difficult is not a particular action of speaking English but, rather, a type of action described as speaking English. Lastly, in (51), Taro does not deny the existence of a particular episode of meeting Hanako but, instead, the existence of any events that are of the type of meeting Hanako.

36. This paragraph is drawn from Iida (2014, chap. 2).

In contrast, an occurrence of "S + *koto*" or "S + *no*" as an object complement of *shiru* ("know") may be argued to denote a particular event, state, or fact. For example, let us consider this sentence:

(52) Taro wa Toukyou ni itta koto
     TOP Tokyo LOC go NOMI

   ga nai.
   NOM NOT
   'Taro has never been to Tokyo.'

In this, the noun phrase *Toukyou ni itta koto* denotes a certain type of event—namely, having been to Tokyo—in general, and it generates no presupposition that there exist events of that type.

Now embed this into a sentence that has *shiru* as its main verb:

(53) Taro ga Toukyou ni itta koto
     NOM Tokyo LOC go NOMI

   ga nai no o Hanako wa
   NOM NOT NOMI ACC   TOP

   shit- te-iru.
   know RESU
   'Hanako knows that Taro has never been to Tokyo.'

Here the object complement of *shiru* denotes a particular fact that Taro has never been to Tokyo, and the sentence as a whole has a presupposition that this fact obtains.

Of course, all this is nothing like an argument. If we wish to verify or falsify our hypothesis in earnest, we have to proceed in a more systematic way. There is, however, another way of defending our hypothesis: to seek some indirect grounds for favoring it in pointing out the merits that it has.

First, our hypothesis explains why a noun phrase of the form "S + *koto*" or "S + *no*" generates a presupposition that S is true when it occurs as an object complement of *shiru*. For it is widely held that a definite noun phrase gives rise to a presupposition that its reference is not empty. Although we do not yet know exactly what this sort of noun phrase refers to, if the truth of S is necessary for "S + *koto*" and "S + *no*" to have reference, then the truth of S should work as a presupposition of the sentence which contains them.

What should be the reference of the definite occurrence of "S + *koto*" or "S + *no*"? As it can be an object complement of *shiru*, this amounts to asking what the object of knowledge is. (Please remember that there is also the content of knowledge, because *shiru* can take a content complement as well, and it is not yet decided whether it is the same as the object of knowledge.)

Some might be tempted to answer that it refers to the proposition that S expresses. It is understandable to be so tempted, because knowledge is usually classified as one of the propositional attitudes. I think this answer cannot be right, however. For, the existence of a proposition is independent of its truth value.

As an example, let us take (42), which I repeat here:

(42) Taro ga   kaet-ta   koto o   Hanako
         NOM went home NOMI ACC

     wa   shit- te-iru.
     TOP   know RESU

Suppose that someone has uttered (42). If she has made a correct statement in doing that, then that Taro went home is its presupposition. So, if Taro has not gone home and is still around, the noun phrase of the form *Taro ga kaet-ta koto* in this particular utterance of (42) should lack a reference, and the entire utterance would be neither true nor false, and this will be exactly a case of a presupposition failure. But, if the proposition that *Taro ga kaet-ta* ("Taro went home") expresses were the reference of this noun phrase, this could not happen, because the proposition exists whether it is true or not.

Hence, the reference of the noun phrase in question cannot be the proposition expressed by S. Then, what does it refer to? In the case of (42), S will be classified as a sentence reporting some concrete events or states (eventualities). Let us call this type of sentence a "state-of-affairs sentence."[37] My proposal is that "S + *koto*" refers to the event of Taro's going home, which exists if S is true. In general, if S is a state-of-affairs sentence, then a definite noun phrase "S + *koto/no*" refers to the events or states that exist if S is true.

Besides state-of-affairs sentences, another main kind of sentence in Japanese are those that attribute some property to a certain subject, which we may call an "attribute sentence." The following example has such a sentence as the object complement of *shiru*:

---

37. For a classification of Japanese sentences into state-of-affairs and attribute sentences, see Iida (2010).

(54) Kujira   ga   honyuu-rui de-aru koto   o
     whale   NOM   mammal   COP   NOMI   ACC

     Hanako   wa   shit-   te-iru.
               TOP   know   RESU
     'Hanako knows that the whale is a mammal.'

What is the reference of *Kujira ga honyuu-rui de aru koto*? I don't think it is something abstract, like the proposition that the whale is a mammal. It should be something that exists only when the whale is a mammal. Perhaps it may be called a "fact."

So I conclude that events, states, and facts can be objects of knowledge. Just as with the English "know," the Japanese *shiru* can take noun phrases that denote persons, things, or places. Thus, they are also possible objects of knowledge. But if our claim about factive verbs that they are two-complement verbs is correct, then knowledge must have also its content. What are they? My guess is that they are the same kinds of entities as those that can be the contents of beliefs. If there is any truth in such an idea, it may give us a fresh perspective for reconsidering the relation between knowledge and belief.

In general, a Japanese verb for a mental activity may take two sorts of sentential complements: an object complement with a nominalizer *koto* or *no*, and a content complement with a quotation marker *to*. We may ask questions like the following about this class of verbs:

1. Which verbs take both sorts of complements? Which ones take only object complements? Which ones take only content complements? Which ones do not take any sentential complement?
2. If a verb takes both sorts of complements, how are its object complement and content complement related to each other?
3. If a verb takes an object complement, should it be a definite noun phrase? Or, should it be an indefinite one? Or, may it should be either?

They are all interesting questions, but some may wonder what relevance answering them can have for philosophy.

Our supposition has been that an object complement represents an object of a mental activity and a content complement its content. But is it justified to proceed in this way from a grammatical distinction to a conceptual one? On the one hand, a grammatical distinction is made differently for different languages; it may be just a reflection of some accidental feature of a particular language. On the other hand, if a grammatical distinction in one language can be relatively easily transferred to another language by means of paraphrase and explanation, it may be regarded as evidence that it has a reality rooted in what is talked about.

Naturally I am inclined to think that the distinction between an object complement and a content complement may belong to the latter category. It may be better, however, not to jump to a conclusion and try to see what picture of our mental life a language that is different from English suggests. It may lead us to discover some conceptual possibilities we may not have noticed or have difficulty doing so if we have only English as our clue.

One such possibility is that mental activities like thinking, feeling an emotion, and communicating to others have both an object and a content. Isn't it possible that taking this possibility seriously might give us a new and interesting account of them?

REFERENCES

Davidson, Donald. (2001). *Subjective, Intersubjective, Objective*. Oxford: Clarendon Press.

Galton, Antony. (1984). *The Logic of Aspect: An Axiomatic Approach*. Oxford: Clarendon Press.

Glock, Hans-Johann. (1996). *A Wittgenstein Dictionary*. Oxford: Blackwell.

Iida, Takashi. (2001). "Nihongo Keishiki Imi-ron no Kokoromi (2)—Doushi- ku no Imiron" [An Essay in Japanese Formal Semantics (2): Semantics of Verbal Phrases]. Unpublished manuscript, Department of Philosophy, Keio University.

Iida, Takashi. (2007). "Towards a Semantics of Japanese Existential Sentences." In *Essays in the Foundations of Logical and Phenomenological Studies. Interdisciplinary Series on Reasoning Studies*, Vol. 3, ed. M. Okada, 67–96. Tokyo: Centre for Integrated Research on the Mind, Keio University.

Iida, Takashi. (2010). "Semantics of Possibility Suffix '(rar)e.'" In *Lecture Notes in Artificial Intelligence*, Vol. 6284, 217–234. Springer.

Iida, Takashi. (2014). "On Singular Quantification in Japanese." Unpublished manuscript.

Inoue, Kazuko. (1976). *Henkei Bunpou to Nihongo. Tougo Kouzou o Chu- ushin ni* [Transformational Grammar and Japanese—Mainly on Syntactic Structures]. Tokyo: Taishuukan.

Kamada, Osamu. (2000). *Nihongo no In-you* [Quotation in Japanese]. Tokyo: Hitsuji Shobou.

Karttunen, Lauri. (1970). "On the Semantics of Complement Sentences." *CLS* 6: 328–339.

Kindaichi, Haruhiko. (1950). "Kokugo doushi no ichi bunrui" [A Classification of Japanese verbs]. *Gengo Kenkyuu* (Linguistic Studies) 15: 48–63.

Kudo, Mayumi. (1995). *Asupekuto Tensu Taikei to Tekusuto* [The Aspect-Tense System and Texts]. Tokyo: Hitsuji Shobou.

Kuno, Susumu. (1973). *Nihon Bunpou Kenkyuu* [Studies in Japanese Grammar]. Tokyo: Taishuukan.

Landman, Fred. (1991). *Structures for Semantics*. Dordrecht: Kluwer.

Maruyama, Naoko. (2002). "Hanashi kotoba no jyoshi —*tte* o chu-ushin ni—." [Particles in Spoken Language: Focusing on *tte*]. *Tokyo Jyoshi Daigaku Nihon Bungaku* (Tokyo Woman's Christian University Japanese Literature) 98: 117–131.

Motomura, Mitsue. (2003). "The Thematic Roles of Sentential *to* /*kooto* Complements in Japanese/Korean." *Japanese/Korean Linguistics* 11: 439–453.

Pietroski, Paul M. (2005). *Events and Semantic Architecture*. Oxford: Oxford University Press.

Sunagawa, Yuriko. (1988). "In-yo-u-bun no kouzou to kinou (2)—in-yo-u-shi to meishi-ku o megutte" [The Structure and Function of Quotation (2)—On Quotation Phrases and Noun Phrases]. *Bungei Gengo Kenkyuu (Gengo hen)* (Studies in Literature and Languages, Languages, University of Tsukuba) 14: 75–91.

Tajima, Ikudo. (1983). "Chishiki" [Knowledge]. In *Kouza Nihongo no Goi 10: Goshi II* (Series Japanese Lexicon 10: History of Individual Words II), ed. Sato Kiyoji, 366–372. Tokyo: Meiji Shoin.

Vendler, Zeno. (1957). "Verbs and Times." *Philosophical Review* 66: 143–160.

CHAPTER 3

Multiple Chinese Verbs Equivalent to the English Verb "Know"

KIYOHIDE ARAKAWA AND MASAHARU MIZUMOTO

1. INTRODUCTION

There are at least three different ways in Chinese to translate the English knowledge verb "know": *renshi* (认识), *zhidao* (知道), and *liaojie* (了解). For instance, we can pick up these verbs from examples in the 2005 Chinese translation of the *Longman Dictionary of Contemporary English*:

I've known her for twenty years.
Wo renshi ta you 20 nian le.
我 认识 她 有20 年了。

Who knows the answer?
Shei   zhidao daan?
谁   知道 答案?

She knows me inside out.
Ta dui wo tai   liaojie le
她 对我 太 了解 了。

In this chapter, we discuss these words from a grammatical and epistemo-logical standpoint. We will then offer some examples of the Japanese verbs *shiru* and *wakaru*, which are counterparts to the English "know," and we will compare them in terms of some aspects of the knowledge verb (for a preliminary work of this chapter, see Arakawa 2012).

2. RENSHI (认识)

We explain *renshi* first because it is the most basic word when we discuss knowledge in Chinese. *Renshi* (认识) emphasizes being able to distinguish someone, some place, or something. When you use this word, you have seen the person, place, or Chinese character before and the image remains in your mind. For example, *Wo renshi ta* (我认识他/她) means "I recognize him (or her)." *Wo renshi zheige difang* (我认识这个地方) means "I distinguish this place from others." *Wo renshi zheige zi* (我认识这个字) means "I distinguish this Chinese character from others." *Ta renshi qu wo jia de lu* (他认识去我家的路) means that "He knows the way (= *lu*) to my home," and so on.

When you don't remember the person, character, or place any longer, you can say *Wo bu renshi ~ le* (我不认识~了), where *bu* 不is a negative adverb and *le* 了 shows the change of the situation. And when you say *wo bu renshi ta* (我不认识他) without *le, wo bu renshi zheige zi* (我不认识这个字), or *wo bu renshi zheige difang* (我不认识这个地方), it means that you have never seen him (or her) or the Chinese character or the place, or that you have seen it, but now you have no memory about it.

Note that the use of *renshi* for someone can be one-sided, so you can say *Wo renshi ta, keshi ta bu renshi wo* (我认识他,可是他不认识我 = "I know him, but he doesn't know me"). For instance, "I know the famous Chinese actress Zhang Ziyi (我认识章子怡), but probably she does not know me (她大概不认识我)."

The term for epistemology in the Chinese language is *renshilun* (认识论). *Lun* (论) means "theory" or "view." *Renshi* in this word is derived from the modern Japanese translation of "epistemology" (認識論) and differs from *renshi,* as just discussed. Presumably, *renshi,* for which we have given many examples, has been used from the Qing (清) dynasty (1616–1912), as follows:

> *Zicong zan ye lia renshi yihou* (自从咱爷俩认识以后 = "After we got acquainted with each other" (*Ernü yingxiongzhuan* 《儿女英雄传》).

Sato (1983, 74) pointed out that one of the *kana* (Japanese translation) for "know" in the 1872 English–Japanese dictionary (『附音挿図英

和字彙』) is *mishiru*. *Mishiru* means "to recognize," and that can also be taken as the translation of the Chinese word *renshi* because the Japanese translations in this dictionary deeply reflect the influence of the English–Chinese dictionary (《英汉字典》 [1866–69]) compiled by W. Lobscheid.

As noted earlier, the word for "epistemology" in Chinese, *renshilun* (认识论), was conceived in Japan (as 認識論) during the early Meiji period (明治时代) (in particular, presumably from the 1870s to 1880s). We can find it, for example, in books like *Tetsugaku jii* (哲学字汇 = *The Terms of Philosophy* [1881]) and *Kyoikugaku* (教育学= *Education* [1882]). The word *renshi*, however, had been used in the Qing dynasty and was imported into Japanese. Japanese people then raised it to a term of philosophy.

One thing to be noted here is that *renshi* only takes a noun object and cannot take a sentence object like *zhidao*. That is to say, its grammatical function is very simple.

3. *ZHIDAO* (知道)

Zhidao is the most common word to know about something generally or roughly. Its original form is *zhi* (知), and *dao* (道) is a kind of suffix, probably added in the Tang (唐) dynasty (618–907). In ancient times, people used only *zhi* (知). A famous example from Confucius is, "I shall teach you what wisdom (*zhi* 知) is. When you know a thing, say that you know it (*zhi zhi* 知之 [the second *zhi* (之) is a pronoun and the object of knowledge]; when you do not know a thing, admit that you do not know it (*bu zhi* 不知). That is wisdom." The *zhi* (知) that is used for wisdom and the *zhi* (知) that is used as a verb are written with the same character here, but today, 智 is usually used for "wisdom."

When you use *zhidao* (知道), you have to have information in your mind as a result of experience or because you have learned it or been told it by someone. So you can say *wo zhidao ta, keshi bu renshi ta* (我知道他, 可是不认识他 = "I know of him, but don't know him personally"). When you use *renshi*, you have to have seen him (or her) before and have his (or her) image in your mind, but when you use *zhidao*, you don't need to have seen him (or her). Thus, you can say *wo zhidao ta* ("I know him"), even if you have obtained the information about him (or her) from other people or books.

Interestingly, *wo zhidao le* (我知道了 = "I have known") is syntactically complete and can be used without any complement, although its English counterpart is not. The Japanese knowledge verb *shiru*, however, cannot be used without its cause when it is used for expressing the event of knowing, even with its complement; for example, *watashi wa sore wo shitta* ("I came to know it") is not a perfect sentence, so we have to say *watashi wa kesa no shinbun de sore wo shitta* ("I learned it from today's newspaper").[1]

The syntactical behavior of *zhidao* varies much and is interesting. First, it can take many kinds of objects. For example, *zhidao* can take not only noun objects, verbs, and adjective objects, but also sentence objects, as follows:

1. Noun objects:
   Wo zhidao ta de mingzi (我知道他的名字) = "I know his name."
   Wo zhidao ta de qingkuang (我知道他的情况) = "I know his circumstances."
   Wo zhidao ni de yisi (我知道你的意思) = "I know your idea."

2. Verb and adjective objects:
   Ni zhi zhidao chi (你只知道吃) = "You only know to eat."
   Ta bu zhidao lei (他不知道累) (*lei* = "be tired") = "He doesn't complain of work."[2]

3. Sentence objects:
   (a) Declarative sentence:
       Wo zhidao ni xianzai hen mang (我知道你现在很忙) = "I know you are very busy now."
   (b) Interrogative sentence:
       Wo zhidao ta zhuzai nar (我知道他住在哪儿) = "I know where he (she) lives now."
       Wo zhidao zenme ban (我知道怎么办) = "I know how to do it."

Note that the complements in (3b) are not literally interrogative sentences but, rather, sentences including an interrogative. If you want to ask someone where he (or she) lives or how to do something, you have to add *ma* (吗) at the end of the sentence:

Ni zhidao ta shi shei ma? (你知道他是谁吗?) = "Do you know who he (she) is?"

The Chinese verb *zhidao* and the English verb "know" are stative verbs. However, the Japanese verb *shiru* is a punctual verb; but if used in this form,

---

1. In contrast, the Japanese verb *wakaru* can be used without other words, as in *watashi wa wakatta* ("I came to know").
2. Note that Japanese *shiru* has the same usage in *Kare wa tsukare wo shiranai* ("He does not know fatigue"). Thus, the relevant area of *zhidao* is not only limited to the mental state but also spreads out to the physical state of the body (for example, allowing one to know physically).

it is a peculiar imperfect active verb, so if you want to refer to the state of knowing, you have to use it in its continuous-perfect form, *shitte-iru*.

4. *LIAOJIE* (了解)

Liaojie is similar to *zhidao*, but it means to know more widely and deeply than *zhidao*. For example, to say *wo liaojie ta* (我了解他), you may need more information about the person than needed to say *wo zhidao ta*.

The syntactical function of *liaojie* is also very simple, as it can only take noun objects, as follows:

> *Wo bu liaojie qingkuang* (我不了解情况) = "I don't understand the situation."
> *Wo hen liaojie ta* (我很了解他) = "I know all about him."

Interestingly, *liaojie* cannot only express a state; it can also express the process of obtaining the information. For example,

> *Ni qu liaojie ta yixia* (你去了解他一下) = "You had better find out about him."
> *Ni qu liaojie yixi* (你去了解一下) = "Look into this and find out."
> *Wo xiang xiang nin liaojie yixia* (我想向您了解一下) = "I would like to ask you something" (asking a question).

Yixia (一下) means "one time" and is used after a verb, indicating an act or an attempt. In other words, it can change the stative verb *liaojie* to express an activity. *Zhidao*, however, cannot be used like *ni zhidao ta yixia* (你知道他一下), so we can say *liaojie* is more active than *zhidao*.

In Japanese, a phrase like *Chugoku wo shiru* ("to know China") is a common form of a title of book or article, which may be put in Chinese, not *Zhidao Zhongguo* (知道中国) but *liaojie Zhongguo* (了解中国), because *zhidao* is a stative verb and therefore its present form cannot explain the future, whereas *liaojie* can explain the future when it is used as a title.

5. STATE AND EVENT

Basically, the English "know" is a stative verb, but it can explain a bounded event or activity when it is used in some sentences. Concerning this point, John Lions (1968) says:

Kiyohide Arakawa and Masaharu Mizumoto

It must also be noted that the "non-progressive" verbs in English are not necessarily stative when they combine with either the past tense or one of the modals: e.g., *As soon as I saw him, I knew that there was something wrong; You will feel a slight pain when I insert the needle* (in these sentences the verbs "knew" and "feel" refer to an "event"—to the beginning of a state, rather than to the state itself). (316)

Zhidao (知道), *liaojie* (了解), and *renshi* (认识) are stative verbs, so if you say

	zhidao		(我知道他)
Wo	liaojie	ta	(我了解他)
	renshi		(我认识他)

it means you already have information about the person, or you know everything about him, or you have seen them and can now recognize him.

Among these verbs, the syntactical function of *zhidao* is simpler than the others. *Liaojie* and *renshi* can easily be changed into expressing an events or activity when you put them in a proper context, as follows:

1. Adding *yixia* after the verb will change it into expressing an activity:
   Ni liaojie ta yixia (你了解他一下) = "You had better know him (or her)."
   Ni renshi ta yixia (你认识他一下) = "You had better get acquainted with him (or her)."

As we pointed out above, *zhidao* cannot combine with *yixia*.

2. Combining with auxiliary verbs (modals) to express an event (the beginning of a state):
   Wo xiang liaojie ta (我想了解他/她) = "I would like to find out about him (or her)."
   Wo xiang renshi ta (我想认识他/她) = "I would like to get acquainted with him (or her)."

Although *zhidao* cannot be used with *yixia*, it can combine with auxiliary verbs (modals), as in:

Wo xiang zhidao ta de mingzi (我想知道他/她的名字) = "I would like to know his (or her) name."

Note, however, *Wo xiang zhidao ta (我想知道他/她) = "I would like to know about him (or her)" is not a natural construction, while the following form is acceptable.[3]

3. Used in the past tense—that is to say, in Chinese, in perfect sentences:
   Wo zhidao le (我知道他/她了) = "I knew him (or her)."
   Wo liaojie ta le (我了解他/她了) = "I knew well about him (or her) [after investigating]."
   Wo zaojiu renshi ta le (我早就认识他/她了) = "I became acquainted with him (or her) long ago."

Renshi can also express an event when it is used in a subordinate clause, as in:

Renshi ni, hen gaoxing (认识你,很高兴) = "Because I have finally become acquainted with you, I am very pleased" (= "Nice to meet you").

6. THE ACTIVITY IMPLICATION

We have considered the Chinese knowledge verbs and contrasted them with their English and Japanese counterparts, mainly in terms of verb classification based on lexical aspect[4] and their corresponding implications of activity. We may then hypothesize that, to the extent that knowing is an activity, the knowledge verbs can naturally be used for an order. However, things are not so straightforward.

For comparison, let us focus on propositional knowledge verbs (in Chinese, zhidao). In Japanese, since shiru is a punctual verb, rather than a stative verb, it is semantically (in its lexical aspect) the same as "shoot," "propose," and so on in English, and we may therefore expect that it can easily express an activity. And it can indeed naturally take the imperative form (shire or shiri nasai), used for giving an order like haji wo shire (= "know shame"), hontou ni hoshii mono wo shirinasai (= "know what you really want"), negai wa kanau noda to shirinasai (= "know that your dreams come true"), and so forth. On the one hand, the English "know," though basically a stative verb, can also be used for an order in more ordinary contexts, like "Know yourself," "Know the answer by tomorrow!," "Know that you are alive" (Konishi 1980, 809), KNOW THIS: Today's Most Interesting and

3. Thus, the reason why 我想知道他/她 is not acceptable while 我知道他/她 and 我知道他/她了 are is a question to be explored in another occasion.
4. For lexical aspect of Japanese knowledge verbs, see footnotes 2–5 of Mizumoto (chapter 5, this volume).

Important Scientific Ideas, Discoveries, and Developments (a book title), "Know the New Features of the 2017 Nissan Frontier" (an advertisement), and so on (though no doubt not so common). On the other hand, *zhidao* does not have the corresponding imperative usage. Thus, these observations suggest that, among the three verbs, the order of strength of activity implication is:

shiru (Japanese) ≥ *know* (English) > *zhidao* (Chinese).

Also, if we examine the "decide to know" construction (and its counterparts), the English "know" has perfectly natural uses, like "I decided to know more about him," which includes the biblical occurrence ("For I decided to know nothing among you except Jesus Christ and him crucified"), and the Japanese counterpart using *shiru* is also possible (*Watashi wa kare wo motto shirou to kimeta*). However, the corresponding Chinese construction (我决心知道 or 我决定知道) is simply not possible. This confirms the hypothetical order of the strength of activity implication just noted.

However, there is also another Japanese knowledge verb for propositional knowledge, *wakatte-iru*, which cannot allow the "want to know" construction (**wakaritai*) when used for expressing the desire for propositional knowledge, even though its basic form, *wakaru*, can express both a state and a bounded event.[5] Thus, one may expect that *zhidao* does not allow such usage, either. However, this is not the case. It can naturally be used in sentence like 我想知道下没下雨 ("I want to know whether it is raining"), just like the English "know" and the Japanese *shiru* (*ame ga hutte iru ka shiritai*).

Also, *wakaru* has its imperative form (*wakare*), but if used as an order, this means "Understand!" or "Appreciate!," rather than "Know!" In this sense, it cannot be used for an order to mean the same thing as "know" or *shire*. Similarly, it cannot meaningfully take the "decide to know" form (**motto wakarou to kimeta*) and mean the same thing as the English phrase, since it means "decided to understand more."[6] See Table 3.1 below for a summary.

These observations apparently support the following order of activity implication:

shiru (Japanese) ≥ know (English) > zhidao (Chinese) > wakaru (Japanese)

However, Mizumoto (chap. 5, this volume) has shown with empirical data that, owing to the ability implication of *wakatte-iru* or its connection with action, the English "know" is closer to *wakatte-iru* than *shitte-iru*. One

5. For more about *wakaru* or its continuous-perfect form, *wakatte-iru*, see chapter 5, this volume.
6. Also note that, when *wakaru* is used as a punctual verb, it expresses an event that is not controllable by the subject (see Mizumoto, this volume).

Table 3.1 SUMMARY OF THE PROPERTIES
OF KNOWLEDGE VERBS

	Order	"decide to"	"want to"
zhidao	✗	✗	✓
know	✓	✓	✓
shiru	✓	✓	✓
wakaru	✗	✗	✗

may therefore doubt that the alleged notion of the strength of activity implication can be consistently held at all. This challenge may be answered empirically through further (analogous) investigation of the use of *zhidao* in relation to *wakatte-iru* and *shitte-iru*, which should be the subject of future investigation.

ACKNOWLEDGMENT

We would like to thank Yang Rui for helpful comments concerning Chinese in the earlier draft of this chapter.

REFERENCES

Arakawa, Kiyohide. (2012). "'Shiru' and 'Zhidao' (知道)." [in Japanese] *Journal of Japanese and Chinese Linguistics and Japanese Language Teaching*, vol. 5: 9–19.
Konishi, Tomoshichi. (1980). *Eigo Kihon Doushi Jiten* [Dictionary of English Basic Verbs]. Kenkyusha.
Lions, John. (1968). *Introduction to Theoretical Linguistics*. New York: Cambridge University Press.
Sato, Toru. (1983). *A Study of the Vocabulary in the Modern Age*. Tokyo: Ohusha.

CHAPTER 4

The Contribution of Confucius to Virtue Epistemology

SHANE RYAN AND CHIENKUO MI

1. CONFUCIAN THOUGHT IS OF EPISTEMOLOGICAL SIGNIFICANCE

While the Confucius of the *Analects* has been regarded as providing a virtue-based approach in ethics, he is not commonly noted as offering anything of epistemological significance (Yao 2000, 33). In this chapter we argue that the Confucian thought of the *Analects* is of epistemological significance—in particular, for virtue epistemology. To begin, we're simply making the case that particular epistemological stances are taken in the *Analects* that are not merely commonsensical or obvious. Yet, in the context of the vast literature on Confucius, our claim is a bold one. We make a claim that runs counter to much ancient and contemporary treatment of Confucius, but we defend this claim at the start. And as we had better also account for why Confucius hasn't been seen as making a contribution to epistemology, we then shift the focus to this task.

Confucius is undoubtedly concerned with moral issues. In fact, on some interpretations of the *Analects*, morality is the main concern. Jeffrey Riegel (2013), in the *Stanford Encyclopedia of Philosophy*, suggests just such an interpretation. He writes that the Confucius of the *Analects* appears most concerned with moral matters. In fact, because of the central place of virtues in Confucian thought, virtues such as *ren* (universal benevolence), and Confucius's discussion of such virtue in relation to the *junzi*, an exemplar of the virtuous person, Confucius is naturally seen as doing virtue ethics.[1] To be clear, we're not saying that those who see Confucius as making a contribution to moral thought are mistaken.

However, it would obviously be a mistake to see Confucius as only having such a concern. Just like Aristotle, Confucius is clearly concerned with what it is to be an exemplary person or a good agent in a much broader sense than a solely moral sense. For example, the inherent partiality of *xiao*, translated as "filial piety," is not obviously a moral virtue, though it is a virtue discussed by Confucius. Depending on whether morality is best viewed as necessarily requiring impartiality, it may be best to see *xiao* as a filial virtue and not a moral virtue. In other words, on this view, *xiao* is a nonmoral virtue, which nevertheless the exemplary person possesses. This provides one basis for thinking that it is a mistake to see Confucius as only being concerned with morality. This claim, however, does not rest on that.

Confucius also lists *zhe*, wisdom, as a virtue. In fact, it is listed in the *Analects* as one of three virtues that lead the way to becoming a *junzi*: "The wise (*zhizhe*) are free from perplexities; the virtuous [actually *ren*] from anxiety; and the bold from fear" (Analects 9.29, discussed in Mi 2015, 365). *Zhe* is, therefore, a significant virtue in Confucian thought and an intellectual virtue at that.

A concern for what it is to be a good agent in a sense that isn't reducible to the moral is still within the domain of ethics. This is surely right in that the notion of good agent used in ethics is not necessarily confined to the moral agent but may also be use when considering the agent who lives well. We categorize discourse on how to live well or theories of the good life as ethics without taking either to necessarily be reducible to moral theory. Confucius is, in fact, concerned with how to live well.

As with Aristotle, part of this living well in Confucian thought is constituted by an epistemic component, of which there is detailed discussion. Confucius, unlike Aristotle however, didn't leave us any writings through which we could discover his ideas. Rather, like Socrates, we learn about Confucius's ideas through records kept by his students. The record kept of Confucius's ideas was a series of short descriptions of situations and what Confucius said in those situations. The form in which we have Confucius's ideas isn't such as to lend itself to comprehensive, unambiguous accounts of theoretical positions; interpretations of Confucian thought are required.

1. Early translations of the *Analects* rendered *junzi* as "gentleman," though a more recent and perhaps more apt translation from Ames and Rosemont (1998) translates *junzi* as "exemplary person" (Wong 2017).

For this reason, we are not making the case that Confucius is a virtue epistemologist, though, given the sophistication of his thought as evidenced in the *Analects*, we're not saying he isn't, either. This is why we defend the more restricted claim mentioned earlier—that some of what Confucius said, as recorded in the *Analects*, is of epistemological significance, particularly of virtue epistemological significance.

Let us now turn to Confucian thought that is of epistemological significance. The view that there is nothing of epistemological significance in the Confucian thought of the *Analects* overlooks the fact that Confucius in the *Analects* does have things to say about epistemological matters. It is true, however, that Confucius does not approach epistemological matters the way epistemologists in the modern era have tended to do so. Confucius shows his concern for epistemological matters within an agent-based approach. This is the same way he shows concern for moral matters. This agent-based approach in Confucian thought is in keeping with the agent-based approach of virtue epistemology more generally.

For example, according to Confucius, the exemplary person, in order to be exemplary, must carefully scrutinize what we would today call first-order beliefs. If we want to have the epistemic status characteristic of the superior man, then those first-order beliefs must be subject to appropriate reflection. This idea is developed by a distinction between two sorts of knowledge, *shi* (識) and *zhi* (知), in the *Analects*. Mi (2015) discusses this distinction in more detail and highlights the parallel with Sosa's distinction between animal and reflective knowledge.[2] *Shi* can be understood as first-order knowledge, or information acquired. *Zhi*, in contrast, is second-order and is ascended to when first-order knowledge has been subject to the right sort of reflection and thereby undergoes development. It is in the following passage that knowledge (*zhi*) is characterized as reflective knowledge:

> The Master said, "You, shall I teach you what knowledge is? When you know a thing, to hold that you know it; and when you do not know a thing, to allow that you do not know it—this is knowledge." (*Analects* 2.17)[3]

2. Mi (2015) highlights that sources of *shi* are the senses and memory. Such knowledge allows us to recognize, identify, differentiate, and simply know certain things. As Mi points out, however, Confucius is not very concerned with first-order knowledge.

3. For further discussion of the epistemological significance of this passage, see Sosa (2015).

In the passage that follows, there is a description that indicates the significance of the *zhi* and *shi* distinction for the exemplary person and, in the second sentence, a characterization of *shi*:

> The Master said, "There may be those who act without knowing why. I do not do so. Hearing much and selecting what is good and following it; seeing much and keeping it in memory—this is the second style of knowledge [or a lower level of knowledge]." (*Analects* 7.28)

What is important to note here is that Confucius, an exemplar too, indicates that *zhi* is required for action, not merely *shi*. He does so by saying that he does not act without *zhi*. In fact, aside from getting a distinction between two different sorts of knowledge, we also get an indication as to why epistemological matters are significant for moral matters. The virtuous person should have the right sort of knowledge, reflective knowledge, before acting. From these passages, fragmentary though they are, we can see that Confucian thought is of epistemological significance. In what follows, we explore the significance of that thought in greater depth.

2. LOCATING THE EPISTEMOLOGICAL SIGNIFICANCE OF CONFUCIAN THOUGHT

Within traditional Chinese scholarship there wasn't an epistemology on the modern Western model, or, to simplify, a science of knowledge. There was no isolated study of knowledge abstracted from daily concerns. It is therefore unsurprising that Chinese scholars did not categorize Confucian thought as making a contribution to epistemology as well as to ethics.

In Western scholarship, certainly since Western scholars first came into contact with Confucian thought and up until very recently, a strongly contrasting practice held sway. Knowledge and related theoretical issues, such as skepticism and justification, have been studied in isolation from what it is to be a good agent. In fact, for this reason, it is understandable that the epistemological significance of Confucian thought has been overlooked. Confucian thought couldn't be seen as being of epistemological significance by Western scholars when that thought looked so unlike epistemology as practiced by Western scholars.

So what has changed? In recent years, epistemology in the West has undergone a significant shift. There has been a virtue turn[4] (Mi et al. 2016).

---

4. Actually, this can also be described as a virtue return, as it marks epistemology's return to the approach of Aristotle and Plato (Mi et al. 2016).

This has meant that in much epistemology there has been a move away from the examination of epistemic issues in isolation from one another to a theoretically unified agent-based examination of epistemological issues.

As mentioned, this agent-based approach in epistemology, marks a new trend in the field. The virtue turn has been a welcome response to the blockages and sclerosis that epistemology faced. The lack of a plausible the-oretically unifying approach in epistemology, and in particular the lack of such an approach that was agent-based, had meant there was an apparent undue, and to many outside the field, a perplexing focus on one particular sort of case, Gettier cases. There also seemed to be an inability to provide a convincing account of a core, perhaps the core concept of epistemology, or justification; and a failure of the narrow, theoretically ununified approach to produce theoretical consistency across areas of specialization, or the value problem.

The virtue turn has led to dialectical progress across all these areas, although unsurprisingly, in none of these areas has the matter become settled. Virtue theorists such as Sosa (2007) and Greco (2010) have offered robust virtue epistemological solutions to Gettier cases, while Pritchard (2010) has put forth an anti-luck virtue epistemological solution.[5] It should be noted that other virtue epistemologists have regarded the decades-long concern with the problem as mistaken and have developed new areas of epistemology that are unconcerned with the analysis of knowledge and with solving the Gettier problem (Baehr 2008).

Arguably, the virtue turn was initiated by Sosa's (1980) article in re-sponse to the problem of epistemic justification mentioned earlier. It was his pioneering work, "The Raft and the Pyramid," that introduced a virtue epistemological approach as a solution to a mainstream epistemo-logical problem. In the article, Sosa argues that both foundationalist and coherentist accounts of justification suffer from fatal flaws, but that a virtue theoretic account can take the best from each approach while avoiding the fatal flaws of each.

Linda Zagzebski (2003), a preeminent virtue theorist, makes the case that a widely supported account of epistemic justification—reliabilism, or an account of justification claimed by its proponents as necessary for knowledge—creates difficulties in accounting for the value of knowledge. Plausibly, a good theory of knowledge will not only be informative with

5. Pritchard (2010, 24) defines robust virtue epistemology as theories of the nature of knowledge that account for knowledge exclusively on the basis of virtue and don't retain a separate anti-luck condition.

regard to the nature of knowledge; it will also allow us to account for the value of knowledge—in particular, the superior value of knowledge vis-à-vis mere true belief. The swamping problem that Zagzebski identifies for reliabilists is addressed by leading virtue theorists such as Greco (2011, 2010, 2009). Greco's agent reliabilist response is to defend the claim that knowledge is a kind of achievement—an achievement being a success from ability—and that achievements have value that mere true beliefs lack.

The virtue turn in epistemology with its agent-based approach enables Western scholars who examine Confucian thought to see its epistemological significance. In fact, engagement by Western scholars with Confucian thought as virtue epistemological has been almost nonexistent up until now. Nonetheless, Sosa (2015), a leading virtue epistemologist, does engage with an epistemological aspect of Confucian thought.

3. CONFUCIAN THOUGHT—PROGRESSING THE DEBATE

Having made the case that Confucian thought is of epistemological significance—in particular, of virtue epistemological significance—we now turn to making the case that Confucian thought can contribute to progressing contemporary virtue epistemological discourse.

The recordings of Confucius's sayings are indicative of well-thought-out positions, which chime with positions in contemporary debates in a number of areas of philosophy. In fact, in our own virtue epistemological work, we have drawn on Confucian thought. The distinction in the *Analects* between different types of knowledge is just one example.

There are, however, areas in Confucian thought, even with regard to the good intellectual agent, that are unique and are worthy of further examination. Confucius, for example, gives special place to reflection in what he has to say about the good epistemic agent. While several philosophers in the contemporary literature are developing positions with regard to reflection (see Kornblith 2012; Kvanvig 2014), Confucius offers innovations in this area. These ideas are not merely of epistemological significance but also have the potential to progress virtue epistemological discourse. To see where Confucian thought can help progressing the virtue epistemological discourse, it is important to provide some background to that discourse.

An interest in the epistemological significance of reflection has been growing in contemporary epistemological discourse. On the one hand, we find a challenge to its epistemological significance posed by Hilary Kornblith (2012), and on the other hand, Sosa (2014, 2011) advocates its epistemological significance. See Mi and Ryan (2016) for examination of these two positions.

As we've discussed, Kornblith (2012, 1) charges philosophers with having a mistaken view of the nature of reflection and its potential as a capacity. For example, philosophers' views of reflection, according to Kornblith, conflict with an empirically informed view according to which reflection is not capable of bringing about philosophical progress. In fact, he claims that many of the processes involved in reflection are "terribly unreliable" (1). In supports of his position, Kornblith (2012, 23) cites various studies purporting to show that belief formation is unduly affected by colors, anchoring effects, and so on.[6]

Kornblith's charge poses a challenge to Sosa's (2014) theory of knowledge, which accords a special place for reflection. Sosa (2014) conceives of reflection as being "something directed or turned on itself" or "meditation, or careful thought." As discussed, Sosa distinguishes animal knowledge from reflective knowledge. The former is a brute knowing, while the latter is a meta-competent knowing.

Sosa (2011, 1–13) articulates this through his AAA model, which treats belief as a kind of performance. According to the AAA model, performances have three aspects by which they can be assessed: accuracy, adroitness, and aptness. Knowledge is a case of a well-performing belief and, as such, each of the three aspects is present in cases of knowledge. In cases of knowledge, belief is accurate and so true, belief is adroit and manifests competence, and a belief is apt—it is true because it is competent. Sosa calls such well-performing belief "animal knowledge."

Reflective knowledge is a meta-competent knowing. It is a type of knowledge that goes beyond animal knowledge. Sosa defines meta-competent knowledge as "apt belief aptly noted." Such belief also follows the AAA model of performance, though the well-performing belief of meta-competent knowledge is an order higher than apt belief, requiring as it does belief. Such meta-competent knowing is belief recognized as apt because of competence. For Sosa, this meta-competence is a reflective competence. If, however, Kornblith is right that the processes involved in reflection are "terribly unreliable," then it is hard to see how reflection could qualify as a competence and, in turn, how we can say there is such thing as reflective knowledge, at least the sort of reflective knowledge that Sosa has in mind. If Kornblith is right that philosophers don't understand the

6. For further discussion of Kornblith on reflection, see Mi and Ryan (2016).

nature of reflection, then the task facing the defender of reflective knowledge looks daunting.

In our own work, we attempt to answer that challenge, and a crucial part in doing so is informed by Confucian thought (Mi and Ryan 2016). In Confucian thought, it is the *junzi*, the virtuous or exemplary person, who is properly reflective. This inspires the move to differentiate between skillful or virtuous reflection and unskillful or unvirtuous reflection, which in any case is a plausible distinction that bears on the empirical data that Kornblith offers in support of his position that reflection is "terribly unreliable."

Our next step is to elaborate on the nature of reflection. Again, Confucian thought shapes the account we set forth. While part of what we say about the nature of reflection, and skillful reflection, draws on dual-process theory, another part draws on what is said about reflection in the *Analects*.

In the *Analects*, there is a distinction between two sorts of reflection (Mi and Ryan 2016; Mi 2015, 364–366). The exemplary person has a reflective capacity with two key components, a perspective component and a retrospective component, as well as dispositional responses. This perspective component involves perception and reasoning, which are directed at a certain goal or good.[7] In other words, reflection that takes place draws on these capacities and does so with a particular goal or goals in mind. The perspective component of reflection disposes the virtuous agent to carefully look ahead when appropriate.

The retrospective component, in contrast, utilizes memories and trained responses. In this case, the responses aren't directed at reaching certain goals but, rather, at moving away from or avoiding their opposites. The retrospective component of reflection disposes the exemplary agent to carefully draw on learning from past mistakes when appropriate.

The Chinese 省 is used for the retrospective component, while 思 is used for the perspective component, as we can see from the *Analects*:

> The philosopher Zeng said, "I daily reflect (省) on myself with regard to three points: whether, in transacting business for others, I may have been not faithful; whether, in intercourse with friends, I may have been not sincere; whether I may have not mastered and practiced the instructions of my teacher." (*Analects*, "Xue Er," 4)

7. The exemplary agent will have goods or appropriate ends as his or her goals.

The Master said, "When we see men of worth, we should *think* (思) of equaling them; when we see men of a contrary character, we should turn inwards and *reflect* (省) on ourselves." (*Analects*, "Li Ren," 17)

Ji Wen thought (思) thrice, and then acted. When the Master was informed of it, he said, "Twice may do." (*Analects*, "Gong Ye Chang," 20)[8]

We've been concerned here to show that not only is the Confucian thought of the *Analects* of epistemological significance but also that it can help us progress contemporary virtue epistemology. By focusing on reflection as a virtue, we can account for the possibility that reflection is "terribly unreliable" in some cases, while defending the claim that in some other cases, for agents with the requisite virtue, it is not.

In our discussion of Sosa's virtue epistemology, we have highlighted the central role that reflection plays in one of the leading theories of knowledge. While the place of reflection in Sosa's theory demonstrates the significance of reflection, the Confucian understanding of reflection is of importance, as it tells us about the nature of this epistemologically significant element. This provides a basis for understanding an aspect, plausibly a central aspect, of the epistemically virtuous agent that has been under explored in the contemporary literature.[9] Next, we highlight a number of other areas in which Confucian thought can progress virtue epistemology.

Aside from helping us understand the nature of reflection as a virtue, Confucian thought on the reflection of the exemplary agent, together with the Confucian distinction between two different sorts of knowledge, helps us diagnose what goes wrong in the Fake Barn County case and why, were there to be knowledge in such a case, it would be of a superior sort of knowledge[10] (Mi and Ryan 2016; see also Mi 2015, 366). Recall that the reflection of the exemplary agent both aims at goods and seeks to avoid bads. While

8. In these translations of the *Analects*, "thinking" is used for 思. Elsewhere we make the case, following John Dewey (1933, 9), that reflection is characterized by "active, persistent, and careful consideration." It is clear that where 思 is being used in the passages, it describes an action with the mentioned characterization, hence we think "reflection" is the appropriate translation.

9. While there is a contribution to contemporary virtue epistemology from the *Analects*, of course what is said there requires careful interpretation and isn't elaborated upon in the way positions in contemporary epistemology tend to be. So while we might like to know more about reflection on Confucian thought, what we have from the *Analects* on reflection is limited. Yet as evidenced from the quoted passages and the discussions of those passages, what we do have is intricate, plausible, and interesting thoughts on reflection that fit well with our pre-theoretical image of the epistemically virtuous agent.

10. The Fake Barn County case appears in an article by Goldman (1976), though the author credits Carl Ginet with the example.

Henry in Fake Barn County is, let's assume, aiming at truth when he forms his belief, a plausible interpretation of the case is that Henry does not exhibit the retrospective component of virtuous reflection, although this is precisely the sort of case where such retrospective reflection is required to avoid going wrong. If he were to engage his retrospective reflection, then we would at least expect him to be more cautious in his belief. It is also the case that, were Henry or any agent to get something right because of competence in the face of a hostile epistemic environment, then that competence would likely involve a reflective capacity to overcome the misleading appearances hostile epistemic environments typically involve. This indicates an epistemic contribution of virtuous reflection.

Confucian thought, this time in *The Great Learning*, also makes a contribution to epistemology[11] (Mi and Ryan forthcoming). In this case, it most obviously does so in the area of social epistemology. While *The Great Learning* is concerned with reflection, it is also concerned with "extended knowledge." At the very beginning of *The Great Learning*, we learn what it is about: "The way of great learning consists in the manifestation of manifesting virtue, in reaching out to others, in achieving ultimate goods" (Legge 2009).

According to the text, when reflection and extended knowledge are appropriately developed, then final goods may be attained. More specifically, second-order virtue, of which virtuous reflection is an example, puts us in a position to work toward obtaining the best kind of epistemic goods. We should begin by trying to comprehend the world around us. This means taking in information or a subject matter in a way that is systematic. By doing so we are better positioned to weed out errors from our own mind and eventually reach understanding and wisdom—the best kind of epistemic goods. The other theme of *The Great Learning* regards "extended knowledge," which concerns epistemic cooperation with others, and which requires reflection and consensus. By establishing consensus, a group has peace or harmony, which allows it to persist as a social unit and facilitates learning cooperation within the group. This attention to the need for consensus within epistemic groups is an alternative to the common-knowledge requirement for group knowledge. While we're not going to make the case for preferring consensus to common knowledge as such a requirement here, our point is to draw the reader's attention to the alternative we get from Confucian thought, which even if ultimately rejected, can help develop the discourse on this topic.

11. Aside from the *Analects*, *The Great Learning*, along with three other texts make up what are regarded as the canonical Confucian texts.

This chapter has made the case, contrary to traditional readings of Confucius, that Confucian thought is of epistemological significance. We provided an explanation as to why it is unsurprising that the epistemological significance of Confucian thought has previously been overlooked, while locating that significance in the contemporary epistemological literature. Each of these tasks was, in fact, complementary, with the epistemological significance of Confucian thought best located within virtue epistemology, and the only recent reemergence of virtue theoretic approaches in epistemology helping us understand the overlooking of the epistemological significance of Confucian thought. Next, we made the case that Confucian thought is not just of epistemological significance, and that it also can contribute to the development of the contemporary discourse. For this, we focused on the significance of reflection in the contemporary debate and what we learn from Confucius about the nature of reflection in the *Analects*.

REFERENCES

Ames, Roger T., and Henry Rosemont. (1998). *The Analects of Confucius: A Philosophical Translation*. New York: Random House Publishing Group.
Baehr, Jason. (2008). "Four Varieties of Character-Based Virtue Epistemology." *Southern Journal of Philosophy* 46(4): 469–502.
Dewey, John (1933). *How We Think: A Restatement of the Relation of Reflective Thinking to the Educative Process*. Lexington, MA: Heath.
Goldman, Alvin I. (1976). "Discrimination and Perceptual Knowledge." *Journal of Philosophy* 73: 771–791.
Greco, John. (2009). "The Value Problem." In *Epistemic Value*, ed. Adrian Haddock, Alan Millar, and Duncan Pritchard, 313–321. Oxford: Oxford University Press.
Greco, John. (2010). *Achieving Knowledge*. Cambridge: Cambridge University Press.
Greco, John. (2011). "The Value Problem." In *The Routledge Companion to Epistemology*, ed. Sven Bernecker and Duncan Pritchard, 219–231. New York: Routledge.
Kornblith, Hilary. (2012). *On Reflection*. Oxford: Oxford University Press.
Kvanvig, J. L. (2014). *Rationality and Reflection: How to Think about What to Think*. Oxford: Oxford University Press.
Legge, James (trans.). (2009). *The Confucian Analects, The Great Learning & The Doctrine of the Mean*. New York: Cosimo.
Mi, Chienkuo. (2015). "What Is Knowledge? When Confucius Meets Ernest Sosa." *Dao: A Journal of Comparative Philosophy* 14(3): 355–367.
Mi, Chienkuo, and Shane Ryan. (2016). "Skillful Reflection as an Epistemic Virtue." In *Moral and Intellectual Virtues in Western and Chinese Philosophy*, ed. Chienkuo Mi, Michael Slote, and Ernest Sosa, 34–48. New York: Routledge.
Mi, Chienkuo, and Shane Ryan. (Forthcoming). "Reflective Knowledge: Knowledge Extended." In *Epistemology Extended*, ed. Andy Clark, Adam Carter, Jesper Kallestrup, Duncan Pritchard, and Orestis Palermos. Oxford University Press.

Mi, Chienkuo, Michael Slote, and Ernest Sosa, eds. (2016). *Moral and Intellectual Virtues in Western and Chinese Philosophy*. New York: Routledge.

Pritchard, Duncan. (2010). "Knowledge and Understanding." In *The Nature and Value of Knowledge: Three Investigations*, ed. A. Haddock, A. Millar, and D. Pritchard, 3–88. Oxford: Oxford University Press.

Riegel, Jeffrey. (2013). "Confucius." In *The Stanford Encyclopedia of Philosophy*, ed. Edward N. Zalta. http://plato.stanford.edu/archives/sum2013/entries/confucius/.

Sosa, Ernest. (1980). "The Raft and the Pyramid: Coherence versus Foundations." *Midwest Studies in Philosophy* 5: 3–25.

Sosa, Ernest. (2007). *Apt Belief and Reflective Knowledge, Vol. 1: A Virtue Epistemology*. Oxford: Oxford University Press.

Sosa, Ernest. (2011). *Knowing Full Well*. Soochow University Lectures in Philosophy. Princeton, NJ: Princeton University Press.

Sosa, Ernest. (2014). "Reflective Knowledge and Its Importance." *Universitas: Monthly Review of Philosophy and Culture* 41(3): 7–16.

Sosa, Ernest. (2015). "Confucius on Knowledge." *Dao: A Journal of Comparative Philosophy* 14(3): 325–330.

Wong, David. (2017). "Chinese Ethics." In *The Stanford Encyclopedia of Philosophy*, ed. Edward N. Zalta (Spring Edition). https://plato.stanford.edu/archives/spr2017/entries/ethics-chinese/.

Yao, Xinzhong. (2000). *An Introduction to Confucianism*. Cambridge: Cambridge University Press.

Zagzebski, Linda. (2003). "The Search for the Source of the Epistemic Good." *Metaphilosophy* 34: 12–28.

CHAPTER 5

"Know" and Its Japanese Counterparts, *Shitte-iru* and *Wakatte-iru*

MASAHARU MIZUMOTO

1. INTRODUCTION: TWO JAPANESE KNOWLEDGE VERBS, *SHITTE-IRU* AND *WAKATTE-IRU*

Ask any Japanese person what the counterpart of the English word "know" is in Japanese. He or she will almost certainly answer "*shitte-iru*," since that is what is written in the dictionary. "Know" and its counterparts in other languages are standardly, conventionally, and almost automatically translated into *shitte-iru* (whose infinite form is *shiru*, meaning, roughly, "come to know" or "learn"). Thus, the Japanese themselves assume there is no gap between "know" and the Japanese counterpart, *shitte-iru*. This may be partly because the noun "knowledge" is expressed in Japanese in Chinese character (which is part of the Japanese writing system) as 知識 (but not necessarily in Chinese language!), and *shitte-iru* is written as 知っている, sharing the crucial character 知.

However, upon reflection, the Japanese also use a similar verb, *wakatte-iru* (or its infinitive form *wakaru*), which is often intersubstitutable with *shitte-iru*.[1] Miura (1983) says that when *wakaru* is translated into English,

---

1. One English–Japanese dictionary at hand (*Taishukan's Unabridged Genius*) does not contain *wakatte-iru* in the list of Japanese translations for "know" but, instead, *rikai-shite-iru*, which is a somewhat formal expression of *wakatte-iru* (the latter is more colloquial), but both of them are the standard translations of English "understand" or "comprehend" into Japanese.

"the most natural equivalent is often either 'understand' or 'know'" (211). He presents the following examples:

1. Nishio-san wa Roshiago ga *wakaru*.
   ("Mr. Nishio understands Russian.")
2. Ano hito ga naze konakatta ka *wakaranai* [the nonpast negative form of *wakaru*].
   ("I don't know/understand why he didn't come.")

Similarly, according to a Japanese–English dictionary, *wakaru* is explained in English as "1. *understand, see, get, appreciate, comprehend*, and 2. *know, see, tell, find, turn out, recognize*." Thus one may find that *wakaru* is roughly an amalgam of "understand" and "know," and if used to express a propositional attitude, in the form of *wakatte-iru*, its main sense is "know." Thus it is said that,

> While in many bilingual dictionaries and Japanese textbooks, *wakaru* is typically translated as "to understand" and *shitte(i)ru* as "to get to know" [. . .], the semantic and functional distinction between the two verbs is not at all clear-cut. In fact, in many cases, either verb can express a lexical meaning similar to English "to know" [. . .]. (Sadler 2010, 110)

Especially when used for propositional knowledge, in most contexts *shitte-iru* and *wakatte-iru* are mutually interchangeable. But then, exactly when are they *not* interchangeable? If there is any difference, how are they related to, and different from, each other? And how are they related to, and different from, the English "know"? These are the questions we are primarily concerned with in this chapter, and we will consider the implications of the results for contemporary epistemology. (Readers who are not interested in the linguistic details of Japanese may skip the following two sections and directly proceed to section 4.) It will turn out that, despite what almost all Japanese think, the use of *wakatte-iru*, rather than *shitte-iru*, is closer to that of English "know." However, since *shitte-iru* is definitely the representative knowledge verb in Japanese, and as we shall see, two opposing positions in many important epistemological debates correspond to the difference between *shitte-iru* and *wakatte-iru*, the existence of such verbs has significant implications to epistemology. We may even think that anglophone epistemologists have suffered from the ambiguity of the English "know," expressing two primitive epistemological concepts captured by *shitte-iru* and *wakatte-iru*.

2. PRAGMATIC CHOICE DATA BETWEEN *SHITTE-IRU* AND *WAKATTE-IRU*

We assume here that there are two (or two *candidates* for, to avoid begging the question) knowledge verbs in Japanese, *shitte-iru* and *wakatte-iru* (or *wakaru*), and we will examine how they are different in use from each other, and from the English "know."

The English "know" in "S knows that *p*" is a stative verb (expressing a state or static situation). The Japanese counterparts like *shitte-iru* and *wakatte-iru* are also stative verbs. However, *shitte-iru* is the non-past continuous-perfect form of *shiru*, which is a punctual verb,[2] expressing an event rather than a state (Miura 1983). Likewise, *wakatte-iru* is the non-past continuous-perfect form of *wakaru*,[3] with the latter mainly used as a punctual verb,[4] though sometimes also used as a stative verb. (English "know" is opposite in this respect, as it is used mainly as a stative verb, but sometimes used as a non-stative verb, expressing an event of getting to know, as in "You will know it tomorrow," "Let me know," etc.). But *shiru* and *wakaru* are very different verbs. *Shiru* means "get to know,"[5] while *wakaru* means "be clear" (as a stative verb) or "become clear" (as a punctual verb) to someone (Miura 1983).[6] If used as a stative verb, *wakaru* means having certain ability (ability to tell, find out, etc.), or just having the relevant information at hand, which is therefore not limited to cognitive ability like "understanding" (as we shall see later). Thus, even though they are usually intersubstitutable when used for propositional knowledge, we may plausibly expect that *shitte-iru* and *wakatte-iru* also have very different, if overlapping, meanings.

The earlier studies on this topic, however, have been done mostly by comparing them in their infinitive forms, *shiru* and *wakaru* (Watanabe 1987; Takahashi 2003; Ashihara 2010; Kung 2013), and while this does not

2. In particular, being telic (having an inherent endpoint), it is an achievement verb. For the verb classification based on lexical aspect, see Filip (2012).

3. Here the *te-iru* part of both *shitte-iru* and *wakatte-iru* is standardly explained as the non-perfective aspect of the infinitives *shiru* and *wakaru*, respectively (*teiru* itself is a complex of the conjunctive morpheme *te*, the existential verb *i*, and the non-past morpheme *ru*). Sadanobu and Malchukov (2011), however, propose an evidential interpretation of this construction.

4. When used as a punctual verb, *wakaru* is an event that is not controllable by the subject (Miura 1983, 211).

5. Or, *shiru* is the acquisition of new knowledge and value through information, experience, and learning (Tien et al. 2007), or the point in time when the information is acquired (Kato 2002).

6. An important grammatical difference is that *wakaru* can take the that-clause as the grammatical subject.

preclude the comparison of *shitte-iru* and *wakatte-iru*, even in such forms they are often used for expressing knowledge of an object (or objects), concrete or abstract, rather than propositional knowledge. Such factors made it difficult to directly apply their analyses to epistemological considerations, in particular the comparison of these Japanese knowledge verbs and the English "know."[7] Also, the judgments of differentiation in earlier studies have been mostly based on researchers' intuitions. In what follows, therefore, we mainly focus on the uses of *shitte-iru* and *wakatte-iru*, and investigate the differences in their uses by examining, empirically, in what kinds of contexts they are *not* intersubstitutable, through the felicity judgments of ordinary people.

Shitte-iru and *wakatte-iru* have often been contrasted and studied in their non-past *negative* forms, *shira-nai* and *wakara-nai* (*wakatte-inai*), respectively. Thus we also start with considering such examples (the percentage in the parenthesis is the acceptance rate, all based on the felicity judgment data of undergraduate students of Kanazawa Gakuin University, where for all the examples, $N = 31$, female = 12.9%, unless otherwise specified).[8]

Example 1
"What are you planning to do in the summer vacation?"[9]
<u>"I don't know yet."</u>

Mada _____.
(1) *wakara-nai* (87%)
(2) **shira-nai* (6%)

---

7. We should also mention here the study of *shitte-iru* in Onishi (1997), which was conducted in the context of the NSM program (see Wierzbicka, this volume). However, it does not discuss, let alone contrast, *shitte-iru* with *wakatte-iru*. The discussion is also focused on evidentiality in relation to some syntactical distinctions. Evidentiality of Japanese is itself an important topic, which is also epistemologically highly interesting, but we cannot discuss it here (but see below).

8. Note that the exact question was: "Please choose one that is the more [or most, when choices are more than two] natural expression as an expression to be filled in the underlined space. But if the choices are equally natural, you may choose both [or more than one], and if they are all unnatural, you may choose none." Thus, this was *neither* a simple felicity judgment *nor* a forced-choice questionnaire. This was because, depending on the surroundings one imagines, almost any grammatically correct constructions can be judged *natural*, while owing to the difference in context, they may mean different things. Of course, the present approach does not completely overcome the difficulty, but we believe it is considerably better insofar as there is a natural context most people come up with when reading the sentences in each example.

9. Lee (2006, 192).

Example 2

A: What are you planning to do during the summer vacation?

B: Several months ago, I had some plan, but I became so busy these days that I <u>don't remember</u> (I <u>don't know</u>) what I was planning to do anymore.

nani wo shiyoo to shite ita no ka _____.

(1) *wasureta* [don't remember / forgot] (79%)

(2) *wakaranaku natta* [past negative form of wakaru] (43%)

(3) **shiranaku natta* [past negative form of shiru] (3%)

Example 3

Hanako is fed up with the selfishness of Taro, and says, "Do whatever you like. I <u>don't care / *don't know</u> anymore whatever happens to you!"[10]

Mou dounattemo_____kara ne!

(1) *shira-nai* (97%)

(2) **wakara-nai* (0%)

What explains these differences? According to Miura (1983), as an answer to the question "What do you plan to do this weekend?" *wakaranai* implies: "I should know the answer but I'm sorry I don't" (cf. Mizutani and Mizutani 1977), while *shiranai* may indicate: "This sort of thing has nothing to do with me." This kind of observation seems to explain these examples.

Lee (1985, 2006), however, explained such differences in a more ambitious, systematic way by appealing to what is called the "territory of information theory," proposed and developed by Akio Kamio.

2.1. The Territory of Information

The notion of "territory" has been used in Japan since the 1930s, in the context of the study of Japanese and English (Sakuma 1936; Hattori 1968; Ando 1986). Kamio (1979) introduced the notion of the "territory of information" and developed it into a general theory (1990, 1994, 1995, 1997, 2002), covering vast topics in linguistics.

This notion is applied to explain many features of linguistic communication, like evidentiality, politeness, modality, and so on. According to Kamio, there are two different kinds of the territory of information: the speaker's and the hearer's. Some information may or may not belong to the

---

10. I owe this example to Tomoyuki Yamada of Hokkaido University (pers. conv.).

Table 5.1 POSSIBLE COMBINATIONS OF TERRITORY OF INFORMATION
(BY KAMIO)

		The speaker's territory	
		Within the territory	Outside the territory
The hearer's territory	Outside the territory	A	D
	Within the territory	B	C

speaker's territory, and also may or may not belong to the hearer's, forming the matrix in Table 5.1.[11]

A piece of information being within one's territory of information means that it is the information *supposedly* (if not actually) possessed by the speaker or the hearer. Kamio (2002, 32) provides the following list of what sorts of information fall into the speaker's or hearer's territory (cf. Kamio 1990, 33, 1997, 39):

(a) Information about (obtained through) internal direct experience
(b) Information about (obtained through) external direct experience
(c) Information that belongs to one's specialty or expertise
(d) Information about one's personal matter

We cannot go into the details of this list, but these rough descriptions are enough for the present purposes. The crucial point here is that although not explicitly stated in the descriptions (but see Kamio 1997, 39), these are sorts of information that fall into the territory of the *speaker* or the *hearer*, and therefore "experience," "specialty," "personal matter," and so on are all those of the speaker's or the hearer's.

2.2. The Territory of Information Theory Applied to *Shira-nai* and *Wakara-nai*

According to Lee (2006), *wakara-nai* is used when a piece of information that is sought falls into the *speaker's* territory of information, while the speaker does not actually have that information at the time of inquiry (196). Thus, in Examples 1 and 2 (the denial of), *wakatte-iru* and its

11. From Kamio (1990), 22.

variant are to be used, since the information in question is the speaker's information (an instance of [d]) in Kamio's classification), falling within the speaker's territory (in this case, A in the table above), whereas it is the hearer's, rather than the speaker's, information (thus in C, rather than A) in Example 3, and therefore (the denial of) *shitte-iru* is the natural choice.

In particular, *shira-nai* in Example 1 sounds as if (as we saw) "that has nothing to do with me" or "that is not my business," just in Example 3. That is why it sounds odd or even rude if a student answers her teacher with *shiri-masen* (the polite form of *shira-nai*) rather than *wakari-masen* (that of *wakara-nai*),[12] especially if the question is what was already taught (Lee 2006, 197). Indeed, the speaker may intentionally violate such norms to produce implicature. In Example 3, for instance, the speaker is rather declaring that the relevant information (about Taro) does not fall within her territory anymore and therefore falls now in C (rather than B) in the table above, by choosing (the denial of) *shitte-iru*. In this way, the speaker can intentionally move the territory boundary for various practical purposes, to express politeness (e.g., saving the hearer's "face"), empathy or anger, and so on (Lee 2006, 201–203; Sadler 2010, 115).

The notion of "territory" is a very general one, observed in various life forms (even insects) and heavily used in ethology. Territory is in this sense a natural kind. If the territory of information is a feature of the reality that is detected by human beings and reflected in their languages, it should also be a natural kind. Thus, if this theory explains our practice of knowledge attribution, irrespective of any particular language, it would be epistemologically interesting, having an obvious connection with the Dretskean information-theoretic account of knowledge (Dretske 1981). Both of them are naturalistic accounts of knowledge (Dretske) or knowledge attribution (territory theory) based on the realistic conception of information. One is metaphysical and focuses on the causal history of acquisition of information, while the other is linguistic and focuses on the location of the information in the subjective space (territory), thus complementing each other.

2.3. The Territory of Information Applied to *Shitte-iru* and *Wakatte-iru*

The success of the explanation of the use of the negative forms of *shitte-iru* and *wakatte-iru* based on the territory of information theory also predicts the choice between the *affirmative* forms of them (as Lee 2006, sec. 4,

---

12. *Masen* is a non-past negative suffix (while *aasu* is a non-past positive suffix) for expressing politeness.

claims). However, the territory of information theory is taken to be a *pragmatic* theory rather than a semantic theory. This is because, as Kamio himself thinks (2002, 42), it is thought as part of the "theory of evidentiality," which is in turn generally regarded as a branch of pragmatics. But if so, it does not seem to have epistemological implications even if it is applied to knowledge verbs.

However, even if the territory of information theory is a theory of knowledge *attribution*, the attributor relativity is compatible with its being a semantic theory (*besides* being a pragmatic theory), thus serving as an epistemological theory, just like epistemic contextualism. Indeed, as we shall see, unlike evidentaility, in the case of the distinction of *shitte-iru* and *wakatte-iru*, we may think that it depends simply on whether the information falls into the territory of the *attributee* of the knowledge, rather than on whether it falls into the speaker's or hearer's territory. If so, the difference of use explained by the territory theory may also be semantic rather than merely pragmatic.

Example 4
The mother says to her son before he goes to bed, "You ought to brush your teeth!" He answers, "I know, I know!"

(1) *Wakatteru, wakatteru!* [simplified colloquial form of *wakatte-iru*] (100%)
(2) **Shitteru, shitteru!* [simplified colloquial form of *shitte-iru*] (0%)

Example 5
You have lost consciousness and have just regained it. Someone else asks: "Do you know who you are?"[13]

Jibun ga dare daka _____masu ka?
(1) wakari (94%)
(2) *wakatte (6%)
(3) *shitte (6%)

Example 6
Taro poisoned the water tank of a government building. Having heard of it, his girlfriend says, "Do you know what you have done?" Being a terrorist, Taro answers, "Yes, of course I know."

---

13. Cf. Lee (1996); Kamio (1990).

Girlfriend: *Jibun ga nani wo shita ka* _____?
Taro: *mochiron* _____ *sa.*

(1) *wakatteru* (94%)
(2) **shitteru* (10%)

In Example 4, the information is about what the speaker ought to do, which he already has in mind. Thus the speaker and the attributor are the same person, and therefore *wakatteru* is the obvious choice. In Example 5, the information is specifically about the person who has lost consciousness, and when the questioner asks whether the person has an ability to recall her own memory (which we shall come back to later), *wakaru* is used as a stative verb. In this context the use of *wakatte-iru* (thus asking *wakatte-masu ka?*) sounds as if "you *ought* to have known it," thereby blaming the person when she cannot recall who she is (see Example 6). Therefore, in this context, *wakari masu ka* (the interrogative polite form of wakaru), which rather asks the *ability* of the person to recall, is clearly the most natural choice. However, using *shitte-iru* in asking whether one knows one's own name (which was the original example of Lee) is like asking whether one has heard of one's own name or not. In Example 6, information about what Taro has done obviously falls in Taro's territory, and hence his girlfriend uses *wakatte-iru*, even though it does not fall into her (the speaker's) territory.

3. SOME FEATURES OF SEMANTIC DIFFERENCES

One may still claim that what we have seen are nevertheless pragmatic differences. Admittedly, they are data of felicity judgments about the speakers' choices between *shitte-iru* and *wakatte-iru*. Thus, for example, even if it is infelicitous to say *shitteru* in Example 4, people would definitely say yes if asked whether the son *shitte-iru* (knows) that he should brush his teeth. Likewise, from the objective or the narrator's perspective, it is arguably perfectly possible to use *shitte-iru* (or its variants) in Examples 5 and 6 in attributing knowledge. Thus, the choices seem to be still "merely" pragmatic, and not based on any *semantic* rules.

However, this line of thought implicitly identifies the semantic content with a truth-condition. But the truth-condition is known to be not fine-grained enough, and therefore even if two sentences share exactly the same truth-condition, that does not ensure that they express the same meaning. Arguably, the distinction between semantic and pragmatic is a technical and artificial one, and for example, there is no such distinction intrinsic to the use theory of meaning. Indeed, historically, the boundary has not been stable and its reality has been questioned even by linguists. Thus, Chomsky says that there is no way of telling pretheoretically whether a felt oddness of a linguistic expression is a matter of syntax, semantics, pragmatics, belief, etc. (Chomsky 1977, 4).

We may then rather expect that the reason for the difference in use (and meaning) explains both the pragmatic difference and the semantic one; and if so, the present data of (the intuitions about) the difference in use can be taken as indicating the reasons for the semantic difference, if there is any. Thus the territory of information theory may also be used for explaining such semantic differences, with territory constituting part of the truth conditions of *shitte-iru* and *wakatte-iru* (and even "know"). In any case, we may thus discern and predict what kind of semantic difference there should be, even through the data of felicity judgments. Indeed, if the choice is based on some specific reason other than communicative or conversational considerations, we may find there are *semantic* reasons for the choice. The following is such an attempt.

3.1. *Shitte-iru* as Having New Information

When we know something as a result of newly obtaining some new information, *shitte-iru* is by far the natural choice, since (as we saw in section 1) its infinite form, *shiru*, is to come to know or learn, whereas *wakaru*, the infinite form of *wakatte-iru*, is to be/become clear, which does not necessarily require new information. See the following examples.

Example 7
"Can you give a talk in our workshop next November? <u>Let me know</u> if you can make it as soon as possible."

"*Narubeku hayaku* _____ *kudasai.*"
(1)   *shirasete* (97%)
(2)   **wakarasete* (0%)

Example 8
"<u>No one knows</u> what happened to him after that. I <u>want to know</u> whether he is still alive."[14]

_____

14. Cf. Miura (1983, 211).

First:

(1) *shira-nai* (81%)

(2) *wakara-nai* (36%)

Second:

(1) *shiri-tai* (97%)[15]

(2) **wakari-tai* (1%)

($N = 67$, First: $p = 0.0000$, $\omega = 0.45$)[16]

In fact, the similar idea has been pointed out in the earlier studies on the distinction of *shiru* and *wakaru*. Takahashi (2003) even uses the notion of information to characterize the first meaning (among four different meanings) of *shiru*, as obtaining new (to the subject of knowledge) information. However, since this kind of characterization makes the explanation of the *negation* of the verb (*shira-nai*) difficult,[17] there is some advantage in the territory of information theory, and we will stick to the explanation based on it here.

3.2. *Wakatte-iru* as Deep Appreciation

The contrast just mentioned implies that one can shift from the state of *not wakatte-iru* (*wakatte-inai*) to that of *wakatte-iru* without gaining any new information, whereas one cannot analogously change from the state of *not shitte-iru* (*shira-ai*) to that of *shitte-iru* without any new information. But this in turn suggests that *wakatte-iru* allows *degree*: *wakattte-iru* is used when we know as a result of becoming clear about something, just like understanding. If so, just like understanding (Kvanvig 2003, 196), *wakatte-iru* comes in degrees (even when used for propositional knowledge). It is a controversial issue whether knowledge allows degree or not (cf. Dretske 1981, chap. 5), or in a more recent debate, whether "know" is a gradable term (cf. Stanley 2004, chap. 2). Detailed examination goes beyond the scope of this chapter, but at least when the topic is the knowledge in the sense of appreciation of a

---

15. *Tai* here is a desiderative suffix.

16. Throughout this chapter (unless explicitly mentioned otherwise), the statistical significance is analyzed by the two-sided Fisher's exact test, and the effect size "ω" means Cohen's φ, where the small effect is 0.1, the medium effect is 0.3, and the large effect is 0.5.

17. For example, in order to explain the meaning of *shira-nai* as lack of experience, Takahashi gives "experiencing something that has not experienced" as the second meaning of *shiru* (2003, 36). Arguably, such uses can be better treated by the territory of information theory.

matter (see the following examples), where we can know something through *deeper* appreciation of it (possibly without gaining further information about it), *wakatte-iru*, rather than *shitte-iru*, seems to be the choice, whether or not such knowledge can be taken as propositional knowledge.

Example 9
A: "<u>You don't know</u> how tragic and miserable the war is."
B: "Yes, <u>I do</u>"
A: "No, <u>You don't!</u>"

A: *Kimi wa sensou ga ikani hisan ka* _____ *nai.*
B: *Iie,* _____ *masu.*
A: *Iya,* _____ *nai!*

(1) *wakatte* (81%)
(2) *shira/shitte* (45%)
($N = 67$, $p = 0.000031$, $\omega = 0.37$)

Example 10
A: "<u>I know</u> smoking is bad for one's health, but I can't help it."
B: "Then <u>you don't really know</u> how bad it is yet."

First:
(1) *wakatte-iru* (76%)
(2) *shitte-iru* (46%)

Second:
(1) *wakatte-nai* (75%)
(2) *shira-nai* (40%)
($N = 67$, First: $p = 0.00069$, $\omega = 0.31$, Second: $p = 0.00010$, $\omega = 0.35$)

Example 11
"<u>Let them know by tomorrow's game</u> that they won't be able to beat us for the next thirty years."[18]

"*Asu no shiai de sero.*"
(1) *shira* (15%)
(2) *wakara* (78%)
($N = 67$, $p = 0.000$, $\omega = 0.63$)

These examples further confirm that the choice between *shitte-iru* and *wakatte-iru* is concerned with whether the information the subject has or

18. Ichiro, baseball player.

is supposed to have falls in that person's territory—for example, whether that person received the information from outside of his or her territory, or whether that person really appreciates the information already in his or her territory, rather than the territory of the speaker or the hearer.

Suppose, for instance, in Example 5, that the person who lost consciousness is described from the third-person perspective. The Japanese translation of "He does not know who he is" is perfectly natural if *wakatte-iru* is used, but not if *shitte-iru* is used. Likewise, in Example 6, if we describe Taro as "He knows what he has done," its Japanese translation is entirely natural with *wakatte-iru*, but not with *shitte-iru*. Or in Example 7, *shitte-iru* is chosen because supposedly the information does not fall in the speaker's territory, whereas the information is obviously the hearer's. However, even if the speaker said "Let my secretary know" instead of "Let me know," the choice (*shirasete*) would not be affected. And similarly for other cases. This is confirmed by Example 11, where the people who are to possess the information are the opponent team—neither the speaker nor the hearer.

We still need further felicity judgment data for the conclusion, but at least it is a highly plausible hypothesis that the crucial factor that divides the use of the two Japanese knowledge verbs is the fact about the possible *attributee* of knowledge, rather than that of the speaker or hearer. If so, the rules governing the distinction encode a much more objective feature of the reality than those governing the phenomena of evidentiality. Thus it seems that, at least in these cases, the choice between *shitte-iru* and *wakatte-iru* is based on the *semantic* reasons, rather than pragmatic principles.

3.3. *Wakatte-iru* as Ability

We may figuratively put the difference we have seen so far between *shitte-iru* and *wakatte-iru* as the difference between *horizontal* and *vertical* knowledge. *Shitte-iru*, as horizontal knowledge, is usually a matter of how much and how widely the subject has obtained information, where obtaining new information can therefore extend the territory, as it were horizontally. *Wakatte-iru*, as vertical knowledge, is a matter of deep appreciation, so that we can go deeper under what is already within one's ken or territory, as if vertically. However, this, and its close relationship with understanding, suggest that *wakatte-iru* also expresses a certain *ability* based on such appreciation, just as *wakaru*. For, if understanding is the achievement of internal coherence and the grasp of such relations, it enables the agent to do reasoning that is "useful as a basis for action" (Kvanvig 2003, 202). But if so, insofar as *wakatte-iru* implies deep appreciation, it must have similar *practical* consequences. It then should follow that, those who *wakatte-iru* can do things that those who merely *shitte-iru* cannot. Thus, this may constitute a further semantic difference between them. Consider the following examples:

Example 12
Taro is trying to solve a difficult puzzle for 10 minutes. But suddenly he shouts, "Now I know how to solve it!"

Tokikata _____!
(1) *wakatta* (97%)
(2) **shitta* (3%)

Example 13
As a result of such an economic mess in Greece, I don't know what's going to happen to it anymore.

Mou nani ga okoru ka _____.
(1) *wakaranai* (97%)
(2) *shiranai* (3%)

Example 14
A: There will be a big earthquake tomorrow.
B: How do you know that?

Doushite _____?
(1) *wakatteru* (6%)
(2) *wakaru* (76%)
(3) *shitteru* (13%)
($N = 67, p = 0.0000$, Cramer's $V = 0.68$ (where $V = 0.3$ is medium and 0.5 is large): comparison between *wakaru* and *shitte-iru*; $p = 0.0000$, $\omega = 0.63$)

Example 15
A: He will actually quit the job by the end of this month.
B: How do you know that?

Doushite _____?
(1) *wakatteru* (0%)
(2) *wakaru* (24%)
(3) *shitteru* (67%)
($N = 67, p = 0.0000$, Cramer's $V = 0.60$: comparison between *wakaru* and *shitte-iru*; $p = 0.000001$, $\omega = 0.43$)

In Example 12, what Taro obtained is not information from the external source, but he figured out the solution by himself, thereby acquiring a new ability. In Example 13, the speaker expresses the lack of ability to predict the future of Greece, which is not to be obtained by merely getting some information from someone else. The contrast between Examples 14 and 15 is especially pertinent here. In Example 14, A is likely to have obtained information from someone, whereas in Example 15, A seems to possess some mysterious ability, which is reflected in the judgment data. Thus, they may provide further evidence for the semantic difference.[19]

We may then think of these principles of the choice between *shitte-iru* and *wakatte-iru* as constituting *semantic* reasons for the choice between them. If so, we can predict that there are situations in which the Japanese speakers judge the use of *shitte-iru* to be *correct* while judging the use of *wakatte-iru* to be *wrong*, or vice versa. Remember, for instance, Examples 2 and 5. There, the person in question was or was doubted to be *unable* to recall the relevant information. But if *shitte-iru* can still be attributed there, that may constitute the gap in the truth-conditions of sentences using these verbs. It would then be especially (epistemologically) interesting if such a semantic gap arises in cases discussed in contemporary epistemology, such as Gettier cases, the TrueTemp case, the Bank case, and the like.

4. STUDIES OF SEMANTIC DIFFERENCES BETWEEN *SHITTE-IRU* AND *WAKATTE-IRU*

4.1. Phone Number Case and Puzzle Case

Before examining such epistemological cases, let us see some specific examples where the felicity judgment data proved to be semantically valid, too. Earlier, in an independent study of felicity judgment (participants were also undergraduates at Kanazawa Gakuin University, N = 39, female = 10.26%),[20] we had found that in the cases where the subject had relevant experience or memory or ability, but was unable to recall (just as in Examples 2 and 5 above), significantly more participants judged the use of *wakara-nai* (the negative form of *wakatte-iru*) natural than those who

---

19. Also, in Examples 12 and 13, it does not matter whether the subject who is ascribed *wakatte-iru* is the speaker or not. We can perfectly naturally describe the situation by using "he" or "she" and ascribe him or her *wakatte-iru*. In Example 14, the distinction is clearly based on the *content* of the information that the subject of knowledge has, which in turn suggests how the subject, whether the hearer or not, obtained the information.

20. See note 16 for the details of statistical analysis.

judged the use of *shira-nai* (that of *shitte-iru*) natural in those situations. Even though that was a study on felicity judgment, we may naturally hypothesize from such results that the Japanese speakers can differentiate the uses of these two verbs by judging that memory preserves the state of *shitte-iru*, but (having lost the relevant ability) not the state of *wakatte-iru*, instantiating a *semantic* difference. To examine this hypothesis, we conducted a new survey, using cases analogous to those used in the felicity judgment study, together with familiar epistemological cases, which will be reported later (note that the Puzzle case, the direct descendent of Example 12, is about *knowledge how*, though this does not make a difference at least for intellectualists like Williamson and Stanley).[21]

Method: Before each question, participants (undergraduates of Kanazawa Gakuin University, $N = 61$, female = 47.5%) were presented the following sentences:

> **Phone Number case:** Taro remembered his previous mobile phone number before, but he has now forgotten it completely.
>
> **Puzzle case:** Hanako knew how to solve a puzzle, but since it was years ago, she is now unable to solve it.

Unlike the earlier felicity judgment studies, where participants were asked to choose the natural expression(s) among given options, as a study of semantic judgment here we first asked whether Taro/Hanako knows or not the relevant thing, in one group using *shitte-iru*, and in another using *wakatte-iru*. (For example, participants were given the sentence "Taro _____ the phone number" for the Phone Number case, and those in the *wakatte-iru* group were asked to choose between *wakatte-iru* and not *wakatte-iru*.) The results serve as between-subject data. But the more important is the results of the second question, where we further asked the participants (of both groups) to choose among the following options, to obtain within-subject data.

> Taro/Hanako now _____the phone number/how to solve the puzzle.
> (1) *shitte-iru* but not *wakatte-iru*
> (2) *wakatte-iru* but not *shitte-iru*
> (3) neither *shitte-iru* nor *wakatte-iru*
> (4) both *shitte-iru* and *wakatte-iru*

21. In fact, about the "knowledge-how" in Japanese, we have found that the relevant modality of the Japanese counterpart of "knowledge-how" is not ability modal, but deontic modal. See Izumi et al. (2017).

Note that, in this second question, the options are the same for both groups. Then, this time, just after "Please choose the one you think is correct," it was explicitly stated, "You may choose an answer that conflicts with your own first answer."

The original purpose of this two-step question strategy was (in addition to obtaining both within-subject and between-subject data) to avoid confusing participants and help them keep track of their own intuitions about the uses of *shitte-iru* and *wakatte-iru*, since we thought that first asking participants to choose among the four options would be confusing for them (choices (1) to (4) are not familiar combinations, even for ordinary Japanese speakers, though there is nothing grammatically wrong), numbing their original intuitions. So we decided to use the first question as a primer to guide or help them keep track of their own intuitions, while allowing them to change their first view in facing the four options in the second question.

Results: We obtained a statistically significant difference in the second question of both the Phone Number case ($p = 0.0094$, $\omega = 0.25$) and the Puzzle case ($p = 0.0000$, $\omega = 0.49$), with the same pattern, significantly more participants attributing *shitte-iru* to the subject than *wakatte-iru* (see Figure 5.1 below).[22] So in both cases, more participants found that Taro/Hanako *wakatte-iru* but not *shitte-iru*, rather than vice versa. These results

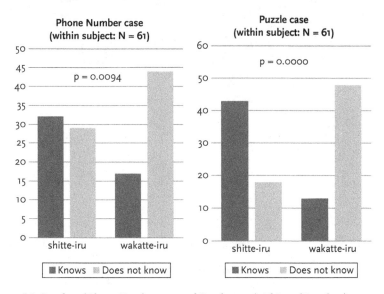

Figure 5.1 Results of Phone Number case and Puzzle case (within-subject data)

22. Predictably, the results of the first question, the between-subject design, showed the same pattern with the similar statistical significance, despite their smaller sample

suggest the semantic difference between the uses of *shitte-iru* and *wakatte-iru*, at least more straightforwardly than previous studies.

In the same study, we have also asked the same two questions for the Fake Barn case, the TrueTemp case, the Furniture Store case, and the Bank case. Before looking at the results, however, let us see somewhat disappointing results we had obtained in a previous study.

Gettier Case

In the study of the Car case used in Weinberg et al. (2001) as a standard Gettier case,[23] where Smith's Ford had been stolen but unbeknownst to John, Smith has got another American car, making John's belief (*Smith owns an American car*) accidentally true, we found utterly no difference between the rates of knowledge attribution whether the question used *shitte-iru* or *wakatte-iru*.[24] (See Figure 5.2.) Note that, given this sample size (*N* = 165), even for the small-effect size of Cohen's φ (ω = 0.1), the statistical

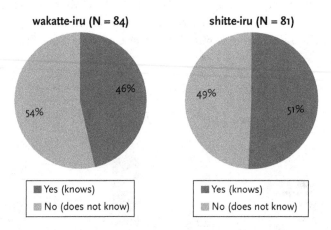

Figure 5.2 Results of Gettier (Car) case (between-subject data)

sizes: $p = 0.018$, $\omega = 0.34$ for the Phone Number case, and $p = 0.00074$, $\omega = 0.46$ for the Puzzle case.

23. Note that, the very category of "Gettier case" is recently questioned; see Turri (2016a). Also, the relatively high rate of knowledge attribution we shall see may be due to the fact that this vignette is a version of *authentic evidence* case (see Starmans and Friedman 2012).

24. Participants were undergraduate students of Tokai University, and the sample sizes indicated are the numbers of participants who passed the two comprehension tests (truth and belief).

power, $1-\beta$ is 0.77, and for the medium-effect size ($\omega = 0.3$), $1-\beta = 0.97$. So it is unlikely that this result was a false negative, and even if it were, the effect size would be ignorably small and would not be epistemologically significant.

Even though, given the territory of information theory, *shitte-iru/shira-nai* would be natural, considering the nature of the information in question (for whether Smith has an American car or not is not particularly related to John), this did not have any valence toward or against attributing *shitte-iru*. Note also that, as another disappointing result, the experiment with US native English speakers (recruited in Amazon M-Turk, $N = 61$, age = 35.9, female = 57.1%) showed, again, utterly no difference from the data of the Japanese,[25] consistently with recent studies.[26]

However, this at least shows that even though *wakaru* (the infinitive of *wakatte-iru*) is commonly used in Japanese in the sense of understanding (see section 1), *wakatte-iru* is different from the English "understanding" if Kvanvig is right in arguing that there are no Gettier cases for understanding (2003, 197–198; see also Pritchard 2010, but see, for criticism, Khalifa 2013). There are philosophers who think that understanding is indeed a species of knowledge (e.g., Grimm 2014), but at least the sense of *John understands that Smith has an American car* is not very clear in that context and (even if it makes sense) is very different from *John knows that Smith has an American car*. Indeed, in most examples in our felicity judgment study, replacing "know" with "understand" does not even make sense. For example, in Example 1, saying "I don't understand yet" in place of "I don't know yet" is simply unintelligible in that context. Such examples not only show the difference between "know" and "understand" but also between *wakatte-iru* and "understand" (we shall come back to this point later).

4.2. Other Results

Results of the Second (within-subject) Question: As for familiar epistemological cases, the results of the second question (within-subject judgment) turned out to show utterly no significant difference between

---

25. For Americans, the rate of yes answers was 57%, and compared with *wakatte-iru*, $p = 0.26$, $\omega = 0.11$, and for this sample size, $1-\beta = 0.65$ for $\omega = 0.1$, and 0.95 for $\omega = 0.3$. Note that the age factor is not well-controlled. However, logistic regression analysis showed that the age factor was not a significant predictor of the knowledge attribution ($p = 0.68$).

26. See Machery et al. (2017) and works cited there.

attributions of *shite-iru* and *wakatte-iru* (see Table 5.2), except in the TrueTemp case ($p = 0.0025$, $\omega = 0.30$, for all other cases, $\omega < 0.07$). Note that the sample size varies, as each case had a comprehension question before the two questions, where those who failed the test were eliminated from the data. But the statistical power is sufficient for the resultant sample size except for the Fake Barn case, where $1-\beta = 0.80$ for $\omega = 0.3$, although only 0.51 for $\omega = 0.1$, which means that the difference with effect size 0.1 can be detected only once in two studies. Still, again, the effect size of 0.1 should be too small to be epistemologically significant even if a statistically significant difference is detected.

Results of the First (between-subject) Question: Surprisingly, however, when we looked at the results of the first question (between-subject comparison), all but the Fake Barn case turned out to be statistically significant! But before looking at individual cases, it is better to rule out false positives arising from multiple comparisons by examining whether the difference between *shitte-iru* and *wakatte-iru* made a difference to the overall data of the between-subject questions. So we conducted a logistic regression analysis by comparing the base model,

$$\text{Logit } (\pi) = \beta_0 + \beta_1 x_1 + \beta_2 x_2 + \beta_3 x_3 + \beta_4 x_4 + \varepsilon,$$

where π is the probability that the participants judge that the subject knows, and the coefficients β_0, β_2, β_3, and β_4 are either of the Furniture Store case, Fake Barn case, Bank case, or TrueTemp case, while β_1 is the coefficient for *shitte-iru* versus *wakatte-iru*, with the interaction model,

$$\text{Logit } (\pi) = \beta_0 + \beta_1 x_1 + \beta_2 x_2 + \beta_3 x_3 + \beta_4 x_4 + \beta_1 {}^* \beta_2 x_5 \\ + \beta_1 {}^* \beta_3 x_6 + \beta_1 {}^* \beta_4 x_7 + \varepsilon.$$

Table 5.2 RESULTS OF THE SECOND QUESTION

Furniture Store case	knows	does not know	TrueTemp case	knows	does not know
wakatte-iru	23	36	*wakatte-iru*	42	16
shitte-iru	22	37	*shitte-iru*	25	33
Bank case	knows	does not know	**Fake Barn case**	knows	does not know
wakatte-iru	16	40	*wakatte-iru*	17	27
shitte-iru	19	37	*shitte-iru*	20	24

The interaction model provided a significantly better fit than the basic model (p = 0.0013, df = 3).[27] Thus, the *shitte-iru/wakatte-iru* factor was a significant contributor to the prediction of whether or not participants would judge the subject in the story to know the relevant fact. Thus, assuming that the significant differences found here are not false positives, let us see the (between-subject) results of cases individually.

Furniture Store Case

Vignette 1 (detailed version): Mr. Yamada is in a furniture store. He is looking at a bright red table under normal lighting conditions. He believes the table is red. However, a white table under red lighting would look *exactly* the same to him, and he has not checked whether the lighting is normal or whether there might be a red spotlight shining on the table.[28]

Question: Does he know (*shitte-iru/wakatte-iru*) that the table is red? (Similarly for questions of all other cases, which will be omitted.) The difference between the answers of *shitte-iru* and *wakatte-iru* was significant (p = 0.049, ω = 0.28) (see Figure 5.3). Even though the sample

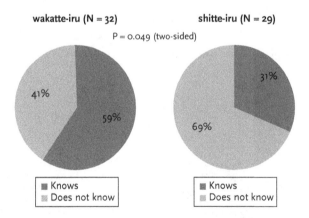

Figure 5.3 The results of the Furniture Store case (detailed version)

27. We did not include in this analysis the data of the Phone Number case and the Puzzle case, since they are somewhat different in nature (based on a simple sentence rather than a detailed vignette). But if we include such data, the statistical significance of the comparison of the corresponding models will be far stronger (p = 3.71E-06), just as expected.

28. The vignette is from Nagel (2010), which was adapted from Cohen (2002).

size is relatively small, we had actually already conducted a more extensive between-subject survey on the Furniture Store case (Kitami Institute of Technology, N = 116), whose results back up the present result. There, we also conducted the plain story version (see next) for comparison, since the detailed story version was originally presented by Nagel (2010) to argue for the effect of salience of the possibility of error.

Vignette 2 (plain version): Mr. Yamada is in a furniture store. He is looking at a bright red table under normal lighting conditions. He believes the table is red.

For the plain story, we had obtained a statistically significant difference between *wakatte-iru* and *shitte-iru* ($p = 0.045$, one-sided, $\omega = 0.20$) (see Figure 5.4). For the detailed story (which was the same vignette as we used in the current survey at Kanazawa Gakuin University), we failed to obtain a statistically significant difference there. But since the pattern of answers (that more people attribute knowledge if asked in *wakatte-iru* than in *shitte-iru*) was the same as the result of the current survey (done at Kanazawa Gakuin), we combined the data from the two surveys and obtained a statistically firmer result ($p = 0.013$, $\omega = 0.19$), albeit with a smaller effect size (see Figure 5.5).

Note also that we have the same pattern (*wakatte-iru* is more tolerantly attributed than *shitte-iru*) in both the plain and the detailed versions, even though there was no statistically significant difference between the results of the plain story and those of the detailed story. This makes an

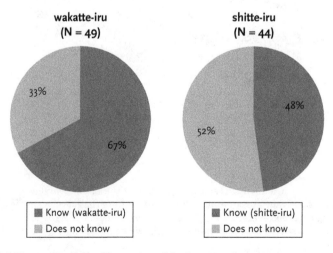

Figure 5.4 The results of the plain version of the Furniture Store case

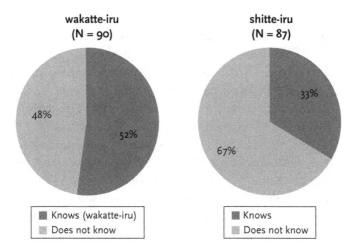

Figure 5.5 Combined results of the detailed version of the Furniture Store case

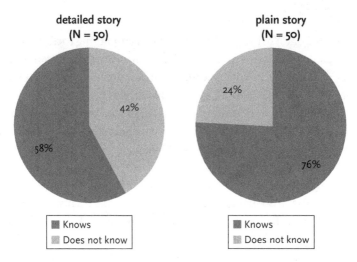

Figure 5.6 US data for the Furniture Store case

interesting contrast with the data of English "know," which we conducted using Amazon M-Turk (N = 100, age = 31.4, female = 48%, all participants were US native English speakers). See Figure 5.6 above.[29]

29. Hereafter, all the English data are of participants recruited via Amazon M-Turk, and we mention only the number of participants after eliminating those who were not US native English speakers. Alexander and his colleagues asked participants to *evaluate the knowledge attribution* rather than make knowledge attribution (as in this study), in fear of a lack of participants' sensitivity to salience of the error possibility (Alexander et al. 2014). Our results show that the fear was unwarranted.

On the one hand, the difference depicted in figure 5.6 is fairly signif-icant (p = 0.001, ω = 0.35), which confirms the result of Alexander et al. (2014, sec. 3.1).[30] On the other hand, in Japanese, neither *shitte-iru* nor *wakatte-iru* showed a statistically significant difference (even though the sample sizes were larger in both cases than in the English survey) between the plain story and the detailed story (for the respective sample size, in the case of *shitte-iru*, 1-β= 0.93 for ω = 0.3; in the case of *wakatte-iru*, 1-β= 0.94 for ω = 0.3). Admittedly, in both cases the rate of knowledge attribu-tion is lower for the detailed story than for the plain story, but the lack of statistical significance and the smaller effect sizes (ω = 0.14 for *shitte-iru*, ω = 0.15 for *wakatte-iru*) than in the English survey show that at least the difference between *shitte-iru* and *wakatte-iru* matters much more than the effect of the salience of the error possibility for the Japanese speakers.

TrueTemp Case

Vignette: One day, Yoshio was hit on the head by a falling rock and knocked out. As a result, his brain was modified in such a way that he is now always right whenever he estimates the temperature. Yoshio is completely una-ware that his brain has been altered in this way. A few weeks after having been hit on the head and knocked out by the rock, he happens to believe that it is 23 degrees (Celsius) in his bedroom. Apart from his estimation, he has no other reason to think that it is 23 degrees in his bedroom. Yet, it is in fact 23 degrees in his bedroom.[31]

For this vignette, we first asked as a comprehension test whether Yoshio can tell the temperature because he trained himself or because he was hit on the head by a rock. The results reported here are only for those who passed the test (see Figure 5.7). The difference between two groups was statistically significant (p = 0.032, Fisher, one-sided, ω = 0.28). Again, the sample size of this survey was small,[32] but this was the only case that turned out to be

---

30. Alexander and his colleagues asked participants to *evaluate the knowledge attri-bution* rather than make knowledge attribution (as in this study), in fear of a lack of participants' sensitivity to salience of the error possibility (Alexander et al. 2014). Our results show that the fear was unwarranted.

31. This vignette and the one used in the Fake Barn case were borrowed from those used in the Intellectual Humility Project by Stich, Machery, and the Intellectual Humility and Cultural Diversity Research Group.

32. Earlier, in a set of between-subject surveys (N = 137 for *shitte-iru*, N = 92 for *wakatte-iru*), we obtained a significant difference (p = 0.012, two-sided, ω = 0.17) with the same pattern (*wakatte-iru* attribution was more tolerant than *shitte-iru*). However, the surveys for two knowledge verbs were conducted in different universities, and in

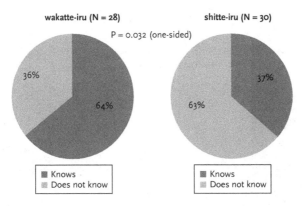

wakatte-iru (N = 28)   shitte-iru (N = 30)

P = 0.032 (one-sided)

36%   37%

64%   63%

Knows   Knows
Does not know   Does not know

Figure 5.7 The results of TrueTemp case

Table 5.3 THE BREAKDOWN OF THE TRUETEMP CASE (BETWEEN-SUBJECT)

shitte-iru as a primer	knows	does not know	*wakatte-iru* as a primer	knows	does not know
wakatte-iru	25	5	*wakatte-iru*	17	11
shitte-iru	8	22	*shitte-iru*	17	11

significant also in the within-subject data (the result of the second question). If we look at the breakdown of the data (see Table 5.3), we find that only participants in the group in which the *shitte-iru* question was a primer distinguished the uses of *shitte-iru* and *wakatte-iru* ($p = 0.00002$, $\omega = 0.60$).[33]

Given the strong statistical significance and the large-effect size, this is unlikely to be a product of sheer accident. Thus, the significant result was either the effect artificially produced by the *shitte-iru* question as a primer (where in fact there was no effect) or the real effect with the other group being distracted by the *wakatte-iru* question as a primer. Expecting that it was the latter, we conducted exactly the same survey this time *without* the first question (that is, with no primer). There, participants were asked to choose *two* options among *shitte-iru*, *wakatte-iru*, and their respective non-past negatives (*shiranai* and *wakatte-inai*).

The participants were again undergraduates of Kanazawa Gakuin University ($N = 36$, female = 58.3%). After eliminating the answers of

this sense were not well controlled. Still, the fact that we obtained the same pattern of responses bolsters our current result.

33. There were no other cases in which the breakdown showed an apparent difference between the two groups, nor was there any group in the breakdown showing a significant difference between the knowledge-attribution judgments of *shitte-iru* and *wakatte-iru*.

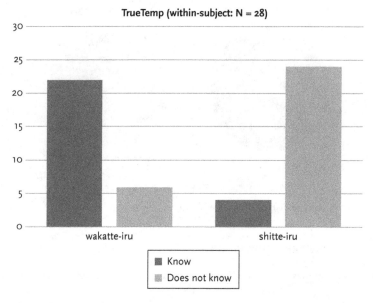

Figure 5.8 The results of the new TrueTemp survey (within-subject)

participants who failed the comprehension test (and those who did not answer the questions) and one participant whose native language was not Japanese, the resulting sample size was $N = 28$. The result obtained was consistent with our hypothesis, and the statistical significance of the difference was overwhelming (see Figure 5.8) , despite the small sample size ($p = 0.000002$, Fisher, two-sided, $\omega = 0.64$).

We may also conjecture here that, since the effect size of this result is no less, or even larger than, the one of the between-subject question with *shitte-iru* as a primer, the *wakatte-iru* question as a primer (but not the *shitte-iru* question) somehow hindered the intuitions of participants. Whether this was true and if so, why this happens is the subject of future study.

Bank Case

Vignette: In one Friday afternoon, Mr. and Mrs. Suzuki drove to the bank to deposit some money, but found a long line inside the bank. Having seen that the bank was open on Saturday two weeks ago, Mr. Suzuki says to his wife, "I know this bank will open tomorrow. Let's come back tomorrow." His wife says, however, "Do you really know it? If it is not open tomorrow, the money will not be deducted, which means that we would lose a big amount of money." Mr. Suzuki answers, "Well, no. Let me go and check."

The first question was a comprehension one, asking whether Mr. Suzuki and his wife would have to pay a large amount of money if they failed to deposit the money by Saturday afternoon. The second question reads as follows:

Suppose that the bank will indeed be open tomorrow. When he said, "Well, no. Let me go and check," Mr. Suzuki:
(1) knew that the bank would be open tomorrow.
(2) did not know that the bank would be open tomorrow.

In one group, *wakatte-iru* was used in both the story and the question. In the other group, *shitte-iru* was used.

The result was statistically significant (p = 0.037, Fisher, one-sided, ω = 0.28) (see Figure 5.9 below).

Given the small sample size, one may doubt that the statistical significance is due to the small rate of "know" answers in both *shitte-iru* and *wakatte-iru* conditions. The small rates of "know" answers are apparently due to the character of the vignette in which Mr. Suzuki apparently changed his view, saying in the end, "Well, no. Let me go and check." However, in an earlier study (participants were undergraduates of Kitami Institute of Technology, N = 141, female = 17%) with the same between-subject design, we gave the following question with four options to choose:

When Mr. Suzuki said, "Well, no. Let me go and check," he:
(1) does not know whether the bank will be open tomorrow, and told a lie.
(2) knows that the bank will be open tomorrow, but has lost confidence.
(3) knew that the bank would be open tomorrow, but has ceased to know now.

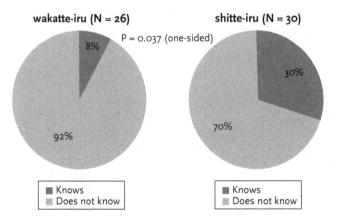

Figure 5.9 The results of the Bank case

(4) did not know whether the bank will be open tomorrow, but has realized that now.

In this case, the rate of "know" answers, which was only option 2 among the four given above, was (after eliminating the data of participants who failed the comprehension test) 65% (N = 60) for *wakatte-iru* and 80% (N = 44) for *shitte-iru*, despite the fact that three other options were the "does not know" answers, which could easily be expected to *increase* the rates of the totality of "does not know" answers.

Even though in this earlier study the difference between the rates of the "know" answer was not statistically significant, since there we had the same pattern, with *wakatte-iru* having the higher rate of the "know" answers than *shitte-iru*, we conducted a logistic regression analysis with the following model,

$$\text{Logit } (\pi) = \beta_0 + \beta_1 x_1 + \beta_2 x_2 + \varepsilon,$$

where β_1 is the coefficient of the *shitte-iru/wakatte-iru* factor, and β_0 and β_2 are coefficients of two bank cases. The Wald test for coefficient β_1 showed that the *shitte-iru/wakatte-iru* factor is a significant predictor of the knowledge-attribution judgement of participants (p = 0.014). Thus, such results further bolster the current hypothesis.

Note that the significant difference between the *shitte-iru* attribution and the *wakatte-iru* attribution in the Bank case is in the *opposite* direction from those of the Furniture Store case and the TrueTemp case. This could have been predicted, however, by the results of the Phone Number case and the Puzzle case. In those cases, the subject was unsure about his own relevant memory or ability. This subjective uncertainty only undermined the attribution of *wakatte-iru*, but not *shitte-iru*, in comparison. The Bank case, or at least the vignette we used, was exactly the same in this sense.[34]

---

34. Note, however, that in the original vignette (the high-stakes condition) of DeRose (1992), the husband not only says, "Well, no. I'd better go in and make sure," but was also described at the same time, as "[r]emaining as confident as [he] was before" (913). Given our hypothesis that the subjective uncertainty of the agent affects attribution of *wakatte-iru* but not so much of *shitte-iru*, this description should play a crucial role for the Japanese speakers in producing the difference in the attributions of these two verbs. Testing this hypothesis is one of the important studies left for future investigation.

There was no significant difference between the answers of the *shitte-iru* group and those of the *wakatte-iru* group (we omit the vignette, which was a standard, but a little lengthy version). This was presumably mainly because of the small sample size (N = 43) owing to the high rate (18/ 61 = 29.5%) of participants who failed to pass the comprehension test (for this sample size, even for the medium-effect size of ω = 0.3, the statistical power $1-\beta$ is only 0.50, which means that it could be detected only once out of two times).[35]

However, given the results of other studies we have already seen, we may predict that the same pattern should be observed as those of the Furniture Store case and the TrueTemp case. Indeed, even though the comparison requires some caution (see later), in earlier independent experiments we had found a statistically significant difference between two independent studies of the Fake Barn case, one using *shitte-iru* and another using *wakatte-iru*.[36] There, the vignettes and questions are identical except the uses of *shitte-iru* and *wakatte-iru*, and there are two questions besides the comprehension question, the first simply asking whether the agent knows or not, and the second asking whether the subject knows or only believes so but does not know. The results of the first question were significantly different (p = 0.0031, two-sided, ω = 0.23), with the participants of the *wakatte-iru* group attributing more knowledge (56%) than the participants of the *shitte-iru* group (32%). The results of the second question were also (but less) significantly different (p = 0.041, two-sided, ω = 0.16), with understandably fewer participants attributing knowledge in both the *wakatte-ru* group (37%) and the *shitte-iru* group (22%).

The problem with this comparison is that these surveys for respective verbs were conducted with participants (undergraduates) at different universities, and therefore the due homogeneity of participants for

---

35. The reason for this, we conjecture, is that the vignette was the exact translation of the English one used in the Intellectual Humility Project (cf. footnote 31), and therefore somehow sounded unnatural for the Japanese. This is inevitable for any cross-linguistic study, where the more literal the translation gets, the more unnatural it will sound. In this particular case, the unnaturalness seems to have imposed a particularly heavy cognitive load on the participants.

36. For the *shitte-iru* group, N = 173, female = 47.4%, 78 participants were from Nagoya University, 95 were from Hokkaido University, 117 passed the comprehension test;, and for the *wakatte-iru* group, N = 101, female 15%, participants were undergraduates of Kitami Institute of Technology, 68 passed the comprehension test. The data of *shitte-iru* belongs to the Intellectual Humility Project mentioned at note 30.

comparison is not ideally controlled.[37] Still, as we shall argue below, the fact that the data were consistent with the results of the Furniture Store case and the TrueTemp case gives us additional (if tentative) support for our view of the semantic difference of these two verbs.

Note also that the Fake Barn case (or the compatibility with the "environmental," rather than "intervening" luck; see Pritchard 2010) was the original reason for Kvanvig to think that understanding is not a species of knowledge (2003, chap. 8). Suppose that the tentative difference between *shitte-iru* and *wakatte-iru* is real. Then, if *wakatte-iru* is the counterpart of the English "understand" and *shitte-iru* is the counterpart of the English "know," that might support Kvanvig's claim. However, as we have seen earlier, there was no difference between *shitte-iru* and *wakatte-iru* in the standard Gettier case, while it was not clear what is meant by the corresponding (English) "understanding" attribution in that context. Thus, it rather seems that *wakatte-iru* is *closer* to the English "know" than to the English "understand," while *wakatte-iru is* also a species of (at least grammatically, a direct derivative of the word for) understanding. All this rather counts against Kvanvig's claim.

4.3. General Discussion

We have seen that, in some cases, significantly more participants attributed *wakatte-iru* but not *shitte-iru* to the subject, and in other cases, the pattern was the opposite, whereas in the Gettier (Car) case, no difference was observed. The overall results are summarized in Table 5.4 (where ∧ means that the rate of the *wakatte-iru* answer was significantly higher than that of the *shitte-iru* answer, and ∨ means that it was significantly lower).

Besides the Phone Number case and the Puzzle case, the fact that, in epistemologically relevant cases participants distinguished *wakatte-iru* and

---

37. Besides, this study included an online survey using *shitte-iru*, whose participants were largely non-student adults, whose average age was 41.6. But its result was significantly different from the data of students, and rather very similar to the student data of *wakatte-iru*. In the combined data of *shitte-iru*, logistic regression analysis showed that the age factor was a significant predictor of the knowledge (*shitte-iru*) attribution ($p = 0.016$ for the first question, $p = 0.00038$ for the second question). That is, the older the age becomes, the more likely the participants will attribute knowledge. Unfortunately, this age effect is in the opposite direction from the one observed by Colaço et al. (2014). Since we do not have the corresponding data for *wakatte-iru*, we did not include the data in the consideration. Whether the effect of the age factor is real, and can also be observed in the case of *wakatte-iru*, etc., are to be investigated in a future study.

Table 5.4 SUMMARY OF THE DIFFERENCES BETWEEN *SHITTE-IRU*
AND *WAKATTE-IRU*

Phone Number case	Puzzle case	Gettier (Car)	Furniture Store case	TrueTemp case	Bank case (High)	Fake Barn case
Shitte-iru						
Wakatte-iru	∨	∨	=	∧	∧	∨(?)

shitte-iru in the between-subject question (except in the Fake Barn case) but were unable to do so (except in the TrueTemp case) when the options were juxtaposed, suggests that the distinction of the use of these two verbs is largely subconscious.

This gives us an important methodological lesson, but apart from the methodology, this insensitivity to meaning has some philosophical implications. Michael Dummett (1978) once claimed,

> It is an undeniable feature of the notion of meaning—obscure as that notion is—that meaning is transparent in the sense that, if someone attaches a meaning to each of two words, he must know whether these meanings are the same. (131)

This is the thesis Williamson (2000) called "luminosity" and criticized in chapter 4 of his book. Apart from Williamson's vagueness-based argument against it, the present question for us is: What does Dummett mean by "know" in the last sentence here? The significant differences in the answers to the between-subject question disappeared in the answers to the within-subject question, in both the Furniture Store case and the Bank case. That is, participants were unable to consciously distinguish the meanings of two verbs. But then remember the Phone Number case and the Puzzle case, where participants were able to distinguish these meanings. When an agent was unable to tell a phone number or solve a puzzle consciously simply because she had forgotten it (thus maintaining the potential ability), participants attributed *shitte-iru*, but not *wakatte-iru*. This means that, when the Japanese are unable to distinguish the meanings of the two verbs consciously, but still can do so potentially, they *know* whether the meanings are the same or not in the sense of *shitte-iru*, but not in the sense of *wakatte-iru*. Thus, the thesis of luminosity is true if Dummett uses "know" in the sense of one Japanese knowledge verb, but false in the sense of another Japanese knowledge verb. Note that Dummett often emphasizes that the speaker's knowledge of the semantic theory is *implicit*. Even so, as long as *wakatte-iru* is a legitimate knowledge verb, the fact remains that the correctness of the luminosity depends on the choice of the knowledge verb.

Also, the fact that among other epistemological cases, only in the TrueTemp case were the two verbs (relatively easily) explicitly differentiated (through the within-subject question) deserves close attention. We have earlier introduced the metaphor of vertical knowledge and horizontal knowledge, and the picture of vertical knowledge fits well the characteristics of *wakatte-iru* (appreciation and cognitive ability based on it); and the paradigmatic case is the TrueTemp case. Unlike the Phone Number case and the Puzzle case, the agent there can consciously (thus has the actual, rather than merely potential, ability to) tell the current temperature, though without consciously accessible reason. In this connection, *wakaru*, the infinite form of *wakatte-iru*, can be used to express (as we saw in section 1), in addition to the state of understanding, knowing, appreciation, and so on, *ability* to get information, appreciate, tell, comprehend, and the like. And the state of *wakatte-iru* can be understood as a product or consequence of this (typically, but not limited to, *cognitive*) ability (cf. section 3.3). On the one hand, since the TrueTemp vignette makes it clear that the agent has the mental content that it is 23 degrees in the room because of the accidentally acquired ability, *wakatte-iru*, derived from the ability sense of *wakaru*, can obviously be attributed. On the other hand, since the transmission of information there is not normal, as would be transmitted from other people or through a book, radio, newspaper, and so on (from outside of the territory) as if horizontally, and its causal history is not clear to the agent, *shittte-iru* was denied attribution there. This case therefore demonstrates a clear semantic difference between these knowledge verbs.

Given this observation, we may say the analogous things about the Furniture Store case. Although we receive information about an object in perception, the paradigmatic way of *receiving* information is from outside of the territory (horizontally), and if the table is already in view, the information is already within the territory of the agent. Thus in such nontypical situations, if participants are asked whether the agent *shitte-iru* or not, they look for alternative possibilities. On the one hand, this explains their stringent judgments even in the plain version of the story. On the other hand, perception in general is just a matter of exercising our own cognitive ability. As long as one is exercising the ability in the normal way, then one can be said to *wakatte-iru*. Exactly the same thing can also be said regarding the Fake Barn case, and therefore the same pattern of results can be predicted, though in this case there is objective reason to consider alternative possibilities.

Given this ability sense of knowledge, we may further characterize *wakatte-iru* as the *agent-based* knowledge, and *shitte-iru* as the *state-based* knowledge (or, allowing degrees, we may say that *wakatte-iru* is *more* agent-based or oriented, and *shitte-iru* is *more* state-based or oriented). Cognitive *ability* is at the personal level, while cognitive *capacity* is usually thought to be at the subpersonal level. Thus conceived, *wakatte-iru* is clearly agent-based knowledge, and we are attributing to the agent an ability when we attribute *wakatte-iru*. This knowledge is therefore undermined when the agent is unable to recall, or do the relevant thing, as in the Phone Number case and the Puzzle case. Shitte-iru, in contrast, is state-based, in the sense that even the agent has lost (if temporarily) the relevant ability, the agent's internal state (at the subpersonal level) assures the state of *shitte-iru*. In the Bank case, for example, the agent loses confidence (or so judged), but his mental state maintains the memory of the relevant experience (seeing the bank open two weeks ago). But being information-theoretic, relevant alternatives affect the quality of information the agent possesses, as in the Fake Barn case, while the stringency of *shitte-iru* judgments in the Furniture Store case is a pragmatic effect.

In this sense, *wakatte-iru* is friendly to virtue epistemology (either virtue reliabilism or responsibilism), where the focus is on the agent (with or without intellectual virtues/vices), or the character or the achievement (apt performance) of the agent, while *shitte-iru* is friendly to information-theoretic conception of knowledge, where the causal etiology of the agent's internal (subpersonal) state, or how the state was caused by the relevant information, is mainly (or even only) what matters.[38] (Or, Ernest Sosa would say that this is rather *animal knowledge*, while *wakatte-iru* expresses *reflective knowledge*. We shall come back to this view later.)

In this connection, John Turri recently has advanced *ablism* by refining or purifying the agent-based perspective of virtue epistemology, or virtue reliabilism in particular (Turri 2015b, 2016b, and 2017). It seems that *wakatte-iru* is a perfect fit for his ablism (remember that *wakatte-iru* is a derivative of the word (mainly) for understanding (cognitive ability), *wakaru*). But if so, is the existence of such a verb good news for Turri? Also, there are recently numerous other philosophers who emphasize the connection between knowledge and action. This includes Jason Stanley, who, connecting his interest-relative invariantism and intellectualism about knowledge-how, even argues against the thought that propositional knowledge is behaviorally

---

38. Though virtue epistemologists may *also* require the appropriate etiology. I would like to thank Shane Ryan for this point.

inert (2011, chap. 4). Thus, the sense of *wakatte-iru* also seems to support his interest-relative invariantism.[39] But if so, is this also good news to Stanley? *Wakatte-iru* will provide a good support for both Turri and Stanley if it is the *true counterpart* of the English "know," and *both wakatte-iru and "know" are instances of THE correct knowledge verb* (if there is such a thing).

Shitte-iru, however, rather behaves like strict (classic, pure) invariantism. Then, suppose that *shitte-iru* is best explained by Dretske's (1981) information theoretic analysis of knowledge. Is this good news to Dretske? What if we say, "It depends which of *shitte-iru* and *wakatte-iru* is the genuine knowledge verb"? Or, there has been a debate in epistemology over whether knowledge requires certainty. As we saw in the Phone Number case and the Puzzle case, and possibly in the Bank case, *wakatte-iru* was vulnerable to the lack of subjective certainty, while *shitte-iru* was relatively resilient to it. We shall see in the next section the extremely stringent attribution of the English "know" in the Phone Number case and the Puzzle case. But then, we may wonder if the existence of such a verb like *shitte-iru* is good news to, say, Jason Stanley (2008), who argues that knowledge does not require (subjective or epistemic) certainty. What if someone says, in response to the question whether knowledge requires certainty, "It depends on which language you use"?

These are serious questions about epistemology, which we discuss in the next section.

5. WHICH ONE IS THE TRUE COUNTERPART OF THE ENGLISH "KNOW"?

Given the *semantic* difference between the two Japanese counterparts of the English "know," *shitte-iru* and *wakatte-iru*, the anglophone epistemologists may naturally ask: Which is the true counterpart of the English "know"? Or, Which is closer to the English "know"?

In the Puzzle case and the Phone Number case, English speakers are *very* stringent; only two people (3.6%) out of 56 US native English speakers (age = 35.0, female = 32.1%) in the Phone case and only one person (1.8%) out of 56 participants answered that the subject knows. This made even the difference with the result of *wakatte-iru* statistically significant ($p = 0.017$, $\omega = 0.30$) in the Puzzle case (but not in the Phone Number case). Still, the difference with the result of *shitte-iru* is no doubt much

---

39. Though the data of Turri and Buckwalter (2017) seem to undermine the direct (if not indirect) influence of the stakes on knowledge attribution. See also section 6

larger ($p = 0.000035$, $\omega = 0.47$ for the Phone Number case, and $p = 0.0000$, $\omega = 0.70$ for the Puzzle case). In this sense, at least, the English "know" is closer to *wakatte-iru* in this respect.

In the Furniture Store case, the English "know" was closer to *wakatte-iru* in the plain version in the sense that it was significantly different from *shitte-iru* but not from *wakatte-iru* (the difference was $p = $ ns, $\omega = 0.10$ for *wakatte-iru*, and $p = 0.0086$, $\omega = 0.29$ for *shitte-iru*). However, in the detailed version, the rate of attribution of "know" (42%) was just in between the rates of *shitte-iru* (33%) and *wakatte-iru* (52%), and was significantly different from neither of them.

In the TrueTemp case, the rate of knowledge attribution by US native English speakers ($N = 87$, age = 34.1, female = 40.2%) who passed the comprehension test ($N = 79$), was 53%. In an earlier, larger scale between-subject survey,[40] the rate for *shitte-iru* was 30% and for *wakatte-iru* 48%.[41] Thus, in this case, English "know" was very similar to *wakatte-iru* in the sense that its difference with *shitte-iru* was statistically significant ($p = 0.0018$, $\omega = 0.22$), while the difference with *wakatte-iru* was not ($\omega = 0.05$).

In the Bank case of the answers only with the "know/does not know" options, the knowledge attribution rate was 11% ($N = 66$, age = 33.1, female = 50.0%, those who passed the comprehension test, N = 56), which is significantly different from *shitte-iru* (30%, $p = 0.028$, one-sided, $\omega = 0.24$), but not from *wakatte-iru* (8%). In the case of the answers with the "know but lost confidence" option, the knowledge attribution rate was 66% (N = 74, age = 34.6, female = 60.8%), roughly the same as that of *wakatte-iru* (65%).

In the survey on the Fake Barn case using US native English speakers (N = 66, age = 35.7, female = 53.0%), to the simple question of whether the agent knows or not, 66% of those who passed the comprehension test (N = 53) answered that the agent knows, in comparison with 32% of *shitte-iru* and 56% of *wakatte-iru* in the earlier between-subject survey. To the second question of whether the agent knows or only believes to know, 49% (N = 53) still answered that the agent knows, in comparison

---

40. For *shitte-iru*, $N = 137$, female = 66.2%, 94 were undergraduates of Kyushu University, 23 from Aoyama Gakuin University, and 23 from Tokyo University, after eliminating non-native Japanese speakers, $N = 128$. For *wakatte-iru*, $N = 92$, female = 14.1%, all undergraduates of Kitami Institute of Technology. Again, the data for *shitte-iru* belongs to the Intellectual Humility Project; see note 31.

41. Again, participants of this between-subject study are not ideally controlled, owing due to the use of different universities for the Japanese participants and the age factor. But as for the latter worry, the result of the logistic regression analysis of the US data shows that the age is not a significant predictor of the knowledge attribution ($p = 0.77$).

Table 5.5 SUMMARY OF THE COMPARISONS OF *SHITTE-IRU/WAKATTE-IRU* WITH THE ENGLISH "KNOW"

	Phone Number case	Puzzle case	Gettier (Car) case	Furniture Store case	TrueTemp case	Bank case (High)	Fake Barn case
Shitte-iru			✓				
Wakatte-iru	✓	✓	✓	✓ (plain version)	✓	✓	✓

with 22% of *shitte-iru* and 37% of *wakatte-iru*. Thus (apart from the worry about the Japanese data mentioned earlier),[42] English "know" is closer to *wakatte-iru* in the sense that it was significantly different from *shitte-iru* in both the first question (p = 0.000084, ω = 0.31) and the second question (p = 0.0006, ω = 0.27), but not from *wakatte-iru* in either question. See the summary presented in Table 5.5 (the check indicates the similarity to English "know").

Even though we need further, better controlled surveys (especially the age factor) with a larger sample size, table 5.5 is impressive in the sense that, although almost all ordinary Japanese usually think that the proper counterpart of English "know" is *shitte-iru*, in fact *wakatte-iru* seems rather closer to it. Does this suggest that the real counterpart of "know" is *wakatte-iru*? If so, some philosophers—in particular, virtue epistemologists and philosophers who emphasize the connection between knowledge and action in general (see the next section)—would be pleased. However, at the same time, it is simply impossible that *shitte-iru* is *not* a knowledge verb. Thus, we would rather like to ask, instead: Why do you want to find the *true counterpart* of the English "know" in the first place? For such an attempt seems to presuppose that "know" is the verb that expresses the proper, legitimate concept for epistemology (as if a paradigmatic exponent of the semantic prime KNOW). But what if it is not? We have already mentioned Kvanvig's challenge to this assumption, by means of "understanding" as the alternative. But it is also perfectly arguable that both "know" and *wakatte-iru* are *impure*, contaminated by some additional (including pragmatic) factors, and therefore not best suited for epistemology. Even if the use of "know" is acceptable, we may also think that the English

42. Concerning the age factor of the English data, the logistic regression analysis showed that it was not a significant contributor to the knowledge attribution (p = 0.66 for the first question, p = 0.98 for the second question).

knowledge verb is *ambiguous*, hovering between two primitive or more fundamental epistemological notions expressed by *shitte-iru* and *wakatte-iru*, with some English speakers using "know" as *shitte-iru* and others using it as *wakatte-iru*. Or indeed, the same person may be using it as *shitte-iru* in some contexts and as *wakatte-iru* in other contexts, without realizing the difference (as we already suggested in the last section, Sosa may fully endorse this possibility).

This may explain the conflicting intuitions (and empirical data) about epistemological cases among ordinary people, and the disagreement among anglophone epistemologists. Note that, given that the difference between these two verbs is semantic, the difference between the properties or relations captured by them should be real, in the sense that normal Japanese speakers have the ability to or can (despite often subconsciously) differentiate their uses in response to different situations, and the difference detected there must be *out there*, available to the speakers. We may then even claim that other knowledge verbs (including "know") that are not sensitive to this distinction are rather ambiguous, mixing up two different senses. Or, one may say such verbs are *polysemous*. Anglophone epistemologists may think that what we have here is allolexy (different words expressing a single semantic prime) of two Japanese knowledge verbs, rather than polysemy of the English "know." And, admittedly, the senses of *shitte-iru* and *wakatte-iru* do overlap, and therefore they are not likely to be both semantic primes at the same time.[43] However, since the sense of "know" also covers more than the overlapping parts of the senses of these two verbs (sharing much more with *wakatte-iru* than *shitte-iru*), the conclusion that the English "know" is *also* polysemous seems unavoidable. Thus, anglophone epistemologists should at least admit that some part of the sense of the English "know" is merely accidental, language-specific, to be ignored in epistemology if it is a universal enterprise.

How, then, could we identify the true semantic prime KNOW? It is just too simple and naïve a principle to stipulate it to be the overlapping part of all the knowledge verbs of languages in the world. The more languages we consider, the smaller core would be left. Then, given that, as Allan Hazlett (2010) points out, even the English "know" has non-factive uses, it is very likely that *no* universal core would be left in the end (then we would have only *family resemblance* of knowledge verbs). If this happens, there is no

43. Note, however, that, as long as semantic content is conceived in terms of truth-condition, meanings of semantic primes in the sense of the NSM program do overlap each other. Consider "see that *p*" and "know that *p*" (SEE and KNOW are semantic primes in NSM).

way anymore to distinguish a verb being mistaken about knowledge from the verb being *not* a knowledge verb in the first place.

Even if this is the case, linguists would not and should not be committed to a *normative* view about what knowledge is (which constrains the use of knowledge verbs). Epistemologists, however, *are* committed to such a view. Most of them take epistemology to be a universal inquiry, independent of a particular language they use. But if so, they seem to be committed to the existence of the case whereby a whole linguistic community is wrong about the use of its knowledge verb. This is equivalent to admitting the "cross-linguistic disagreement," where the use of the knowledge verb of one language differs from that of another language, with no relevant ignorance, no performance error, and the like on the part of the speakers of both sides. As long as we assume the language-independent universal concept of knowledge, this disagreement is genuine (one over whether an agent possesses the relevant knowledge), rather than merely apparent (discussing different topics).

However, what we found in Japanese is, in a sense, the "*intra*-linguistic disagreement" of two knowledge verbs. But this disagreement is merely apparent, there being no question of which is right. If so, however, why cannot we think the same way about all other apparent cross-linguistic disagreements? Indeed, this seems the most plausible understanding of the data of cross-linguistic differences of knowledge verbs.

But if this is really the case, it does not make sense to talk about cross-linguistic disagreement anymore, which has far-reaching consequences even for epistemological debates that are not directly concerned with the linguistic issue, let alone the possible linguistic diversity of knowledge verbs. We have seen in section 4 that *wakatte-iru* apparently supports virtue epistemology, Turri's ablism, and Stanley's interest-relative invariantism, while *shitte-iru* apparently supports Dretskean information-theoretic analysis of knowledge and Stanley's view of the relation between knowledge and certainty. But if we are right, there is no single correct view or theory about knowledge here, unless a specific language (here, English) is assumed.

More generally, John Turri and Wesley Buckwalter (2017) pit Descartes, who claims that knowledge is "fundamentally separable from action and other practical concerns," with Locke, who opposes this view and tries to "reunite" these two. They stand on the side of Locke and argue for it with good empirical evidence. Despite their psychologically rigorous procedure, however, their results (that apparently support the Lockean view) are only data about the English "know." Even if Lockeans proved to be correct based on their empirical data, this connection with action and practical interests is a character of but one knowledge verb, "know." We saw that *wakatte-iru* was also such a verb, having a close connection with cognitive and practical abilities and therefore actions. However, *shitte-iru* was not such a verb, maintained even if the agent lacks the relevant ability. On the one hand, it rather supports the Cartesian conception of knowledge in the sense of Turri and Buckwalter (thus it is very likely that their data will be reproduced with Japanese subjects only if *wakatte-iru*, but not *shitte-iru*, was used as the knowledge verb). If, on the other hand, Lockeans claim that our data show that *shitte-iru* is still action-infused *enough*, then they admit that there is a *continuum* of knowledge verbs that vary with their closeness to action, and we can also conceive of a knowledge verb (at the one end) that has no (or almost no) connection with action in some language. Lockeans can no longer claim here that such a verb is not a knowledge verb, given the possibility implicated by two Japanese knowledge verbs. But then, there should be no question of which (Lockeans or Cartesians) is right there.

In general, if there is no genuine cross-linguistic disagreement, there is no epistemological question about whether an agent possesses relevant knowledge in a particular situation, independent of any particular language. If so, however, we cannot and should not expect *one* answer to the epistemological question about the nature of knowledge, for we have only a family of multiple, consistent, overlapping concepts, none of which is *the* concept of knowledge. One might then think that there is no epistemology either,[44] but there are only *epistemologies* (cf. Manifesto, this volume). There, epistemologists are in fact doing a version of anthropology, or *ethno-epistemology*. But is *this* epistemology at all?

Hazlett (2010) seems to admit such epistemology (or epistemologies) when he proposes the "divorce" between language-specific epistemologies and language-independent universal epistemology. But the latter, if there is such epistemology, assumes the universal "core" knowledge, and to identify such knowledge would be difficult where languages disagree about whether an agent possesses the relevant knowledge. We would then need some language-independent method or theory. Let us briefly consider what such epistemology, in particular the theory of knowledge, would and should be like.

---

44. Of course, epistemology is also concerned with other notions like belief, justification, truth, and so on. But given the linguistic diversity of knowledge verbs, terms for belief and justification should *all the more* vary from language to language, and we already have data suggesting that even Japanese counterparts of "is true" and "is correct" significantly differ from English ones in their usage (Mizumoto, *manuscript*).

6. WHAT SHOULD LANGUAGE-INDEPENDENT EPISTEMOLOGY BE LIKE?

Given the problems posed regarding epistemology by the linguistic diversity of knowledge verbs, epistemologists may naturally claim that such linguistic contingencies, and therefore the data of linguistic diversity in general, are irrelevant to epistemology and should be ignored.

However, any apparent language-independent approach in epistemology is still not free from the knowledge verbs in the languages used, at least as long as it emphasizes the practical aspect of knowledge.[45] Practical considerations may be essential for knowledge attribution in the case of the English "know" (and Japanese *wakatte-iru*), but for epistemology per se, such a contingent aspect must be ignored. Practical concerns must be based on knowledge, but not vice versa (at least for *shitte-iru* and possibly other knowledge verbs in other languages). If so, the data (armchair of experimental) of knowledge *attributions* or *ascriptions* should be ignored in epistemology, or at least on the one side of the Hazlett's divorce. But how, then, can we proceed in epistemology without all such data?

At this point we may appeal to formal language. Thus, one might claim that an artificial, formal language of formal epistemology is the scientific language for epistemology. But formalization is formalization of informal concept, and our question was whether that informal concept was language-independent or not. Still, if the concept of knowledge or knowledge itself is captured by or even *consists of* a formal property, this approach can be justified.

Another possible approach that is divorced from linguistic considerations is the information-theoretic approach (not incompatible with the formal one) to knowledge (see, *inter alia*, Dretske 1981). Information is a language-independent entity *out there* in the environment, which individuals may gain, possess, lack, or communicate with others. (Territory of information theory was also meant to be such a universally applicable theory.) According to Dretske, knowledge is a belief *properly caused* by such information. This theory is therefore presumably independent of our knowledge-attribution practices, let alone contingencies of language to ascribe knowledge.

---

45. This includes approaches like Edward Craig's, who criticizes the project of analysis of knowledge, and instead proposes us to consider what the concept of knowledge *does* (Craig 1990). This kind of approaches focuses on the functional role of knowledge in the form of life, in which our practical interests and concerns are intrinsically embedded.

Apart from his controversial rejection of the epistemic closure principle,[46] however, this theory has some difficulties in explaining nonperceptual and nontestimonial knowledge, like knowledge about the future, mathematical knowledge, knowledge of general fact, and the like. But this feature of his theory is by no means the limit of the information-theoretic approach in general. Surely the information-theoretic account or analysis of knowledge that overcomes such difficulties is possible (indeed, such a theory can easily be formalized as a monotonic belief with respect to the information in the environment, while accommodating the anti-Gettier condition, which therefore synthesizes the formal and information-theoretic approaches).[47] Such a theory does not accommodate any practical concerns, and therefore practical aspects of our knowledge-attribution practices are largely irrelevant (except Gettier cases) to it. And we should think so, at least for one party to the divorce. Pure information-theoretic epistemology should oppose the intrusion of pragmatic concerns.[48]

If this is what scientific epistemology should look like if we are to reject the linguistic considerations in "core" universal epistemology, some epistemologists might find it boring and no longer interesting. This is understandable, since according to this picture most debates in contemporary

46. See, however, recent experimental work to support the rejection in Turri (2015a).
47. For example, we may start with the most basic and general principle, *accumulability*, that knowledge is essentially accumulable (whereas belief is not). Arguably, it is part of the common usage of any language that knowledge can be stored, shared by people, and transmitted from one person, group, or even a generation to another. In particular, gaining new knowledge should be compatible with earlier knowledge. From this follows the principle of *no lucky ignorance*, that one cannot know by virtue of being, luckily, ignorant of some facts. That is, we cannot know *by virtue of ignorance*. Elsewhere (2011), I have argued that this principle accommodates the anti-Gettier condition. Formally, this accumulability of knowledge is called *monotonicity*, whereas belief is non-monotonic. We may also assume, at least for epistemological purposes, that information properly understood is also monotonic. Thus we have three layers of information, belief, and knowledge, with only the middle layer, belief, being non-monotonic. Given the idealization of belief to be consistent, and the stipulation of "belief" to be understood as full belief, this entails a formal theory of knowledge and belief change, in which a belief is formed or abandoned upon receiving new information, and the monotonic belief with respect to the totality of (actual) information is identified as knowledge. Given the formalization of the theory of belief change as formal derivations of beliefs from the totality of information one possesses, knowledge is also formally represented as monotonic belief with respect to the totality of information, which I called "sustainability." See for similar proposals, Rott (2004) and Stalnaker (2006), though they do not ultimately endorse the proposed analyses. As for the subtle difference between my analysis and theirs, see sections 5.3 and 5.4 of Mizumoto (2011).
48. Turri's primatological, evolutionary approach in his contribution to this volume might be another candidate. We believe that theory based on this approach and the one based on the information-theoretic approach will ultimately converge.

epistemology would be redundant or irrelevant. What, then, are such epistemologists doing? One answer that has already been suggested is that they are doing *ethno-epistemology*, or one of such epistemolog*ies*, which should be the other side of Hazlett's divorce. Arguably, however, such epistemology may well be a legitimate, even scientific investigation of the universal facts of human beings, in the sense that anthropology can still reveal the universal core of human cultures. There, of course, the data of folk practices of knowledge attribution should be valuable. Thus, it seems that we have only two options for legitimate scientific epistemology: either formal, abstract, information-theoretic epistemology or X-Phi-based, multi-linguistic, empirical epistemology (ethno-epistemology). Then everything in between has value only insofar as it contributes to either of them.

7. CONCLUSION

When Kvanvig was proposing *understanding* as the proper subject of epistemology, he lamented the *lack of diversity* in epistemology (2003, 188). He cites Fogelin (1994) to refer to the controversy over the right translation of Greek *episteme* (185), where some scholars argue that the term ought to be translated into "understanding" rather than "knowledge." However, merely adding another *English* notion, which is one of the two possible translations of a *single* Greek term, should not be enough to stop the lament of the lack of diversity in epistemology.

Our observations here suggest that we should expect many further different concepts of knowledge to be found in the world. In this connection, cross-linguistic studies of knowledge verbs have always been haunted by two difficulties. Any apparent data of linguistic divergence of the use of two knowledge verbs in two different languages may be explained away either by the problem of the translations of terms other than the knowledge verbs or by the difference in extra-linguistic factors, like cultural-psychological difference, or even difference in sociopolitical systems as backgrounds. Thus, it is difficult to establish that there are in fact different knowledge verbs cross-linguistically. However, in the case of *shitte-iru* and *wakatte-iru*, these difficulties would not arise, since speakers share all other terms in knowledge-attribution sentences, as well as cultural background and other extra-linguistic factors. The Japanese are in this sense all *bilinguals* of two (otherwise identical) languages with their respective knowledge verbs, and therefore are ideal for the comparison of different concepts of knowledge. We have seen that these two verbs express different concepts of (propositional) knowledge, and that is enough to establish that there are multiple, distinct concepts of knowledge. Moreover, we have seen that *shitte-iru* often supports one side of epistemological debates while *wakatte-iru* supports the other side. But if so, that raises the question about the nature of disagreement in epistemology, even *within* the Western tradition.

The consequence is that we are left with either language-independent universal epistemology, which should be simple but boring, or the multi-linguistic epistemology as an interlinguistic enterprise. But note that, in the latter, we should not have any prior assumption that there is a universal core captured by all knowledge verbs of languages in the world. Whether there is such a thing is an empirical matter. We might only have *family resemblance*, or worse, we might have to admit that there is no plausible meta-concept KNOW, unifying (even if loosely) all the similar concepts expressed by relevant verbs in languages of the world. In that case, epistemology cannot be a universal enterprise, essentially assuming some particular languages. In contrast, there is even a hope that the research in multi-linguistic empirical epistemology will eventually meet and *reunite* with the divorced half—the abstract, formal, information-theoretic armchair epistemology. Thus, either way, we will need data of knowledge verbs of not only English and Japanese but also of many other languages, and here epistemology solely based on the use of the knowledge verb of one particular language is out of question. This should be an inevitable course of events in contemporary epistemology, and the serious investigation of the other half of Hazlett's divorce—the enterprise of the multi-linguistic epistemology—has only begun!

ACKNOWLEDGMENTS

I would like to thank Stephen Stich and Edouard Machery for kindly allowing the use of the vignettes and data from the Intellectual Humility Project, and Toshiyuki Sadabobu, John Turri, Wesley Buckwalter, Mi Chienkuo, and Shane Ryan, for kind and helpful comments; and Terrillon Jean-Christophe for helpful comments and corrections of my English. Also I thank Kaori Karasawa, Naoki Usui, and Takaaki Hashimoto for their co-operation in translating English vignettes into Japanese in the Intellectual Humility Project, and Kenji Yamada, Naoyuki Nakamura, and Shogo Tanaka for kindly helping collect data. This work was supported by JSPS KAKENHI (C) Grant Number JP26370010.

REFERENCES

Alexander, J., C. Gonnerman, and J. Waterman. (2014). "Salience and Epistemic Egocentrism: An Empirical Study." In *Advances in Experimental Epistemology*, ed. James Beebe, 97–117. London: Bloomsbury.

Ando, Sadao. (1986). "Nishieigo no daikushisu" [Deixis of Japanese and English words]. *Eigo Kyoiku* 34(12): 70–75.

Ashihara, Kyoko. (2010). "Nhichijo kaiwa ni okeru 'wakaru' to 'shiru' no tsukai wake – dannwa no bunseki wo tooshite." *Ryugakusei Kyoiku* 7: 17–32.

Chomsky, Noam. (1977). *Essays on Forms and Interpretation*. Amsterdam: North Holland.

Cohen, S. (2002). "Basic Knowledge and the Problem of Easy Knowledge." *Philosophy and Phenomenological Research* 65: 302–329.

Colaço, D., W. Buckwalter, S. Stich, and E. Machery. (2014). "Epistemic Intuitions in Fake-Barn Thought Experiments." *Episteme* 11(2): 199–212.

Craig, E. (1990). *Knowledge and the State of Nature: An Essay in Conceptual Synthesis*. Oxford: Oxford University Press.

DeRose, K. (1992). "Contextualism and Knowledge Attributions." *Philosophy and Phenomenological Research* 52: 913–929.

Dretske, F. (1981). *Knowledge and the Flow of Information*. Cambridge, MA: MIT Press.

Dummett, Michael. (1978). *Truth and Other Enigmas*. London: Duckworth.

Filip, H. (2012). "Lexical Aspect." In *The Oxford Handbook of Tense and Aspect*, ed. R. I. Binnick, 721–751. Oxford: Oxford University Press.

Fogelin, Robert. (1994). *Pyrrhonian Reflections on Knowledge and Justification*. Oxford: Oxford University Press.

Grimm, Stephen R. (2014). "Understanding as Knowledge of Causes." In *Virtue Epistemology Naturalized: Bridges between virtue epistemology and philosophy of science* (Vol. 366), 329–345. Springer.

Hattori, Shiro. (1968). *Eigo Kiso-goi no Kenkyu* [A Study in the Basic Vocabulary of English]. Tokyo: Sanseido.

Hazlett, Allan. (2010). "The Myth of Factive Verbs." *Philosophy and Phenomenological Research* 80(3): 497–522.

Izumi, Y., S. Tsugita, and M. Mizumoto. (2017). "Knowing How in Japanese." *Unpublished manuscript*.

Kamio, Akio. (1979). "On the Notion Speaker's Territory of Information: A Functional Analysis of Certain Sentence-Final Forms in Japanese." In *Explorations in linguistics: Papers in Honor of Kazuko Inoue*, ed. George Bedell, Eichi Kobayashi, and Masatake Muraki, 213–231. Tokyo: Kenkyuusha.

Kamio, Akio. (1990). *Zyoohoo no Nawabari-riron: Gengo no kinooteki bunseki*. Tokyo: Taishuukan Shoten.

Kamio, Akio. (1994). "The Theory of Territory of Information: The Case of Japanese." *Journal of Pragmatics* 21(1): 67–100.

Kamio, Akio. (1995). "Territory of Information in English and Japanese and Psychological Utterances." *Journal of Pragmatics* 24(3): 235–264.

Kamio, Akio. (1997). *Territory of Information*. Amsterdam and Philadelphia: John Benjamins.

Kamio, Akio. (2002). *Zoku zyoohoo no Nawabari-riron: Gengo no kinooteki bunseki*. Tokyo: Taishuukan Shoten.

Kato, Yukiko. (2002). "'Chigai-ga wakaru otoko' wa donna otoko ka" [What Kind of Person Is Someone Who Is Called 'chigai-ga wakaru otoko']. *Bulletin of the International Student Center Gifu University* 97–109.

Khalifa, K. (2013). "Understanding, Grasping, and Luck." *Episteme* 10(1): 1–17.

Kvanvig, J. (2003). *The Value of Knowledge and the Pursuit of Understanding.* Cambridge: Cambridge University Press.

Kung, Po-Rong. (2013). "Analysis of Meaning of Japanese Verb 'Shiru' and 'Wakaru.'" Master's thesis, Soochow University.

Lee, Kiri. (1985). "The Speaker's Territory of Information Observed in the Use of *Shira/lai* and *Wakam/wi* in Japanese." Paper presented at the University of Massachusetts Workshop on Oriental Languages.

Lee, Kiri. (2006). "Territory of Information Theory and Emotive Expressions in Japanese: A Case Observed in *Shiranai* and *Wakaranai*." In *Emotive Communication in Japanese*, ed. S. Suzuki, 191–207. Amsterdam and Philadelphia: John Benjamins.

Machery, E., S. Stich, D. Rose, A. Chatterjee, K. Karasawa, N. Struchiner, S. Shirker, N. Usui, and T. Hashimoto. (2017). "Gettier Across Cultures." *Nous* 51(3): 645–664.

Miura, Akira. (1983). *Japanese Words & Their Uses.* Rutland, VT: Charles E. Tuttle.

Mizumoto, M. (2011). *A Theory of Knowledge and Belief Change: Formal and Experimental Perspectives.* Hokkaido: Hokkaido University Press.

Mizumoto, M. (2018). "A prolegomenon to (empirical) cross-linguistic study of truth." Unpublished manuscript.

Mizutani, O., and N. Mizutani. (1977). *An Introduction to Modern Japanese.* Tokyo: Japan Times.

Nagel, J. (2010). "Knowledge Ascriptions and the Psychological Consequences of Thinking about Error." *Philosophical Quarterly* 60(239): 286–306.

Onishi, M. (1997). "The Grammar of Mental Predicates in Japanese." *Language Sciences* 19(3): 219–233.

Pritchard, D. (2010). "Knowledge and Understanding." In *The Nature and Value of Knowledge: Three Investigations*, ed. D. Pritchard, A. Millar, and A. Haddock, 5–88. Oxford: Oxford University Press.

Rott, H. (2004). "Stability, Strength and Sensitivity: Converting Belief into Knowledge." *Erkenntnis* 61: 469–493.

Sadanobu, T., and A. Malchukov. (2011). "Evidential Extension of Aspecto-Temporal Forms in Japanese from a Typological Perspective." *In the Mood for Mood (Cahier Chronos)* 23: 141–158.

Sadler, M. (2010). "Subjective and Intersubjective Uses of Japanese Verbs of Cognition in Conversation." *Pragmatics* 20(1): 109–128.

Sakuma, Kanae (1936). *Gendai nihongo no hyogen to goho* [The Expression and Usage of Modern Japanese Language]. Tokyo: Koseikaku.

Stalnaker, R. (2006). "On Logics of Knowledge and Belief." *Philosophical Studies* 128: 169–199.

Stanley, J. (2004). *Knowledge and Practical Interests.* New York and Oxford: Oxford University Press.

Starmans, C., and O. Friedman. (2012). "The Folk Conception of Knowledge." *Cognition* 124(3): 272–283.

Stich, E., E. Machery, and the Intellectual Humility and Cultural Diversity Research Group. Unpublished data.

Takahashi, Keisuke (2003). "Ruigigo 'shiru' to 'wakaru' no imi bunseki." *Nihongo Kyoiku* 119: 31–40.

Tien, C., S. Izuhara, and S. Kim, eds. (2007). *Ruigigo tsukaiwake jiten* [Synonym "How to Chose" Dictionary]. Tokyo: Kenkyusha.

Turri, John. (2015a). "An Open and Shut Case: Epistemic Closure in the Manifest Image." *Philosophers' Imprint* 15(2): 1–18.

Turri, John. (2015b). "From Virtue Epistemology to Abilism." In *Character: New Directions from Philosophy, Psychology, and Theology*, ed. Christian B. Miller, R. Michael Furr, Angela Knobel, and William Fleeson. Oxford Scholarship Online: November 2015.

Turri, John. (2016a). "Knowledge Judgments in 'Gettier' Cases." In *A Companion to Experimental Philosophy*, ed. J. Sytsma and W. Buckwalter, 337–348. Malden, MA: Wiley-Blackwell.

Turri, J. (2016b). "A New Paradigm for Epistemology: From Reliabilism to Abilism." *Ergo* 3(8): 189–231.

Turri, John. (2017). "Epistemic Situationism and Cognitive Ability." In *Epistemic Situationism*, ed. Abrol Fairweather and Mark Alfano, 158–167. Oxford: Oxford University Press.

Turri, John, and Wesley Buckwalter. (2017). "Descartes's Schism, Locke's Reunion: Completing the Pragmatic Turn in Epistemology." *American Philosophical Quarterly* 54(1): 25–45.

Watanabe, Shinji. (1987). "Shiru-Wakaru." In *Imi Bunseki*, ed. Kunihiro Tetsuya, 9–11. Research Report of Department of Linguistics, University of Tokyo.

Weinberg, J. M., Nichols, S., and Stich, S. (2001). Normativity and epistemic intuitions. *Philosophical Topics* 29(1/2): 429–460.

Williamson, Timothy. (2000). *Knowledge and its Limits*. Oxford: Oxford University Press.

CHAPTER 6

Gettier Was Framed!

EDOUARD MACHERY, STEPHEN STICH, DAVID ROSE,
AMITA CHATTERJEE, KAORI KARASAWA,
NOEL STRUCHINER, SMITA SIRKER, NAOKI USUI,
AND TAKAAKI HASHIMOTO

1. INTRODUCTION

Gettier cases describe situations in which an agent possesses a justified true belief that *p* without, at least according to mainstream analytic epistemology, knowing that *p* (Gettier 1963; Shope 1983; Zagzebski 1994). We will call judgments that a protagonist in a Gettier case does not know the relevant proposition "Gettier intuitions." Gettier intuitions have played a central role in epistemology since the 1960s. Gettier cases seem to show that knowing that *p* cannot be reduced to having a true justified belief that *p*, and in response to Gettier cases, philosophers have attempted to formulate additional conditions that, when conjoined with justification, truth, and belief, would yield an account of knowledge immune to Gettier-style counterexamples.

More recently, Gettier cases have migrated from analytic epistemology to the experimental study of knowledge ascription (e.g., Weinberg et al. 2001; Starmans and Friedman 2012; Turri 2013; Nagel et al. 2013; Turri et al. 2015; Machery et al. 2015, 2017). Weinberg and colleagues' (2001) article has been particularly influential because it reported that participants with Western cultural backgrounds agreed with philosophers that the relevant beliefs of protagonists in Gettier cases are not cases of knowledge, while a majority of participants with East Asian and South Asian cultural backgrounds took these beliefs to be cases of knowledge. The apparent cultural variation of the Gettier intuition has played a central role in the criticism of the method of cases—roughly, the use of cases such as the Gettier case to support or undermine philosophical theories—by experimental philosophers: if cases elicit different judgments across cultures, then we may not be warranted to take our own judgment at face value (for discussion, see, e.g., Weinberg et al. 2001; Machery 2011, 2017; Sosa 2007; Weinberg 2007; Alexander 2012; Williamson 2011; Cappelen 2012; Deutsch 2015; Colaço and Machery 2017; Stich and Tobia 2016).

Experimental philosophers' case against the method of cases has weakened in the last few years. There is now a growing consensus that the Gettier intuition may well be universal for at least some types of Gettier case (Seyedsayamdost 2015; Kim and Yuan 2015; Machery et al. 2015, 2017). In particular, we have shown in recent work that people in Brazil, India, Japan, and the United States share the Gettier intuition when presented with a pair of Gettier cases (Machery et al. 2015; see figure 6.1).

Our goal in this chapter is to show that even if Gettier intuitions do not vary across cultural groups, this provides little comfort to proponents of the method of cases. Demographic variation, including cultural variation, is only one of two kinds of effects that raise doubts about this method (Machery 2017). It is also challenged when people make different judgments about a given case when this case is presented differently. Framing effects (variations in judgment due to variations in the irrelevant narrative details of a given case) and order effects (variations in judgment due to variations in the order in which cases are presented) illustrate this second phenomenon, which we will call "presentation effects" (Machery 2017). Experimental philosophers have shown that a number of cases are subject to presentation effects (e.g., Nichols and Knobe 2007; Nadelhoffer and Feltz 2008; Tobia et al. 2012). Here are a few examples of order effects involving cases in epistemology and ethics (see also Feltz and Cokely 2011; Schwitzgebel and Cushman 2012, 2015). The Truetemp case, which describes a situation in which an agent can reliably form true beliefs without being aware that she has this capacity, has often been viewed as a serious challenge to reliabilist theories of knowledge. Swain and colleagues (2008) report that participants are more willing to ascribe knowledge to the protagonist in the Truetemp case when they have first read a case of clear non-knowledge instead of a case of clear knowledge. Some evidence suggests that the switch and footbridge versions of the Trolley case elicit the same judgments across various demographic groups (Hauser et al. 2007), but Lanteri et al. (2008) have shown that people are more likely to judge that it is morally acceptable to pull the switch in the switch version

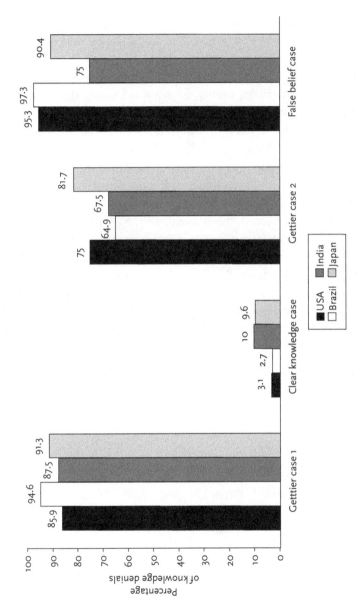

Figure 6.1 Proportion of knowledge denials for two Gettier cases, a Clear Knowledge case, and a Justified False Belief case in the United States, Japan, Brazil, and India (based on Machery et al. 2015)

of the Trolley case when it is presented before the footbridge version of the Trolley case (94%) than after (78%) (see also Lombrozo 2009; Wiegmann et al. 2012). Liao and colleagues (2012) have also shown that judgments about the loop version of the Trolley case vary: people are more likely to agree that it is morally permissible to send a runaway trolley on a loop, where it would be stopped by hitting a person, after having read the switch version than the footbridge version.

This chapter reports the first body of evidence that Gettier intuitions are subject to presentation effects; that is, we can make the Gettier intuition compelling or underwhelming by presenting it in different contexts. We report a surprising order effect: people find the Gettier intuition less compelling when a case describing a justified but false belief is presented before a Gettier case. We also report a surprising framing effect: two Gettier cases that differ only in their philosophically irrelevant narrative details elicit substantially different judgments.

Here is how we will proceed. In section 2, we report on a cross-cultural study suggesting that in four different cultures with four different languages, people react differently when a Gettier case is presented first or after a justified false belief case (Study 1). Section 3 investigates this phenomenon by controlling a potential confound in Study 1 (Study 2). We provide further evidence for the order effect and we also provide evidence for a framing effect, showing that different cases elicit different judgments. Section 4 shows that the Gettier intuition is not influenced by cases of clear knowledge (Study 3). Section 5 examines the philosophical implications of these findings.

2. STUDY 1

We begin by examining whether the Gettier intuition is liable to order effects in four different countries.

2.1. Participants and Materials

We collected data from 520 participants in four countries: Brazil, Japan, India, and the United States. US participants were recruited on Amazon Mechanical Turk (www.mturk.com) and received a small compensation. All the other participants completed paper-and-pencil versions of the survey, and they were volunteers. We excluded data from participants who failed to complete the questionnaire or did not answer correctly the comprehension questions for any of the three cases. Since we are interested in the prevalence of Gettier intuitions across cultures and languages, we also excluded the answers of those participants who judged that the protagonist's belief was not justified in any of the three cases (answer $\leq$ 4 to the justification questions).[1] Our final sample consisted of 350 respondents. Table 6.1 presents basic descriptive statistics for participants in each country.[2]

Three vignettes were presented in a fixed order: the Gettier/Hospital case, the Justified False Belief case, and the Gettier/Clock case. The first and the third vignettes are Gettier cases; the second case describes a situation in which a protagonist has a justified but false belief. The two Gettier cases read as follows:

Gettier/Hospital Case

Paul Jones was worried because it was 10 p.m. and his wife Mary was not home from work yet. Usually she is home by 6 p.m. He tried her cell phone but just kept getting her voicemail. Starting to worry that something might have happened to her, he decided to call some local hospitals to ask whether any patient by the name of "Mary Jones" had been admitted that evening. At the University Hospital, the person who answered his call confirmed that someone by that name had been admitted with major but not life-threatening injuries following a car crash. Paul grabbed his coat and rushed out to drive to University hospital. As it turned out, the patient at University Hospital was not Paul's wife, but another woman with the same name. In fact, Paul's wife had a heart attack as she was leaving work, and was at that moment receiving treatment in Metropolitan Hospital, a few miles away.

Gettier/Clock Case

Wanda is out for a weekend afternoon walk. As she passes near the train station, she wonders what time it is. She glances up at the clock on the train station wall, sees that it says 4:15 p.m., and concludes that it is 4:15 p.m. What she doesn't realize is that this clock is broken and has been showing 4:15 p.m. for the last two days. But by sheer coincidence, it is in fact 4:15 p.m. just at the moment when she glances at the clock.

---

1. The results are similar when participants who failed to answer that the protagonist's belief was not justified are included (see Appendix).
2. Age information was accidentally not collected for US participants.

Table 6.1 DEMOGRAPHIC INFORMATION FOR PARTICIPANTS IN STUDY 1

Country	Method	Location / Source	N	% Male	Age Range	M	SD
Brazil	Paper-pencil	Law School of the Federal University of Rio de Janeiro	47	21.3	20–37	22.0	2.5
Japan	Paper-pencil	The University of Tokyo, Fukuyama University, Toyo University, Kyushu University, and public places	142	58.5	20–78	27.84	12.6
India	Paper-pencil	Jadavpur University, Vidyasagar University, University of Kalyani	69	42.0	16–58	25.5	9.1
USA	Web-based	Amazon Mechanical Turk	92	47.8	na–na	na	na

The Justified False Belief case reads as follows:

Justified False Belief Case

Emma is shopping for jewelry. She goes into a nice-looking store. She looks at several displays, then selects a necklace from a tray marked "Diamond Earrings and Pendants." "What a lovely diamond!" she says as she tries it on. Zirconium is a substance from which fake diamonds can be made. Emma could not tell the difference between a real diamond and a zirconium fake just by looking or touching. In fact, this particular store has a dishonest employee who has been stealing real diamonds and replacing them with fakes; in the tray Emma chose from, all of the necklaces—including the one she tried on—had zirconium stones rather than diamonds.

Each scenario was followed by four questions:

(1) A binary comprehension question
(2) A binary question asking whether or not the protagonist knows the relevant proposition; the response options were "Yes, [s]he knows" and "No, [s]he doesn't know" (we call this question *Knowledge 1*).

(3) A question about justification ("How justified is [name of the protagonist] in thinking that [relevant proposition]?") followed by a 7-point scale ranging from "completely unjustified" to "completely justified."

(4) The question: "In your view, which of the following sentences better describes [the protagonist's] situation?" followed by two choices: (i) "[Protagonist] knows that [relevant proposition]," and (ii) [Protagonist] feels like s[he] knows that [relevant proposition] but [s]he doesn't actually know [this] (we call this question *Knowledge 2*).

To illustrate, the comprehension question of the Justified False Belief case was as follows (possible answers in parentheses): "According to the story, what kind of stone is in the necklace that Emma tries on?" ("Diamond"/ "Zirconium"); the Knowledge 1 probe was: "Does Emma know whether or not the stone is a diamond?" ("Yes, she knows"/"No, she doesn't know"); the justification probe was: "How justified is Emma in thinking that the stone is a diamond?" (7-point scale); finally, the Knowledge 2 probe read as follows: "In your view, which of the following sentences better describes Emma's situation?" ("Emma knows that the stone is a diamond"/"Emma feels like she knows that the stone is a diamond, but she doesn't actually know that it is.")

The Knowledge 2 probe is loosely inspired by the procedure used in Nagel et al. (2013), where participants were first asked a knowledge question with the response options "Yes, she knows," "No, she doesn't know," and "Unclear," and then, if they had answered "Yes, she knows," they were presented with what we are calling the Knowledge 2 question. Nagel et al. (2013) motivate the use of the Knowledge 2 question by noting that "know" can be used to express the judgment that a protagonist feels like she knows some proposition—a phenomenon known as "protagonist projection" (Holton 1997; Buckwalter 2014)—and the Knowledge 2 question gives us some insight into whether this is what a participant is doing when she responds to the Knowledge 1 question. However, as Starmans and Friedman (2013, 664) argue, asking the Knowledge 2 question only when participants indicate that the protagonist does have knowledge is methodologically problematic. Thus, in contrast to Nagel et al. (2013), participants in our study were *always* asked the Knowledge 2 question. The final page of our questionnaire asked participants to report various demographic characteristics.

2.2. Results

We first examined whether people respond to the two Gettier cases differently across all cultures. People were significantly more likely to have the

Gettier intuition when the Gettier case was read first (the Gettier/Hospital case) than when it followed the Justified False Belief case (the Gettier/Clock case). Focusing on the Knowledge 1 question, 69.4% of participants reported that the protagonist does not know the relevant proposition for the first Gettier case, but only 33.7% for the second ($\chi^2(1, 700) = 89.4$, $p < 0.001$). The Knowledge 2 question revealed the same pattern: 89.1% of participants reported that the protagonist does not know the relevant proposition for the first Gettier case, but only 52.3% for the second ($\chi^2(1, 700) = 114.8$, $p < 0.001$).

We then examined whether people respond to the two Gettier cases differently, country by country (figure 6.2). US participants were significantly more likely to have the Gettier intuition when the Gettier case was read first (the Gettier/Hospital case) than when it followed the Justified False Belief case (the Gettier/Clock case). Focusing on the Knowledge 1 question, 72.8% of US participants reported that the protagonist does not know the relevant proposition for the first Gettier case, but only 38.0% for the second ($\chi^2(1, 184) = 22.6$, $p < 0.001$). The Knowledge 2 question revealed the same pattern: 85.9% of US participants reported that the protagonist does not know the relevant proposition for the first Gettier case, but only 54.3% for the second ($\chi^2(1, 184) = 21.8$, $p < 0.001$). Similarly, Brazilian participants were significantly more likely to have the Gettier intuition when the Gettier case was read first (the Gettier/Hospital case) than when it followed the Justified False Belief case (the Gettier/Clock case). Focusing on the Knowledge 1 question, 85.1% of Brazilian participants reported that the protagonist does not know the relevant proposition for the first Gettier case, but only 36.2% for the second ($\chi^2(1, 94) = 23.6$, $p < 0.001$). The Knowledge 2 question revealed the same pattern: 95.7% of Brazilian participants reported that the protagonist does not know the relevant proposition for the first Gettier case, but only 57.4% for the second ($\chi^2(1, 94) = 19.2$, $p < 0.001$). The results are more complicated with Indian participants. They were significantly more likely to have the Gettier intuition when the Gettier case was read first (the Gettier/Hospital case) than when it followed the Justified False Belief case (the Gettier/Clock case) for the Knowledge 2 question, but not for the Knowledge 1 question. Focusing on the Knowledge 1 question, 36.2% of Indian participants reported that the protagonist does not know the relevant proposition for the first Gettier case and 27.5% for the second ($\chi^2(1, 138) = 1.2$, ns). The Knowledge 2 question revealed a different pattern: 88.4% of Indian participants reported that the protagonist does not know the relevant proposition for the first Gettier case and 56.5% for the second ($\chi^2(1, 138) = 17.6$, $p < 0.001$). Finally, Japanese participants behaved like US and Brazilian participants.

Focusing on the Knowledge 1 question, 78.2% of Japanese participants reported that the protagonist does not know the relevant proposition for the first Gettier case, but only 33.1% for the second ($\chi^2(1, 284) = 58.4$, $p < 0.001$). The Knowledge 2 question revealed the same pattern: 89.4% of Japanese participants reported that the protagonist does not know the relevant proposition for the first Gettier case, but only 47.2% for the second ($\chi^2(1, 284) = 58.6$, $p < 0.001$).

For the sake of completeness, we also report the descriptive statistics for the Justified False Belief case (see figure 6.3)

2.3 Discussion

Across four countries, characterized by very different cultures and languages, people express very different judgments about Gettier cases when a Gettier case is read first or when it follows a case describing a justified but false belief. In the four countries, people were much more likely to express the Gettier intuition in the former situation than in the latter when they answered the Knowledge 2 question. Furthermore, the differences between the two Gettier cases are very large: people are nearly twice as likely to report the Gettier intuition when it is read first, compared to when it follows a case describing a justified but false belief.

It is more difficult to interpret the answers to the Knowledge 1 question. A similar pattern was observed for US, Brazilian, and Japanese participants in the two knowledge questions. However, Indian participants were equally unlikely to report the Gettier intuition when "know" was contrasted to "does not know" (Knowledge 1 question), and there was no difference between the two orders of presentation. As we noted elsewhere (Machery et al. 2015), we suspect that this can be explained by the fact that the words commonly used to translate "to know" in Bengali (*jánā*) and in Sanskrit *jñā* (the verbal root of the Bengali word) are used somewhat differently from "to know" in English. In particular, the distinction between "to believe" and "to know" is not always retained when *jánā* or *jñā* are used, which plausibly explains why in Gettier cases a majority of Bengali participants readily "ascribed knowledge" to the protagonist when simply asked whether the protagonist knows (*jánā*) the relevant proposition. At the same time, *jánā* can be used to single out an epistemic state that differs from true justified belief, as shown by participants' answers to the Knowledge 2 question. Thus, *jánā* may in fact express two rather different concepts in Bengali, one of which is closer to the concept expressed in English by "know" and the other closer to the concept expressed in English by "believe." While

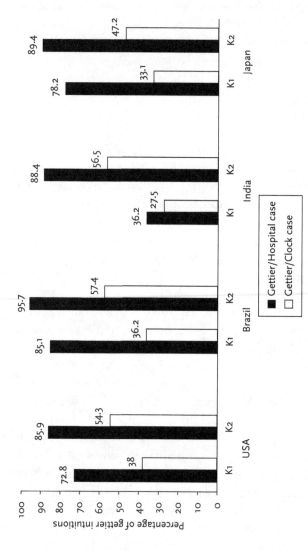

Figure 6.2 Proportion of Gettier intuitions for the two Gettier cases and the four populations (first pair for each country: Knowledge 1; second pair: Knowledge 2)

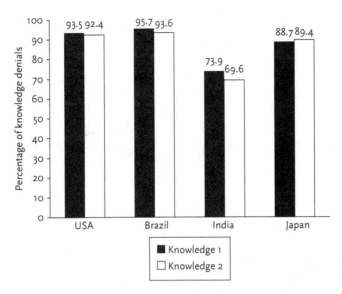

Figure 6.3 Proportion of knowledge denials for the Justified False Belief case and the four populations

the distinction is apparently not highly salient for Bengali speakers, the different responses to the Knowledge 1 and Knowledge 2 questions suggest that they are somehow aware of the distinction.

What explains this order effect? We hypothesize that people decide whether someone knows by comparing her belief to a prototype of knowledge. This prototype has various weighted features (truth, justification, etc.) that determine the similarity between the protagonist's belief and the prototype of knowledge. When the protagonist's belief has a sufficient number of features—that is, when it is sufficiently similar to the prototype of knowledge—people judge that her belief is an instance of knowledge. Now, people who read the Justified False Belief case tend to judge that the protagonist's justified but false belief is not an instance of knowledge (see figure 6.3). When they make this judgment, the truth-value of the belief becomes salient: people judge that the protagonist does not know because her belief is *false*. That is, the weight of the truth-value of the belief increases—being true becomes more important for a belief to be judged an instance of knowledge. When participants then read the Gattier/Clock case, the truth of the protagonist's belief ensures that it is sufficiently similar to the prototype of knowledge, and people are more likely to judge that the protagonist's belief is an instance of knowledge. Future research should test this account of the order effect.

Study 1 is limited in two important respects. Most important, two different Gettier cases were used: the Hospital case and the Clock case. It may be that the differences found are not due to the fact that participants read the Justified False Belief case before reading the Clock case. Rather, people may simply be less likely to ascribe knowledge when they read the Clock case. Furthermore, Study 1 was within-subjects. It would be important to show that the order effect is also found in a between-subjects experiment. Study 2 addresses these two shortcomings.

3. STUDY 2

3.1. Participants and Materials

A total of 306 participants located in the United States were recruited on Amazon Turk, and received a small compensation. We excluded data from participants who failed to complete the questionnaire, were less than eighteen years old, and did not answer correctly any of the comprehension questions. Our final sample consisted of 298 respondents. Table 6.2 presents basic descriptive statistics for the participants. The study was conducted in English.

Subjects were randomly assigned to one of four conditions. Participants in condition 1 (N = 82) were presented with the Justified False Belief case used in Study 1, followed by the Gettier/Hospital case; participants in condition 2 (N = 66) were presented with the Gettier/Hospital case followed by the Justified False Belief case; participants in condition 3 (N = 79) were presented with the Justified False Belief case followed by the Gettier/Clock case; participants in condition 4 (N = 71) were presented with the Gettier/Clock case followed by the Justified False Belief case. Each scenario was followed by the four questions used in Study 1.

Table 6.2 DEMOGRAPHIC CHARACTERISTICS OF PARTICIPANTS IN STUDY 2

Location/ Source	% English as Native Language	% Born in the USA	% Male	Age		
				Range	*M*	*SD*
Amazon Mechanical Turk	99.1	98.4	63.4	18–68	29.8	10.8

3.2. Results

We first examined whether people treat the Clock and the Hospital cases differently (figure 6.4). Aggregating across the two orders of presentations, participants were less likely to have the Gettier intuition when reading the Clock case than the Hospital case. Focusing first on the Knowledge 1 question, 76.4% of participants reported that the protagonist does not know the relevant proposition for the Hospital case, but only 35.3% for the Clock case ($\chi^2(1, 298) = 50.8$, $p < 0.001$). The pattern is similar for the Knowledge 2 question: 85.1% of participants reported that the protagonist does not know the relevant proposition for the Hospital case, but only 63.3% for the Clock case ($\chi^2(1, 298) = 18.5$, $p < 0.001$). This finding confirms the concern that the results of Study 1 are at least in part due to the differences between the Hospital and Clock cases.

We then examined whether people are less likely to have the Gettier intuition when the Gettier case is read after the Justified False Belief case compared to when it is read before (figure 6.5). Aggregating across the two Gettier cases, participants were less likely to have the Gettier intuition when reading a Gettier case after the Justified False Belief case than before. Focusing first on the Knowledge 1 question, 61.5% of participants reported that the protagonist does not know the relevant proposition when reading a Gettier case first, but only 49.7% when reading it second ($\chi^2(1, 298) = 4.2$, $p = 0.041$). The pattern is similar for the Knowledge 2 question: 79.1% of

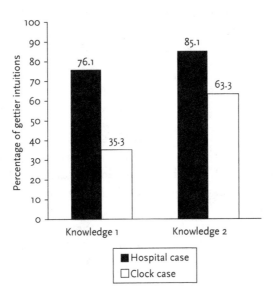

Figure 6.4 Proportion of Gettier intuitions for the Hospital and Clock cases in Study 2

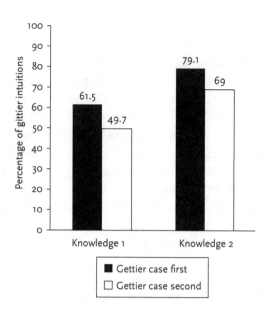

Figure 6.5 Proportion of Gettier intuitions when a Gettier case is presented first and second

participants reported that the protagonist does not know the relevant proposition when reading a Gettier case first, but only 69.0% when reading it second ($\chi^2(1, 298) = 4.0$, $p = 0.046$).

This finding shows that the results of Study 1 are not merely due to the differences between the Hospital and the Clock case; rather, people are less likely to have the Gettier intuition when they read a Gettier case after having read a case describing a false but justified belief. However, the effect size is smaller than what was suggested by Study 1 (about 10%).

3.3. Discussion

This between-subjects study examined the possible confounds of Study 1. It shows that people are much less likely to have the Gettier intuition in response to the Clock case than to the Hospital case. This framing effect is surprising. What might explain it? We hypothesize that we treat the Hospital and the Clock cases differently because the former, but not the latter, is similar to familiar situations where the agent has no knowledge. The Hospital case involves the formation of a belief on the basis of testimony, and it is in this respect (but not in other respects) similar to the common situation where somebody forms a false belief (e.g., the belief that Barack Obama is a Muslim) based on testimony. Because people did not acquire any knowledge in the latter type of situation, people are inclined to deny knowledge in the Hospital case despite the differences between the situations. The Clock case is not similar to any salient situation, and people cannot generalize from their practice of ascribing knowledge in everyday situations. Other hypotheses are conceivable. It may be that people think that testimony-based knowledge is more easily defeated than perceptual knowledge, and that the Hospital case describes a clear situation where testimony-based knowledge is defeated, while the Clock case does not describe an equally clear situation where perceptual knowledge is defeated. Alternatively, it may be that it is salient to the participants that the protagonist in the Hospital case has a false belief (namely, the belief that his wife is at the University Hospital), and that the saliency of this false belief explains why the participant is judged to have no knowledge. Naturally, the protagonist in the Clock case also has a false belief (namely, the belief that the clock is working properly), but this belief may not be salient to participants. Future research should test these different accounts of the framing effect.

Study 2 also shows that there is a genuine order effect, but that its magnitude is smaller than what Study 1 suggested. When people read about a justified but false belief, they are then less likely to deny that a Gettierized belief is an instance of knowledge, perhaps because the truth-value of belief becomes more important for deciding whether a belief is an instance of knowledge.

Study 2 suffers from a possible confound: It may be that people would be less likely to have the Gettier intuition after reading *any* text rather than after reading a case describing a justified but false belief specifically. Study 3 examines this potential confound.

4. STUDY 3

4.1. Participants and Materials

A total of 308 participants located in the United States were recruited on Amazon Turk, and received a small compensation. We excluded data from participants who failed to complete the questionnaire, were less than eighteen years old, and did not answer correctly any of the comprehension questions. Our final sample consisted of 303 respondents. Table 6.3 presents basic descriptive statistics for participants. The study was conducted in English.

Subjects were randomly assigned to one of four conditions. Participants in condition 1 (N = 71) were presented with the Clear Knowledge case

Table 6.3 PARTICIPANTS' DEMOGRAPHIC CHARACTERISTICS IN STUDY 3

Location / Source	% English as Native Language	% Born in the USA	% Male	Age Range	M	SD
Amazon Mechanical Turk	96.2	94.5	68.9	18–67	30.5	11.3

followed by the Gettier/Hospital case; participants in condition 2 (*N* = 73) were presented with the Gettier/Hospital case followed by the Clear Knowledge case; participants in condition 3 (*N* = 74) were presented with the Clear Knowledge case followed by the Gettier/Clock case; participants in condition 4 (*N* = 85) were presented with the Gettier/Clock case followed by the Clear Knowledge case. Each scenario was followed by the four questions used in Study 1.

The Clear Knowledge case describes a commonsense situation where the protagonist acquires perceptual knowledge. It reads as follows:

Clear Knowledge Case

Albert is in a furniture store with his wife. He is looking at a bright red table in a display. He believes the table is just the shade of red he was looking for. The showroom features contemporary furniture pieces, with clear, natural lighting throughout the entire store, and plenty of space around each piece on display. Albert usually likes traditional furniture designs, however the modern design of this particular table appeals to him for some reason. He checks the dimensions and price of the table, and starts to consider buying it. Albert asks his wife, "Do you like this red table?"

Participants were asked whether Albert knows that the table is red.

4.2. Results

We first attempted to replicate the results of Study 2 about the differences between the Hospital and Clock cases (figure 6.6). Aggregating across the two orders of presentations, participants were less likely to have the Gettier intuition when reading the Clock case than the Hospital case. Focusing first on the Knowledge 1 question, 74.3% of participants reported that the protagonist does not know the relevant proposition for the Hospital case, but

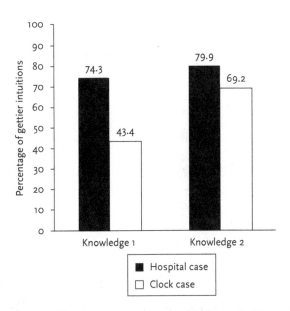

Figure 6.6 Proportion of Gettier intuitions for the Hospital and Clock cases in Study 3

only 43.4% for the Clock case ($\chi^2(1, 303) = 29.7$, $p < 0.001$). The pattern is similar for the Knowledge 2 question: 79.9% of participants reported that the protagonist does not know the relevant proposition for the Hospital case, but only 69.2% for the Clock case ($\chi^2(1, 303) = 4.5$, $p = 0.03$). This finding confirms the results of Study 2.

We then examined whether people are less likely to have the Gettier intuition when the Gettier case is read after the Clear Knowledge case compared to when it is read before (figure 6.7). There was no order effect: aggregating across the two Gettier cases, participants were not less likely to have the Gettier intuition when reading a Gettier case after the Clear Knowledge case than before. Focusing first on the Knowledge 1 question, 57.1% of participants reported that the protagonist does not know the relevant proposition when reading a Gettier case first, and 59.2% when reading it second ($\chi^2(1, 303) = 0.1$, ns). The pattern is similar for the Knowledge 2 question: 73.7% of participants reported that the protagonist does not know the relevant proposition when reading a Gettier case first, and 69.0% when reading it second ($\chi^2(1, 303) = 0.05$, ns).

4.3. Discussion

Study 3 controls for the potential confound of Study 2 mentioned at the end of section 3. The order effect found in Study 2 is not the mere result

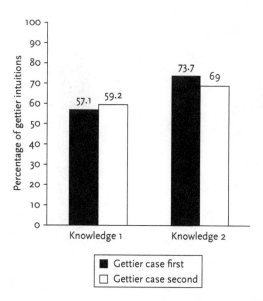

Figure 6.7 Proportion of Gettier intuitions when a Gettier case is presented first and second

of reading the Gettier case after any text since the proportion of Gettier intuitions was the same when people read a Gettier case before or after a Clear Knowledge case.

The negative result reported in Study 3 is consistent with the explanatory hypothesis proposed in section 3. Judging that the protagonist's belief is an instance of knowledge in the Clear Knowledge case does not make any feature of the prototype of knowledge salient (since the case describes a prototypical instance of knowledge), and as a result reading the Clear Knowledge case before a Gettier case does not influence participants' knowledge ascription.

5. PRESENTATION EFFECTS AND THE METHOD OF CASES

5.1. Framing Gettier

Two main results emerge from the three studies presented in this chapter. First, people respond very differently to two Gettier cases, the Clock case and the Hospital case. The philosophically relevant features—the protagonist has formed a true belief based on misleading evidence—are shared by the two cases, which differ only in irrelevant features of the narrative, the Hospital case involving the accidental formation of a true belief on the basis of testimony and the Clock case on the basis of one's perceptual experience.[3] This framing effect is robust—it is found with the two ways of eliciting the Gettier intuition (Knowledge 1 and 2 questions)—and its size is substantial: 30–40% when the question contrasts knowing and not knowing (Knowledge 1 question), 10–20% when it contrasts knowing and thinking one knows but not knowing (Knowledge 2 question).

Furthermore, people answer differently when a Gettier case is presented without any context and when it is presented after a case describing a justified but false belief. In the latter condition, people are somewhat less likely to have the Gettier intuition (about 10%). This finding extends the growing body of evidence that judgments elicited by philosophical cases are subject to order effects. While most studies have focused on cases in ethics, the results reported in this chapter extend Swain and colleagues' (2008) claim that cases in epistemology are also subject to order effects.

Study 1 suggests, without establishing conclusively, that the framing and order effects are found across cultures and languages. Study 1 showed that in four countries with four very different languages, people responded very differently to the Hospital case and to the Clock case, which followed a case describing a justified but false belief. This robust result is probably due to both the order effect and the framing effect distinguished in Study 2.

5.2. The Gettier Intuition and the Method of Cases

Does the protagonist in the Hospital case know that his wife is in the hospital or does he merely believe it? Does the protagonist in the Clock case know that it is 4:15 p.m. when she looks at the clock or does she merely believe it? Nearly all philosophers agree that the second answers are correct: In a Gettier case, the protagonist does not know the relevant proposition. The findings reported in this chapter cast this consensus into doubt. When the Clock case is presented after a case describing a justified but false belief, most people judge that the protagonist's belief *is* an instance of knowledge; when the Hospital case is presented independently, most people judge that the protagonist's belief is *not* an instance of knowledge (figure 6.8). Which of these two judgments is correct? Without an answer to this question, we should suspend judgment about whether the protagonist knows the relevant proposition in a Gettier case.

---

3. Of course, the difference between testimony-based knowledge and perceptual knowledge is, in general, philosophically relevant, but it is not taken to be relevant in the context of Gettier cases. Indeed, the Clock case is often viewed as a paradigmatic Gettier case.

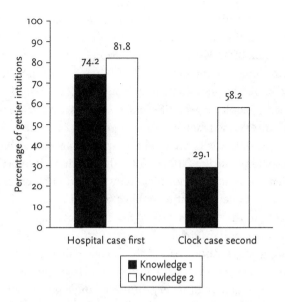

Figure 6.8 Proportion of Gettier intuitions in the Hospital case presented first and the Clock case presented second in Study 2

It is tempting to argue that one of these two judgments is mistaken, but it is quite difficult to explain which one it is. Perhaps we should prefer the judgment elicited by a Gettier case considered on its own to the judgment elicited by a Gettier case in the context of a Justified False Belief case since the former but not the latter is not influenced by factors extraneous to the case. Conversely, to decide correctly whether a belief is an instance of knowledge, the truth-value of the belief may need to be properly salient, and if our explanation of the order effect presented in this chapter is right (section 3.3), reading the Justified False Belief case raises the salience of truth-value. The Hospital and the Clock case are equally unusual: both involve an extremely unlikely situation where a protagonist forms a belief that turns out to be true by an extraordinarily lucky set of circumstances. On the one hand, perhaps we should prefer the judgment elicited by the Hospital case since it is in some respects similar to common situations—that is, situations where we form a false belief as a result of misleading testimony. On the other hand, if our explanation of the framing effect presented in this chapter is right (section 4.3), we judge that the protagonist's belief in the Hospital case is not an instance of knowledge, in part because it is similar to a *false* belief acquired by testimony. So, perhaps we should discount the judgment we make in response to the Hospital case, and favor the judgment elicited by the Clock case.

An alternative response would hold that the judgments elicited by the Hospital case read first and the Clock case read second are both correct: these two cases describe two distinct situations, and whether or not an agent knows p depends on the context in which knowledge is ascribed. So, the protagonist of the Hospital case read first really has a mere belief, while the protagonist of the Clock case knows what time it is.

However, we do not see what differences would make it the case that the protagonist's belief counts as an instance of knowledge in the Clock case, but not in the Hospital case. The differences between the two cases seem irrelevant for knowledge ascription. Further, until we are told how reading a Justified False Belief case relevantly changes the context of knowledge ascription, appealing to context remains unconvincing.

As noted in the introduction to this chapter, Gettier intuitions have played an important role in the meta-philosophical dispute about the method of cases. Gettier cases are paradigmatic examples of the cases used in philosophical argumentation. If we must suspend judgment about Gettier cases, as we have just argued (see also Weinberg 2017), and a number of cases are subject to presentation effects (section 2), we must probably suspend judgment about many cases used in philosophical argumentation.

5.3. Objections and Responses

One could object that the effects reported in this chapter are small. Particularly, once it is disentangled from the framing effect, the order effect is small: the proportion of Gettier intuitions is only 10% smaller when a Gettier case is presented after a case describing a justified but false belief. True, the context in which a Gettier case is presented does influence whether people have the Gettier intuition, but a majority of participants agree that in a Gettier case the participant does not know the relevant proposition, independent of the context in which the case is presented. It would be a mistake, so the argument continues, to suspend judgment when the liability to order effect is so small.

Small effects matter, however, because they add up. Considered by itself, the order effect is indeed small, but combined with the framing effect, the effect is substantial. Consider figure 6.8, which reports the proportion of Gettier intuitions for the Clock case presented last and for the Hospital case presented first.

When people are asked whether the protagonist in a Gettier case knows versus does not know, a large majority of people accept the Gettier intuition when the Hospital case is presented first, and deny it when the Clock case is presented last.

The first objection assumed that if order effects were large, this would cast doubt on the judgments elicited by philosophical cases, but denied that these effects were large. The second objection we will consider challenges the assumption that large order effects would cast doubt on the judgments elicited by philosophical cases. Horne and colleagues have argued that the order effects found in the experimental literature do not cast doubt on the judgments elicited by philosophical cases (Horne et al. 2013; Horne and Livengood 2017). In a nutshell, they argue that studies reporting an order effect compare participants' judgments in response to a target case (e.g., the Gettier case) when it is presented first or when it follows another case ("the contextual case"), as we ourselves did. Any difference between these two conditions, they maintain, may be due to participants *learning* something important when they read the contextual case. If this is the case, then it is not irrational to give a different answer to the target case when it comes first versus when it comes second; rather, one judges differently in the latter condition because one has learned something by reading the contextual case.

Whatever bite Horne and colleagues' argument may have against other studies reporting order effects, it is toothless against the results reported here. It is unclear what participants could learn by considering the Justified False Belief case that would make it rational to judge differently when a Gettier case is presented after such a case and when it is presented independently. So, the influence of the Justified False Belief case on Gettier intuitions is not properly thought of as an instance of learning.

6. CONCLUSION

Gettier intuitions may well be universal—some cases elicit it in very different cultures with very different languages (Machery et al. 2015, 2017)—but it is also liable to framing and order effects. Although our first study did not disentangle these two types of effects, it suggests that the liability of the Gettier intuition to framing and order effects is robust across languages and cultures. This liability casts doubt on whether or not in a Gettier case the protagonist's belief counts as an instance of knowledge.

ACKNOWLEDGMENTS

We are grateful to the following colleagues for assistance with translation and data collection, and for many helpful suggestions: Kazuya Horike (Tokyo University), Masashi Kasaki (Kyoto University), Masaharu Mizumoto (Japan Advanced Institute of Science and Technology), Yukiko Muramoto (University of Tokyo), Aya Nodera (Fukuyama University), Pedro Henrique Veiga Chrismann (Pontifícia Universidade Católica do Rio de Janeiro), Hiroyuki Yamaguchi (Kyushu University).

APPENDIX

This appendix reanalyzes the data from the original 520 participants of Study 1. We excluded data from participants who failed to complete the questionnaire and who did not answer correctly the comprehension questions about any of the three cases, but we did not exclude the answers of those participants who judged that the protagonist's belief was not justified. Our final sample consisted of 478 respondents. The results are similar to the results reported in Study 1 (figure 6.9).

American participants were significantly more likely to have the Gettier intuition when the Gettier case was read first (the Gettier/Hospital case) than when it followed the Justified False Belief case (the Gettier/Clock case): For the Knowledge 1 question, $\chi^2(1, 200) = 26.1$, $p < 0.001$; for the Knowledge 2 question, $\chi^2(1, 200) = 20.7$, $p < 0.001$. Similarly, Brazilian participants were significantly more likely to have the Gettier intuition when the Gettier case was read first (the Gettier/Hospital case) than when it followed the Justified False Belief case (the Gettier/Clock case): for the Knowledge 1 question, $\chi^2(1, 108) = 26.8$, $p < 0.001$); for the Knowledge 2, $\chi^2(1, 108) = 21.4$, $p < 0.001$. Indian participants were significantly more likely to have the Gettier intuition when the Gettier case was read first (the Gettier/Hospital case) than when it followed the Justified False Belief case (the Gettier/Clock case) for the Knowledge 2 question, but not for the Knowledge 1 question: for the Knowledge 1 question, $\chi^2(1, 200) = 1.7$, *ns*; for the Knowledge 2, $\chi^2(1, 200) = 18.7$, $p < 0.001$. Finally, Japanese participants behaved like US and Brazilian participants: for the Knowledge 1 question, $\chi^2(1, 448) = 77.8$, $p < 0.001$; for the Knowledge 2 question, $\chi^2(1, 448) = 79.8$, $p < 0.001$.

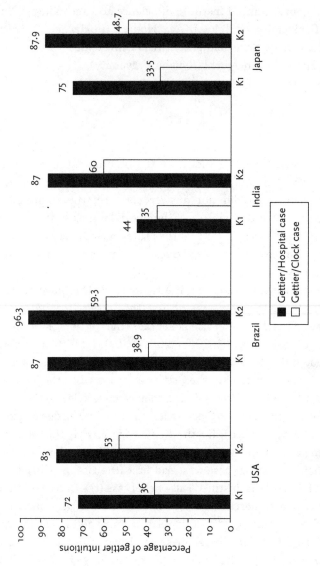

Figure 6.9 Proportion of Gettier intuitions for the two Gettier cases and the four populations (first pair for each country: Knowledge 1; second pair: Knowledge 2)

REFERENCES

Alexander, J. (2012). *Experimental Philosophy: An Introduction*. Cambridge: Polity.

Buckwalter, W. (2014). "Factive Verbs and Protagonist Projection." *Episteme* 11: 391–409.

Cappelen, H. (2012). *Philosophy Without Intuitions*. Oxford: Oxford University Press.

Colaço, D., and E. Machery. (2017). "The Intuitive Is a Red Herring." *Inquiry* 60: 403–419.

Deutsch, M. (2015). *The Myth of the Intuitive*. Cambridge, MA: MIT Press.

Feltz, A., and E. Cokely. (2011). "Individual Differences in Theory-of-mind Judgments: Order Effects and Side Effects." *Philosophical Psychology* 24: 343–355.

Gettier, E. L. (1963). "Is Justified True Belief Knowledge?" *Analysis* 23: 121–123.

Hauser, M., F. Cushman, L. Young, R. Kang-Xing Jin, and J. Mikhail. (2007). "A Dissociation Between Moral Judgments and Justifications." *Mind & Language* 22: 1–21.

Holton, R. (1997). "Some Telling Examples: A Reply to Tsohatzidis." *Journal of Pragmatics* 28: 625–628.

Horne, Z., and J. Livengood. (2017). "Ordering Effects, Updating Effects, and the Specter of Global Skepticism." *Synthese* 194: 1189–1218.

Horne, Z., D. Powell, and J. Spino. (2013). "Belief Updating in Moral Dilemmas." *Review of Philosophy and Psychology* 4: 705–714.

Kim, M., and Y. Yuan. (2015). "No Cross-cultural Differences in the Gettier Car Case Intuition: A Replication Study of Weinberg et al. 2001." *Episteme* 12: 355–361.

Lanteri, A., C. Chelini, and S. Rizzello. (2008). "An Experimental Investigation of Emotions and Reasoning in the Trolley Problem." *Journal of Business Ethics* 83: 789–804.

Liao, S. M., A. Wiegmann, J. Alexander, and G. Vong. (2012). "Putting the Trolley in Order: Experimental Philosophy and the Loop Case." *Philosophical Psychology* 25: 661–671.

Lombrozo, T. (2009). "The Role of Moral Commitments in Moral Judgment." *Cognitive Science* 33: 273–286.

Machery, E. (2011). "Thought Experiments and Philosophical Knowledge." *Metaphilosophy* 42: 191–214.

Machery, E. (2017). *Philosophy within Its Proper Bounds*. Oxford: Oxford University Press.

Machery, E., S. P. Stich, D. Rose, A. Chatterjee, K. Karasawa, N. Struchiner, S. Sirker, N. Usui, and T. Hashimoto. (2015). "Gettier across Cultures." *Nous*. doi: 10.1111/nous.12110.

Machery, E., Stich, S. P., Rose, D., Alai, M., Angelucci, A., Berniunas, R., Buchtel, E. E., Chatterjee, A., Cheon, H., Cho, I.-R., Cohnitz, D., Cova, F., Dranselka, V., Lagos, A. E., Ghadakpour, L., Grinberg, M., Hashimoto, T., Horowitz, A., Hristova, E., Jraissati, Y., Kadreva, V., Karasawa, K., Kim, H., Kim, Y., Lee, M., Mauro, C., Mizumoto, M., Moruzzi, S., Olivola, C. Y., Ornelas J., Osimani, B., Romero, C., Rosas Lopez, A., Sangoi, M., Sereni, A., Songhorian, S., Sousa, P., Struchiner, N., Tripodi, V., Usui, N., Vazquez del Mercado, A., Volpe, G., Vosperichian, H. A., Zhang, X., and Zhu, J. 2017. The Gettier intuition from South America to Asia. *Journal of the Indian Council of Philosophical Research*, 34, 517–541.

Nadelhoffer, T., and A. Feltz. (2008). "The Actor-Observer Bias and Moral Intuitions." *Neuroethics* 1: 133–144.

Nagel, J., V. S. Juan, and R. A. Mar. (2013). "Lay Denial of Knowledge for Justified True Beliefs." *Cognition* 129: 652–661.

Nichols, S., and J. Knobe. (2007). "Moral Responsibility and Determinism: The Cognitive Science of Folk Intuitions." *Nous* 41: 663–685.

Schwitzgebel, E., and F. Cushman. (2012). "Expertise in Moral Reasoning?" *Mind & Language* 27: 135–153.

Schwitzgebel, E., and F. Cushman. (2015). "Philosophers' Biased Judgments Persist Despite Training, Expertise and Reflection." *Cognition* 141: 127–137.

Seyedsayamdost, H. (2015). "On Normativity and Epistemic Intuitions: Failure of Replication." *Episteme* 12: 95–116.

Shope, R. K. (1983). *The Analysis of Knowing. A Decade of Research*. Princeton, NJ: Princeton University Press.

Sosa, E. (2007). "Experimental Philosophy and Philosophical Intuition." *Philosophical Studies* 132: 99–107.

Starmans, C., and O. Friedman. (2012). "The Folk Conception of Knowledge." *Cognition* 124: 272–283.

Starmans, C., and O. Friedman. (2013). "Taking 'Know' for an Answer: A Reply to Nagel, San Juan, and Mar." *Cognition* 129: 662–665.

Stich, S. , and K. Tobia. (2016). "Experimental Philosophy and the Philosophical Tradition." In *Blackwell Companion to Experimental Philosophy*, ed. W. Buckwalter and J. Sytsma, 5–21. Malden, MA: Blackwell.

Swain, S., J. Alexander, and J. M. Weinberg. (2008). "The Instability of Philosophical Intuitions: Running Hot and Cold on Truetemp." *Philosophy and Phenomenological Research* 76: 138–155.

Tobia, K., W. Buckwalter, and S. Stich. (2012). "Moral Intuitions: Are Philosophers Experts?" *Philosophical Psychology* 30: 1–10.

Turri, J. (2013). "A Conspicuous Art: Putting Gettier to the Test." *Philosophers' Imprint* 13: 1–16.

Turri, J., W. Buckwalter, and P. Blouw. (2015). "Knowledge and Luck." *Psychonomic Bulletin & Review* 22: 378–390.

Weinberg, J. M. (2007). "How to Challenge Intuitions Empirically without Risking Skepticism." *Midwest Studies in Philosophy* 31: 318–343.

Weinberg, J. M. (2017). "Knowledge, Noise, and Curve-fitting: A Methodological Argument for JTB?" In *Explaining Knowledge: New Essays on the Gettier Problem*, ed. R. Borges, C. de Almeida, and P. Klein, 253–272. Oxford: Oxford University Press.

Weinberg, J. M., S. Nichols, and S. Stich. (2001). "Normativity and Epistemic Intuitions." *Philosophical Topics* 29: 429–460.

Wiegmann, A., J. Okan, and J. Nagel. (2012). "Order effects in Moral Judgment." *Philosophical Psychology* 25: 813–836.

Williamson, T. (2011). "Philosophical Expertise and the Burden of Proof." *Metaphilosophy* 42: 215–229.

Zagzebski, L. (1994). "The Inescapability of Gettier Problems." *Philosophical Quarterly* 44: 65–73.

CHAPTER 7

Justification and Truth

Evidence from Languages of the World

LISA MATTHEWSON AND JENNIFER GLOUGIE

1. INTRODUCTION

Our goal in this chapter is to investigate some cross-linguistic data relating
to epistemological concepts. We will not be directly addressing the word *know*
or its translations, but instead will investigate two properties that have often
been claimed to form *part* of the requirements for knowledge: justification
and truth.

Ever since Gettier (1963) it has been at the very least controversial that
knowledge can be reduced to justified true belief. However, it is still commonly accepted that one cannot know something that is not true, and
that knowledge requires some form of justification (see Hazlett 2015 for
an overview). Consequently, it appears fruitful to investigate whether and
how human languages encode the potentially more primitive notions of
justification and truth.

We will argue that the tracking of justification is widespread in languages
of the world. In many languages, justification is tracked by (certain types
of) evidentials. We will also argue that many languages explicitly encode
truth—or at least, the speaker's certainty that the proposition presented is
true—in the form of so-called verum focus, and moreover that they do so
in very similar ways. While "universality" is of course not yet proven, there
are at the very least striking cross-linguistically recurrent patterns in both

the areas we investigate. We will also argue that the discourse conditions under which speakers tend to encode truth are similar to the discourse conditions under which they encode justification. Both justification-based evidentials and verum focus arise in contexts in which the speaker feels the need to defend his or her assertions against implied or explicit disagreement or skepticism. To the best of our knowledge these parallelisms between justification- and truth-marking have not been commented on before.

The cross-linguistic similarities we will document suggest that linguistic evidence has the potential to reveal insights into what humans count as justification and what humans count as truth. If justification and truth are necessary conditions for knowledge, then our findings may in turn bear on what humans count as knowledge. The extent to which our results bear on the question of what justification, truth, and knowledge *are* (as opposed to what humans *believe* they are) is, however, an issue that goes beyond the bounds of this chapter (and of our expertise). The divide between linguistic evidence and philosophical concepts in epistemology is highlighted by Hazlett (2010), who argues that there is a mismatch between the English word *know* (which he claims is non-factive) and knowledge itself (which is factive). However, we believe Hazlett is too hasty in drawing from this the conclusion that "epistemologists may have reason to stop looking at linguistic phenomena altogether" (499). English *know* is just one word in one language, and its properties may not be shared cross-linguistically, as pointed out by Stich et al. (manifesto, this volume). We therefore maintain that the first step in establishing whether linguistic phenomena can shed light on epistemological concepts is to look beyond English to cross-linguistic data, as we do here.

The chapter is structured as follows. In the remainder of the introduction, we provide background on the languages we discuss, and our methodology. In section 2, we introduce evidentials, elements that encode the speaker's source of belief. In section 3, we discuss a subset of evidentials, which we argue directly encode the speaker's assessment of their level of justification for the proposition they are advancing. We show that justification is tracked in remarkably parallel ways cross-linguistically, even in supposedly "non-evidential" languages like English. Section 4 turns to verum operators, again showing striking cross-linguistic similarities. Section 5 discusses the partially similar discourse conditions under which verum emphasis and justification-based evidentials are used. And the final section 6 summarizes and outlines avenues for further investigation.

1.1. Languages Discussed and Methodology

We discuss data from seven languages: English, Cuzco Quechua, St'át'imcets, Gitksan, Nivacle, and Nɬeʔkepmxcín. Here, we provide background information on the lesser-known languages in our sample, and we outline our data-collection methodologies for each language.

Our English data come from native-speaker introspection by both authors and from a corpus of witness interviews by police officers collected by the second author; see Glougie (2016) for details about the corpus.

Cuzco Quechua is a Quechuan language spoken in and around the city of Cuzco, Peru. Our Cuzco Quechua data come from secondary sources (Faller 2002).

St'át'imcets (a.k.a. Lillooet) is a Northern Interior Salish language spoken in the southwest interior of British Columbia, Canada. It currently has fewer than 100 first-language speakers. Our St'át'imcets data come from primary fieldwork by the first author. Fieldwork was with speakers of both the Upper St'át'imcets dialect (Carl Alexander, the late Beverley Frank, the late Gertrude Ned, and the late Rose Agnes Whitley) and the Lower St'át'imcets dialect (Laura Thevarge).

Gitksan is the term used to cover that part of the Nass-Gitksan dialect continuum that is spoken along the upper drainage of the Skeena River in northwestern interior British Columbia. Gitksan currently has fewer than 400 speakers (First Peoples' Cultural Council 2014). Our Gitksan data come from fieldwork by the first author with four speakers of three dialects: Barbara Sennott, from Ansbayaxw (Kispiox), Vincent Gogag, from Git-anyaaw (Kitwancool), Hector Hill, from Gijigyukwhla (Gitsegukla), and Ray Jones, from Prince Rupert and Gijigyukwhla.

The fieldwork methodologies utilized for St'át'imcets and Gitksan include translation tasks (in both directions), acceptability judgment tasks (in which the consultant evaluates a target language utterance in a particular discourse context), and storyboard tasks (in which targeted contexts are provided to the consultant by a series of pictures, in response to which the consultant tells a story). See Matthewson (2004), Burton and Matthewson (2015), and Tonhauser and Matthewson (2016) for further details.

Nivacle is a Matacoan-Mataguayan language spoken in the Argentinean and Paraguayan Chaco. Our Nivacle data were collected by Analía Gutiérrez and published in Gutiérrez and Matthewson (2012).

Nɬeʔkepmxcín (a.k.a. Thompson River Salish) is a Northern Interior Salish language, closely related to St'át'imcets, spoken in the southern interior of British Columbia. Our Nɬeʔkepmxcín data are taken from Mackie (2010), who conducted original fieldwork on the language, and supplemented his data with material from Thompson and Thompson (1996).

2. EVIDENTIALS AS ELEMENTS THAT ENCODE SOURCE OF EVIDENCE

We begin our cross-linguistic investigation of epistemological concepts with an introduction to evidentials. In the next section we will focus on a subset of evidentials that explicitly encode the speaker's assessment of his or her level of justification for the proposition being advanced.

An *evidential* is traditionally defined as an element that encodes information about the speaker's source of evidence for his or her statement (e.g., Aikhenvald 2004). Most European languages, including English, are usually assumed not to possess grammaticalized evidential systems. In many languages of the world, however, source of evidence is grammatically encoded in an obligatory or near-obligatory way. This means that in such languages, one cannot simply assert a proposition such as "It's raining in Vancouver." Instead, one has to indicate grammatically whether the speaker, for example, witnessed the rain herself, was told about it by somebody else, or inferred it using indirect evidence (such as the fact that everyone coming in off the Vancouver streets is carrying a wet umbrella).

One example of an evidential language is St'át'imcets. As shown in (1), the absence of any overt evidential marking strongly implies that the speaker has direct personal evidence for the rain. If the speaker was told about the rain by a third person, she will use the reportative evidential *ku7*, as in (2), and if she used inference, she will tend to use the inferential evidential *k'a*, as in (3). See Matthewson et al. (2007) for in-depth discussion of the St'át'imcets evidential system.[1]

(1) Wa7 kwis.
     IPFV rain
     'It's raining.'   [usually means I witnessed it]

---

1. St'át'imcets data are presented in the orthography designed by Jan van Eijk (see van Eijk 1997) and adopted by the Upper St'át'imc Language Authority. The symbol 7 stands for a glottal stop, c(w) is a (rounded) velar fricative, x(w) is a (rounded) uvular fricative, and t' is an ejective lateral affricate. Abbreviations used here that are not covered by the Leipzig glossing conventions (www.eva.mpg.de/lingua/resources/glossing-rules.php) are listed in the Appendix.

(2) Wá7=**ku7**   kwis.
    IPFV=**REPORT** rain
    'It's raining.'   [somebody told me]

(3) Wá7=**k'a**   kwis.
    IPFV=**INFER** rain
    'It's raining.'   [I used inference]

Languages are not restricted to just these three types of evidential. On the contrary, they can encode a range of subtle and precise evidential distinctions. For example, St'át'imcets has an additional evidential *lákw7a* which requires sensory evidence, but disallows visual evidence of the event itself. Thus, *lákw7a* allows direct perception of the event (as long as it's nonvisual), or indirect evidence about the event (as long as it's sensory). Some examples illustrating these properties of *lákw7a* are given in (4)–(11). First, (4)–(7) show that direct witness via each nonvisual sense licenses *lákw7a*.

(4) Wa7 **lákw7a**   k=wa   ílal.
    IPFV **SENS.NON.VIS** DET=IPFV cry
    'Somebody is crying over there.' *(Context: You hear it)*

(5) Tsem-s=kán   **lákw7a**   ti=ts'í7=a.
    burn-CAUS=1SG.SU   **SENS.NON.VIS** DET=meat=EXIS
    'I burnt the meat.' *(Context: You smell it)*

(6) Wa7 **lákw7a**   ku=sq'áq'pa7 lts7a ti=ts'í7=a.
    be   **SENS.NON.VIS** DET=dirt   here   DET=meat=EXIS
    'This meat tastes as if there's dirt in it.'

(7) *Context: You are blindfolded. I ask you to tell me which of three cups a stone is in. You feel around and touch the stone and you say:*

    Nilh **lákw7a**   lts7a.
    FOC   **SENS.NON.VIS** here
    'It's in this one.'

(8) shows that visual evidence of the event itself is disallowed, and (9) and (10) show that sensory evidence of the results of the event is licit, even if that evidence is visual.

(8) Áolsem=lhkacw **lákw7a**.
   sick=2SG.SU **SENS.NON.VIS**
   'You must be sick.'
   Rejected if the speaker sees someone is shivering and sweaty. Accepted if
   the speaker hears them coughing.

(9) Cw7áy=t'u7 **lákw7a**   k=s=cin'=s   kw=s=wa7
   NEG=just **SENS.NON.VIS** DET=NMLZ=long.time=3POSS DET=NMLZ=be

         l=ti=qú7=a –   wá7=t'u7 wa7   k'ac!
         in=DET=water=EXIS IPFV=just IPFV   dry
   'It couldn't have been under the water long – it's dry!'
   (Speaker didn't witness how long it was under water, but feels the dryness.)

(10) *Context: You had five pieces of ts'wan (wind-dried salmon) left when you*
   checked yesterday. Today, you go to get some ts'wan to make soup and you
   notice they are all gone. You are not sure who took them, but you see some
   ts'wan skins in John's room.

   Ts'áqw-an'-as **lákw7a**   i=ts'wán=a   k=John.
   eat-DIR-3ERG **SENS.NON.VIS** DET.PL=ts'wan=EXIS DET=John
   'Looks like John might have eaten the ts'wan.'

Finally, (11) confirms that pure inference or reasoning is not allowed with
lákw7a.

(11) *Context: I show you a coin and three small cups. I put the coin under one of*
   the cups and then I mix them around and around very fast so you can't see
   any more which one it's under. I ask you to guess. You guess one cup, and
   I lift it up and show you that it's not under there. You guess a second one,
   the same. You point at the last cup and say:

   # Láti7 **lákw7a**   lh=as   legw.
   there **SENS.NON.VIS** COMP=3SBJN hide
   'It must be under that one.' *(Volunteered with inferential k'a.)*

Not only do some languages encode subtle and precise evidential
distinctions, but different languages can encode evidential distinctions
that are slightly different from each other. For example, in the closely related language Nɬeʔkepmxcín, there is an evidential *nuk^w* which requires
sensory evidence and disallows direct visual evidence (just like *lákw7a*), as
shown in (12)–(13).

(12) qeʔ-nim-ne **nukʷ** xeʔ e Mr. Strang
hear-TR-1.SU **SENS.EV** DEM DET Mr. Strang
'I hear Mr. Strang.' (Mackie 2010)

(13) * wik-t-ne **nukʷ** xeʔ e s-ʔaaʔ
see-1.SU **SENS.EV** DEM DET NMLZ-crow
'I see a crow.' (Mackie 2010)

However, unlike *lákw7a*, *nukʷ* allows some visual perception of the event itself, as long as some other sense is involved in addition. This is shown in (14), where the speaker smells the rotten food as well as seeing it. A sentence parallel to this would be ruled out with St'át'imcets *lákw7a*.

(14) *Context: I return from a few weeks' vacation and open the fridge to a terrible odour. I see a bag of something in the back of the fridge, and it's clear that that's what smells.*

ʔes-naqʼ **nukʷ** xeʔe
STAT-rotten **SENS.EV** DEM
'Something's gone rotten.' (Mackie 2010)

Also unlike *lákw7a*, *nukʷ* allows 'gut feelings' or intuition, as shown in (15).

(15) puys-t-xʷ **nukʷ** sexʷsuxʷ
kill-TR-2.SU **SENS.EV** grizzly.bear
'[Premonition tells me] you've killed a grizzly.'
(Mackie 2010, citing Thompson and Thompson 1996)

Other languages also have evidentials that largely but not completely overlap with *lákw7a*'s territory. For example, Gitksan has an evidential *'nakw* which requires sensory evidence and normally disallows visual evidence of the event itself, just like *lákw7a*. However, it can be uttered in a visual-evidence situation, and then gives rise to a mirative (surprise) interpretation (missing with St'át'imcets *lákw7a*) (Peterson 2010).

The point of this discussion is that many languages provide their speakers with grammatical means to encode detailed information about how they acquired their evidence for the propositions they are advancing. Languages also display both similarities and differences in the precise evidential distinctions they encode. If we consider that the evidential basis for one's assertions has a close connection to the justification one has for those assertions, then already we have reason to believe that human languages are sensitive to the epistemological notion of justification. In the next section we will focus on a subset of evidential elements that reflect speaker justification in an even more direct way. We will also see that languages from unrelated language families deal with justification in similar ways. This suggests that the linguistic evidence may reveal core ideas that humans share about what counts as "justified" belief.

3. EVIDENTIALS THAT ENCODE JUSTIFICATION

Some evidentials encode, instead of primarily evidence source, evidence reliability or trustworthiness (Matthewson 2013). Here, we interpret this as meaning that these evidentials encode the speaker's view of how justified he or she is in advancing the proposition. In this section we present evidence that a speaker's linguistic choices are sensitive to justification in three unrelated languages.

3.1. Justification-based Evidentials in Cuzco Quechua, Nivacle, and English

Our first example of justification-based evidentials comes from Cuzco Quechua; the discussion is based on the work of Martina Faller (2002, 2011). Faller argues that the Cuzco Quechua evidential =*mi* requires the speaker to have the "best possible grounds" for advancing the proposition. The best possible grounds evidential =*mi* allows three subtypes of evidence, listed in (16).

(16)   Cuzco Quechua =*mi* encodes:

   (i)   direct evidence, in cases where the described event is directly observable or otherwise directly accessible
   (ii)   the next best thing, in cases where the event is not observable
   (iii) undisputed common and learnt knowledge

Data illustrating each of these subcases are given in (17)–(21). (17) is a prototypical direct evidence situation: the speaker personally witnessed the bread-eating by Pilar.

(17)   *Direct evidence:*
       Pilar-qa   t'anta-ta-**n**   mikhu-rqa-n
       Pilar-TOP   bread-ACC-**BPG**   eat-PST1-3
       'Pilar ate bread.' *(Context: Speaker saw it.)*   (Faller 2002, 18)

In (18), the speaker did not witness Inés going to Cuzco tomorrow, since it isn't possible to have already witnessed a future event. However, a report by Inés about her plans counts as the next best thing. (Faller [2011, 664] observes that reports by others would not license the use of *=mi* in (18).) The same holds for (19); one cannot directly witness another's sadness, but a report by the person herself is the next best thing.

(18) *The next best thing:*
    Paqarin   Inés   Qusuq-ta=**n**   ri-nqa.
    tomorrow   Inés   Cuzco-ACC=**BPG**   go-3FUT
    'Inés will go to Cuzco tomorrow.' *(Context: Inés told the speaker.)*
                                                            (Faller 2011, 664)

(19) *The next best thing:*
    Inés   llaki-ku-n=**mi**.
    Inés   be.sad-REFL-3=**BPG**
    'Inés is sad.' *(Context: Inés told the speaker.)*   (Faller 2011, 664)

Finally, undisputed common and learned knowledge is shown in (20)–(21).

(20) *Undisputed common and learned knowledge:*
    1945   wata-pi=**n**   segunda guerra mundial=qa   tuku-rqa-n.
    1945   year-LOC=**BPG**   second war world=TOP   end-PST-3
    'World War II ended in 1945.' *(Context: Learned in school.)*   (Faller 2011)

(21) *Undisputed common and learnt knowledge:*
    Yunka-pi=**n**   k'usillu-kuna=qa   ka-n.
    rainforest-LOC=**BPG**   monkey-PL=TOP   be-3
    'There are monkeys in the rainforest.' *Context: Everyone knows that.)*
                                                                (Faller 2011)

These data clearly show that *=mi* does not require direct witness by the speaker. What all three types of *=mi*-contexts have in common is that the evidence is considered reliable by the speaker—either due to personal witness, the next best thing, or being undisputed common knowledge. We interpret this as indicating that the speaker believes him or herself to have a high level of justification for the assertion when he or she uses *=mi*.

Our second case study comes from Nivacle, and involves evidential determiners. According to Gutiérrez (2010) and Gutiérrez and Matthewson (2012), determiners in Nivacle encode whether the speaker has had, at some point in the relevant individual's life span, the best possible sensory evidence for the existence of that individual. Three of the four determiners in the language require the best possible sensory evidence (*na, xa,* and *ka;* these differ from each other in deictic properties), while the fourth, *pa,* is used when the speaker *lacks* the best possible sensory evidence. Gutiérrez and Matthewson analyze the distinction between *na/xa/ka* and *pa* as being one of evidence reliability.

In support of the claim that evidence reliability is what is at stake, Gutiérrez and Matthewson point out that what counts as "good enough" evidence is context-dependent, rather than being determined strictly by the type of evidence source. For example, visual evidence usually, but not always, counts as the best possible evidence. This is illustrated in (22)–(29). First, the contrast between (22) and (23) shows that even the existence of presumably quite reliable reports does not license the use of a best-sensory-evidence determiner when referring to a sister one has not personally seen.

(22) *Speaker who has seen his sister before:*
ka?ax   ɬ-**xa**=be?ɬa   ʧita?
have   F-**BEST.SENS.DET**=one elder.sister
'I have one elder sister.'

(23) *Speaker who has never seen his sister before (she fled from the family or was kidnapped by the military before he was born):*
ka?ax   ɬan   ɬ-**pa**=be?ɬa   ʧita?
have   REPORT   F-**NOT.BEST.SENS.DET**=one   elder.sister
'I have an elder sister.' (I have been told.)

The primacy of visual evidence is also illustrated in (24) versus (25). In both cases, the speaker currently has only auditory evidence for the crying baby. But in (24) the speaker has had visual evidence, at some point in the baby's lifetime, for its existence, so the best-sensory-determiner is licensed.

(24) *Context: The speaker has seen the baby at some point in the past (even though the current evidence is only auditory).*

xa=ɬo?os   ɬ-xa=Patricia   jip-?in
BEST.SENS.DET=child   F-BEST.SENS.DET=Patricia   cry-IPFV
'Patricia's child is crying.'

(25) *Context: The speaker hears a crying baby, but has never seen the baby before.*

jip-?in   **pa**=tɑklax
cry-IPFV   **NOT.BEST.SENS.DET**=baby
'A baby is crying.'

However, the most reliable evidence is not *always* visual. In the context of determining what one is eating or drinking for example, taste is the best evidence one can have. This is shown in (26)–(27), where best-sensory determiners are felicitous.

(26) *Context: You are blindfolded. You need to guess what food/liquid you are being given.*

    k'a-joxi   **na**=jinoʔot
    1SG-drink   **BEST.SENS.DET**=water
    'I am drinking water (I can feel it).'

(27) *Context: As in (26).*

    nokeʃ xa-k'aɬtana **ɬa**=ɬaʔ
    now   1SG-try   **F.BEST.SENS.DET**=fruit
    'Now I am tasting a fruit.'

A final pair illustrating that nonvisual evidence can count as sufficient justification to license the best-sensory determiners is given in (28)–(29). In (28), as we expect, feeling a tickling in the dark does not count as sufficient justification for best-sensory determiners when asserting the existence of a spider. But in (29), the speaker considers that feeling the shape of the spider's feet is sufficient to license the best-sensory determiner *na*.

(28) *Context: You wake up in the middle of the night because you feel that your leg tickles. It is dark and you cannot see what is going on.*

    kaʔax   t'ape   ɬ-**pa**=siβoǩlok
    there.is DUB   F-**NOT.BEST.SENS.DET**=spider
    'There is a spider.'

(29) *Context: The speaker feels the round feet that red spiders have.*

    kaʔax   t'e   **na**=ʔojeqtsin
    there.is DUB **BEST.SENS.DET**=red.spider
    'There is a red spider.'

So far in this section we have seen that evidentials in some languages, such as Quechua and Nivacle, can encode whether the speaker has the best possible evidence for the propositions he advances. We interpret this as an encoding of the speaker's sense of his level of justification. In the remainder of the section, we discuss the overt encoding of justification level in supposedly "non-evidential" languages—in particular, English. We begin with the epistemic modal *must*.

In an important contribution to the literature on evidentiality in English, von Fintel and Gillies (2010, 3) write that "*must* carries an *evidential signal*, in particular it signals that the speaker has reached her conclusion via an indirect inference." They provide evidence such as in (30), where direct visual witness of the event precludes the use of *must*.

(30) *Context: Seeing the pouring rain.*

   ?? It must be raining.   (von Fintel and Gillies 2010, 3)

According to von Fintel and Gillies, *must* requires that the speaker's evidence for the prejacent proposition be indirect. In support of the claim that it is really indirectness of evidence, and not uncertainty about the truth of the prejacent, which counts, they observe that in (31), *must* is licensed even though the speaker is sure about the prejacent.

(31) *Context: Chris has lost her ball, but she knows with full certainty that it is in either Box A or B or C. She says:*

   The ball is in A or B or C. It is not in A . . . It is not in B. So, it must be in C.   (von Fintel and Gillies 2010,14)

In (31), the speaker is not uncertain about the truth of the prejacent; she knows the ball is in Box C. What *must* signals is that the speaker knows this by means of indirect evidence; in this case, reasoning.

Following Matthewson (2013, 2015), we propose that von Fintel and Gillies's findings should be reinterpreted as showing not that *must* requires indirect inference but, instead, that it is infelicitous whenever the speaker has the most reliable, or justified, evidence for her assertion in the circumstances. In line with this, observe that what counts as "good enough" evidence for the purposes of disallowing *must* includes a number of different types of evidence source. First, any direct sensory evidence of the event itself is disallowed, as shown in (32) (Matthewson 2013, 2015).

(32) a. *Context: The speaker sees the rain.*
          # It must be raining.

      b. *Context: The speaker hears people playing Tchaikovsky.*
          # They must be playing Tchaikovksy.

c. *Context: The speaker smells a good smell.*
   # Something must smell good.

d. *Context: The speaker tastes something good.*
   # Something must taste good.

e. *Context: The speaker feels that a coat is wet.*
   # The coat must be wet.

In addition to being disallowed by direct sensory evidence, *must* is also disallowed when the speaker's source of information for his assertion is a trustworthy report with the content of the prejacent.

(33) *Context: Belinda, Bob's wife, tells the speaker that Bob is home.*
      # Bob must be home.

Finally, *must* is disallowed where the speaker proffers information that is common or general knowledge, as shown in (34).

(34) *Context: It is general knowledge that World War II ended in 1945.*
      # World War II must have ended in 1945.

In summary, *must* seems to disallow the most trustworthy or reliable evidence, which, depending on the context, may be information obtained by direct observation in the utterance situation, trustworthy report, or general knowledge. *Must* is allowed when the speaker does not have trustworthy evidence for her assertion, even though she may know the prejacent assertion to be true.

Must, therefore, is the inverse of the Quechua =*mi*. =*Mi* requires reliable evidence, while *must* disallows it. In other words, =*mi* is felicitous where the speaker can justify the prejacent proposition on the basis of her evidence, while *must* is felicitous where the speaker cannot. This is interesting for our purposes because it shows that two unrelated languages display the same concern for the speaker's justification level for the proposition she advances. Moreover, as von Fintel and Gillies (2010) and Glougie (2016) show, even "non-evidential" languages like English track this distinction.

English also has elements that encode a sufficient level of justification, more akin to Cuzco Quechua =*mi*. Glougie (2016) argues that discourse markers like *actually* mark that the speaker has reliable evidence for the assertions she makes. Glougie's police interview corpus data show that speakers use *actually* where they have the best possible evidence for the assertion in the circumstances. Her findings are summarized in (35), with examples from the corpus data.

(35) English *actually* encodes:

    a. *Speaker performance (events the speaker participates in):*
Finally I'd **actually** fallen asleep for a night where I could've gotten more than 2 or 3 hours together. (Glougie 2016, 88)

    b. *Sensory observation:*
. . . and then Casey **actually** had an obituary and believe it or not I remember seeing the obituary. (Glougie 2016, 78)

    c. *Trustworthy reports:*
He said there was a... big change in pattern. You guys will need to look at those phone records ... there was **actually** a change in Casey's pattern on the phone. (Glougie 2016, 80)

    d. *General knowledge:*
But submerged in water however deep I don't care if it's six inches or what the dog will show some reaction. Water or moisture **actually** magnifies the dog's ability to smell even more. (Glougie 2016, 85)

Actually is licensed in very much the same contexts as Quechua *=mi*, with one exception: *actually* is also allowed where the speaker's evidence for the assertion is that he performed the event described in the assertion (as in (35)a). This does not appear to be the case for *=mi*. However, as Faller points out, performing the act "might in fact be the most direct evidence possible" (2002, 46).

Like *=mi, actually* is not allowed where the speaker does not have the best possible evidence for the assertion. *Actually* is unattested in the police interview corpus where the speaker's evidence for the assertion is reasoning, inference, or a nontrustworthy report. In those cases, speakers use *must, supposedly,* or *apparently* to introduce their assertions.

(36) *Types of evidence disallowed by* actually:
- nontrustworthy reports
- inference or reasoning

Thus, the types of "reliable information" that license *actually* largely parallel those that license Cuzco Quechua *=mi* (Glougie 2016, 42) and which disallow *must*. We see that unrelated languages rely on, and encode, the very same notions of justification.

3.2. Conclusions About Justification

We have shown that three unrelated languages (Cuzco Quechua, Nivacle, and English) track justification in strikingly parallel ways. In all three languages, there are elements that encode a notion of "best" or "most reliable" evidence. In Quechua, the "best possible grounds" evidential =*mi* marks that the speaker believes she has the best possible evidence for asserting the prejacent proposition. In Nivacle, the "best sensory evidence" determiners are used when the speaker has had, at some point within the relevant individual's life span, the best possible sensory evidence for that individual's existence. And although English is not regarded as a language that obligatorily grammaticizes evidential notions, we showed that it possesses two elements that encode opposite ends of the justification spectrum. The epistemic modal *must* requires a lack of reliable evidence for the prejacent, and thus encodes the absence of sufficient justification (similar to the determiner *pa* in Nivacle). And the discourse particle *actually* requires the existence of reliable evidence for the prejacent, with licensing conditions that are almost exactly parallel to those of Cuzco Quechua =*mi*.

As with the more traditional "evidence-type" evidentials discussed in section 2, justification-based evidentials vary in certain details cross-linguistically. As we have seen, the Nivacle best-sensory determiners encode not only a justification-based requirement but also the requirement that the evidence be sensory. This is missing from, for example, Cuzco Quechua =*mi* or English *actually*. However, the conclusion we draw from the foregoing discussion is that human languages are sensitive to, and often explicitly encode, the notion of justification for the speaker's assertions.

This is the linguistic conclusion. We will return to some speculative remarks about the epistemological consequences of the linguistic findings in section 6.

4. LINGUISTIC ENCODING OF TRUTH: VERUM

We turn now to another notion required for knowledge: truth. In this section, we investigate the linguistic encoding of the speaker's desire to place emphasis on the truth of his assertions.

4.1. Verum in German and English

According to Höhle (1992), who bases his discussion on German data, all declarative sentences contain a silent VERUM operator, defined in (37).

(37)   [[VERUM (p)]] ≈ 'It is true that p'

In German, one can focus the verum operator by placing a H*L accent on an element in C position, usually the finite verb / auxiliary. This leads to emphasis on the expression of truth, and is illustrated in (38)–(39). Notice that we see the same effect in the English translations; English also emphasizes truth by accenting a finite verb or an auxiliary.

(38)   A: Ich habe Hanna gefragt, was Karl grade macht, und sie hat die
              albeme Behauptung aufgestellt, daß er ein Drehbuch schreibt.
              'I asked Hanna what Karl is doing at the moment, and she
              made the idiotic claim that he is writing a screenplay.'

        B: (Das stimmt.)   Karl   SCHREIBT   ein   Drehbuch.
              (That's right.)   Karl   writes   a   screenplay
              '(That's right.) Karl IS writing a screenplay.'
                          (Höhle 1992, 112; glosses and translations added)

(39)   A: Ich habe Hanna gefragt, was Karl letztes Jahr gemacht hat,
              und sie hat die albeme Behauptung aufgestellt, daß er ein
              Drehbuch geschrieben hat.
              'I asked Hanna what Karl did last year, and she made the idiotic
              claim that he wrote a screenplay.'

        B: (Das stimmt.)   Karl   HAT   ein   Drehbuch   geschrieben.
              (That's right.)   Karl   has   a   screenplay   written
              '(That's right.) Karl DID write a screenplay.'
              (adapted from Höhle 1992, 112)

Some recent linguistic analyses derive the "emphasis on truth" effect indirectly, rather than viewing it as the result of focusing a VERUM operator (Romero and Han 2004; Gutzmann 2012; Repp 2013; Lohnstein 2015; Romero 2015, among many others). But still, we see a functional effect that is relevant for current purposes: "in emphasizing, the speaker wants to affirm the truth of his thought" (Lohnstein 2015, 1). Or in the words of Hartmann (2013, 110), the presence of verum emphasis[2] "explicitly excludes the possibility that the opposite truth value of the proposition holds."

Assuming, then, that the verum emphasis construction serves to emphasize the speaker's belief that her assertion is true, our goal in the remainder of this section is to show that verum effects show up in completely unrelated languages, with very similar properties. This again suggests that the linguistic evidence reveals some potentially important insights about how humans view truth. We will be comparing verum emphasis in German and English with its corresponding construction in Gitksan.

In (40), we list ten properties of verum emphasis in German and English (environments where it either is or is not licensed to appear). This list is an expanded version of a set of diagnostics presented by Zimmermann and Hole (2008). We then proceed to show that verum emphasis in Gitksan shows up in almost an identical set of environments.

(40) Properties of verum emphasis in English and German

Contexts where verum emphasis is allowed:
i.   Correcting a previous utterance
ii.   Corrections of negative expectations
iii.   Emphatic agreement
iv.   Confirmation of expected path of events
v.   Answers to questions (with emphatic effect)
vi.   Answers to indirect questions
vii.   In the antecedent of conditionals ('stressing the conditionality')
viii. Inside *yes-no* questions (with an 'Is it really?' effect)

Contexts where verum emphasis is disallowed:
ix.   Discourse-initially
x.   Neutral answers to questions

---

2. From now on, we refer to the phenomenon under discussion as "verum emphasis" in order to remain neutral with respect to the precise analysis of the construction, and with respect to whether a focusing operation is involved.

4.2. Verum Emphasis in Gitksan

In Gitksan, verum emphasis is not marked by focus accenting but, instead, by an overt verum operator _k'ap_. This is not unheard of cross-linguistically; Hartmann (2013), for example, argues that various Chadic languages mark verum emphasis in ways that are unconnected to the ordinary focus strategies in the languages. For example, Bura, just like Gitksan, encodes verum emphasis via a dedicated morpheme, _kú_.

The Gitksan element _k'ap_, which we will argue encodes verum emphasis, has variant pronunciations based on dialect and speech rate: either _k'ap_ or _ap_. Syntactically, it is a "preverbal" (Rigsby 1986). These elements "precede[] all other pre-predicate morphemes" (Tarpent 1987, 376). Since the language is predicate-initial, _k'ap_ almost always appears clause-initially. It can appear in declarative sentences and _yes-no_ questions, but is marginal in _wh_-questions, and it is dispreferred for some speakers in imperatives.[3]

_K'ap_ is glossed as "certainly, indeed, for sure" by Rigsby (1986, 381), and its counterpart in the closely related language Nisga'a is glossed as "must, have to, absolutely, simply, really, no getting out of it, no two ways about it, no choice about it" by Tarpent (1987, 383). An initial example of its usage, along with the speaker's volunteered translation into English, is given in (41).

(41) **Ap**   xatxw   'nii'y.
      VERUM   cold   1SG.III
      'I am really/actually/very cold.'

The first core context where verum emphasis arises in English and German is when a speaker is correcting the content of a previous utterance. _K'ap_ is licensed and often volunteered in such contexts, as shown in (42)–(44).

(42) Lisa: Nee=dii-t   hlis-in=s   Aidan=hl   an-hahla'alji-t.
             NEG=FOC-3.II   finish-TR=PN   Aidan=CN   NMLZ-work-3.II
             'Aidan didn't finish his work.'

      Michael: **Ap**   hlis-in-d=ist!
                VERUM   finish-TR-3.II=QUDD
                'He DID finish it!'   (volunteered)

---

3. In its marginality in _wh_-questions, _k'ap_ differs from verum emphasis in German and English; we set this aside here as requiring future research. The restriction may be syntactic, because _k'ap_ and the _wh_-word compete for the clause-initial position.

(43) Barbara: Dim   'witxw-t   Aidan ji   hlaa   am=hl   ga-'nagw-it.
              PROSP arrive-3.II Aidan IRR   INCEP   good=CN   PL-long-SX
              'Aidan will come later.'

    Lisa: Nee, **ap**   nem=dii   'witxw-t.   Yukw=hl siipxw-t.
          NEG **VERUM** NEG.PROSP=FOC arrive-3.II IPFV=CN   sick-3.II
          'No, he won't come. He's sick.'

(44) *Context: You're complaining that I didn't go to visit you.*

    A: Nee=dii   'witxw-in   go'o=hl   wilb-'y.
       NEG=FOC   arrive-2SG.II   LOC=CN   house-1SG.II
       'You did not come to my house.'

    B: **K'ap**   'witxw   'nii'y   go'o=hl   wilb-in   gi.
       VERUM   arrive   1SG.III   LOC=CN   house-2SG.II   PR.EVID
       'I DID come to your house.' (volunteered)

K'ap is also used to correct negative expectations arising from a previous utterance. In (45)–(47) we see that *k'ap* is consistently volunteered when responding to utterances that strongly implicate the negation of *k'ap*'s prejacent. Speakers in fact prefer *k'ap* to be present in such cases, and sometimes even reject the *k'ap*-less versions.

(45) *Context: Adam and Betty are talking about their friend Charlie.*

    A: Siipxw-good-i-s   Charlie,   hiis-siipxw-t.
       sick-heart-TR-PN   Charlie   pretend-sick-3.II
       'Charlie is pretending to be sick.'

    B: **K'ap**   siipxw   'nid=is.
       VERUM   sick   3SG.III-QUDD
       'He IS sick.' (volunteered)

(46) A: Ha-'nii-good=s   Peter   ji   amxsiiwaa-t.
       INS-on-heart=PN   Peter   IRR   white.person-3.II
       'Peter thinks he's a white guy.'

    B: **Ap**   amxsiiwaa   'nid=ist.
       VERUM   white.person   3SG.III=QUDD
       'He IS a white guy.' (volunteered)

(47) *Context: We're wondering about whether Aidan finished his work for the Gitksan Lab.*

    Lisa: Nee-dii   ha-'nii-good-'y   ji-t   hlis-in=hl   hahla'alji-t.
           NEG=FOC INS-on-heart-1SG.II IRR-3.II finish-TR=CN work-3.II
           'I don't think he finished his work.'

    Henry: **Ap**   hlis-in-d=ist.
           VERUM finish-TR-3.II=QUDD
           'He DID finish it.'   (volunteered)

The use of verum emphasis to correct previous expectations extends to answers to "leading questions," questions whose presuppositions the addressee/answerer does not share. This is illustrated in (48).

(48) Barbara: Nda=hl   wi=s   Aidan   gan   wi=hl
             WH=CN   COMP=PN Aidan   REAS COMP=CN

             nem=dii   'witxw-t?
             NEG.PROSP=FOC arrive-3.II
             'Why isn't Aidan coming today?'

    Lisa: Dim   **ap**   'witxw 'nid=ist.
           PROSP **VERUM** arrive   3.III=QUDD
           'He IS coming.'

The third verum emphasis environment is in contexts of emphatic agreement. Focal stress on the verb or auxiliary is licensed here in English and German, and similarly, *k̲'ap* appears in Gitksan, as shown in (49).

(49) *Context: Katie is pregnant and about to have her baby very soon.*

    A: Am=hl   wila   jabi=s   Katie k'yoots.
        good=CN MANNER do=PN   Katie yesterday
        'Katie was looking good yesterday.'

    B: Ee, **k'ap**   lukw'il   am.
        yes **VERUM** very   good
        'Yes, she WAS looking good.'   (volunteered)

<u>K'</u>ap is also used to confirm an expected path of events, as shown in (50).

(50) *Context: We are expecting Aidan and he hasn't shown up yet.*

Ee'eesxw	'nit	dim	'witxw-t=ist,	dim	ii
promise	3.III	PROSP	arrive-3.II=QUDD	PROSP	CL.CNJ

#**(ap)**   'witxw-t.
#**(VERUM)** arrive-3.II
'He promised to come and he WILL come.'
(adapted from Zimmermann and Hole 2008)

When answering a *yes-no* question, <u>k'</u>ap is possible, and has an emphatic effect, similar to verum focus in German or English. This is illustrated in (51)–(52).

(51) A: Guu   limx   'nii'n   aa?
          HABIT sing   2SG.III YNQ
          'Can you sing?'

     B: Ee'aa, **(k'ap)**   guu   limx 'nii'y.
          yes   **(VERUM)** HABIT sing 1SG.III
          'Yes, I can sing.'

Consultant's comment on <u>k'</u>ap-version: "It's like saying 'Yeah, it's true, I *am* a singer.'"

(52) A: Oo,   siipxw Charlie aa?
          oh   sick   Charlie YNQ
          'Is Charlie sick?'

     B: Ee,   **(k'ap)**   siipxw 'nit.
          yes   **(VERUM)** sick   3SG.III
          'Yeah, he is sick.'

Consultant's comment on *k'ap*-version: "This is where she's telling that it's bad. It's really sick. <u>K'</u>ap means it's really, actually, it's happening, it's not good."

K'ap can also be used in answer to a *wh*-question, but again only when there is an emphatic effect. This is shown for example by the consultant's comment in (53):

(53) Lisa: T   naa   sil-ga-hahla'alsd-n   sa   tun?
             DM   who   COM-DISTR-work-2SG.II   day   DEM.PROX
             'Who did you work with today?'

    Barbara: (Ap)   t   Aidan   sil-ga-hahla'alsd-'y.
              (VERUM)   DM   Aidan   COM-DISTR-work-2SG.II
              'I worked with Aidan.'

Consultant's comment on Barbara's utterance: "*Ap* is usually used
for emphasis. So you're just trying to get ahead of the guy. You're
anticipating that he would question that and so instead of having
to say it again, you say *Ap t Aidan.*"

The consultant's comment here appears to target the type of discourse context, or speaker mindset, which would license a stressed *DID* in English in (53).

The same emphatic effect arises when *k̲'ap* appears on answers to indirect questions, as shown in (54).

(54) A: Nee=dii-n   wilaax ji   dim   'witxw=s   Henry.
         NEG=FOC-1SG.I   know   IRR   PROSP   arrive=PN   Henry
         'I don't know if Henry is coming today.'

    B: **K̲'ap**   dim   'witxw=is.
        VERUM   PROSP   arrive=QUDD
        'He IS coming.'
        (adapted from Zimmermann and Hole 2008; Gutzmann 2012, 5)

Consultant's comment: "Yes, 'cause you told him to be. And you
know for sure."

Note that completely implicit questions are usually marginal with *k̲'ap*, as
shown in (55); we return to this issue later.

(55) *Context: A and B walk in to see that their dog is badly injured. (Implicit
     question: Who punched the dog? / Did you punch the dog?) A says:*

    (**K̲'ap**)   nee=dii-n   t'is=hl   os=is.
    (**VERUM**)   NEG=FOC-1SG.I   hit=CN   dog=QUDD
    'I didn't punch the dog.'

One consultant commented about the *k̲'ap*-version of (55), "If she's
accusing him, he could say that." This comment appears to parallel the

situation in English, where uttering (55) in the given context is not entirely good with verum emphasis either; it works better if A has been explicitly accused.

Verum also appears in German and English inside the antecedent of a conditional, to "stress the conditionality" (Zimmermann and Hole 2008). In Gitksan, adding k̲'ap to a conditional antecedent gives rise to the same effect:

(56) *Context: You think Aidan probably won't come.*

Ji	daa	**ap**	'witxw=s	Aidan,	dim	ii
IRR	SPT	**VERUM**	arrive=PN	Aidan	PROSP	CL.CNJ

ha'w-'y,	ii	ap
go.home-1SG.II	CL.CNJ	VERUM

nee=dii	ha'niigood-'y	dim	'witxw-t.
NEG=FOC	think-1SG.II	PROSP	arrive-3.II

'IF Aidan comes, I will leave (but I don't think he will come).'
(adapted from Zimmermann and Hole 2008)

Consultant's comment: "Yes, it's ok too [i.e., as well as the k̲'ap-less version]. But there's a little more emphasis on the 'if.'"

The final environment where verum emphasis appears is inside *yes-no* questions, with an effect of asking whether the addressee is really sure that something is true. Examples are given in (57)–(58).

(57) B:

Siipxw=t	Tsaalii.
sick=DM	Charlie

'Charlie is sick.'

  A:

Oo,	**ap**	siipxw=t	Tsaalii	aa?
oh	**VERUM**	sick=DM	Charlie	YNQ

'Is he really?'

(58) A:

Mahl-di=s	T.J.	win	Bellingham	hla-miinimts'ep	Washington.
say-TR=PN	T.J.	COMP	Bellingham	NMLZ-capital	Washington

'T.J. said that Bellingham is the capital of Washington.'

  B:

K̲'ap	Bellingham	hla-miinimts'ep=hl	Washington	aa?
VERUM	Bellingham	NMLZ-capital=CN	Washington	YNQ

'IS Bellingham the capital of Washington?' (volunteered)
(adapted from Gutzmann and Castroviejo-Miró 2011, 162)

Finally, we turn to two environments where verum emphasis is predicted *not* to appear—namely, discourse-initially and in the answer to a neutral question. Discourse-initial contexts are illustrated in (59)–(60); we see that *k̓ap* is infelicitous, just as it would be in the English translations.

(59) *Context: Adam and Betty are eating dinner quietly. Nobody has said anything yet. Betty suddenly says:*

     (#**K̓ap**)   siipxw=t   Charlie.
     (#**VERUM**) sick=DM   Charlie
     'Charlie is sick.'

(60) *Context: We are sitting working and Michael is also in the room. Michael suddenly says out of the blue:*

     (#**K̓ap**)   ban=hl   t̓imges-'y.
     (#**VERUM**) hurt=CN   head-1SG.II
     'I have a headache.'

K̓ap is also infelicitous in answers to neutral questions, whether *yes-no* or *wh*-questions. This was shown earlier for *yes-no* questions by the consultant's comments in (51) and (52); the comments indicate the non-neutral effect of *k̓ap*. Similarly, the non-neutral effect of *k̓ap* in answers to *wh*-questions was shown by the consultant's comment on (53). The infelicity of *k̓ap* in answers to neutral *wh*-questions is further illustrated in (61)–(62).[4]

(61) *Context: Talking about what kind of pet Michael has. We know the pet is called Spot. Aidan recently was at Michael's house and saw the pet, so you ask him 'What is Spot?' Aidan replies:*

     (?**Ap**)   os-t   Spod=is.
     (?**VERUM**) dog-3.II   Spot=QUDD
     'Spot is a dog.'

(62) *Context: Michael is telling Katie that he has a pet called Fluffy. Katie wonders what kind of animal Fluffy is, so she asks Michael what Fluffy is. Michael replies:*

     (#**K̓ap**)   lelt/lalt=t   Fluffy(=ist).
     (#**VERUM**) snake=DM   Fluffy(=QUDD)
     'Fluffy is a snake.'

4. The exception to this is where the speaker is answering a leading *wh*-question, not by providing new information but by challenging the presupposition in the leading question itself. This was already illustrated in (48), and we discuss it further in section 6.

Consultants' comments on versions with k'ap:
"No. it would just be *Lalt Fluffy ist*. And then if she doubts it, he can say *Ap lalt Fluffy ist*."
"No. Not unless you start arguing and then you say *Oo, k'ap lelt*."

We have now checked all the ten diagnostic environments where verum emphasis is or is not found in English and German, and found that the results for Gitksan k'ap are strikingly similar. In the next subsection, we discuss the potential consequences of these findings for the study of the representation of truth in human language.

4.3. On the Relation Between Verum and Truth

We started our investigation of verum emphasis by observing that according to Höhle's original analysis, a silent VERUM operator contributes semantics related to truth. When a speaker places focus on the VERUM operator, she emphasizes that the assertion is true (or, in questions or imperatives, asks the hearer to confirm that a proposition is true or to make it true that an event happens). Subsequent researchers have derived the perceived effect of an emphasis on truth more indirectly than Höhle did. For example, Romero and Han (2004, 627) argue that the VERUM operator "is used not to assert that the speaker is entirely certain about the truth of *p*, but to assert that the speaker is certain that *p* should be added to the Common Ground." Romero and Han nevertheless observe (631) that the VERUM operator has the "intuitive effect" of insisting on the truth of a proposition. Similarly, Gutzmann and Castroviejo-Miró (2011, 143) argue that VERUM gives rise only indirectly to an emphasis on truth. They argue that VERUM is a use-conditional operator that "takes as argument a proposition *p* and expresses the interpretational instruction to downdate the corresponding question ?*p* from the question under discussion." The truth effect follows because a speaker who asserts that *p*, and also indicates that she wants to downdate ?*p* "must be sure that *p* should be added to the C[ommon] G[round]. This emphasizes that *p* is true, because we have the impression of a double assertion that *p*" (162).

Even if the field is divided on whether verum emphasis constructions *directly* encode the speaker's belief about the truth of her assertions, we believe that verum effects have the potential to be relevant to epistemological questions. We propose that the cross-linguistic similarities in both justification encoding and verum behavior suggest that these phenomena reveal something about how humans view the concepts of justification, truth, and ultimately perhaps knowledge. In the next section, we further propose that the encoding of verum emphasis is similar in its discourse conditions and speaker motivation to the encoding of justification. Specifically, both verum emphasis constructions and justification-based evidentials like *actually* are used when speakers are compelled to explicitly express commitment to their assertions, usually because they are attempting to convince a skeptical interlocutor of their point of view.

5. JUSTIFICATION AND TRUTH AS MEANS TO CONVINCE

In this section, we discuss the discourse conditions under which justification-based evidentials (such as *actually*) and verum emphasis are licensed. We argue that both justification and verum emphasis are encoded in contexts in which the speaker is compelled to expressly commit to his assertion. We will also, however, uncover some differences in the precise contexts in which justification versus truth are appealed to.

5.1. Discourse Conditions for *Actually*

When we discussed *actually* in section 3, we did not talk about its discourse properties. However, it is obviously the case that speakers don't use *actually* every time they have good evidence for their assertions. In particular, for example, *actually* is typically not good out of the blue. In fact, in our judgment, the (in)felicity of *actually* largely parallels the behavior of verum emphasis constructions, as summarized in (40).

Normally, a bare assertion is sufficient to establish the speaker's commitment to the informations he asserts (Schiffrin 1987, 18). The normal conditions on assertion will suffice in any neutral context to indicate the speaker's commitment to the propositions she advances. For economy reasons, speakers will rarely explicitly justify their discourse contributions unless there is a specific reason to do so.

We propose that speakers use *actually* only when they have a reason to justify their positions; they use *actually* to support their claims by marking that they have reliable evidence for them. Glougie (2016) shows that speakers use *actually* to achieve the discourse goals of correcting information previously given; responding to a challenge; or persuading their discourse partners to adopt their assertions. Illustrative data are given in (63).

(63) a. *Correction*

   I went and picked up uhm, my sister's laptop. Well, it's **actually**
   my mom's laptop, but you know, my sister was, she's had it for
   the past month or so . . .

   (Glougie 2016, 163)

   b. *Challenge*
   A: . . . how many times did she drive, or did you drive her car,
        were you in her car? . . .
   B: I never drove, I **actually** never drove her car.

   (Glougie 2016, 175)

   c. *Persuasion*
   A: . . . you wouldn't have known my [maiden] name until
        October . . .
   B: No, you **actually** told me, you **actually** told me . . .

   (Glougie 2016, 184)

In the absence of some reason to emphasize the reliability of one's evidence/justification, *actually* will tend not to be used. When a speaker does use *actually* where the need to emphasize the reliability of their information is not obvious, it is generally understood as indicating that something about the claim will be surprising to the addressee.

5.2. Discourse Conditions for Verum

Like *actually*, verum emphasis marking is also infelicitous in neutral or out-of-the-blue contexts. This infelicity is captured by current analyses in various ways. Within Gutzmann and Castroviejo Miró's (2011) Question Under Discussion–based analysis, the infelicity of discourse-initial verum emphasis follows from the fact that prejacent of VERUM is not the QUD in a discourse-initial context.

   However, something more appears to be needed to fully capture the discourse conditions of verum emphasis. Consider the example in (64). Here, B is answering the QUD, but verum emphasis is not licit. An important feature of this type of context is that B's answer provides information novel to the discourse, on which neither discourse participant has yet taken a position. In such neutral contexts, normal conditions of assertion are sufficient to convey that B is committed to the truth of the proposition advanced.

(64) A: Why didn't you go to school today?
      B: # I DIDN'T want to.

The contexts in which verum emphasis *is* allowed (the contexts in (40i-viii) above) seem to share the property that the information being conveyed is controversial. We contend that verum emphasis is used only when the speaker wishes to prevent the "wrong" proposition from entering the Common Ground. This is summarized in (65).

(65) Discourse condition on VERUM:
      ?p is the maximal QUD, and the speaker wants to prevent ¬p from entering the Common Ground.

The proposal in (65) predicts that VERUM(p) is only felicitous when the speaker has reason to believe ¬p is threatening to enter the Common Ground, and he wishes to prevent this. In line with this, observe the contrast between a response to a leading question where the addressee does not accept the underlying presupposition, as in (66), and a response where the addressee does accept the underlying presupposition, as in (64). We see in (66) that verum emphasis is licit in response to leading questions where the speaker's answer takes the form of a challenge to the presupposition. Verum emphasis is felicitous here because the speaker is responding to (denying) the presupposition explicitly put into the discourse in the question.

(66) A: Why didn't you go to school today?
      B: I DID go to school today.

In summary, the generalization is that verum emphasis constructions are used in discourse contexts where the content of the speaker's current contribution is controversial. In such contexts, the speaker may not want to rely on the normal conditions on assertion as a means to convey her commitment to the truth of the propositions she advances. By placing emphasis on the truth of the relevant proposition, the speaker aims to convince her addressee of her point of view.

5.3. Differences Between Verum Emphasis and *Actually*

Although justification-based evidentials and verum emphasis differ in that only the former reference evidence (therefore only the former relate to justification level), they share the common property that they are both used to strengthen the normal commitments of speakers to their assertions. Speakers can choose to strengthen their commitments by referencing either of the core notions underlying knowledge: justification or truth.[5]

Although speakers use both verum emphasis and *actually* to justify their discourse contributions and to strengthen the normal commitments of their utterances, their conditions of use are not identical. Where they differ is with respect to the types of information they are responding to and on what basis. Speakers use verum emphasis to accept or challenge information explicitly offered by their interlocutors. Verum emphasis requires the explicit assertion of information by the speaker's discourse partner and indicates that the speaker accepts or rejects that information on the basis of what the speaker believes to be true. *Actually*, in contrast, is much more permissive; *actually* can be used to respond to implicit, anticipated, or even imagined disagreements, as long as the speaker has reliable evidence for her claim. Therefore, *actually* is licensed in a wider range of contexts than is verum focus.

The difference between verum emphasis and *actually* shows up with discourse-novel information such as in (67).

(67) *Context: You watch someone throw a rock through a store window and run into an alley. The police arrive and ask where the vandal went. You say:*

    a.   He ran into the alley.
    b.   He **actually** ran into the alley.
    c.   # He **DID** run into the alley.

A bare assertion (as in (67a) is fine in response to the police officer's question. However, *actually* is also felicitous when the speaker can justify his answer on the basis of reliable evidence (67b). Verum emphasis, however, is not felicitous, regardless of whether the speaker believes his assertion to be true (67c).

In a similar vein, observe that unlike verum emphasis, *actually* is felicitous in response to neutral *wh*-questions, even where the information provided in the response is novel to the discourse. Consider the snake example given in Gitksan in (62) above. We see in (68) that verum emphasis is infelicitous in English, just as ḵ'ap was in Gitskan. *Actually*, however, is perfectly fine.

5. Our discussion of the commitments of assertion needs to be extended to cover the use of verum emphasis and justification-based evidentials in questions and imperatives. We don't see any looming problems here, but for reasons of space we leave the task for future research.

(68)   *Context: Michael is telling Katie that he has a pet called Fluffy. Katie*
       wonders what kind of animal Fluffy is, so she asks Michael what Fluffy is.

   a.   # Fluffy **IS** a snake.
   b.   Fluffy is **actually** a snake.

As we predict based on our analysis of *actually* given in section 3, *actually*
is only felicitous in (68) if the speaker has reliable evidence that Fluffy is
a snake. Consider a slightly different scenario in which Michael agreed to
buy a pet named Fluffy from an animal shelter in order to avoid the pet's
being euthanized. Michael agreed to buy Fluffy without asking or caring
about Fluffy's species. Michael arrives at the shelter to take possession
of Fluffy and is told she's with the veterinarian but will be ready to leave
shortly. While he waits, Michael sees an empty snake habitat with the
name "Fluffy" in the corner. Katie, who has accompanied Michael to the
shelter, asks what Fluffy is. It is infelicitous in that context for Michael to
use *actually*. Instead, a marker of *lack* of justification must be used: either
the epistemic modal *must* (cf. discussion in section 3) or *apparently* (which
Glougie 2016 analyzes as a marker of less than reliable evidence).

(69)   *Context: As described.*

   a.   # Fluffy is **actually** a snake.
   b.   Fluffy **must** be a snake.
   c.   Fluffy is **apparently** a snake.

The difference between verum emphasis and *actually*, then, is what they
may respond to. Verum emphasis requires an explicit assertion by the
speaker's discourse partner. However, *actually* is much more permissive;
as long as the speaker has reliable evidence for his claim, *actually* can be
used to respond to implicit, anticipated, or even imagined disagreements.
In (68), for example, Michael may expect Katie to disbelieve his answer
to her question on the basis that it is unexpected for a snake to be named
Fluffy. Using *actually*, Michael can anticipate Katie's resistance and cut it
off at the pass by marking that he knows Fluffy is a snake on the basis of
good evidence. The same is true in (67): verum emphasis would be acceptable here if someone had either explicitly denied that the vandal ran into
the alley, or presupposed or strongly implicated that he didn't, or asked
whether he did, or even simply stated that he did or didn't (either of which
raises the question of whether he did). But *actually* can be used merely because the speaker suspects that the information might be mildly surprising
to the addressee.

Related to this is the fact that *actually*, unlike verum emphasis, can respond to utterances that don't directly contain or ask about *actually*'s prejacent proposition. In (70), for example, we see that *actually* can respond to an eyebrow raise, which implicitly asks a question, even though the speaker's assertion does not directly answer that implicit question.

(70) *Context: The window above my seat on the bus is open. Another person comes in and sits next to me. They stand up, point to the window and raise their eyebrows (as if to ask if they can close it). I say:*

    a. It's **actually** really warm in here.[6]
    b. # It **IS** really warm in here.[7]

Verum emphasis is infelicitous here, and the reason is not just that the previous "utterance" was merely an eyebrow raise. In our judgment, verum emphasis *can* sometimes respond to mere facial gestures, but only if the proposition being asserted in the verum utterance directly responds to the implicit question raised by the facial expression. This is shown in (71).

(71) *Context: The last cookie is missing from the cookie jar. I ask if you ate the last cookie and you say no. I raise my eyebrow (as if to ask if you're telling the truth). You say:*

    a. I **DIDN'T.**
    b. I **actually** didn't.

The problem for verum emphasis in (70), then, is parallel to the problem in (67) and (68): verum is only used when the proposition being advanced directly responds to a prior utterance. This requirement of verum emphasis has been discussed in the literature under the guise of "givenness"; for example, Gutzmann and Castroviejo Miró (2011, 160) write that verum emphasis "is only felicitous if the lexical material that constitutes the propositional content of the sentence is already given in the discourse context"; see also Richter (1993), Egg and Zimmermann (2012), and Littell (2016), among others. *Actually* is not subject to as strict a givenness requirement.

---

6. *Actually* has a certain amount of freedom with respect to its placement within the clause, and its different positions correlate to a certain extent with different semantic or pragmatic effects. We are abstracting away from these issues here; see for example, Greenbaum (1969), Taglicht (2001) and Glougie (2016) for discussion.

7. (70b) should be read with ordinary falling intonation at the end of the sentence. It can be rescued with a special (fall-rise) intonation at the end, which adds extra discourse effects.

However, *actually* is in one respect more restricted than verum emphasis, because *actually* requires some expressed, implied, or anticipated disagreement, whereas verum doesn't. The interaction of these two factors (direct vs. indirect response, agreement vs. disagreement) is illustrated in (72). Here, the immediately previous utterance contains an indirect embedded question (whether Charlie stole my purse). We see that verum emphasis is felicitous when the speaker is responding directly to the embedded question, whether to agree with the positive bias of the question (72a), or to disagree (72b). However, verum emphasis is completely incoherent in (72c), where the response only indirectly answers the embedded question. *Actually* has no problem answering indirectly (72f), but is dispreferred when the answer and the positive bias of the embedded question align (72d).

(72)　*Context: I notice that my purse is missing, and Charlie is one of my suspects. I say 'I wonder whether Charlie stole my purse.' You reply:*

　　　a.　　He DID steal it.
　　　b.　　He DIDN'T steal it.
　　　c.　# He IS in the hospital.[8]
　　　d.　??He actually stole it.
　　　e.　　He actually didn't steal it.
　　　f.　　He is actually in the hospital.

In summary, speakers can use *actually* in the absence of any explicit relevant proposition in a way that verum does not permit, but *actually* seems to require challenge or disagreement (explicit or anticipated) in a way that verum does not. It is unknown at this stage whether these differences in discourse licensing conditions between truth-markers and justification-evidentials are universal and, if so, why that would be. To our knowledge, no one has considered those issues before (or has even considered the partial parallels between the discourse conditions for verum emphasis vs. justification-evidentials), and we leave further investigation to future research.

5.4. Summary

We propose that justification marking and truth marking are common— perhaps universal—strategies that humans use when they are making

---

8. Again, this example should be read with normal intonation at the end of the sentence.

an effort to be believed by their interlocutors. Humans like to get their assertions believed by others, and this is more important in some discourse contexts than in others. In discourse contexts where extra emphasis is needed, we support our assertions by linguistically encoding either "I have justification" or more directly, simply "What I'm saying is true."

So, the study of things like justification-based evidentials and verum marking can help reveal what humans count as bolstering their claims— what will help them be believed. It seems that we frequently attempt to convince others either by indicating that we have reliable evidence for what we say or by emphasizing that what we say is true. These are, of course, two of the subcomponents of a traditional definition of knowledge.

6. CONCLUSION

We have shown that the linguistic strategies speakers use to justify their assertions look very similar in unrelated languages. We've seen that Quechua =mi, English *must*, and English *actually* are all sensitive to justification. Does this mean that *all* languages encode justification? Of course, we don't know, and future research is necessary to attempt to empirically falsify that proposal. However, the fact that unrelated languages like Quechua, Nivacle, and English mark speaker justification is sufficient to allow us to hypothesize that all languages have some way to encode the speaker's sense of his or her justification for the propositions he or she makes.

Even if all languages have some way to encode speaker justification, it is clear that languages differ in the details of how they do so. We've seen that Quechua =mi, the Nivacle determiners, English *must*, and English *actually* count very similar types of evidence as "justified enough." But there are also differences in the details: *actually* allows speaker performance, while Quechua =mi apparently does not; the Nivacle best-evidence determiners require sensory evidence, while the others do not. Even if languages all encode speaker justification, we don't know the extent to which languages can vary in accomplishing that goal.

Nonetheless, there are certain features of justification that we observe to hold in all the languages we have surveyed so far. First, the cases we presented all count general knowledge as justified enough. In fact, the Tibeto-Burman language Yongning Na even has an evidential specifically dedicated to propositions that are common knowledge (Lidz 2010). Second, none of the languages surveyed counts inference or reasoning as justified enough. Therefore, we hypothesize that languages will differ in how they lexically cut up the "justification cline," but not in the order of elements in the cline.

We also query, for future research, whether evidentials can tell us anything about the famous Gettier cases—that is, cases involving justified true belief that nevertheless does not count as knowledge. McCready (2014) investigates how Japanese speakers use evidentials in Gettier cases such as that in (73) (containing the inferential evidential *mitai*), and concludes that "[u]nsurprisingly, the Gettiered individual can assert an evidential with respect to his putative knowledge" (167).

(73)   *Context: Johnny is traveling in the country when he sees what looks to him like a horse on top of a hill and hears a horse neigh. However, what he sees is a horse-shaped rock, and the neigh is just the wind whistling through that pipe over there. But there is – coincidentally – a horse standing behind the rock.*

ano	oka-no	ue-ni	uma-ga	iru	**mitai**	da
that	hill-GEN	TOP-DAT	horse-NOM	exists	**EVID**	COP

'There appears to be a horse on top of that hill.'

(McCready 2014, 167)

McCready argues that (73) is only assertable by Johnny because, in his Gettiered state, he believes he has sufficient evidence to make it true. A non-Gettiered observer cannot utter (73) sincerely. Moreover, McCready argues that the Gettiered speaker and a non-Gettiered observer will evaluate the truth of (73) differently; for Johnny, (73) will be true and for the non-Gettiered observer, it will be false.

It may be that evidentials won't tell us much about the core question of whether a Gettiered speaker *knows* a proposition like that in (73). As pointed out by McCready, all we seem to be able to find out is whether the speaker *believes* she knows it. However, Gettier cases may still provide useful insights with respect to speaker justification. The point here is that Gettier cases crucially involve *justified* true belief, and it is often left up to the researcher's intuition what counts as "justified." Recent experimental studies (e.g., Nagel et al. 2013; Machery et al. 2015) instead ask participants directly about how justified the Gettiered individual was. In that vein, we propose research projects that might consider the following.

First, we could present Gettier cases involving a range of evidence types (visual, non-visual sensory, reliable report, unreliable report, inference/reasoning) to speakers of languages with evidence-source–based evidentials and to speakers of languages with justification-based evidentials, in order to determine how speakers use these evidentials in Gettier cases. Specifically, we want to determine which evidentials speakers use, which evidentials they accept, and whether there is a correlation between evidential use and Gettier judgments.

For example, consider the Gettier/Hospital case from Machery et al. (2015), in which Paul Jones is worried about his wife Mary, who has not come home from work. He calls University Hospital and they tell him that someone with her name has been admitted with major injuries following a car crash. As it turns out, the patient at University Hospital is not Paul's wife but, rather, another woman with the same name. In fact, Paul's wife had a heart attack and is at that moment receiving treatment at Metropolitan Hospital, a few miles away.

In our judgment, Paul can say in this context "My wife is actually in the hospital," and he cannot say "My wife must be in the hospital." This is as we expect, because Paul is Gettiered and believes himself to have good justification. However, evidence-source-based languages might require Paul to use a reportative evidential when asserting that his wife is in the hospital. It is an open question whether such an evidential system could affect—or reflect—differing opinions about the extent to which Paul is justified in his assertion. Similarly, it remains to be seen whether speakers of different language types would react differently if the context is minimally changed so that Paul has only inferential evidence that his wife is in the hospital. These questions, which may reveal something about whether speakers make a connection between overtly encoded justification, on the one hand, and truth/knowledge, on the other, remain to be empirically tested.

In addition to testing speaker reactions to Gettier cases, more empirical work would shed light on how speakers react to the Clear Knowledge case discussed by Machery et al. (2015). They give the following as an example:

> Albert is in a furniture store with his wife. He is looking at a bright red table in a display. He believes the table is just the shade of red he was looking for. The showroom . . . [has] clear, natural lighting throughout the entire store, and plenty of space around each piece on display. . . . He checks the dimensions and price of the table, and starts to consider buying it. Albert asks his wife, "Do you like this red table?" (5)

In this Clear Knowledge case, Albert's evidence for his assumption that the table is red is visual. For English, we predict speakers will treat this context the same as they do the Gettier case described earlier. Sure enough, in our judgment, Albert can say "This table is actually red" and he cannot say "This table must be red." However, in some languages, the Hospital scenario and the Clear Knowledge scenario would obligatorily receive a different form of evidential marking. Does this result in a difference with respect to speaker judgments? This remains to be tested.

ACKNOWLEDGMENTS

We are very grateful to St'át'imcets consultants Carl Alexander, Laura Thevarge, the late Beverley Frank, the late Gertrude Ned and the late Rose Agnes Whitley, and to Gitksan consultants Vincent Gogag, Hector Hill, Ray Jones, and Barbara Sennott. We are also very grateful to the organizers of, and participants in, the workshop on the Geography of Philosophy: Knowledge, Person, and Wisdom at the University of Pittsburgh, and to the editors of the current volume. The research reported on here was supported in part by SSHRC grant #410-2011-0431 and the Jacobs Research Fund.

APPENDIX: ABBREVIATIONS USED

BEST.SENS.DET = best sensory determiner, BPG = best possible grounds, CL. CNJ = clausal conjunction, CN = common noun connective, DIR = directive transitivizer, DM = determinate marker, DUB = dubitative, EXIS = assertion of existence, HAB = habitual, I/II/III = series I/I/III pronoun, INFER = inferential evidential, NOT.BEST.SENS.DET = not best sensory determiner, PN = proper name, PR.EVID = prior evidence, PROSP = prospective aspect, QUDD = Question Under Discussion downdate, REAS = reason clause, REPORT = reportative evidential, SENS.EV = sensory evidential, SENS.NON.VIS = sensory nonvisual evidential, SPT = spatiotemporal, SX = subject extraction, YNQ = *yes-no* question.

REFERENCES

Aikhenvald, Alexandra. (2004). *Evidentiality*. Oxford: Oxford University Press.
Burton, Strang, and Lisa Matthewson. (2015). "Targeted Construction Storyboards in Semantic Fieldwork." In *Semantic Fieldwork Methodology*, ed. R. Bochnak and L. Matthewson, 135–156. Oxford University Press.
Egg, Markus, and Malte Zimmermann. (2012). "Stressed Out!" Accented Discourse Particles: The Case of *doch*." *Proceedings of Sinn und Bedeutung* 16: 225–238.
Faller, Martina. (2002). "Semantics and Pragmatics of Evidentials in Cuzco Quechua." PhD dissertation, Stanford University.

Faller, Martina. (2011). "A Possible Worlds Semantics for Cuzco Quechua Evidentials." *Proceedings of SALT* 20: 660–683. [Ithaca, NY: Cornell University, CLC Publications]

First Peoples' Cultural Council. (2014). *Report on the Status of B.C. First Nations Languages 2014*, 2nd ed. Brentwood Bay, BC: FPCC.

Gettier, E. L. (1963). "Is Justified True Belief Knowledge?" *Analysis* 23: 121–123.

Glougie, Jennifer. (2016). "The Semantics and Pragmatics of English Evidential Expressions." PhD dissertation, University of British Columbia.

Greenbaum, S. (1969). *Studies in English Adverbial Usage*. London: Longmans.

Gutiérrez, Analía. (2010). "Evidentiality Distinctions in Nivacle Determiners." Qualifying paper, University of British Columbia.

Gutiérrez, Analía, and Lisa Matthewson (2012). "Evidential Determiners: Best (Sensory) Evidence." *Proceedings of SULA 6: The Semantics of Under-Represented Languages in the Americas,* 63–79. [Amherst, MA: GLSA]

Gutzmann, Daniel. (2012). "Verum – Fokus – Verum-Fokus? Fokus-basierte und lexikalische Ansätze." In *Wahrheit – Fokus – Negation*, ed. Hardarik Blühdorn and Horst Lohnstein, 67–103. Linguistische Berichte Sonderheft 18. Hamburg: Buske.

Gutzmann, Daniel, and Elena Castroviejo Miró. (2011). "The Dimensions of Verum." In *Empirical Issues in Syntax and Semantics 8*, ed. Oliver Bonami and Patricia Cabredo Hofherr, 143–165. www.cssp.cnrs.fr/eiss8.

Hartmann, Katharina. (2013). "Verum Blocking Effects in Chadic Languages." *Lingua* 136: 103–124.

Hazlett, Allan. (2010). "The Myth of Factive Verbs." *Philosophy and Phenomenological Research* 80(3): 497–522.

Hazlett, Allan. (2015). "The Maturation of the Gettier Problem." *Philosophical Studies* 172: 1–6.

Höhle, Tilman N. (1992). "Über Verum-Fokus im Deutschen." In *Information-sstruktur und Grammatik*, ed. Joachim Jacobs, 112–141. Opladen: Westdeutscher Verlag.

Lidz, Liberty. (2010). "A Descriptive Grammar of Yongning Na (Mosuo)." PhD dissertation, University of Texas at Austin.

Littell, Patrick. (2016). "Focus, Predication, and Polarity in Kwak'wala." PhD dissertation, University of British Columbia.

Lohnstein, Horst. (2015). "Verum Focus." In *Handbook of Information Structure*, ed. Caroline Fery and Shinichiro Ishihara, 290–313. Oxford: Oxford University Press.

Machery, Edouard, Stephen Stich, David Rose, Amita Chatterjee, Kaori Karasawa, Noel Struchiner, Smita Sirker, Naoki Usui, and Takaaki Hashimoto. (2015). "Gettier Across Cultures. *Nous* 51(3): 1–20. doi: 10.1111/nous.12110.

Mackie, Scott. (2010). "Sensory Evidence in Thompson River Salish." Qualifying paper, University of British Columbia.

Matthewson, Lisa. (2004). "On the Methodology of Semantic Fieldwork." *International Journal of American Linguistics* 70: 369–415.

Matthewson, Lisa. (2013). "Evidence Type, Evidence Location, Evidence Strength." In *Evidentials and Modals: Crosslinguistic Explorations*, ed. Chungmin Lee and Jinho Park. Unpublished manuscript, University of British Columbia.

Matthewson, Lisa. (2015). "Evidential Restrictions on Epistemic Modals." In *Epistemic Indefinites*, ed. Luis Alonso-Ovalle and Paula Menendez-Benito, 141–160. Oxford: Oxford University Press.

Matthewson, Lisa, Henry Davis, and Hotze Rullmann. (2007). "Evidentials as Epistemic Modals: Evidence from St'át'imcets." *Linguistic Variation Yearbook* 7: 201–254.

McCready, Eric. (2014). "What Is Evidence in Natural Language?" In *Formal Approaches to Semantics and Pragmatics: Japanese and Beyond*, ed. Eric McCready, Katsuhiko Yabushita, and Kei Yoshimoto, 155–180. Studies in Linguistics and Philosophy series. Dordrecht: Springer.

Nagel, Jennifer, Valerie San Juan, and Raymond A. Mar. (2013). "Lay Denial of Knowledge for Justified True Beliefs." *Cognition* 129: 652–661.

Peterson, Tyler. (2010). "Epistemic Modality and Evidentiality in Gitksan at the Semantics-Pragmatics Interface." PhD dissertation, University of British Columbia.

Repp, Sophie. (2013). "Common Ground Management: Modal Particles, Illocutionary Negation and Verum." In *Beyond Expressives. Explorations in Use-Conditional Meaning*, ed. Danial Gutzmann and Hans-Martin Gärtner, 231–274. Leiden: Brill.

Richter, Frank. (1993). "Settling the truth: Verum Focus in German." Unpublished manuscript, Amherst, MA.

Rigsby, Bruce. (1986.) "Gitksan Grammar." Unpublished manuscript, University of Queensland, Australia.

Romero, Maribel, and Chung-hye Han. (2004). "On Negative Yes/No Wuestions." *Linguistics and Philosophy* 27(5): 609–658.

Romero, Maribel. (2015). "High Negation in Subjunctive Conditionals and Polar Questions." In *Proceedings of Sinn und Bedeutung* 19: 499–516.

Schiffrin, D. (1987). *Discourse Markers*. Cambridge: University of Cambridge Press.

Taglicht, J. (2001). "*Actually*, There's More to It than Meets the Eye." *English Language and Linguistics* 5(1): 1–16.

Tarpent, Marie-Lucie. (1989). "A Grammar of the Nisgha Language." PhD dissertation, University of Victoria.

Thompson, Laurence C., and M. Terry Thompson. (1996). "Thompson River Salish Dictionary." University of Montana Occasional Papers in Linguistics 12, Linguistics Laboratory, University of Montana, Missoula.

Tonhauser, Judith, and Lisa Matthewson. (2015). "Empirical Evidence in Research on Meaning. Unpublished manuscript, Ohio State University and University of British Columbia.

van Eijk, Jan. (1997). *The Lillooet Language: Phonology, Morphology, Syntax*. Vancouver: University of British Columbia Press.

von Fintel, Kai, and Anthony Gillies. (2010). "Must ... Stay ... Strong!" *Natural Language Semantics* 18: 351–383.

Zimmermann, Malte, and Daniel Hole. (2008). "Predicate Focus, Verum Focus, Verb Focus. Similarities and Difference." Paper presented at the Potsdam-London IS Meeting, December 2008.

CHAPTER 8

Knowledge, Certainty, and Skepticism

A Cross-Cultural Study

JOHN WATERMAN, CHAD GONNERMAN, KAREN YAN,
AND JOSHUA ALEXANDER

1. INTRODUCTION

In one of the most celebrated articles in experimental philosophy, Weinberg et al. (2001) described evidence of cross-cultural intuitional diversity about a variety of famous epistemological cases. This evidence led many philosophers to deny what we call *epistemic universalism,* the view that epistemic intuitions are culturally universal, and it became one of the central parts of the growing restrictionist challenge in experimental philosophy (Alexander 2012; Alexander and Weinberg 2014). It is easy to see why people might think that cross-cultural intuitional diversity would be worrisome: if different groups of people have intuitions that are subtly sensitive to different sorts of factors, and if we are going to avoid epistemic relativism, then someone's intuitions have to turn out to be sensitive to the wrong things, or at least inappropriately sensitive to the right things, and the challenge is at least in part to determine whose intuitions to trust and when to trust them. Not everyone has been convinced, and lots of time and energy have gone into trying to explain this evidence away. Among the most powerful responses has been the suggestion that the results do not replicate. Nagel (2012), for example, points to a number of failed attempts to replicate the results of these cross-cultural studies, and argues that this should be unsurprising since we have good reason for thinking that our epistemic intuitions about knowledge are largely the product of a natural, mostly universal folk psychological capacity for "mindreading"—something that should render core epistemic intuitions highly stable across cultures. (For additional discussion of attempts to replicate these results, see Machery et al. 2016; Nagel 2013; Nagel et al. 2013; Stich 2013; Alexander and Weinberg 2014; Boyd and Nagel 2014; Kim and Yuan 2015; and Seyedsayamdost 2015).

The stakes in the debate over epistemic universalism are high; after all, part of what underwrites the traditional practice of pursuing epistemological questions through the lens of our epistemic intuitions is the thought that these intuitions are more or less universally shared. Given the high stakes and the unsettled experimental landscape, we wanted to take another look at epistemic universalism. Here, we present several new studies focusing on "salience effects"—the decreased tendency to attribute knowledge to someone when an unrealized possibility of error has been made salient in a given conversational context. These studies suggest a more complicated picture of epistemic universalism: there may be *structural universals*—universal epistemic parameters that influence epistemic intuitions—but that these parameters vary in such a way that epistemic intuitions, in either their strength or propositional content, can display patterns of genuine cross-cultural diversity.

2. SALIENCE AND KNOWLEDGE ATTRIBUTION

There has been a great deal of discussion in contemporary epistemology about whether standards for knowledge attribution depend on what possibilities have been made salient in a given conversational context. Some philosophers contend that they do, arguing that whether it is right to say that someone knows something depends in part on whether our conversational context includes mention of the possibility that she might be wrong (DeRose 1992; Cohen 1998). Other philosophers contend that they do not, arguing that what possibilities are mentioned in a given conversational context do not affect whether someone knows something (Hawthorne 2004; Williamson 2005). Both sides accept the idea that people are generally more willing to say that someone "knows" in conversational contexts that do not include mention of a possibility of error than in contexts that do. The debate has hinged on whether this is something that needs to be explained or explained away. Given this shared starting point, it was all the more striking that, when experimental philosophers began to study the relationship between folk knowledge attribution and discussion of unrealized possibilities of error, these studies seemed to suggest that this common starting point is wrong and that people are just as willing to attribute knowledge when an unrealized error possibility is salient as when it is not (for review, see Buckwalter 2012).

These early experimental studies focused on pairs of cases involving a married couple stopping by a bank on a Friday afternoon to deposit their paychecks. In both cases, the couple notices that the lines inside are quite long and the husband suggests coming back the following day to make the deposit, noting that he knows that the bank will be open on Saturday because he was there two Saturdays ago. One relevant difference between the two cases is that, in one of the cases but not the other, the wife mentions to her husband the possibility that he might be wrong, noting that banks sometimes change their hours. The common starting point to the philosophical debate outlined is that folk knowledge attributions will track this difference, and that people will be less inclined to say that the husband knows that the bank will be open on Saturday when the possibility of being wrong has been made salient than when that possibility goes unmentioned. The central question has been whether folk knowledge attributions are tracking changing standards for knowledge attribution or are displaying some kind of performance error.[1] But in these early empirical studies, mention of an error possibility did not affect people's willingness to attribute knowledge, suggesting that the debate rests on a mistake (Buckwalter 2010; Feltz and Zarpentine 2010; May et al. 2010).

However, several reasons warn against drawing this conclusion too quickly. One is that the early studies failed to make sufficiently salient the possibility that the bank will be closed on Saturday: merely mentioning a possibility doesn't necessarily make that possibility salient, particularly when that possibility seems strange or improbable (Schaffer and Knobe 2012). And it does seem that people are less inclined to say that the husband knows that the bank will be open on Saturday when more care is given to making the possibility that he might be wrong salient—for instance, by embedding it in the context of a personal anecdote (Schaffer and Knobe 2012; Buckwalter 2014). A second reason for wanting to tread carefully here is that the early experimental studies involved asking participants to make knowledge attributions rather than to evaluate knowledge attributions, and that when participants were asked to evaluate knowledge attributions they were asked to do so in situations where it was natural to

---

1. See for discussion of the difficulties involved in trying to determine precisely what is part of our conceptual competence and what is part of our conceptual performance.

deny knowledge (DeRose 2011). When adjustments are made to address these worries, it again seems that people are less inclined to say that the husband knows that the bank will be open on Saturday when the possibility of being wrong has been made salient than when the possibility goes unmentioned (Buckwalter 2014).

In light of this unsettled experimental landscape, Alexander et al. (2014) took another look at whether standards for knowledge attribution depend on what possibilities have been made salient in a given conversational context using a pair of cases discussed by Nagel (2010: 287):

> *"Plain Story*: John A. Doe is in a furniture store. He is looking at a bright red table under normal lighting conditions. He believes the table is red. Q: Does he know that the table is red?

> *More Detailed Story*: John B. Doe is in a furniture store. He is looking at a bright red table under normal lighting conditions. He believes that the table is red. However, a white table under red lighting conditions would look exactly the same to him, and he has not checked whether the lighting is normal, or whether there might be a red spotlight shining on the table. Q: Does he know that the table is red?"

Contrary to the results of the first set of experimental studies, but consistent with the results of more recent studies, Alexander et al. found that participants were significantly more willing to attribute knowledge in the plain story than in the more detailed story. Their results support the conclusion that the sensitivity of folk knowledge attributions to what possibilities have been made salient in a given conversational context can be explained in part in terms of *epistemic egocentrism*, or what is sometimes called the *curse of knowledge*, an egocentric bias to attribute our own mental states to other people (and sometimes our own future and past selves). In effect, what seems to be happening is that, when we are asked to consider a story in which someone is making a judgment and we are told that it is possible for her judgment to be wrong, we treat our own concerns as hers and penalize her for failing to appropriately respond to those concerns.

For present purposes, these results are important because the more recent experimental work on salience moves beyond traditional bank cases, where issues of salience get wrapped up with considerations about what is at stake for the story's protagonists, and this shows both that salience can act alone to influence the shape of folk knowledge attributions and that salience effects themselves are not tied to any idiosyncratic features of bank cases. Having said that, even these more recent empirical studies leave a number of questions unanswered. Salience effects have still only been studied across a limited variety of cases, and recent controversies over folk intuitions else-where in experimental epistemology (for instance, over Gettier intuitions; see the debate between Starmans and Friedman 2012, 2013 and Nagel et al. 2013a, 2013b) council against basing broad conclusions on a narrow exper-imental base. Are salience effects robust? Does mentioning an unrealized possibility of error merely cause us to *temper* our willingness to attribute knowledge or *withhold* knowledge attribution entirely?

2.1. Study 1: The Generality of Salience Effects, and the Possibility of Misunderstanding

To test the generality of salience effects, and to rule out the possibility that misunderstanding contributes to generating them, we took another look at whether attributions of knowledge depend on what possibilities have been made salient in a given conversational context using pairs of cases modeled on scenarios discussed by Dretske (1970, 1981) and Putnam (1975), to-gether with those used by Alexander et al. (2014).

Furniture Case, Normal Version: John A. Doe is in a furniture store. He is looking at a bright red table under normal lighting conditions. He believes the table is red.

Furniture Case, Skeptical Version: John B. Doe is in a furniture store. He is looking at a bright red table under normal lighting conditions. He believes the table is red. However, a white table under red lighting conditions would look *exactly* the same to him, and he has not checked whether the lighting is normal, or whether there might be a red spotlight shining on the table.

Bird Watching Case, Normal Version: John is an outdoor enthusiast. He hears on the radio that a very rare breed of bird, the tufted Siberian grebe, is roosting in the area and can be seen swimming on a nearby lake. The radio report describes the Siberian grebes as having black top feathers and white wing-tip feathers. John is an avid pho-tographer, so he drives out to the lake, sees a Siberian grebe, and takes a picture of it.

Bird Watching Case, Skeptical Version: John is an outdoor enthusiast. He hears on the radio that a very rare breed of bird, the tufted Siberian grebe, is roosting in the area and can be seen swimming on a nearby lake. The radio report describes the Siberian grebes as having black top feathers and white wing-tip feathers. John is an avid photographer, so he drives out to the lake, sees a Siberian grebe, and takes a picture of it. However, the radio report doesn't mention that gad-wall ducks are very common in the area, and that gadwall ducks are almost indistinguishable from Siberian grebes. John is not a birdwatcher, and if the bird had been a gadwall duck, he wouldn't have been able to tell the difference.

Zoo Case, Normal Version: John and his friend go to the zoo. As they walk around, they pause in front of an exhibit marked "Brazilian Jaguar Enclosure." John and his friend read about jaguars from the sign, and look out and see a jaguar sleeping on the branch of a tree in the enclosure.

Zoo Case, Skeptical Version: John and his friend go to the zoo. As they walk around, they pause in front of an exhibit marked "Brazilian Jaguar Enclosure." John and his friend read about jaguars from the sign, and look out and see a jaguar sleeping on the branch of a tree in the enclosure. However, African leopards look very much like Brazilian jaguars, and the signs in the zoo have recently been replaced by an inexperienced crew of workers. If a zoo official had accidentally switched the signs on their exhibits, John wouldn't have been able to tell the difference between the jaguar he did see and a leopard.

Arboretum Case, Normal Version: It is a beautiful Saturday early in spring, and John goes to the local arboretum to see the plants flowering and to enjoy the weather. As he walks around, he pauses in front of a yellow flowering bush. The sign next to the bush is labeled "Gorse." In his guidebook he reads that gorse is native to Scotland, and that it is a genus of flowering plants in the family Fabaceae.

Arboretum Case, Skeptical Version: It is a beautiful Saturday early in spring, and John goes to the local arboretum to see the plants flowering and to enjoy the weather. As he walks around, he pauses in front of a yellow flowering bush. The sign next to the bush is labeled "Gorse." In his guidebook he reads that gorse is native to Scotland, and that it is a genus of flowering plants in the family Fabaceae. However, nearby in the arboretum there is an exhibit of Asian forsythia that looks remarkably similar to gorse. If the arboretum staff had mixed up the signs, John wouldn't have been able to tell the difference between the gorse bush he did see and a forsythia bush.

Participants (N = 327, age M = 29, female = 32%) received one of the eight vignettes, and were asked to indicate the extent to which they agreed or disagreed with the claim that John knows the relevant proposition, together with a comprehension question and set of standard demographic questions.[2] Answers were assessed using a six-point Likert scale, with 1 = strongly disagree and 6 = strongly agree. As expected, knowledge

2. Thirty-six participants were excluded for failing the comprehension question or for possibly taking the survey more than once as indicated by repeat IP addresses. Exclusion criteria were decided prior to analysis, and do not affect our results: we still observed a significant difference ($t(322.1)$ = 13.43, $p < 0.001$, d = 1.51, a "large" effect) in knowledge attribution between the normal conditions (M = 4.95, SD = 1.22) and the skeptical conditions (M = 2.88, SD = 1.47). See note 4 for further discussion of the exclusion criteria.

attribution was higher in the normal conditions (n = 136, M = 5.06, SD = 1.13) than in the Skeptical conditions (n = 154, M = 2.91, SD = 1.61). A planned comparison showed that the difference was significant, $t(274)$ = 13.29, p < 0.001, d = 1.54, a "large" effect. We found this same pattern within each of our four pairs of conditions. Replicating Alexander et al. (2014), we found knowledge attribution was significantly higher ($t(40.6)$ = 5.34, p < 0.001, d = 1.57, a "large" effect) in the normal Furniture condition (n = 17, M = 5.18, SD = 0.88) than in the skeptical Furniture condition (n = 26, M = 3.23, SD = 1.51). The three new cases repeated this pattern: in the Zoo cases, knowledge attribution was significantly higher ($t(37.7)$ = 9.17, p < 0.001, d = 2.2, a "large" effect) in the normal condition (n = 47, M = 5.66, SD = 0.52) than in the Skeptical condition (n = 34, M = 2.94, SD = 1.67); in the Bird Watching cases, knowledge attribution was significantly higher ($t(78)$ = 8.16, p < 0.001, d = 1.92, a "large" effect) in the normal condition (n = 33, M = 4.52, SD = 1.00) than in the skeptical condition (n = 47, M = 2.13, SD = 1.45); in the Arboretum cases, knowledge attribution was significantly higher ($t(85)$ = 3.93, p < 0.001, d = 0.86, a "large" effect) in the normal condition (n = 40, M = 4.75, SD = 1.48) than in the skeptical condition (n = 47, M = 3.49, SD = 1.45). These results can be visualized as shown in figure 8.1.

2.2. Study 2: Balanced Cases

There is another possible explanation for the Alexander et al. (2014) results—namely, that salience effects are not the result of differences in epistemic intuition but are, instead, the result of processing differences owing to the differing lengths and complexities in the basic pairs that were used in those studies.[3] Perhaps shallow processing of the shorter normal cases encourages participants to attribute knowledge when they otherwise would not have, or perhaps the longer skeptical cases increase cognitive load to the point where participants withhold knowledge attribution when the might otherwise have attributed it. To test this possibility, we used a pair of cases balanced for word length and modeled on the Furniture cases used in the previous Alexander et al. studies.

Balanced Furniture, Normal Version: John A. Doe is in a furniture store, looking for a new table for his kitchen. He asks the salesperson to show him quite a wide

---

3. Thanks to John Turri for bringing this worry to our attention.

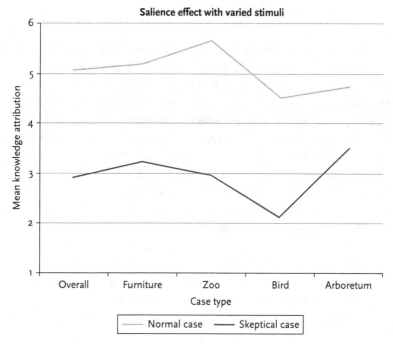

Figure 8.1 Salience effects with varied stimuli. The horizontal bars indicate the mean knowledge attribution by case type; the distance between the bars is an indication of the size of the effect.

variety of different options, which she does, showing him one new kitchen table at a time. At the moment, John is looking at a bright red table under normal lighting conditions. He believes the table is red.

Balanced Furniture, Skeptical Version: John B. Doe is in a furniture store, looking for a new table. The salesperson shows him several options. Currently, John is looking at a bright red table under normal lighting conditions. He believes the table is red. However, a white table under red lighting conditions would look the same to him, and he has not checked whether the lightning conditions are normal.

Participants ($N = 99$, age $M = 28.8$, female = 26%) were recruited via Amazon Mechanical Turk. They received one of the vignettes, and were then asked to indicate the extent to which they agreed or disagreed with the claim that John knows that the table is red together with a comprehension question and set of standard demographic questions.[4] Answers were assessed using

---

4. Two participants were eliminated from the analysis for ignoring basic instructions. Including their responses does not affect the results.

a six-point Likert scale with 1 = strongly disagree and 6 = strongly agree. Consistent with our expectations, we found that knowledge attribution was higher in the normal scenario ($n = 53$, $M = 4.96$, $SD = 1.43$) than in the skeptical scenario ($n = 44$, $M = 3.52$, $SD = 1.42$). An independent samples t-test showed the difference was significant ($t(95) = 4.95$, $p < 0.001$); moreover, the effect size ($d = 1.01$) was comparable to our previous results, suggesting that small differences in length and complexity do not materially influence knowledge attribution.

These two studies suggest that salience effects generalize across a variety of skeptical vignettes where conversational context involves mention of an unrealized possibility of error, and that salience effects are not due simply to some misunderstanding about the nature of the kinds of error possibilities that are frequently used in these kinds of skeptical vignettes. Comprehension checks were used to ensure that participants understood that the salient alternatives were *unrealized* and not merely *uneliminated*, and the fact that we find salience effects across a variety of skeptical cases suggests that salience effects do not depend on idiosyncratic content. Perhaps more important, the studies also suggest that salience effects do more than cause us simply to temper knowledge attribution, where we attribute knowledge but at a lower level or with less confidence; these studies suggest instead that salience effects cause us to genuinely withhold attribution of knowledge. This is important because the role that salience effects play in the diagnosis of skeptical arguments depends on their ability to cause us to withhold knowledge attribution rather than merely temper our willingness to attribute knowledge in skeptical vignettes. (It is worth mentioning that previous discussions of salience effects have tended to focus on whether they exist, rather than on their size or their ability to play this theoretical role in explaining the appeal of skeptical arguments from ignorance that many philosophers have suggested.) These studies reveal that 61% of participants withheld knowledge attribution in skeptical conditions, where this was operationalized as responding below the midpoint of 3.5 on a six-point Likert scale. Looking within each of the four pairs of conditions used in Study 1, we find large effect sizes, and in all but the Arboretum cases (45%), a majority of participants withhold knowledge attribution in the skeptical conditions. This shows that mentioning an unrealized possibility of error does not merely cause us to temper our willingness to attribute knowledge; it causes us to genuinely withhold knowledge attribution entirely. Indeed, given the size of these effects, it is surprising that Bank cases, which have been so persuasive in the philosophical literature, lead to such equivocal results when explored empirically.

3. SALIENCE AND CULTURE

Having found evidence for the generality and strength of salience effects, it is natural to wonder whether there might be cross-cultural differences in how salience effects influence folk knowledge attribution. One reason for wondering whether there is a relationship between culture and salience comes from philosophical work on culture and skeptical doubt. Some people have argued that philosophical concern with global skeptical arguments is both recent and Western. To take just two examples, Burnyeat (1982) argues that doubts about the external world skepticism are original to Descartes, and Hansen (1981) argues that some Chinese philosophical traditions lack a concern for global skepticism because they focus on kinds of pragmatic implications of knowledge that diminish the significance of the distinction between knowledge and belief. But other philosophers defend the idea that skepticism and its refutation are not merely Western preoccupations, in part because they think that the attraction of skeptical arguments is rooted in a core human conception of knowledge (see, e.g., Williams 1978).

Another reason for wondering whether there is a relationship between culture and salience comes from earlier work in experimental philosophy. Among other things, Weinberg et al. (2001) studied the relationship between salience and folk knowledge attribution, looking at the epistemic intuitions of American college students with different cultural backgrounds. They presented participants with a vignette modeled after Dretske's famous Zebra case, and found evidence of cross-cultural differences in how people responded to mention of the possibility that the zebra might be a cleverly painted mule; in particular, they found that students from South Asian cultural backgrounds were significantly more willing to say that the protagonist knew that the animal was a zebra than were students from Western European backgrounds. Nichols et al. (2003) think that this suggests cross-cultural variation in the epistemic intuitions grounding skeptical arguments, and that this variation might well be grounds for rethinking the importance of philosophical skepticism. While many recent attempts to replicate Weinberg et al.'s cross-cultural results have failed, the lone attempt to replicate their results about the relationships between culture, salience, and folk knowledge attribution were inconclusive, and suggest that further experimental work is needed. Seyedsayamdost (2015) did not find significant cross-cultural differences in how salience effects influence folk knowledge attribution when comparing participants from East Asian and Western European backgrounds, but he did not include enough participants from South Asian backgrounds to directly engage Weinberg et al.'s results, which focused on differences between participants from South Asian and Western European backgrounds. There are also methodological limits to studying cultural differences by proxy. Both Weinberg et al. and Seyedsayamdost use standard demographic instruments to determine cultural background, and while accurate as measures of affinity, they are nevertheless imprecise as a proxy for cultural involvement. Individuals and families differ in their efforts to preserve cultural connections, and while some might be relative newcomers, others might be many generations removed from their country of origin. Given the ambiguous nature of these results and the methodological concerns with previous studies, we decided to explore salience effects in situ and in the native languages of our participants.

3.1. Study 3: Culture, Salience, and Folk Knowledge Attribution

To test the relationship between culture and salience, participants ($N = 275$, age $M = 29.5$, female = 36%) were recruited from the United States ($n = 73$), India ($n = 95$), and China ($n = 88$) using Amazon Mechanical Turk (US and India) and www.zhubajie.com (China).[5] Participants in the United States and India received their studies in English, and participants in China received them in Mandarin.[6] Participants received one of Nagel's cases, and

5. Nineteen participants were excluded for failing comprehension questions or for disregarding basic instructions. Exclusion criteria were decided in advance of analysis. We instructed participants that they could only participate in the study once, so they would encounter a normal case or a skeptical case, but not both. This decision was based on prior work suggesting that if participants encountered both they might interpret experimenters as intending a contrast between the two cases, and attempt to accommodate that expectation (see Alexander et al. 2007 for a discussion of order effects; see Hansen and Chemla (2013) for empirical evidence that Bank cases can produce salience effects when there is an explicit contrast between a normal and skeptical version). Our worry, then, was that allowing repeated participation would bias our studies *toward* finding salience effects. Prior experience with American MTurk users suggested that some individuals do respond to surveys repeatedly using different browsers and different account IDs. Examining IP addresses, we found a number of participants retook the test using a different browser. These repeat participants, along with those who failed the attention checks, were excluded from the final analysis. Doing so alters some of our findings. We still observe salience effects in each culture: US normal ($M = 5.23$, $SD = 1.17$), US skeptical ($M = 3.14$, $SD = 1.81$), $t(60.6) = 5.96$, $p < 0.001$; China normal ($M = 4.40$, $SD = 0.63$), China skeptical ($M = 2.91$, $SD = 1.80$), $t(90) = 4.05$, $p < 0.001$; India normal ($M = 4.95$, $SD = 1.1$), India skeptical ($M = 3.71$, $SD = 1.63$), $t(86.7) = 4.56$, $p < 0.001$. However, we no longer find an interaction between culture and case type on knowledge attribution, $F[2, 269] = 1.77$, $p = 0.17$. Because this result concerns one of the crucial questions of this chapter, we take up this question again in the next studies.
6. All translations were prepared by two native speakers, and differences were resolved in consultation with the authors. Stimulus materials are available upon request.

were asked to indicate the extent to which they agreed or disagreed with the claim that John knows that the table is red, together with a comprehension question and set of standard demographic questions. Answers were assessed using a six-point Likert scale, with 1 = strongly disagree and 6 = strongly agree. The results were striking.

A two-way ANOVA revealed a main effect for scenario type on knowledge attribution, $F[1, 250] = 66.36$, $p < 0.001$, $\eta^2 = 0.210$ (a "medium" to "large" effect). We also found evidence of salience effects in all three cultural conditions. Participants from the United States were more inclined to attribute knowledge in the normal condition ($n = 38$, $M = 5.32$, $SD = 1.07$) than in the skeptical condition ($n = 35$, $M = 3.11$, $SD = 1.83$). A planned comparison showed a significant difference between conditions $F[1, 71] = 40.25$, $p < 0.001$, and a "large" effect size (Cohen's $d = 1.43$). Participants from China were also more inclined to attribute knowledge in the normal condition ($n = 55$, $M = 4.44$, $SD = 1.64$) than in the skeptical condition ($n = 33$, $M = 2.82$, $SD = 1.74$). A planned comparison showed a significant difference between conditions $F [1, 86] = 19.16$, $p < 0.001$, and a "large" effect size (Cohen's $d = 0.96$). And, participants from India were also more inclined to attribute knowledge in the normal condition ($n = 53$, $M = 4.92$, $SD = 1.11$) than the skeptical condition ($n = 42$, $M = 4.10$, $SD = 1.53$). A planned comparison showed a significant difference between conditions $F [1, 93] = 9.41$, $p < 0.003$, and a "medium" effect size (Cohen's $d = 0.61$). There was also a significant main effect of culture on knowledge attribution, $F[2, 250] = 7.83$, $p < 0.001$, $\eta^2 = 0.06$. Participants from India tended to attribute knowledge at a higher level ($M = 4.56$, $SD = 1.37$) than either those from the United States ($M = 4.26$, $SD = 1.84$) or China ($M = 3.83$, $SD = 1.84$). Post-hoc tests revealed that the only significant difference in means is between China and India ($p < 0.01$).

Most important, there was a significant interaction effect between culture and case type on knowledge attribution, $F[2, 250] = 4.44$, $p < 0.015$, $\eta^2 = 0.03$. This suggests that while participants from China, the United States, and India all exhibited salience effects, participants from different cultures nevertheless respond differently when error possibilities are introduced into the conversational context. One plausible explanation for this result is that the mean difference between normal and skeptical conditions in India is much smaller than in either the United States or China; in other words, people from India are more likely to attribute knowledge when the conversational contexts includes the possibility that the protagonist is wrong than are people from either the United States or China. In order to examine this possibility, we ran a series of two-way ANOVAs. There was no significant interaction between the United States and China ($F[1, 157] = 1.30$,

p = 0.256), while there was a marginally significant interaction between China and India ($F[1, 179]$ = 3.04, p = 0.083, η^2= 0.02) and a significant interaction between the United States and India ($F[1, 164]$ = 10.05, p = 0.002, η^2= 0.06). These results can be visualized as shown in figure 8.2.

Putting all of this together, here's what we found. We found salience effects across cultures, but also found evidence of important differences in the magnitude of the salience effect between cultures. Both of these results are philosophically important. As we've already noted, salience effects play an important role in diagnosing the appeal of radical skepticism, and these findings further support the conclusion that salience effects are genuine. Moreover, finding that unrealized error possibilities have somewhat similar effects on folk intuitions about knowledge attribution in three largely disparate cultures suggests they are the product of a shared mechanism—what we might call a shared *epistemic parameter*. (For additional discussion of this kind of inference from cross-cultural agreement to the existence of core epistemic parameters, see Machery et al., in press.) A natural question to ask, given that there is evidence of both similarity and difference, is what this means for *epistemic universalism*, at least with respect to folk knowledge attribution. Here the picture becomes more complicated, since we also found important differences in the magnitude of salience effects

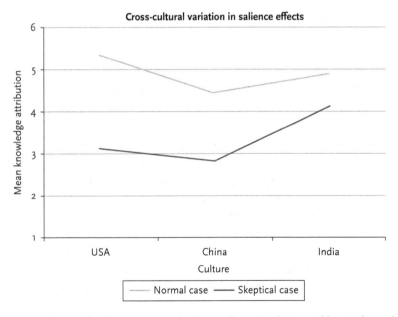

Figure 8.2 Cross-cultural comparison of salience effects. The horizontal bars indicate the mean knowledge attribution by culture; the distance between the bars is an indication of the size of the effect

across culture. As we've noted earlier, one of the most important findings from Studies 1 and 2 is the evidence that salience effects do more than merely cause us to temper knowledge attribution; it seems like salience effects cause us to genuinely withhold attribution of knowledge. But the results from Study 3 suggest that this might not be true across different cultures. Looking within cultural conditions, we find that a majority of both American (60%) and Chinese (67%) participants withhold knowledge attribution in the skeptical condition, where this is again operationalized as responding below the theoretical midpoint of 3.5 on a six-point Likert scale. By contrast, only a minority of Indian participants (31%) withhold knowledge attribution in the skeptical condition. Comparing knowledge attribution between normal and skeptical conditions points to the same result: the size of salience effects seem to be largest in the United States, somewhat smaller in China, and smaller still in India. Why might this be important? Salience effects are not an all-or-nothing phenomenon. As the results from Study 1 show, and past work on Bank cases can attest, the force of salience effects vary from case to case and person to person. This suggests that the force of salience effects can vary by degree, and if that force varies by culture, then it is possible that cultures differ in their susceptibility to skeptical doubts.

3.2. Study 4: Culture, Salience, and Folk Knowledge Attribution, Version 2.0

The interaction between culture and case type on knowledge attribution observed in Study 3 was in part driven by the results of Indian participants, who tended generally to be more willing to attribute knowledge across conditions. One worry about this study is that it involves surveying Indian participants in English. Some studies of survey response style suggest that participants responding in a second language tend to agree more with survey items than they otherwise would when responding in a home language (Harzing 2006). Although English is one of the national languages of India, fluency varies from region to region, and it is possible that some of the Indian participants were uncomfortable with the language of the study. Another reason to worry about Study 3, and one we by no means wish to minimize given recent concerns over experimental replication, is that the observed interaction between culture and case type was no longer significant when responses from repeat participants and comprehension failures are included (see note 5). While remaining open to the possibility of Type I error, we believe that the most likely explanation, given the observed effect size, is that the study simply did not have the necessary power to overcome the added noise of the excluded data.

To test each of these possibilities, and to further examine the generality of salience effects, we translated the cases used in Study 1 into Mandarin and into Standard Hindi. Participants (N = 599, age M = 28.6, female = 40%) were recruited from India (n = 181) using Amazon Mechanical Turk, and from China (n = 228) using www.zhubajie.com.[7] We used a randomizer on the data collected in the United States in Study 1 to produce a pool of approximately the same size (n = 190). Participants received one of the vignettes and were asked to indicate the extent to which they agreed or disagreed with the claim that John knows the relevant proposition, together with two comprehension questions and set of standard demographic questions. Answers were assessed using a six-point Likert scale, with 1 = strongly disagree and 6 = strongly agree.

The results support the findings of Study 3. A two-way ANOVA revealed a main effect for scenario type on knowledge attribution, $F[1, 426]$ = 62.70, $p < 0.001$, η^2 = 0.13 (a "medium" effect). As before, we found strong evidence for salience effects in all three cultures. Participants from the United States were more inclined to attribute knowledge in the normal condition (n = 82, M = 5.09, SD = 0.98) than in the skeptical condition (n = 79, M = 3.05, SD = 1.58). A planned comparison showed a significant difference between conditions $F[1, 159]$ = 95.60, $p < 0.001$, and a "large" effect (Cohen's

---

7. A total of 167 responses were excluded for failing a comprehension question or for repeated participation using different account IDs. This study used the same exclusion criteria as the previous study. Reanalysis with the excluded responses does not alter the observed results. A two-way ANOVA on knowledge attribution revealed main effects for culture ($F[2, 593]$ = 7.98, $p < 0.001$, η^2 = 0.03), and for case type ($F[1, 593]$ = 77.04, $p < 0.001$, η^2 = 0.12). Importantly, incorporating the excluded dated does not alter the significant interaction between culture and case type on knowledge attribution ($F[2, 593]$ = 9.51, $p < 0.001$, η^2 = 0.03). This suggests that Study 3 lacked the necessary power (only 0.37 compared to 0.98 in Study 2) to detect the interaction, given the noise from the exclusions. Although understandable under the circumstance, the 27% exclusion rate does deserve some discussion. Half the excluded responses (20 from the US, 24 from India, and 41 from China) were repeat responses from approximately 20 individuals. A further third of the exclusions (9 from the US, 16 from India, and 26 from China) failed an additional attention check (not used in Study 2) that was added to determine whether participants understood that the error possibility was unrealized. Because failure of this check indicates participants believed the error possibility was actual, including these results would create the appearance that salience effects are larger than they are in fact; mean knowledge attribution for the group bears this out (n = 51, M = 2.8, SD = 1.43). Nevertheless, reanalysis with the exclusions presents the same general pattern of results as for Study 3: salience effects are largest among the US sample (a mean difference in knowledge attribution between cases of 1.94), smaller among Chinese participants (a mean difference of 0.87), and smallest among Indian participants (a mean difference of 0.61).

$d = 1.55$) comparable to the one observed in Study 3. Participants from China were also more inclined to attribute knowledge in the normal condition ($n = 97$, $M = 4.10$, $SD = 1.85$) than in the skeptical condition ($n = 57$, $M = 3.49$, $SD = 1.74$). A planned comparison showed a significant difference between conditions $F [1, 152] = 4.11$, $p < 0.05$, and a "small" effect size (Cohen's $d = 0.34$). Chinese participants in this study ascribed knowledge in the skeptical scenario at a much higher level than in the previous study ($M = 2.82$), leading to the smaller effect size. This may be partially explained by the high number of participants in the skeptical condition that failed an added attention check ($n = 26$) designed to assure that participants understood the protagonist's belief was true. Finally, Indian participants attributed knowledge at a higher level in the normal condition ($n = 66$, $M = 4.77$, $SD = 1.43$) than in the skeptical condition ($n = 51$, $M = 3.75$, $SD = 1.70$). A planned comparison showed a significant difference between conditions $F [1, 115] = 12.6$, $p < 0.001$, and a "medium" effect ($d = 0.65$) comparable to the one observed in Study 3. As before, and again unlike participants from the United States or China, in the skeptical scenario a majority of Indian participants attributed knowledge to the agent (55%), and mean knowledge attribution was above the midline. There was also a marginally significant main effect for culture on knowledge attribution, $F[2, 426] = 2.85$, $p = 0.059$. As before, participants from India attributed knowledge at the highest level ($M = 4.32$, $SD = 1.63$) largely because of higher attribution levels in the skeptical conditions. Americans attributed knowledge at somewhat lower level ($M = 4.09$, $SD = 1.66$), and participants from China did so at the lowest level ($M = 3.88$, $SD = 1.72$).

Most important, for present purposes, and as we found in Study 3, there was a significant interaction between culture and scenario type on knowledge attribution, $F[2, 426] = 8.28$, $p < 0.001$, $\eta^2 = 0.04$ (a "small" effect). The result supports our earlier conclusion that the strength of salience effects varies by culture. To further explore the interaction, we ran a series of two-way ANOVAs. Comparing US and Chinese participants we found a significant interaction between case type and culture ($F[1, 311] = 15.48$, $p < 0.001$, $\eta^2 = 0.05$) but no main effect on culture ($F[1, 311] = 2.24$, $p = 0.135$). This suggests that the difference between US and Chinese participants is primarily a function of the size of salience effects. Comparing Indian and Chinese participants, there was no significant interaction between culture and case type ($F[1, 267] = 0.95$, $p = 0.33$), but a modestly significant difference for culture ($F[1, 267] = 4.70$, $p = 0.03$, $\eta^2 = 0.17$). Finally, there was a significant interaction between culture and case type for US and Indian participants ($F[1, 274] = 8.45$, $p < 0.005$, $\eta^2 = 0.03$), but no main effect on culture ($F[1, 274] = 1.22$, $p = 0.27$). This also is consistent with the hypothesis that

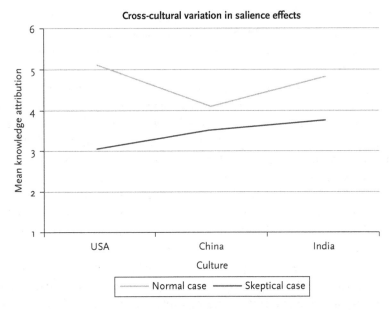

Figure 8.3 Cross-cultural comparison of salience effects. The horizontal bars indicate the mean knowledge attribution by culture; the distance between the bars is an indication of the size of the effect

salience effects are weaker for participants from India.[8] These results can be visualized as shown in figure 8.3.

There are a number of things worth noting here. The first is that these results replicate the findings of Study 3, particularly the observed inter- action between culture and case type on knowledge attribution, some- thing that further strengthens the conclusion that salience effects vary in strength across culture. The second thing worth noting is that the results of surveying Indian participants in Hindi are largely the same as those from Study 3 using English; this suggests that a feeling of disfluency was not leading to an acquiescence bias, and thereby driving the observed in- teraction effect. We also conducted one post-hoc analysis to further guard against the influence of known survey response-style differences. In partic- ular, US survey takers are sometimes associated with an *extreme response style* (ERS)—the tendency to use only the endpoints of a scale—while

8. Because some of the results appeared non-normal, we followed the recommen- dation of Conover (1999, 419) and confirmed the result by rerunning the two-way ANOVA using rank-transformed knowledge attribution as a DV. The procedure does not materially alter the mainline analyses, and specifically we still observe an inter- action between culture and case type on knowledge attribution ($F[2, 426] = 7.18$, $p < 0.001$).

East Asian survey takers are sometimes associated with a *mild response style*—the tendency to avoid the endpoints of a scale (See Chen et al. 1995, Harzing 2006). It is possible to worry that an ERS led participants from the United States to use the endpoints at a higher rate, thereby contributing to larger salience effects than we found among Chinese or Indian participants. To examine this possibility, we compared the use of endpoints among the participants, which is a common procedure for detecting ERS (for procedure, see Van Vaerenbergh and Thomas 2013; Reynolds and Smith 2010). If an American ERS were driving the results, we'd expect participants from the United States to use the endpoints at a higher rate than either Chinese or Indian participants. Looking at the data in Study 4, we don't see this pattern: Mandarin speakers used the endpoints at the highest rate (44%), while English speakers (38%) and Hindi speakers (36%) did so at approximately the same rate.[9] The final thing worth mentioning here is that, by finding salience effects using a broader array of stimulus materials, these results both extend the results of Study 1 and support the conclusion that differences in salience effects across cultures are not the result of culture-specific responses to the content of the stimulus materials.

How do salience effects differ across cultures? Stated simply, salience effects are much larger in the United States than in either India or China (see figure 8.3). One way to think about this result is in terms of relative effect size: introducing an unrealized error possibility had a very large effect on knowledge attribution among Americans in both studies (S3: $d = 1.55$; S4: $d = 1.43$), but had a smaller effect, comparatively speaking,

---

9. In a recent cross-cultural study, Machery et al. (in press) found that while a majority of Indian participants attribute knowledge in Gettier cases when asked "Does X know P" (yes/no), the same participants tended to deny knowledge when they were next asked "Which better describes X's situation" (X knows that P / X feels like she knows P, but she doesn't actually know P). Machery et al. 2016 attribute the difference to the fact that the most common translation of "to know" in Bengali, *jáná*, does not always distinguish knowledge from belief, and that the second question helped participants tacitly resolve the ambiguity. The most common translation of "to know" in Hindi, the language of our studies, is *jānanā*, which shares a common Sanskrit root with the Bengali term. Might this explain the greater tendency to attribute knowledge in skeptical cases among Indian participants? The possibility deserves careful further study. We would make two observations in this respect. The first is that we observed the same pattern of results when surveying Indian participants in English. This suggests that whatever differences there are in marking the distinction between knowledge and belief, they occur at the level of culture, not language. Consequently, a difference in marking this distinction may in fact be a kind of cross-cultural variation that deserves notice. The second is that in subsequent empirical studies it might be useful to only use a second form of question in surveying participants. Asking repeatedly whether a participant thinks an agent knows that P may lead to a form of directional accommodation, where the participants guess that there is a desired response.

on Chinese (S3: d = 0.96; S4: d = 0.34) and Indian participants (S3: d = 0.61; S4: d = 0.65). For the purposes of considering their philosophical significance, it is also useful to look at absolute levels of knowledge attribution and denial in the skeptical conditions. We find that 61% of US participants denied the protagonist knew the relevant proposition in the skeptical conditions, as compared with 54% of Chinese participants and only 45% of Indian participants. These results support the conclusion that there is a shared epistemic parameter that influences salience effects across the studied cultures, and further supports the conclusion that this parameter can vary in its sensitivity across cultures.

4. SALIENCE, CERTAINTY, AND CULTURE

Let's pause for a moment to take stock of where we are at this point. The first two studies suggest that salience effects are genuine (they do not depend on participant misunderstanding), are robust (they can be found across a diverse set of skeptical vignettes), and do not merely cause us to temper our willingness to attribute knowledge (they cause us to genuinely withhold knowledge attribution altogether). The second two studies suggest that salience effects are culturally universal, but that the strength of salience effects is not. One interesting question is why not, and one way to try to answer this question would be to identify the mechanism response for salience effects, and then look for culture differences related to the way that mechanism operates. But what mechanism is responsible for salience effects in folk knowledge attribution?

There are actually a number of competing accounts in the philosophical literature. Hawthorne (2004) and Williamson (2005) point to the availability heuristic in attempting to explain away salience effects, and Gerken (2011) suggests that they can be explained away in terms of an epistemic focal bias, while Nagel (2010) argues that they arise out of epistemic egocentrism (a position supported by the empirical results of Alexander et al., 2014). Among more linguistically oriented theories, Schaffer (2005) argues that contrast effects give rise to salience effects; Hazlett (2009) claims that they are the product of pragmatic errors of interpretation; and Malcolm (1952) sees them as emerging out of an ambiguity in "know" between a strong and weak sense. And then there are fallibilists like Cohen (1999) and DeRose (2009), who take salience effects to rest on shifting standards of warrant or justification, and infallibilists like Lewis (1996), who take them to arise out of shifting standards concerning which error possibilities are relevant and in need of elimination in a particular context.

With so many compelling possibilities defended by so many smart philosophers, it might seem that we are heading straight for a deadlock. The way out, then, is to recognize that these accounts are, in the first instance, explanations of a psychological phenomenon with possible epistemological import. Salience effects with respect to knowledge attribution arise when there is a decreased tendency to attribute knowledge after mention of an unrealized, uneliminated possibility of error, and an accurate epistemological theory of about the nature of salience effects on folk knowledge attribution should include the merits of a good psychological theory. Chief among these is *empirical adequacy*, in the sense that the philosophical story should manage to account for the observed results. The studies reported here indicate that these results include not only the finding that salience effects exist for people from different cultural backgrounds and across a range of different skeptical vignettes but also that they differ in magnitude across certain cultures. The upshot is that if any philosophical proposal, whether currently in the literature or not, can account for these two results, then that should count in its favor. But where to look for this proposal? Inspired by context-sensitive infallibilist proposals made by Peter Unger (1975) and David Lewis (1979, 1996), we decided to explore the possibility that salience effects with respect to knowledge are in part driven by a salience effect on certainty, where the impact that mention of unrealized possibilities of error on attributions of certainty can vary across cultures.

4.1. Study 5: Salience, Certainty, and Folk Knowledge Attribution

In light of this, we designed a study to explore whether culture moderates judgments of subjective certainty when error possibilities are salient, and whether these judgments have a further effect on folk attributions of knowledge. More specifically, we designed a study to explore the following hypotheses:

H1: There is an indirect effect of vignette type (normal or skeptical) on knowledge attributions via certainty attributions. In other words, certainty attributions mediate a relation between vignette type and knowledge attributions.

H2: There is an interaction between vignette type and nationality on certainty attributions. Otherwise put, the nationality of the attributor moderates a relation between vignette type and certainty attributions. The negative impact that mention of an unrealized possibility of error has on certainty attributions (relative to there being no such mention) will vary in magnitude according to the nationality of the attributor, with the magnitude greatest among Americans.

In view of the fact that when X has an indirect effect on Y via M with W moderating the relation between X and M, it follows that W moderates the indirect effect of X on Y (Hayes 2013), we can combine H1 and H2, giving us:

H3: There is an indirect relation between vignette type and knowledge attributions via certainty attributions that is moderated by nationality. The indirect relation is largest for American participants.

Participants (N = 457; age M = 29.2, female = 40%) were recruited from the United States (n = 165) and India (n = 126) using Amazon Mechanical Turk, and from China (n = 166) using www.zhubajie.com.[10] Participants received either the normal or the skeptical Furniture case used in previous studies. Americans received their materials in English, Indians in standard Hindi, and Chinese in Mandarin using simplified Chinese characters. After reading the vignette, in addition to being asked to indicate the extent to which they agreed or disagreed with the claim that John *knows* that the table is red, participants were asked to indicate the extent to which they agreed or disagreed with the claim that John can be *certain* that the table is red, together with two comprehension questions and a set of standard demographic questions. Answers were assessed using a six-point Likert scale, with 1 = strongly disagree and 6 = strongly agree. To test H1, H2, and H3, we used the PROCESS macro for SPSS (Hayes 2013).

We began with a simple mediation analysis to test H1, focusing on the question of whether the responses gathered from our participants were consistent with vignette type (VT) exerting an indirect effect on attributions of knowledge (KA) through attributions of certainty (CA). Based on the results of this analysis, there is reason to think that VT did indirectly influence KA via CA. As can be seen in figure 8.4, participants who received the skeptical vignette were less inclined to say that John can be certain that the table is red (a = -1.053), and their attributions of certainty positively predicted their attributions of knowledge while controlling for any direct influence of vignette type on attributions of knowledge (b = 0.531). A 95% bias-corrected bootstrap confidence interval for the indirect effect (ab = -0.559), based on 1,000 bootstrap samples, was entirely below zero (-0.339

10. Eighty-nine participants were excluded for failing comprehension questions or disregarding basic instructions: the same exclusion criteria of previous studies. Including them in the simple mediation, moderation, and moderated mediation analyses generated the same pattern of results. We do not report them since it would take up too much space to do so. The results of these analysis are available upon request.

Panel A: R^2 Increase due to interactions

	R^2 Change	F	p
VT×D_1	0.017	10.17	0.0015
VT×D_2	0.018	10.83	0.0011
Both	0.024	7.16	0.0009

Panel B: Conditional effects of vignette type on certainty attributions

	Effect (SE)	t	p
Chinese	−0.68 (0.24)	−2.78	0.0056
Indians	−0.56 (0.28)	−1.96	0.0503
Americans	−1.78 (0.25)	−7.26	<0.0001

Figure 8.4 Results of moderation analysis

to -0.761), which is consistent with H1, or there being an indirect effect of vignette type on knowledge attributions via certainty attributions.

Next, to test whether the responses gathered from our participants were consistent with the hypothesis that nationality moderates an effect of vignette type on attributions of certainty (H2), we conducted a moderation analysis. Since the proposed moderator—nationality—was a categorical variable with three levels, following the procedure described in Hayes (2015), we recoded nationality into two dummy variables: D_1 and D_2. Chinese participants were captured by the pattern $D_1 = 1$ and $D_2 = 0$, Indian participants by $D_1 = 0$ and $D_2 = 1$, and US participants by $D_1 = 0$ and $D_2 = 0$. With this coding structure in place, we tested H2 by estimating a regression model predicting certainty attributions from vignette type (VT), D_1, D_2, and their products (VT×D_1 and VT×D_2). The most pertinent results for the test of H2 are the reported in table 8.1. In Panel A, the row labeled "Both" reports the results of a test of the null hypothesis that nationality does not moderate an effect of vignette type on attributions of certainty (see Hayes 2015). That hypothesis can be rejected: $F(2, 451) = 7.163, p = 0.0009$. In other words, the responses provided by our participants are consistent with the first part of H2, that nationality moderates an effect of vignette type on attributions of certainty. Moreover, if we probe the moderation effect by estimating the conditional effect of vignette type on certainty attributions among US, Chinese, and Indian participants (see Panel B of table 8.1), it appears that the negative effect that mention of an unrealized possibility of error has on certainty attributions (relative to there being no such mention) is largest among Americans, which is consistent with the second part of H2.

Table 8.1 RESULTS OF MODERATION
ANALYSIS

Panel A: R^2 Increase Due to Interactions

	R^2 Change	F	p
VT×D_1	0.017	10.17	0.0015
VT×D_2	0.018	10.83	0.0011
Both	0.024	7.16	0.0009

Panel B: Conditional Effects of Vignette Type on Certainty Attributions

	Effect (SE)	t	p
Chinese	−0.68 (0.24)	−2.78	0.0056
Indians	−0.56 (0.28)	−1.96	0.0503
Americans	−1.78 (0.25)	−7.26	<0.0001

The final analysis that we conducted was a moderated mediation analysis. The simple mediation analysis provided reason to think that vignette type has an indirect effect on knowledge attributions through certainty attributions. The moderation analysis gives us reason to think that nationality moderates an effect of vignette type on certainty attributions. All together, there is thus reason to think that the mediation is moderated, that there is an indirect effect of vignette type on knowledge attributions through certainty attributions that depends on the nationality of the attributor. When this occurs, Preacher et al. (2007) suggest an estimation of conditional indirect effects (i.e., the value of the indirect effect conditioned on values of the moderator), as well as testing whether these indirect effects significantly differ from zero. As can be seen by examining table 8.2, the 95% bias-corrected bootstrap confidence intervals for the conditional indirect effects of vignette type on knowledge attributions based on 1,000 bootstrap samples are entirely below zero for each of the nationalities, and hence are statistically significant for each of them. Also observe that the conditional indirect effect is largest among Americans. These results support H3.

The moderated mediation model developed here suggests subjective certainty plays a role in determining whether people are willing to attribute knowledge when error possibilities have been made salient; as people become less certain that p, they become less willing to attribution knowledge that p to someone else. These results support a picture with important

Table 8.2 CONDITIONAL INDIRECT EFFECTS
OF VIGNETTE TYPE ON KNOWLEDGE
ATTRIBUTIONS

| | | 95% Bias-corrected bootstrap confidence interval | |
	Effect (SE)	Lower	Upper
Chinese	−0.36 (0.14)	−0.66	−0.10
Indians	−0.29 (0.12)	−0.57	−0.06
Americans	−0.94 (0.15)	−1.25	−0.66

Note: 1,000 bootstrap samples.

similarities to the context-sensitive infallibilism of Lewis (1996). On the picture we advocate, salience of error acts on our sense of subjective certainty to influence folk knowledge attribution, and the strength of this interaction is influenced by culture. The results also suggest an interesting complication for our understanding of folk knowledge attribution by challenging the orthodox view that knowledge does not require certainty, a normative move that was thought necessary to block the most thoroughgoing kinds of philosophical skepticism. Whatever normative merits epistemic fallibilism might have, these results suggest that it seems to run up against a robust picture of the psychology involved in folk knowledge attribution. In the present context, what is perhaps most interesting is that they suggest that the influence that subjective certainty has on the relationship between salience and folk knowledge attribution changes in magnitude from one culture to the next, something that suggests that folk epistemic intuitions might display interesting patterns of cultural difference even when there are widespread cultural similarities to the folk epistemic intuitions themselves.

5. CONCLUSION

The studies presented here provide growing support for the idea that salience effects influence folk knowledge attribution, and suggest that while salience effects influence folk knowledge attribution across cultures, the influence that salience effects have on folk knowledge attribution changes in magnitude from one culture to the next. This supports a rather more complicated and interesting picture of the relationship between cultural background and folk epistemic intuitions than has been at stake in the current debate over epistemic universalism. Since both sides to that debate agree that folk epistemic intuitions have their basic root in some kind of psychological capacity that is either innate (Machery et al., in press) or otherwise naturally constrained in such a way that leads to universal expression (Nagel 2013), the debate about epistemic universalism has hinged on whether this universal psychological capacity permits of any interesting patterns of cultural diversity. Our studies suggest that the influence that subjective certainty has on the relationship between salience and folk knowledge attribution changes in magnitude from one culture to the next, something that supports the idea that there are shared psychological mechanisms that influence folk epistemic intuitions, but that the function of these mechanisms can vary in such a way that certain folk epistemic intuitions display patterns of genuine cross-cultural diversity. We hope that this important discovery can move us past the old model of thinking about epistemic universalism, where it was treated as an all-or-nothing proposal, and toward a model of thinking about epistemic universalism that allows for interesting patterns similarity *and* difference. We think that this is a way toward real progress in our understanding of the manner in which culture influences philosophical cognition.

ACKNOWLEDGMENTS

We are grateful to Steven Gross, Divya Gupta, Jonathon Hricko, Barry Lam, Wenjuan Ma, Edouard Machery, Jennifer Nagel, Shaun Nichols, Shane Reuter, Chitra Venkataramani, Jonathan Weinberg, and audiences at the Epistemology for the Rest of the World Conference in Tokyo, the Society for Philosophy and Psychology in Vancouver, the Central Division Meeting of the APA in St. Louis, and the Buffalo Experimental Philosophy Conference for valuable input during the project. Support for some of the work included here was provided by the Fuller Theological Seminary/Thrive Center in concert with the John Templeton Foundation and by the Center for Philosophy of Science at the University of Pittsburgh.

REFERENCES

Alexander, Joshua. (2012). *Experimental Philosophy: An Introduction.* Cambridge, UK: Polity Press.
Alexander, Joshua, Chad Gonnerman, and John Waterman. (2014). "Salience and Epistemic Egocentrism: An Empirical Study." In *Advances in Experimental Epistemology,* ed. James Beebe, 97–118. New York, NY: Continuum Press.

Alexander, Joshua, Ronald Mallon, and Jonathan Weinberg. (2010). "Accentuate the Negative." *Review of Philosophy and Psychology* 1(2): 297–314.

Alexander, Joshua, and Jonathan Weinberg. (2007). "Analytic Epistemology and Experimental Philosophy." *Philosophy Compass* 2(1): 56–80.

Alexander, Joshua, and Jonathan Weinberg. (2014). "The 'Unreliability' of Epistemic Intuitions." In *Current Controversies in Experimental Philosophy*, ed. Elizabeth O'Neill and Edouard Machery, 128–145. New York, NY: Routledge.

Boyd, Kenneth, and Jennifer Nagel. (2014). "The Reliability of Epistemic Intuitions." In *Current Controversies in Experimental Philosophy*, ed. Elizabeth O'Neill and Edouard Machery, 109–127. New York, NY: Routledge.

Buckwalter, Wesley. (2010). "Knowledge Isn't Closed on Saturday." *Review of Philosophy and Psychology* 1: 395–406.

Buckwalter, Wesley. (2012). "Non-traditional Factors in Judgments about Knowledge." *Philosophy Compass* 7: 278–289.

Buckwalter, Wesley. (2014). "The Mysteries of Stakes and Error in Ascriber Intuitions." In *Advances in Experimental Epistemology*, ed. James Beebe, 145–174. New York, NY: Continuum Press.

Burnyeat, Miles. (1982). "Idealism and Greek Philosophy: What Descartes Saw and Berkeley Missed." *Philosophical Review* 91: 3–40.

Chen, Chaunsheng, Shin-Ying Lee, and Harold Stevenson. (1995). "Response Style and Cross-cultural Comparisons of Rating Scales Among East Asian and North American Students." *Psychology Science* 6: 170–175.

Cohen, Stewart. (1998). "Contextualist Solutions to Epistemological Puzzles: Skepticism, Gettier, and the Lottery." *Australasian Journal of Philosophy* 76: 289–306.

Cohen, Stewart. (1999). "Contextualism, Skepticism, and the Structure of Reasons." *Nous* 33: 57–89.

Conover, W. J. (1999). *Practical Nonparametric Statistics*, 3rd ed. New York: John Wiley.

DeRose, Keith. (1992). "Contextualism and Knowledge Attributions." *Philosophy and Phenomenological Research* 52: 172–198.

DeRose, Keith. (2009). *The Case for Contextualism: Knowledge, Skepticism, and Context*, Vol. 1. New York, NY: Oxford University Press.

DeRose, Keith. (2011). "Contextualism, Contrastivism, and X-Phi Surveys." *Philosophical Studies* 56: 81–110.

Dretske, Fred. (1970). "Epistemic Operators." *Journal of Philosophy* 67: 1007–1023.

Dretske, Fred. (1981). "The Pragmatic Dimension of Knowledge." *Philosophical Studies* 40: 363–378.

Feltz, Adam, and Chris Zarpentine. (2010). "Do You Know More When It Matters Less?" *Philosophical Psychology* 23: 683–706.

Gerken, Mikkel. (2011). "Epistemic Focal Bias." *Australasian Journal of Philosophy* 91: 41–61.

Hansen, Chad. (1981). "Linguistic Skepticism in the *Lao Tzu*." *Philosophy East and West* 31: 321–336.

Hansen, Nat, and Emmanuel Chemla. (2013). "Experimenting on Contextualism." *Mind and Language* 28: 286–321.

Harzing, Anne-Wil. (2006). "Response Styles in Cross-national Survey Research: A 26-Country Study." *International Journal of Cross-Cultural Management* 6: 243–266.

Hawthorne, John. (2004). *Knowledge and Lotteries*. New York, NY: Oxford University Press.

Hayes, Andrew. (2013). *Introduction to Mediation, Moderation, and Conditional Process Analysis: A Regression-Based Approach*. New York: Guilford.

Hayes, Andrew. (2015). "Hacking PROCESS to Estimate a Simple Moderation Model with a Three-category Moderator." Unpublished white paper. www.afhayes.com/public/multicatmodhack.pdf.

Hazlett, Allan. (2009). "Knowledge and Conversation." *Philosophy and Phenomenological Research* 78: 591–620.

Kim, Minsun, and Yuan Yuan. (2015). "No Cross-cultural Differences in the Gettier Car Case Intuition: A Replication Study of Weinberg et al. 2001." *Episteme* 12: 355–361.

Lewis, David. (1979). "Scorekeeping in a Language Game." *Journal of Philosophical Logic* 8: 339–359.

Lewis, David. (1996). "Elusive Knowledge." *Australasian Journal of Philosophy* 74: 549–567.

Machery, Edouard, Stephen Stich, David Rose, Amita Chatterjee, Kaori Karasawa, Noel Struchiner, Smita Sirker, Naoki Usui, and Takaaki Hashimoto. (2016). "Gettier Across Cultures." *Nous* 51(3): 645–664.

Malcolm, Norman. (1952). "Knowledge and Belief." *Mind* 61: 178–189.

May, Joshua, Walter Sinnott-Armstrong, Jay Hull, and Aaron Zimmerman. (2010). "Practical Interests, Relevant Alternatives, and Knowledge Attributions: An Empirical Study." *Review of Philosophy and Psychology* 1: 265–273.

Nagel, Jennifer. (2010). "Knowledge Ascriptions and the Psychological Consequences of Thinking About Error." *Philosophical Quarterly* 60: 286–306.

Nagel, Jennifer. (2012). "Intuitions and Experiments: A Defense of the Case Method in Epistemology." *Philosophy and Phenomenological Research* 85: 495–527.

Nagel, Jennifer. (2013). "Defending the Evidential Value of Epistemic Intuitions: A Reply to Stich." *Philosophy and Phenomenological Research* 86: 179–199.

Nagel, Jennifer, Valarie San Juan, and Raymond Mar. (2013a). "Lay Denial of Knowledge for Justified True Beliefs." *Cognition* 129: 652–661.

Nagel, Jennifer, Valarie San Juan, and Raymond Mar. (2013b). "Authentic Gettier Cases: A Reply to Starmans and Friedman." *Cognition* 129: 666–669.

Nichols, Shaun, Jonathan Weinberg, and Stephen Stich. (2003). "Meta-skepticism: Meditations on Ethno-epistemology." In *The Skeptics*, ed. Stephen Luper, 227–247. Burlington, VT: Ashgate.

Preacher, Kristopher J., Derek D. Rucker, and Andrew F. Hayes. (2007). "Addressing Moderated Mediation Hypotheses: Theory, Methods, and Prescriptions." *Multivariate Behavioral Research* 42(1): 185–227.

Putnam, Hilary. (1975). "The meaning of 'Meaning.'" *Minnesota Studies in the Philosophy of Science* 7: 131–193.

Reynolds, Nina, and Anne Smith. (2010). "Assessing the Impact of Response Styles on Cross-cultural Service Quality Evaluation: A Simplified Approach to Eliminating the Problem." *Journal of Service Research* 13: 230–243.

Schaffer, Jonathan. (2005). "Contrastive Knowledge." In *Oxford Studies in Epistemology 1*, ed. Tamar Szabo Gendler and John Hawthorne, 235–272. New York, NY: Oxford University Press.

Schaffer, Jonathan, and Joshua Knobe. (2012). "Contrastive Knowledge Surveyed." *Nous* 46: 675–708.

Seyedsayamdost, Hamid. (2015). "On Normativity and Epistemic Intuitions: Failure of Replication." *Episteme* 12: 95–116.

Starmans, Christina, and Ori Friedman. (2012). "The Folk Conception of Knowledge." *Cognition* 124: 272–283.

Starmans, Christina, and Ori Friedman. (2013). "Taking "Know" for an Answer: A Reply to Nagel, San Juan, and Mar." *Cognition* 129: 662–665.

Stich, Stephen. (2013). "Do Different Groups Have Different Epistemic Intuitions? A Reply to Nagel." *Philosophy and Phenomenological Research* 87: 151–178.

Unger, Peter. (1975). *Ignorance*: A Case for Scepticism. New York, NY: Oxford University Press.

Van Vaerenbergh, Yves, and Roy Thomas. (2013). "Response Styles in Survey Research: A Literature Review of Antecedents, Consequences, and Remedies." *International Journal of Public Opinion Research* 25: 195–217.

Weinberg, Jonathan, Shaun Nichols, and Stephen Stich. (2001). "Normativity and Epistemic Intuitions." *Philosophical Topics* 29: 429–460.

Williams, Bernard. (1978). *Descartes: The Project of Pure Enquiry*. Harmondsworth: Pelican.

Williamson, Timothy. (2005). "Contextualism, Subject-sensitive Invariantism and Knowledge of Knowledge." *Philosophical Quarterly* 55: 213–235.

CHAPTER 9

I KNOW

A Human Universal

ANNA WIERZBICKA

1. INTRODUCTION: AN "INNATE CORE EPISTEMOLOGY"

In their article "Gettier Across Cultures," Machery et al. (2015, 1–2) note that "for much of the history of Western philosophy, the dominant account of knowledge was that knowledge is justified true belief" and that in an article published in 1963, Edmund Gettier challenged this traditional account, arguing that "having justified true belief is not sufficient for having knowledge."

Machery et al. (2015) build on what they call "the Gettier intuition" (that "justified true belief" does not guarantee "knowledge") and argue that this intuition reflects an underlying innate and universal folk episte-mology. They state: "people across cultures share a core epistemology, just as they share a folk physics and a folk history" (655). I believe that this statement is true and that it is of fundamental importance for philosophy, and for the human sciences in general. At the same time, this statement needs clarification, and such clarification requires some attention to the language in which our questions and answers on this theme (as on any other) are formulated. More specifically, we need to ask about the meaning of words in which these questions and answers are formulated and also, on what grounds we have chosen these particular words with which to ask our questions and to frame our answers.

Thus, a philosophical account of human epistemology needs to be complemented by a linguistic one, and more particularly, one informed by the analytical and empirical experience of cross-linguistic semantics. In this chapter I outline such a complementary account; and in doing so, I adopt the "Gettier Across Cultures" article as my point of reference, along with an article on Gettier by Polish linguist Andrzej Bogusławski (2002), entitled "There Is No Getting Round Gettier."[1]

My main claim will be that KNOW is an indefinable and universal human concept, and that there are four "canonical" frames in which this concept occurs across languages. Sections 2–7 discuss different aspects of the methodology that enables us to reach these conclusions, and sections 8–15 examine different ways in which KNOW is used in English and in other languages. Section 16 ties up the different strands of the discussion and draws a final thumbnail sketch of KNOW as a fundamental, invariable and universal human concept.

2. WHERE DO WE START?

Every inquiry has to start somewhere, and I don't think that an inquiry into fundamental philosophical concepts can start with the concept of "epistemology." As powerfully argued by Leibniz, to explain anything at all we need to base our explanations on concepts that are self-explanatory, and presumably no one would want to argue that "epistemology" is one of those.[2]

How can we tell which concepts are self-explanatory and which are not? Here, too, an unbeatable answer, I believe, was provided by Leibniz: we can find out only by trial and error—that is, by trying to explain (i.e., paraphrase) some concepts in terms of others, without vicious circles (*circuli vitiosi*), and taking the process of explanation as far as it will go. Proceeding in this way (in any language), we can reach a given language's conceptual core—that is, its conceptual primes, which cannot be explained any

1. There is an enormous multidisciplinary literature on the concept of "knowledge" (and "knowing"), and surveying it is beyond the scope of this chapter. Consequently, I will list in the references at the end only those items that are particularly relevant to the present discussion.

2. *The Oxford Companion to Philosophy* (Honderich 1995, 242) defines *epistemology* as "that branch of philosophy concerned with the nature of knowledge, its possibility, scope, and general basis." At the same time, it defines *knowledge* as "the principal intellectual attainment studied by epistemology" (227). Such circularity is typical of philosophical publications that do not recognize the need for indefinables that are self-explanatory.

further, and in terms of which all the other concepts embedded in this language can be explained.

Leibniz called this set of conceptual primes "the alphabet of human thoughts," or *Alphabetum Cogitationum Humanarum*. The human mind, he held, is equipped with a set of simple concepts that are, as it were, "letters" of an innate mental alphabet, and all human thoughts constitute combinations of those simplest concepts. I adduce here a few key quotes from Couturat's 1903 edition of Leibniz's inedita (my translation):

a. Although infinitely many concepts can be understood, it is possible that only a few can be understood in themselves. This is so because an infinite number can be constructed by combining a few elements. Indeed, it is not only possible but probable, because nature usually achieves as much as possible with as few elements as possible, that is to say, it usually operates in the simplest possible way. (430)

b. The alphabet of human thoughts is the catalogue of primitive concepts— that is, those concepts which cannot be made clearer by means of any definitions. (435)

c. The alphabet of human thoughts is the catalogue of those concepts which can be understood by themselves, and from whose combinations our other ideas arise. (430)

Leibniz maintained that these simplest concepts are the limit of human understanding of anything: they are inherently intelligible to human beings and everything else can be understood only through them. If there were no concepts which were self-explanatory, we couldn't understand anything at all.

d. If nothing could be understood in itself, nothing at all could ever be understood. Because what can only be understood via something else can be understood only to the extent to which that other thing can be understood, and so on; accordingly, we can say that we have understood something only when we have broken it down into parts which can be understood in themselves. (430)

Thus, people can understand an infinite number of ideas because they possess a small number of simple concepts that are understandable by themselves. Different combinations of these simple concepts can generate an infinite number of complex ones.

In Leibniz's view, if we want to understand anything, we should always proceed like this: we should reduce everything that is complex to what is simple—that is, present complex ideas as configurations of very simple ones that are absolutely necessary for the expression of thoughts.

> e. All other concepts should be reduced to those which are absolutely necessary for expressing thoughts conceived by the human mind. (281)

How, then, can it be determined which concepts are absolutely necessary for articulating the full range of human thoughts? Leibniz's answer to this question was very simple: it can be determined only by trial and error—that is, by experimenting with various provisional definitions.

> f. The primary terms, the indefinables, cannot be easily recognized by us except in the way that the prime numbers are: we can only recognize them as such if we try to divide them [by the smaller ones]. (187)

As we know from his unpublished manuscripts, Leibniz experimented in this way all his life, and sometimes despaired of the human capacity to ever identify the set of simple and necessary concepts.

Leibniz was convinced that the task of identifying those simplest, absolutely necessary concepts is extremely important, and he found it surprising that only very few people think about this.

> g. This consideration [how some concepts arise from others] allows us to avoid vicious circles, which are constantly taken recourse to, and the mind can fasten to some firm and fixed concepts which can be determined. How very important this is, few people understand, because few people reflect how very important it might be to determine what the first elements in all things are. (160)

As various commentators have noted, Leibniz avoided "the obvious question as to the number and type of fundamental concepts" (Martin 1964, 26). From his own perspective, two obstacles stood in the way of his program during his lifetime: first, the absence of collaborators; and second, lack of data from many diverse languages of the world. Notwithstanding Leibniz's own intense interest in languages, including Chinese, wide-ranging typological cross-linguistic investigations were still in the distant future, and the longed-for collaborators did not materialize. In the end, Leibniz died without leaving so much as a sketch of the "alphabet of human thoughts," and subsequently, the whole program fell into oblivion for three hundred years.

3. A CROSS-LINGUISTIC SEARCH FOR THE INNATE "ALPHABET OF HUMAN THOUGHTS"

A search for an innate and universal "alphabet of human thoughts" based on empirical cross-linguistic investigations was undertaken, three hundred years after Leibniz, in a research program in linguistic semantics known under the acronym NSM, or Natural Semantic Metalanguage (Wierzbicka 1972; Goddard and Wierzbicka 1994, 2002; Wierzbicka 1996; Peeters 2006; Goddard 2008; Goddard and Wierzbicka 2014). The main methodological tool of this program is reductive paraphrase: complex meanings are elucidated in NSM-based work in paraphrases based on simpler ones, down to the level of self-explanatory "conceptual primitives."[3]

After decades of intensive analytical and empirical investigations, NSM researchers have identified—through progressive approximations—sixty-five concepts that meet Leibniz's criteria as elements of the "alphabet of human thought": they are intuitively intelligible; they cannot be explained (paraphrased) without leading, directly or indirectly, to vicious circles; and they can serve as tools for explaining (or, in NSM terms, "explicating") all complex concepts from any semantic domain. They can also be found as words or wordlike elements in all sampled languages (cf. Goddard and Wierzbicka 2014).

The findings of the half-century-long search for the "alphabet of human thought" begun in my 1972 *Semantic Primitives* are summarized in table 9.1. The key feature of this table is that it can be given, in an exactly matching form, in other languages, as illustrated in table 9.2.

It will be noticed that the concept KNOW is included on this list, along with six other "mental predicates," in the seventh row of table 9.1. During half a century of a cross-linguistic search for the "alphabet of human thought," from *Semantic Primitives* to *Words and Meanings* (Goddard and Wierzbicka 2014), the set of elements recognized as conceptual primes was gradually expanding; KNOW joined the expanding set of primes in 1989. Before that, KNOW (or, strictly speaking, "know that") was posited as a semantic prime by Bogusławski (1981), who in more recent work has called it "the most fundamental semantic prime" (2002, abstract), and even "the Central Relation Constituting the Reality" (2007, 8).

---

3. Leibniz's idea that there was an innate and universal "alphabet of human thought" was recalled in the early 1960s by the previously mentioned Polish linguist Andrzej Bogusławski. The NSM program is deeply indebted to Bogusławski's vision in general (1970) and to his account of "knowing" in particular.

Table 9.1 SEMANTIC PRIMES (ENGLISH EXPONENTS)

I, YOU, SOMEONE, SOMETHING~THING, PEOPLE, BODY	substantives
KINDS, PARTS	relational substantives
THIS, THE SAME, OTHER~ELSE	determiners
ONE, TWO, SOME, ALL, MUCH~MANY, LITTLE~FEW	quantifiers
GOOD, BAD	evaluators
BIG, SMALL	descriptors
KNOW, THINK, WANT, DON'T WANT, FEEL, SEE, HEAR	mental predicates
SAY, WORDS, TRUE	speech
DO, HAPPEN, MOVE	actions, events, movement
BE (SOMEWHERE), THERE IS, BE (SOMEONE/ SOMETHING)	location, existence, specification
(IS) MINE	possession
LIVE, DIE	life and death
WHEN~TIME, NOW, BEFORE, AFTER, A LONG TIME, A SHORT TIME, FOR SOME TIME, MOMENT	time
WHERE~PLACE, HERE, ABOVE, BELOW, FAR, NEAR, SIDE, INSIDE, TOUCH	place
NOT, MAYBE, CAN, BECAUSE, IF	logical concepts
VERY, MORE	augmentor, intensifier
LIKE	similarity

Notes: Exponents of primes can be polysemous—i.e., they can have other, additional meanings. Exponents of primes may be words, bound morphemes, or phrasemes. They can be formally—i.e., morphologically—complex. They can have combinatorial variants or allolexes (indicated with ~). Each prime has well-specified syntactic (combinatorial) properties.
Source: Goddard and Wierzbicka (2014).

4. NOT "KNOWLEDGE" BUT "KNOWING"

In their article "Gettier Across Cultures," in which they posit an "innate and universal *core folk epistemology*," Machery et al. (2015, 8) speak also of "a central epistemic concept" and state that "in most cultures that concept will be expressed by the epistemic term commonly translated into English as 'know'" (8). This is consistent with the findings of the NSM program: according to these findings, all (sampled) languages have a word indistinguishable in meaning from the English word *know* (as used in specifiable, "canonical" sentences such as "I know (it)" and "he knows (it)."

The way these findings are formulated is important: the NSM claim is not that there is a universal "concept of knowledge," as Machery et al. (2015, 10) put it, but rather, that there is a universal concept of "knowing," as, for example, in "I know (it)" and "he knows (it)."

Table 9.2 POLISH SEMANTIC PRIMES, WITH ENGLISH EQUIVALENTS

JA, TY, KTOŚ, COŚ, LUDZIE, CIAŁO I, YOU, SOMEONE, SOMETHING~THING, PEOPLE, BODY	substantives
RODZAJE, CZĘŚĆI KINDS, PARTS	relational substantives
TEN, TEN SAM, INNY THIS, THE SAME, OTHER~ELSE	determiners
JEDEN, DWA, NIEKTÓRE~NIEKTÓRZY, WSZYSTKIE~WSZYSCY, DUŻO, MAŁO ONE, TWO, SOME, ALL, MUCH~MANY, LITTLE~FEW	quantifiers
DOBRY, ZŁY GOOD, BAD	evaluators
DUŻY, MAŁY BIG, SMALL	descriptors
MYŚLEĆ, WIEDZIEĆ, CHCIEĆ, NIE CHCIEĆ, CZUĆ, WIDZIEĆ, SŁYSZEĆ KNOW, THINK, WANT, DON'T WANT, FEEL, SEE, HEAR	mental predicates
POWIEDZIEĆ~MÓWIĆ, SŁOWO, PRAWDA SAY, WORDS, TRUE	speech
ROBIĆ, STAĆ SIĘ, RUSZAĆ SIĘ DO, HAPPEN, MOVE	actions, events, movement

BYĆ (GDZIEŚ), BYĆ, BYĆ (KIMŚ/CZYMŚ)
BE (SOMEWHERE), THERE IS, BE (SOMEONE/
   SOMETHING)
	location, existence,
	   specification

(JEST) MOJE (IS) MINE	possession
ŻYĆ, UMRZEĆ LIVE, DIE	life and death

**KIEDY~CZAS, TERAZ, PRZEDTEM, POTEM, DŁUGO,
   KRÓTKO, PRZEZ PEWIEN CZAS, CHWILA**
WHEN~TIME, NOW, BEFORE, AFTER, A LONG TIME,
   A SHORT TIME, FOR SOME TIME, MOMENT
	time

**GDZIE~MIEJSCE, TUTAJ, NAD, POD, DALEKO, BLISKO,
   STRONA, DOTYKAĆ**
WHERE~PLACE, HERE, ABOVE, BELOW, FAR, NEAR, SIDE,
   INSIDE, TOUCH
	place

NIE, BYĆ MOŻE, MÓC, BO, JEŻELI NOT, MAYBE, CAN, BECAUSE, IF	logical concepts
BARDZO, WIĘCEJ VERY, MORE	intensifier, augmentor
TAK JAK	similarity

But while evidence strongly suggests that there is a universal concept of "knowing," there is no universal concept of "knowledge": the English word *knowledge* is an abstract noun that has no counterparts in most languages of the world (for example, in languages of Australia such as Warlpiri [Laughren et al. 2006]), and which has only very approximate counterparts in several other European languages.

It is particularly interesting to note that philosophical classics known to Anglophone philosophy students under titles such as *The Problem of Knowledge* (Ernst Cassirer, 1950), *Two Fundamental Problems of the Theory of Knowledge* (Karl Popper, 2009), or *Knowledge and Human Interests* (Jürgen Habermas, 1972) were in fact published in the original German under titles including the word *Erkenntnis* (*Das Erkenntnis Problem, Die beide Grundprobleme der Erkenntnistheorie*, and *Erkenntnis and Interesse*, respectively). The German noun *Erkenntnis* is derived from the verb *erkennen*, glossed in *Harrap's Standard German and English Dictionary* (1963) as "to discern, to make out, to perceive, to recognize, to detect" (and not as "to know"), and the noun *Erkenntnis* itself is glossed, in the first place, as "perception, recognition, realization."

Similarly, in French there are three words listed in French-English dictionaries as possible renderings of the English *knowledge*, in different contexts: *savoir* (derived from the verb *savoir*, "to know something"), *connaissance* (from the verb *connaître*, which is used for "knowing someone" but in many other contexts as well), and *science*, a "false friend" of the English *science*.

A good illustration of the lack of correspondence between the English word *knowledge* and its closest counterpart in French is provided by the opening sentence of the volume entitled *Logique et connaissance scientifique* (Logic and scientific knowledge) in the *Encyclopédie de la Pléiade*, edited by Jean Poirier (1967, 3): "La logique, la méthodologie et la théorie de la connaissance, ou épistémologie, constituent trois branches du savoir." The literal English translation would read: "Logic, methodology and theory of knowledge [*connaissance*] or epistemology, are three branches of knowledge [*savoir*]."

Thus, "epistemology" is equated here with the theory of "connaissance," and "scientific knowledge" appears to be "connaissance scientifique," but "savoir" appears to be "knowledge" in some higher, overarching sense. From an English speaker's point of view, the only thing that is clear here is that neither *connaissance* nor *savoir* matches up with *knowledge*.

To mention briefly one more example, in Russian there are two nouns corresponding to the English *knowledge*, both derived from the verb *znat'*, "to know," but used differently: *znanija* (plural) and *znanie* (singular).

(Ožegov's Russian dictionary (1978) illustrates the use of *znanija* (plural) with the phrase *obladat' znanijami* ("to have knowledge") and the use of *znanie* (sg.) with the phrase *oblast' znanija*, "a field of knowledge.")

In English, too, the range of usage of the noun *knowledge* is quite different from that of the verb *to know*, and much more restricted. The word is used a lot in the context of education, in university studies, in philosophy, in encyclopedias, and so on, but far less commonly in everyday life or with reference to momentary states of affairs. For example, if I know what time it is, that doesn't mean I "have knowledge of what time it is"—at least not in ordinary language.

So "knowledge" is not a shared human concept, innate, universal, and indefinable, and of course English-speaking children acquire it much later than the concept of "knowing." (As anyone who spends time with preschool children can attest, sentences like "I know" and "I don't know" are common in their speech, but only a most unusual preschooler would talk of his or her "knowledge" (cf. Wellman 1990, 1995).

Having said this, I must acknowledge that when one writes in English, it is sometimes more convenient to use the word *knowledge* rather than *knowing* when one means "knowing." In what follows, I will sometimes use phrases like "tacit knowledge," "verbalized knowledge," and "verbalizable knowledge"—partly for the sake of convenience and partly to connect with the traditional philosophical usage. In my explications, however, I will use only the verb *know*, never the noun *knowledge*.[4]

5. IDENTIFYING UNIVERSAL CONCEPTS THROUGH UNIVERSAL CANONICAL FRAMES

Machery et al. (2015, 11) write: "our findings do not support the claim that the words used to translate 'to know' express the same concept." From an NSM perspective, it is essential to bring the notion of "canonical sentences" into the picture here. If we want to test translatability and universality of the concept "know," we have to do so within specified and cross-translatable contexts.

Of course this condition assumes that we do have some such cross-translatable contexts at our disposal. Contexts such as "I know (it)" and "this someone knows (it)" *are*, evidence suggests, cross-translatable: in

4. Philosophers usually prefer to talk about "knowledge" rather than "knowing," and, for example, tend to define "epistemology" as "theory of knowledge." For a notable exception, see Shope (1983).

all the languages that have been investigated from this point of view, bilingual consultants and experts have had no difficulty in providing exact equivalents for them, and were not able to find any differences in meaning between them.

Machery et al. (2015, 8) note that "the words commonly used to translate 'to know' in Bengali ('jáná') and in Sanskrit ('jña') . . . are used somewhat differently from 'to know' in English" and that "the distinction between 'to believe' and 'to know' is not always retained when 'jáná' or 'jña' are used." From an NSM point of view, however, the key question is whether there is any identifiable (paraphrasable) difference between *know* and *jáná* (or *jña*) in canonical frames (such as "I know (it)," or "he/she knows (it)"). To the best of my knowledge there is none.[5]

In this chapter, I will seek to identify the universal concept of "knowing" through its universal frames, such as "I know," "this someone knows it," "this someone knows something," and "this someone knows something about something."

6. IS THE CONCEPT OF "KNOWING" CULTURALLY VARIABLE?

In their article "Gettier Across Cultures," Machery et al. (2015) write:

> It is important to recognize that even if Gettier intuitions have a central epistemic concept that requires more than JTB ["justified true belief"], this does not entail that people in all cultures have the same knowledge concept. For it might be the case that, while core folk epistemology requires a knowledge concept that is more demanding than JTB, it permits considerable variation in the details, with different cultures elaborating on the JTB theme in different ways. (8)

From a semantic (NSM) point of view, whether or not "all cultures have the same knowledge concept" is not quite the right question. What we should really be asking is: Do all cultures have the same concept of "knowing" (as in "I know (it)" and "he/she knows (it)")? Further, we should not be comparing cultures in terms of "JTB" ("justified true belief"), because neither "justified" nor "belief" are universal human concepts. The words *justified* and *belief* are English words, which embed Anglo-English concepts. To compare concepts, and ideas, across cultures, we need a *tertium*

---

5. For a helpful discussion on this point I am indebted to the Sanskrit specialist McComas Taylor.

comparationis—a common measure—that is independent of English (and other European languages), and that can be "justified" from a universal perspective. The word *true* (in the canonical frames "this is true" and "this is not true") can well serve as a tool for cross-cultural comparison because it is attested in all sampled languages, but "belief" and "justified" are not: they have an entirely different status.

Machery et al. (2015) write (citing many references) that "other plausible components of core folk epistemology are evidential markers . . . and epistemic modals." But evidential markers are known to be extremely variable across languages, presenting different configurations of meanings, such as "I know," "I think," "I see," "people say" (cf. Wierzbicka 1996, chap. 15). Further, as Helen Bromhead (2009) has shown in her study of "epistemic expressions" in sixteenth- and seventeenth-century English, the "folk epistemology" embedded in English has changed considerably after the seventeenth century. Epistemic concepts such as "believe," "suppose," and "assume" (in the post-Enlightenment sense of these words) reflect a folk epistemology embedded in modern English, not that of earlier times. Such historical ("vertical") shifts in folk epistemology are as important and worthy of thorough investigation as variations across cultures in a "horizontal" perspective. As for "epistemic modals," cross-linguistic investigations show that, strictly speaking, there are only two that are universally available: MAYBE and CAN; and of these two, only MAYBE is always "epistemological", because CAN be used in other functions as well.

Thus, universal meanings such as KNOW, THINK, TRUE, and MAYBE give us better tools for investigating "core folk epistemology" across cultures than language- and culture-specific ones like "believe," "justified belief," or "knowledge." And not only across cultures, but also across times. But to investigate such differences and shifts, we need conceptual tools valid across both time and space. The concept KNOW is one of such stable and reliable tools (as are also TRUE, THINK, and MAYBE).

This doesn't mean, however, that there are no cross-cultural differences in the use of sentences like "I know it" or "he/she knows it." To take an example from a well-known text, in St. John's Gospel, Jesus says to Martha, about her dead brother Lazarus, "Your brother will rise," and Martha replies, "I know he will rise, in the resurrection on the last day" (John 11:23–24). Does Martha "know" that her brother will rise or does she simply "believe" it? From the point of view of many English speakers in the twenty-first century, she probably "believes" it rather than "knows" it. From Martha's own point of view, however, when she says "I know," she doesn't mean "I believe"; she means "I know."

My point is that there is no difference in meaning between Martha's "I know" in "I know he will rise" and the "I know" of a present-day English speaker who says "I know that the earth is round, not flat." It is not Martha's "concept of knowing" which differs from that of well-educated and epistemically cautious present-day speakers of English. Rather, the difference lies in different cultural attitudes toward saying "I know" in relation to something that cannot be logically proved or experimentally demonstrated.

It is certainly possible, and important, to investigate different attitudes toward saying "I know" in different cultures and societies. But such comparisons are only possible if we have a common measure, a *tertium comparationis*, to compare such attitudes across languages and cultures. The canonical sentence "I know (it)" provides such a common measure.

The more general point here is that different cultural attitudes are re-flected in complex concepts, and not in the elementary ones. For example, as Anna Gladkova (2007) has shown in relation to Russian, the Russian word *sčitat'* is different in meaning from the English word *believe*, as they both reflect different ways of thinking about thinking and knowing, but the Russian word *dumat'* (used in the canonical frames) matches the English *think* exactly (and the Russian word *znat'* matches, exactly, the English *know*). When we rely in our analysis on stable concepts like "know," "true," and "think," we can pinpoint, with precision, changing and variable cultural attitudes, as Bromhead (2009) has done in relation to the episte-mological "thought world" of sixteenth- and seventeenth-century England.

In my own work on the historical shifts in epistemological culture re-flected in the history of English (Wierzbicka 2002a, 2002b) I have studied the decline in the use of the words *true* and *truly* and the rise of *real* and *really*, and also the rise of *right* and *wrong* (and the corresponding decline of *true* and *not true*). In another study (Wierzbicka 2002c), I have shown that the "discourses of truth" in Russian and in English are profoundly different. I have also studied the semantic trajectory of the noun *evidence* in English and the rise of the powerful new concept of "evidence" (as in "What's the evidence?") in modern English (Wierzbicka 2010).

All such comparisons, both "horizontal" and "vertical," require some stable conceptual reference points. The universal primes TRUE, THINK, and KNOW (as used in their canonical frames) make such cross-cultural and his-torical comparisons possible.

Anthropological and linguistic literature has amassed a great deal of in-formation on different attitudes toward "knowing" prevailing in different cultures and societies. Often, however, this literature suffers from lack of clarity because different cultural attitudes to "knowing" are described as a "different concept of knowing" or a "different meaning of the verb 'to know.'"

There are also, however, positive examples, such as Sophie Nicholls' work on the Roper River Kriol in Australia (2013, 296–297). Since Nicholls clearly recognizes the cross-linguistic stability of the concept KNOW (as used in canonical frames), she is able to use the concept to pinpoint, with clarity and precision, the cross-cultural differences in the attitudes toward "knowing." For example, Nicholls proposes the following "cultural scripts" related to the "ownership of knowledge" and the rights and responsibilities associated with it:

Cultural script regarding "owners of information and talking for others"

a. people here think like this:
b. some people know many things about some places/things
c. these people can say things about these places/things to other people
d. it can be bad if some other people say things about these places/things
e. some people can't know anything about these places/things

Nicholls explains:

> The first few components indicate that there are some people with superior knowledge to others. These particular people can say things about the things that they know. In component (d) the script indicates that other people are not at liberty to tell others about such things, and that "it can be bad" if they do. The final component (e) shows that this information is restricted, and some people shouldn't know anything about it. (297)

It is important to note the central role of the frame "to know something about something" in this script. (I will return to this point in section 10.)

7. DIFFERENT FRAMES OF KNOWING: SIMPLE AND COMPLEX, UNIVERSAL AND NONUNIVERSAL

A concept cannot be identified apart from the frames within which it can occur. For example, the universal concept SAY comes, so to speak, with a package including "say something," "say something to someone," and "say something about something" (Goddard 2008, 14; Goddard and Wierzbicka 2014, 159); and THINK comes with a package of frames including "(I) think like this" and "(I'm) thinking about it" (Goddard 2008, 14; Goddard and Karlsson 2008).

What are the universal frames of the concept KNOW? The long-time champion of KNOW as a fundamental and irreducible human concept, Andrzej Bogusławski has always focused on "know that" (that is, "know" with a "that"-clause) as the basic frame, and in fact, has been identifying the concept in question as "know that" rather than simply "know" (cf., e.g., 1981, 2002, 2007).

This insistence on "know that" saved Bogusławski from falling into the trap of identifying "knowing that" (in French, *savoir*; in German, *wissen*) with "knowing someone" (in French, *connaître*; in German, *kennen*), as NSM researchers have done for many years. Since these researchers were, for many years, not able to explicate "knowing someone" in terms of "knowing that," they assumed that lexical distinctions such as *savoir* and *connaître* in French or *wissen* and *kennen* in German were not linked with genuine differences in meaning—not even in contexts such as "knowing something" and "knowing someone."

It was only in 2013 that an analysis was proposed that enabled NSM researchers to recognize that, in this context—though not necessarily in others—words like *connaître* and *kennen* were in fact paraphrasable in terms of *savoir* and *wissen* (Goddard and Wierzbicka 2013; Goddard 2015b). As a result, KNOW as a universal semantic prime posited in NSM lost the combinatorial options "to know someone" and "to know a place" with which it had been earlier credited (see section 12).

It should be noted, however, that paraphrasing verbs like *connaître* and *kennen* (in the context of "knowing someone") in terms of *savoir* and *wissen* is not tantamount to reducing "knowing someone" (and "knowing a place") to "knowing that" (with a that-clause). As we will see in section 13, "knowing someone" can be paraphrased in terms of "knowing something about someone," and not in terms of "knowing that," and as discussed in section 10, the frame "to know something about something" is also irreducible and fundamental. Further, as I will discuss in section 9, the "know that" construction is itself semantically complex and can be reduced to (paraphrased in terms of) a simple construction "to know it."

I will report on the basics of this analysis of "knowing someone" through "knowing something about someone" shortly. First, however, let me present several common frames of KNOW as they are understood in current NSM work. I will discuss the frames in which KNOW can occur across languages in sections 8–14, under the following headings:

- Dialogical uses of KNOW ("I know," "I don't know")
- Knowledge fully or partially expressed in words ("knowing that," "knowing it")

- Knowledge not expressed in words ("knowing something," "knowing something about something")
- Asking for knowledge expressed in words, ("wanting to know," asking questions)
- Knowledge that could be expressed in words ("knowing where/when/who" etc.)
- Nonverbalizable knowledge ("knowing someone," "knowing a place")
- Knowing how to do something ("knowing how")

Evidence suggests that all these frames are widespread across languages, and that some of them are universal.

8. DIALOGICAL USES OF KNOW ("I KNOW," "I DON'T KNOW")

To begin with, KNOW plays an important role in dialogical exchanges between "I" and "you." This is particularly striking in the case of "I don't know," which is probably one of the most common recurring responses in all face-to-face exchanges in any language. Significantly, it is "I don't know" rather than "I don't know it," even in a language like English, where "transitive" verbs usually do require a complement. The dialogical response meaning "I don't know" is so common in human speech that it often takes the form of a single particle, or particle-like word, like *dunno* in spoken English and *chépa* in spoken French. *The Warlpiri Dictionary* (Laughren et al. 2006) includes, for example, *murra-ja*, glossed as "I don't know, search me, nothing to do with me." In many languages, as in English, there are also multiple elaborations on the basic meaning "I don't know," such as "who knows," "God knows," "no idea," and so on.

Nonetheless, while the positive response "I know" is no doubt far less common than "I don't know," it too often occurs in face-to-face exchanges, with or without an "object."

I will adduce two examples from English, one from a collection of stories by the Australian writer Tim Winton, and the other from Shakespeare. Winton's story entitled "More," from the volume *Minimum of Two* (1990, 130), includes the following dialogical exchange between a man and a woman, Jerra and Rachel:

[RACHEL:] "I like her. I like them both."
[JERRA:] "Yeah, I know."

Clearly, "I" in "I know" does not refer to the same person as "I" in "I like," so what Jerra knows does not correspond exactly (literally) to the previous sentence (see section 9).

The second example comes from *King Lear* (Act v, scene iii, 176–177). When the Duke of Albany says to Edgar, son of Gloucester, "Let sorrow split my heart if ever I did hate thee or thy father," Edgar replies: "Worthy prince, I know't." What Edgar knows is summed up in the (phonetically reduced) word "it." This "it," however, is not a substitute for a that-clause. What Edgar means is that Albany never hated him or his father, but this does not correspond directly to the sentence uttered by Albany. Thus, the word *know* as used by Edgar does not stand for "know that." Its meaning is indefinable, and the frame—"I know (it)"—is no doubt universal. Does Edgar's "I know't" stand for verbalized knowledge? Partly, yes, but perhaps not entirely. Even leaving aside the question of "referential opacity" (to be discussed in section 9), Albany didn't say, exactly, "I never hated you or your father," although he said something that implied it.

Conversational uses of expressions referring to the speaker's, and the addressee's, knowledge require a thorough cross-linguistic investigation. For the moment, it seems safe to say that both "I don't know" and "I know" are used in many, and possibly all, languages as moves in dialogical exchanges, and that they cannot be seen as elliptical versions of "I know that" sentences.[6]

9. KNOWLEDGE FULLY OR PARTIALLY EXPRESSED IN WORDS ("KNOWING THAT," "KNOWING IT")

In languages like English, the frame "knowing that . . . " (with a complement clause) is probably the most common frame in which the word *know* appears. Since the complement clause states in words what the person in question knows, a "know"-sentence with a "that"-clause appears to present

6. Evidence suggests that in many languages there is also another common dialogical "move" involving KNOW: "you know" (in French, *tu sais*; in Italian, *sai*; in Spanish, *sabes*; in Russian, *znaeš*. In some languages, as in English, this move relies on the verb *to know*; in others, it is made by means of a particle or particle-like expression, such as *ne* in Japanese (Asano-Cavanagh 2011) and *panya* or *panya-tja* in Pitjantjatjara (Goddard 1996), which can be glossed in English as "you know." Unlike "I know" and "I don't know," however, "you know" can be regarded as an abbreviated version of a longer expression, most likely "you can know." The matter requires further investigation.

fully verbalized knowledge that this person has. So, for example, in the sentence "John knows that Oslo is the capital of Norway," the complement clause "(that) Oslo is the capital of Norway" expresses the full knowledge attributed by the speaker to John in this sentence. In philosophical discourse, sentences of this kind are usually linked with the term "propositional knowledge": the "proposition" expressed in the "that"-clause is something that the knower (in this case, John) could say in just these words.

There are good reasons to think, however, that a "know that . . ." sentence is not as simple conceptually as it seems, but rather, embodies some elements not visible on the surface, to wit:

John knows that Oslo is the capital of Norway
it is like this: Oslo is the capital of Norway
John knows it

The need for such "decomposition" of "know that . . ." into "it is like this, . . . someone knows it" becomes particularly clear when one considers sentences with what Roman Jakobson (1984[1957]) called "shifters," such as "you," "I," "this," "here," and "now." For example, the sentence "John knows that I live here" may seem to imply that the content of the sentence "I live here" is part of what John knows. In fact, however, it is not, because the "proposition" "I live here" belongs to "me" (the speaker), not to John. What John knows is something that *I* (not John) can represent by means of the sentence "I live here."

Roughly speaking, we might say that frames like "know that . . ." in English and in other languages indicate "verbalized knowledge" without indicating who verbalizes it, and so to whom the perspective reflected in this verbalization belongs. The identity of the "knower" and the "verbalizer" is guaranteed only in the case of first-person utterances, where the "knower" and the "verbalizer" coincide.

Thus, the assumption that the frame "he knows that . . ." is not basic but is derived from "he knows it" (where "it" refers to a declarative sentence either fully or partially retrievable from context) allows us, among other things, to deal with the well-known chestnut of "referential opacity" (cf., e.g., Quine 1964). For example, a sentence like "John knows that I live here" purports to represent what John knows, but it reflects my own, rather than John's, way of thinking: John doesn't think of me as "I," so the subordinate clause "that I live here" represents an amalgam of what John knows and how I think about it. By contrast, a sentence like "John knows it" does not seek to verbalize

John's knowledge; and while it is certainly vague, it doesn't represent an amalgam of two perspectives:

John knows that I live here.
it is like this: I live here
John knows it

I live here, John knows it.
I live here
John knows it

In a sense, both constructions, "know that . . ." and "know it," aim at verbalized knowledge, but they do it in different ways. A sentence like "John knows that I live here" refers to John's knowledge verbalized by someone other than John, but verbalized in the same syntactically complex (hypotactic) sentence. A syntactically simpler (paratactic) sequence "I live here, John knows it" says, essentially, the same thing: here, too, John's knowledge ("it") is verbalized, but only in the adjacent sentence ("I live here"), not in the same sentence ("John knows it"). If there is a slight semantic difference between the two constructions—the paratactic and the hypotactic one—it has to do with the framing of the knowledge: in the paratactic construction it is, as it were, asserted, whereas in the hypotactic one ("John knows that I live here"), it is taken for granted. In the explications above this difference is shown by means of the phrase "it is like this."

Apart from the old philosophical theme of "referential opacity," the relation between knowledge and verbalization raises particularly interesting and difficult questions in relation to "indigenous knowledge"—questions that are not often discussed in either philosophical or anthropological literature. For if the supposed "indigenous" knowledge is described through English words that have no equivalents in indigenous languages, then the outcome does not represent authentic indigenous knowledge but rather, an amalgam of indigenous knowledge and Anglo conceptualization (reflected in English-specific verbalization). By analogy with "referential opacity," we could call this "cultural opacity." I will illustrate this problem with two very simple examples.

A. P. Elkin's classic book *The Australian Aborigines* (1974[1938]) includes a chapter entitled "Knowledge of Nature," in which the author speaks with obvious admiration of "the amount and the depth of knowledge about the environment and all that is therein which is required by food-gatherers and hunters living continuously off the land," and comments: "Nature to the Aborigines is a system in which natural species and phenomena are related, or associated, in space and time" (32).

But there are no words like "nature," "environment," "system," or "phenomena" in Australian languages, and phrases like "knowledge of nature" reflect a European cultural perspective. Paradoxically, perhaps, anthropologists could stay closer to authentic local thinking and local knowledge by relying on simple and universal concepts such as "places," "places where they live," "living things," "living things of many kinds," and so on (cf. Goddard and Wierzbicka 2015).

The second example is the piece of anthropological "knowledge" quoted, mockingly, by the great anthropologist Clifford Geertz in his book *Local Knowledge* (1983, 181): "in Australia, they eat worms." The point is that indigenous Australians eat small creatures of many kinds, some of which could be described by English speakers as "worms." The statement quoted by Geertz is misleading because it presents English speakers' construal, which includes something like repugnance, as part of what can be "objectively" known. The implication appears to be that Aboriginal Australians eat things that are inherently repugnant. By contrast, the "local knowledge" is that people can eat very small creatures of some kinds that live in the ground. Such knowledge cannot be accurately portrayed using English words like *worms*, which have no exact semantic equivalents in the languages in which the relevant "local knowledge" is stored; it *can*, however, be accurately portrayed in a more controlled English (Minimal English) relying on cross-translatable words.[7]

Unfortunately, despite the reverence with which many anthropologists and linguists speak these days about "cultural knowledge" and the need for documenting it, they often seek to do so in culture-specific English words (such as, for example, *nature* and *worms*), without recognizing the problem of "cultural opacity" inherent in describing one body of "local knowledge" (embedded, for example, in an Australian language) in terms taken from another body of "local knowledge": that embedded in global English.

10. KNOWLEDGE NOT EXPRESSED IN WORDS ("KNOWING SOMETHING," "KNOWING SOMETHING ABOUT SOMETHING")

Cross-linguistic, as well as intra-linguistic, evidence suggests that in addition to the basic frames "I know (it)" and "he/she knows (it)," KNOW has two other basic and irreducible frames that can be represented

7. On the notion of "Minimal English," see Goddard (2018); see also Wierzbicka (2014).

schematically as "someone knows something" and "someone knows something about something" (or "about someone").

Of these two, the second appears to relate to more sophisticated ways of knowing, possibly combined with the ability to think about something. While "knowing something about someone" does not imply an ability to say, in words, what it is that one knows about this someone, it appears to imply that one can "bring something to mind"—perhaps an image. For example, one can imagine the following dialogue:

—Do you know anything about the new director?
—I know what she looks like.

Saying "I know what she looks like" does not imply that I can describe the appearance of the new director with words, but it does seem to imply that I can create an image in my mind and think: "she looks like this."

Evidence suggests that the configuration "to know something about something" is important in human thinking across cultures, and plays a special role in talking about traditional knowledge. For example, in Australian Aboriginal culture, it is held that old men and old women know a lot about things that happened in the *Jukurrpa*, or "Dreamtime" (Goddard and Wierzbicka 2015).

In fact, when one reads the entries related to KNOW in the monumental online dictionary of another Australian language (Laughren et al 2006), one is struck by the fact that most examples refer to people who "know a lot about something" (or "know how to do something"), and very few to "knowing that" or "knowing it." Is this an accident? It is impossible to be sure, but it seems clear that the idea of some people being "knowledgeable about something" is very salient in Warlpiri culture, perhaps more so than that of "knowing that."[8] The importance of the frame "know something about something" in Aboriginal culture is clearly related to ideas about the "ownership of knowledge" and the rights of certain people (but not others) to know about some things, as mentioned in section 6 with reference to Nicholls (2013).

But as important and as irreducible as the frame "to know something about something" is in human thought and speech, the fact remains that in some contexts—from theology to microbiology—people also want to

---

8. One can't help wondering in this context whether the idea of human expertise—knowing many things about things of some kinds—doesn't have some conceptual links with the ability to say many things about things these kinds. If it does, then the exact nature of these links requires further investigation.

talk about "knowing something" without the additional phrase "about something."

For example, when talking about God, people may want to say that "God knows everything" without having to add: "about everything." Cross-linguistic testing suggests that while the concept of "God" is of course culture-specific, the sentence "God knows everything" is cross-translatable (regardless of what word is chosen to render "God") (cf. Wierzbicka 2001).

In biology, people may want to say that a fly, or a worm, "knows something" (or "some things"), without having to say that it "knows something about something," and again, the sentence "it knows something" appears to be cross-translatable.

Leaving the superhuman and the subhuman realm, at the human level, too, speakers may want to say that someone "knows something" or "knows nothing" without having to specify the topic of this "knowing." For example, in her autobiography *The Story of a Soul* (2010, 2) St. Thérèse of Lisieux writes that God "has, in fact, created the child who knows nothing and can only make feeble cries" (in the original, "Il a créé l'enfant qui ne sait rien et ne fait entendre que de faibles cris" [Sainte Thérèse 2012, 21]). One may disagree with the statement, but one must acknowledge phrases like "knows nothing" as meaningful and self-contained: they are not elliptical versions of "knows nothing about anything" ("ne sait rien de rien"). It also seems clear that "knows" is not used here in the frame "know that" but, rather, in the simple and irreducible frame "know something."

Finally, as I will discuss in the next section, in all languages people have means of asking questions, and questions generally convey the message: "I want to know something." Thus, the combination of "know" and "something" appears to be needed in human thought and speech and to be generally available. Accordingly, I see both combinations discussed in this section as irreducible, and I will use them both in the explications of complex "know" constructions in the sections that follow.

Thus, while Bogusławski's decades-long insistence on KNOW as a fundamental human concept must be properly acknowledged, his interpretation of this concept as inherently linked with a "that"-clause ("know that") appears mistaken. By limiting "KNOW" to "know that" we would be reducing all ways of "knowing" to just one: "knowing" that is verbalized (though not necessarily by the knower him- or herself). But there are many "ways of knowing," not all of them verbalizable. Granted, the frames "knowing a person" and "knowing a place" *can* be paraphrased away, but the frame "knowing something about someone (something)" is as basic and irreducible as "knowing it" (where "it" refers to something partly verbalized in the surrounding context).

11. ASKING FOR KNOWLEDGE EXPRESSED IN WORDS
("WANTING TO KNOW," ASKING QUESTIONS)

The importance of the concept of "knowing" in all cultures is reflected not only in the lexicons of all languages but also in their grammars. In the lexicon, the pride of place belongs to the verb (and in some languages, adjective) meaning "know," usable in basic frames such as "I know it" and "I know something about it." In grammar, the universality of questions witnesses to the importance of "wanting to know." Generally speaking, all questions can be said to include in their meaning the following three components (combined):

> I want to know something
> I can know it if you say something
> [. . . . .]
> I want you to say it

Or, to avoid any unnecessary quibbles about the term "questions," we can say that all languages have means (either grammatical or prosodic, and usually both) to express these three components. In addition, different kinds of questions include some more specific components, usually linked with "question words" such as "where?," "when?," "who?," "what?," "how?," and "why?" For example, the question "where is Mary?" carries, arguably, the following additional components:

I think like this:
    "Mary is somewhere
    you can say about a place: 'in this place' because you know it"

Thus, a full explication of a "where" question may look like this:

Where is Mary?

I want to know something
I can know it if you say something

I think like this:
    "Mary is somewhere
    you can say about a place: 'in this place' because you know it"

I want you to say it

The same general template can apply to other types of *wh*-questions as well. For example:

Who did it?

I want to know something
I can know it if you say something

I think like this:
  "someone did it,
  you can say about someone: 'this someone' because you know it"

I want you to say it

According to the analysis reflected in all these explications, in asking a question the speaker does not assume that the addressee knows the answer. Rather, the speaker *thinks* that the addressee knows something about it. This is different from "embedded questions"—for example, "John knows where Mary lives"—as will be discussed in the next section. First, however, a quick note about yes/no questions.

Building on Goddard's (2002) NSM-based analysis, I would propose that yes/no questions include the same three "interrogative" components posited here for *wh*-questions ("I want to know something," "I can know it if you say something," and "I want you to say it"), but add to them three further ones, based on the word *maybe* and the two twin phrases "it is like this" and "it is not like this," as follows:

Do you love me?

I want to know something
I can know it if you say something
I want you to say it

I think like this now: "maybe it is like this: you love me"
if it is like this, I want you to say: "it is like this"
if it is not like this, I want you to say: "it is not like this"

Questions of this kind envisage two possible answers—in English, "yes" and "no"— which (as suggested by Goddard) build on the two options inherent in the questions themselves ("it is like this," "it is not like this"). But since such answers are inherently dialogical in meaning, I would also posit for them a dialogical semantic component "you can know it," echoing the component "I can know it if you say something" included in the question:

> *Yes*
> it is like this, you can know it
>
> *No*
> it is not like this, you can know it

12. KNOWLEDGE THAT COULD BE EXPRESSED IN WORDS, BUT IS NOT (I KNOW WHERE/WHEN, ETC.)

In a great many languages, like in English, so-called *wh*-questions (e.g., "where is Mary") have their counterparts in the so-called embedded questions (e.g., "They know where Mary is"). Intuitively, the two types are closely related. Speaking loosely, we can say that while the former request "verbalizable knowledge," the latter refer to "verbalizable knowledge" stored in people's heads. Given the close relationship between the two types, their explications should also be closely related, taking account, however, of the differences, as well as the similarities.

One important difference is that a question is normally directed from a particular speaker ("I") to a particular addressee ("you"), whereas those so-called embedded questions do not imply a particular speaker and addressee. For example, if we say "John knows where Mary lives," no "you" and "I" are being referred to, and there are no "I want" and "you can say it" components. As a result, the explication can be much shorter than that of a corresponding question, but the core components are the same, as the following examples illustrate:

1. a. *John knows where Mary lives*

      it is like this: Mary lives somewhere
      John can say about a place: "in this place" because he knows it

   b. *John doesn't know where Mary lives*

      it is like this: Mary lives somewhere
      John can't say about a place: "in this place" because he doesn't know it

2. *Where does Mary live?*

> I want to know something
> I can know it if you say it

> I think about it like this:
>> "Mary lives somewhere
>> you can say about a place: 'in this place' because you know it"

> I want you to say it

As one can see comparing the explications in (1) and (2), in questions that are being asked the speaker thinks that the addressee will know the answer, and provides a ready-made form this answer should take (for example, "this place," as a response to "Where does Mary live?"); in the so-called embedded questions (as in "John knows where Mary lives"), in contrast, there is no "dialogue" and an "objective" state of affairs is being referred to: "it is like this."

13. KNOWLEDGE THAT COULD NOT BE EXPRESSED IN WORDS ("KNOWING SOMEONE," "KNOWING A PLACE")

As mentioned earlier, many languages use different words for "knowing something" (or "knowing that") and "knowing someone" (or "knowing a place"). For example, in French, to say "I know that Mary is married," one uses the verb *savoir*, whereas to say "I know this man," one uses the verb *connaître*; and in German, one uses *wissen* in the first case and *kennen* in the second.

Intuitively, in sentences of this kind, the two verbs in each pair are different in meaning. If one knows something (for example, that Mary is married), one can put this into words (by saying "Mary is married"), and one can pass this "knowing" on to other people by saying something to them (e.g., "Mary is married"). This is not the case, however, with "knowing someone." For example, if John knows Mary, then he can't pass his personal acquaintance with Mary on to other people by telling them something with words. "Knowing someone" is based on personal experience and can only be acquired through personal experience, not through words. Similarly, if someone says about a place: "I know this place" (in French, *connaître*; in

German, *kennen*), he or she is referring to some "knowing," which can only be acquired through experience and which cannot be put into words.

As mentioned earlier, despite such differences between "knowing something" (in French, *savoir*; in German, *wissen*) and "knowing someone," or "knowing a place" (in French, *connaître*; in German, *kennen*), in the past, lexical distinctions such as those between *savoir* and *connaître*, or between *wissen* and *kennen*, were treated in NSM literature as variants (allolexes) of the same semantic prime KNOW, and in English, the verb *to know* was treated as monosemous. The reason for this was that for many years, NSM researchers were not able to paraphrase "knowing someone" in terms of "knowing something" (*connaître* in terms of *savoir*, *kennen* in terms of *wissen*). In the last few years, however, the NSM position on this point has changed, because after many unsuccessful attempts to explicate away "knowing someone" and "knowing a place" by reducing them to something more basic, one proved viable.

> *I know these people (je connais ces gens, ich kenne diese Leute)*
> I know some things about these people because I have been (=was) with them before
> because of this, I can think about these people like this: "these people are like this"

The same analysis is applicable to "knowing a place," as follows:

> *I know this place (je connais cet endroit, ich kenne diesen Platz)*
> I know some things about this place because I have been (=was) in this place before
> because of this, I can think about these people like this: "this place is like this"

A key feature of this kind of tacit, nonverbalized "knowledge" is its experiential character: one knows a person because one has been with the person before, one knows a place because one has been in this place before. As a result of such personal knowledge (cf. Polanyi 1958), the knower can, so to speak, close his or her eyes and bring the person or place in question to mind, and think: "he/(she, it) is like this," without having to put into words what this "like this" stands for.

As the explications above show, in the analysis proposed here the complex frames "know someone" and "know a place" are not being reduced to the basic and irreducible frame "I know it" (where "it" stands for a sentence retrievable from context) but, rather, to the frame "I know something about this someone/this place," also basic and irreducible.

In his book *Our Knowledge of the External World* (1914), Bertrand Russell famously drew a distinction between "knowledge by description" and "knowledge by acquaintance." According to Russell, "knowledge by acquaintance, which is what we derive from sense, does not . . . imply even the smallest 'knowledge about,' i.e., it does not imply knowledge of any proposition concerning the object with which we are acquainted" (151). According to the analysis proposed here, however, "experiential knowledge" of people and places does imply "knowing some things about them," although not any propositions concerning them.

14. KNOWING HOW TO DO SOMETHING

In many languages, including English, there is also a construction dedicated to, roughly speaking, "skills": knowing how to do something may or may not be verbalizable, but it can always be demonstrated. For example, if I can't unscrew a tricky jar, or unlock a tricky door, someone may be able to give me verbal instructions which will enable me to do it; but I may also know what movements to make with my hand to achieve the same goal, even if I couldn't adequately describe those movements with words. At least this is how the "know how" construction appears in English (and also, for example, in French and Spanish). In other languages—for example, in my native Polish—there is a separate verb dedicated to nonverbalizable "skills" (*umieć*), whereas the basic KNOW verb—*wiedzieć*—tends to be reserved for verbalizable "doing knowledge." Thus, one can use *wiedzieć* to translate the sentence: "she knows how to open it," but not the sentence "she knows how to swim": in the latter case, *umieć* would have to be used. For English "know how" (and its equivalents in many other languages), the following explication can be proposed:

She knows how to do it.

she can do it if she wants because she knows something,
    like people can know some things about something if they have done
    it before

This explication presents "knowing how to do something" as analogous, in some ways, to "knowing someone" and "knowing a place," since it, too, refers to personal experience. Yet there are two important differences here.

First, in the case of "knowing someone" or "knowing a place," it is assumed that normally there is a causal link between the present "knowledge" and the earlier experience; in the case of "knowing how to do something," however, previous experience is likely but not necessary. For example, one can say that a newborn baby "knows how to suck," even though it had not sucked before. Thus, personal experience is a touchstone—rather than a prerequisite—for knowing how to do something. To "know a place," however, one must have been in this place before, and to "know someone," one must have been with this someone before.

Second, according to the analysis presented here, true experiential "knowledge," as in "knowing someone" and "knowing a place," includes a "thinking" component, referring to the ability to bring to mind a mental image. No mental image, however, needs to be attributed to a duckling who "knows how to swim."

Like many other uses of the verb *know*, "knowing how" is the subject of many discussions in Anglophone philosophical literature (cf., e.g., Ryle 1945; Polanyi 1958; Stanley 2011). Interesting as these discussions are, they cannot be reviewed here for reasons of space.

15. MANY WAYS OF KNOWING THE WORLD

In Ian McEwan's novel *Solar* (2010, 207), the protagonist is a scientist convinced of the superiority of scientific knowledge over all other ways of knowing. His wife Maisie, a literary scholar, sees his attitude as narrow and linked with an "alienation from his own feelings" and an "unconscious assumption of his own 'centrality.'" She questions "his unexamined belief in the importance of his work, in his objectivity, and in rationality itself." According to Maisie, "he failed to grasp that knowing himself was a vital undertaking. There were other ways of knowing the world, women's ways, which he treated dismissively."

The phrase "other ways of knowing the world" raises interesting questions, both philosophical and semantic. To begin with, it is not a phrase that is readily translatable into other languages, not even one as culturally close to English as French. If we try to grasp the intended meaning of this phrase through French, we must ask, first of all: Is it about different ways of *savoir* or different ways of *connaître*? And if it is a matter of *connaître*, then *connaître* in which sense of the word? "Il y a d'autres façons de savoir" and "il y a d'autres façons de connaître le monde" are both plausible translations here.

If scientific knowledge is understood as "knowledge" (knowing) that can be put into words (other conditions applying as well), then those "other ways of knowing" would seem to refer to "knowledge" (knowing) that is inherently unverbalizable. I am not talking here about "knowing someone" or "knowing a place" in which, as shown in section 13, the word *know* is used in a different, more complex, meaning. The phrase "other ways of knowing" implies that there are various ways of "knowing" in the same sense of the word *know*.

In a classic meditation on, one might say, ways of knowing, Pascal famously wrote (1947, 151; emphasis added):

> Nous *connaissons* la vérité, non seulement par la raison, mais encore par le cœur; c'est de cette dernière sorte que nous *connaissons* les premiers principes, et c'est en vain que le raisonnement qui n'y a point de part essaye de les combattre. (. . .) Nous *savons* que nous ne rêvons point; quelque impuissance où nous soyons de le prouver par raison, cette impuissance ne conclut autre chose que la faiblesse de notre raison, mais non point l'incertitude de toutes nos *connaissances* . . . .
>
> Car la *connaissance* des premiers principes, comme qu'il y a espace, temps, movements, nombres, est aussi ferme qu'aucune de celles que nos raisonnements nous donnent. Et c'est sur ces connaissances du cœur et de l'instinct qu'il faut que la raison s'appuie, et qu'elle y fonde tous son discours. (151)

In an English translation by Honor Levi (1995), this passage reads as follows:

> We know the truth not only by means of the reason but also by means of the heart. It is through the heart that we know the first principles, and reason which has no part in this knowledge vainly tries to contest them. . . . We know that we are not dreaming, however powerless we are to prove it by reason. This powerlessness proves only the weakness of our reason, not the uncertainty of our entire knowledge . . . .
>
> For the knowledge of first principles such as space, time, movement, number is as certain as any that our reasoning can give us, and it is on this knowledge by means of the heart and instinct that reason has to rely, and must base all its argument. (35–36)

Evidently, for Pascal, the word *connaissance* covers different ways of knowing, without being polysemous. Further, for Pascal, this broad concept of "connaissance" is linked both with the verb *connaître* and with the verb *savoir* (both rendered in the English translation of the relevant passage with *know*).

From a linguistic, and cross-linguistic, point of view, what matters most is that there are different ways of knowing linked with different grammatical frames, some verbalizable and some not.

16. CONCLUSIONS

KNOW is a fundamental and indefinable human concept. It shows up as a word in all languages, in four universal frames. Schematically, these frames can be presented as follows:

1. Dialogical (first-person): "I know," "I don't know"
2. Partially verbalized: "to know it" (e.g., this someone knows it)
3. Nonverbalized and "non-topicalized": "to know something" (e.g., this someone knows something)
4. Nonverbalized but "topicalized": "to know something about something" (e.g., he/she knows something about it)

In many languages, the same word that expresses KNOW in the four canonical frames can also be used in some other frames, such as "to know that . . ." "to know someone," "to know a place," "to know where . . . " and "to know how . . . " Two of the four indefinable frames—(1) and (2)—link "knowing" with "saying": one knows something that has been said, or can be said. The other two—(3) and (4)—are independent of "saying," and thus allow for "ways of knowing" that are not verbalizable.

Evidence from the world's languages suggests that everywhere in the world people conceptualize "knowing" not as restricted to things that can be put into words but rather, as extending over a wide range of "sayables" and "non-sayables." Within this range, there is room for "scientific knowledge" and for "intuitive knowledge," for "knowledge" that can be transmitted through words and "knowledge" that cannot be so transmitted, for "knowledge" that is objectively verifiable and "knowledge" that can only be verified subjectively and experientially.[9]

It is of course open to scientists (in the English sense of the word *scientist*) to value empirical ways of knowing over nonempirical ones; and it is open to analytical philosophers to value verbalized "knowledge"

9. On nonverbalizable knowledge, see in particular Polanyi (1958, 1964); see also Torrance (1980); Polkinghorne (1986); Clarke (2005). From an NSM point of view, the whole area of "ways of knowing" requires a great deal of further investigation, grounded in cross-translatable concepts.

over nonverbalized, or nonverbalizable "knowledge." But to be able to communicate at all, we need some conceptual givens, derived neither from historically shaped Anglo English, nor from the European philosophical tradition, nor from modern science, which is not entirely language- and culture-independent, either. This chapter contends that reliable conceptual givens can be found in the lexico-grammatical intersection of all languages, in self-explanatory and indefinable words such as *say, think, want, feel,* and *know,* as used in their "canonical" grammatical frames. Many questions remain, of course, but if we rely on such self-explanatory indefinables we can ask questions that are clearer, more precise, and more verifiable than if we proceed along more traditional lines, without any stable and universal reference points. A philosophical inquiry into "knowledge" needs to go hand in hand with an active interest in language universals, as they emerge from empirical cross-linguistic investigations.

16.1. A Coda: The Priority of the First-Person Perspective

Although this chapter is entitled "I KNOW: A Human Universal," I have not yet given a lot of attention to the phrase "I know" as such. Unquestionably, the "central epistemological concept" that manifests itself in human speech is expressed in the word *know* and its equivalents in other languages (in frames like "know (it)," "know something," and "know something about something"), and not in the first-person phrase "I know" as such. Yet, as intimated in section 8, there are good reasons to think that among all the combinations of "know" with words specifying the "knowers"—"I know," "you know," "he/she knows," "people know," and so on—the phrase with the first-person-singular knower, "I know," has a privileged position, with perhaps "I want to know" a close second.

The priority of first-person frames like "I know," "I know it," and "I want to know" may not show in their frequencies in English (and other) corpora, but it is clearly reflected in the grammar and prosody of many languages, including English. For example, if one asks in English: "Are they coming?" both the grammatical structure and the prosody convey the meaning "I want to know something"; and if one asks "They are coming?" the intonation itself carries the same semantic component. Broadly speaking, if "interrogative" sentences carry the component "I want to know something," the so-called declarative ones (e.g., "They are not coming") carry the component "I know (it)," as evidenced, for example, by the perfectly legitimate response: "How do you know?"

The qualification "broadly speaking," however, is very important here. To begin with, the "I know" message applies only to those utterances where there is an identifiable "I." For example, a sentence in an encyclopedia that says that Madrid is the capital of Spain does not include the component "I know it" because the whole genre—encyclopedia articles—excludes such a frame by definition. In this genre, the dominant frame is "people can know it" or "it is like this: people can know it."

There are many other genres of communication, both written and spoken, that depart from the basic "I say this to you" model, and that cannot be read as implying "I know (it)." Clearly, there is no "I know" in public signs, such as "Roadwork Ahead," in ritual speech, in prophetic speech, and so on. In all such situations, a key to the proper interpretation is provided by the genre. In face-to-face communication, however, where there is clearly an "I" speaking to a "you," the person addressed ("you") must be able to recognize the "key."

Furthermore, even when there is an embodied individual speaker on the scene, a "declarative" sentence with a first-person subject does not always imply an "I know" frame. There are many types of sentences with "I" as a subject that exclude the presence of an "I know" component. This applies, in particular, to sentences with "epistemological qualifiers" of various kinds, whether adverbial like *maybe, probably, presumably,* or *allegedly* (cf. Wierzbicka 2006, chap. 8), verbal like "I think," "I suppose," "I assume," (cf. Wierzbicka 2006, chap. 7), or others.

One final point: the meaning of the intonation. The basic fact is that first-person meanings such as "I know" and "I want to know" can be conveyed by the intonation, with the speaker's body and voice showing who the "I" in a given situation is. Can the intonation convey meanings other than first-person ones?

Presumably, under some circumstances it can, because sometimes one can indicate with one's voice that one is not speaking in one's own voice. One can imitate someone else's voice, one can speak in a sing-song voice, one can sing, chant, declaim, and so on. But all such vocal strategies signal a departure from the default mode of speaking, which is a first-person one.

Linguistic evidence suggests that the priority of the first-person applies not only to the Cartesian *cogito* ("I think"),[10] but also to *volo* ("I want"),

---

10. It appears that "I know" plays also a crucial role in human reasoning, where a person passes from "I know this" to "because of this, I can think like this: I know some other things." Again, this first-person orientation in reasoning appears to have no third-person parallels (no "he knows this, because of this, he can know some other things").

sentio ("I feel"),[11] and, last but not least, *scio* ("I know"). The traditional philosophical preference for abstract nouns, and phrases like "human knowledge," "scientific knowledge," and "propositional knowledge," tends to obscure, it seems to me, the fundamental importance of the first-person epistemological key "I know" in human communication, as it does the importance of "knowing something" and "knowing something about something" in human cultures and cognition.

ACKNOWLEDGMENTS

This chapter owes a great deal to extensive discussions with Cliff Goddard, and is based, in part, on our joint work on the semantic grammar of KNOW over many years. An earlier version of the chapter was also read by Bert Peeters, who offered many very helpful comments and suggestions.

REFERENCES

Asano-Cavanagh, Yuko. (2011). "An Analysis of Three Japanese Tags: *ne, yone*, and *daroo*." *Pragmatics & Cognition* 19(3): 448–475.

Bogusławski, Andrzej. (1970). "On Semantic Primitives and Meaningfulness." In *Sign, Language and Culture*, ed. A. Greimas, R. Jakobson, M. R. Mayenowa, and S. Żółkiewski, 143–152. The Hague: Mouton.

Bogusławski, Andrzej. (1981). "Wissen, Wahrheit, Glauben: zur semantischen Beschaffenheit des kognitiven Vocabulars." In *Wissenschaftssprache. Beiträge zur Methodologie, Theoretischen Fundierung und Deskription*, ed. Theo Bungarten, 54–84. München: Fink Verlag.

Bogusławski, Andrzej. (2002). "There Is Go Getting Round Gettier." *Journal of Pragmatics* 34(8): 921–937.

Bogusławski, Andrzej. (2007). *A Study in the Linguistics-Philosophy Interface*. Warsaw: BEL Studio.

Bromhead, Helen. (2009). *The Reign of Truth and Faith: Epistemic Expressions in 16th and 17th Century English*. Berlin: Mouton de Gruyter.

Clarke, Chris, ed. (2005). *Ways of Knowing: Science and Mysticism Today*. Exeter: Imprint Academic.

Couturat, Louis, ed. (1903). *Opuscules et fragments inédits de Leibniz*. Paris. [Reprinted 1961, Hildesheim: Georg Olms]

Elkin, A. P. (1974[1938]). *The Australian Aborigines*. Sydney: Angus and Robertson.

---

11. The privileged position of "I feel" is evidenced, for example, in interjections, exclamations, and swearing (cf., e.g., Goddard 2014, 2015a), and that of "I want," in the grammar of imperatives and speech act verbs (cf. Goddard and Wierzbicka 2014).

Geertz, Clifford. (1983). *Local Knowledge: Further Essays in Interpretive Anthropology*. New York: Basic Books.

Gladkova, Anna. (2007). "Universal and Language-specific Aspects of 'Propositional Attitudes': Russian vs. English." In *Mental States, Vol. 2: Language and Cognitive Structure*, ed. Andrea Schalley and Drew Khlentzos, 61–83. Amsterdam: John Benjamins.

Goddard, Cliff. (1996). *Pitjantjatjara/Yankunytjatjara to English Dictionary*, rev. 2nd ed. Alice Springs, Australia: IAD Press.

Goddard, Cliff. (2002). "Yes or No? The Complex Semantics of a Simple Question." In *Proceedings of the 2002 Conference of the Australian Linguistic Society*, ed. Peter Collins and Mengistu Amberber, 1–7. Australia: Australian Linguistic Society. http://www.als.asn.au/proceedings/als2002/Goddard.pdf

Goddard, Cliff. (2008). "Natural Semantic Metalanguage: The State of the Art." In *Cross-Linguistic Semantics*, ed. Cliff Goddard, 1–34. Amsterdam: John Benjamins.

Goddard, Cliff. (2014). "Interjections and Emotions (with Special Reference to 'Surprise' and 'Disgust')." *Emotion Review* 6(1): 53–63.

Goddard, Cliff. (2015a). "'Swear Words' and 'Curse Words' in Australian (and American) English: At the Crossroads of Pragmatics, Semantics and Sociolinguistics." *Intercultural Pragmatics* 12(2): 189–218.

Goddard, Cliff. (2015b). "Lexicosyntactic Molecules with KNOW and MINE." Paper presented at the NSM Workshop, Australian National University, July 4.

Goddard, Cliff, ed. (2008). *Cross-linguistic Semantics*. Amsterdam: John Benjamins.

Goddard, Cliff, ed. (2017). *Minimal English for a Global World*. London: Palgrave Macmillan.

Goddard, Cliff, and Susanna Karlsson. (2008). "Re-thinking THINK in Contrastive Perspective: Swedish vs. English." In, *Cross-Linguistic Semantics*, ed. Cliff Goddard, 225–240. Amsterdam: John Benjamins.

Goddard, Cliff, and Anna Wierzbicka. (2013). "NSM4.0 (or: Some Current Developments in NSM in Historical Perspective)." Paper presented at NSM Semantic Workshop, Australian National University, April 5.

Goddard, Cliff, and Anna Wierzbicka. (2014). *Words and Meanings: Lexical Semantics Across Domains, Languages, and Cultures*. Oxford: Oxford University Press.

Goddard, Cliff, and Anna Wierzbicka. (2015). "What does *Jukurrpa* ('Dreamtime,' "the Dreaming") Mean? A Semantic and Conceptual Journey of Discovery." *Australian Aboriginal Studies* 2015(1): 43–65.

Goddard, Cliff, and Anna Wierzbicka, eds. (1994). *Semantic and Lexical Universals— Theory and Empirical Findings*. Amsterdam: John Benjamins.

Goddard, Cliff, and Anna Wierzbicka, eds. (2002). *Meaning and Universal Grammar: Theory and Empirical Findings*, 2 vols. Amsterdam: John Benjamins.

Harrap's Standard German and English Dictionary. (1963). London: Harrap.

Honderich, Ted, ed. (1995). *The Oxford Companion to Philosophy*. Oxford and New York: Oxford University Press.

Jakobson, Roman. (1984[1957]). "Shifters: Verbal Categories and the Russian Verb." In *Russian and Slavic Grammar*, by Roman Jakobson, 41–58. Berlin: Mouton.

Laughren, Mary, Kenneth Hale, and Warlpiri Lexicography Group. (2006). *Warlpiri-English Encyclopaedic Dictionary. Electronic files*. St Lucia, Australia: University of Queensland.

Machery, Edouard, Stephen Stich, David Rose, Amita Chatterjee, Kaori Karasawa, Noel Struchiner, Smita Sirker, Naoki Usui and Takaaki Hashimoto. (2015). "Gettier Across Cultures." *Nous* 50(4): 645–664. doi.: 10.1111/nous.12110

Martin, Gottfried. (1964). *Leibniz: Logic and Metaphysics*. Translated by K. J. Northcott and P. G. Lucas. Manchester: Manchester University Press.

McEwan, Ian. (2010). *Solar*. London: Jonathan Cape.

Nicholls, Sophie. (2013). "Cultural Scripts, Social Cognition and Social Interaction in Roper Kriol." *Australian Journal of Linguistics* 33(3): 282–301.

Ožegov, S. I. (1978). *Slovar' russkogo jazyka* [Russian dictionary]. Moscow: Russkij Jazyk.

Pascal, Blaise. (1947). *Pensées*. Paris: Delmas.

Pascal, Blaise. (1995). *Pensées and Other Writings*. Translated by Honor Levi. Oxford: Oxford University Press.

Peeters, Bert, ed. (2006). *Semantic Primes and Universal Grammar: Empirical Evidence from the Romance Languages*. Amsterdam: John Benjamins.

Poirier, Jean. (1967). *Encyclopédie de la Pléiade*. Paris: Gallimard.

Polanyi, Michael. (1958). *Personal Knowledge: Towards a Post-critical Philosophy*. London: Routledge and Kegan Paul.

Polanyi, Michael. (1964). *Science, Faith and Society*. Chicago: University of Chicago Press.

Polkinghorne, John. (1986). *One World: The Interaction of Science and Theology*. London: SPCK.

Quine, W. V. (1964). "Reference and Modality." In *From a Logical Point of View*, 2nd ed. Cambridge, MA: Harvard University Press.

Russell, Bertrand. (1914). *Our Knowledge of the External World*. London: G. Allen & Unwin.

Ryle, G. (1945). "Knowing How and Knowing that: The Presidential Address." *Proceedings of the Aristotelian Society* 46: 1–16.

Saint Thérèse of Lisieux. (2010). *The Story of a Soul: The Autobiography of the Little Flower*. Translated by Michael Day. Charlotte, NC: TAN Books.

Sainte Thérèse. (2012). *Histoire d'une âme*. N.p.: Cerf et Desclée De Brouwer.

Shope, Robert. (1983). *The Analysis of Knowing: A Decade of Research*. Princeton, NJ: Princeton University Press.

Stanley, Jason (2011). *Know How*. Oxford: Oxford University Press.

Torrance, Thomas F., ed. (1980). *Belief in Science and in Christian Life: The Relevance of Michael Polanyi's Thought for Christian Faith and Life*. Edinburgh: Handsel Press.

Wellman, Henry. (1990). *The Child's Theory of Mind*. Cambridge, MA: MIT Press.

Wellman, Henry. (1995). "Young Children's Conception of Mind and Emotion: Evidence from English speakers." In *Everyday Conceptions of Emotion*, ed. J. A. Russell, J. Fernandez-Dols, A. S. R. Manstead, and J. C. Wellenkamp, 289–313. Dordecht, The Netherlands: Kluwer.

Wierzbicka, Anna. (1972). *Semantic Primitives*. Frankfurt: Athenäum.

Wierzbicka, Anna. (1996). *Semantics: Primes and Universals*. Oxford: Oxford University Press.

Wierzbicka, Anna. (2001). *What Did Jesus Mean?: Explaining the Sermon on the Mount and the Parables in Simple and Universal Human Concepts*. New York: Oxford University Press.

Wierzbicka, Anna. (2002a). "Right and Wrong: From Philosophy to Everyday Discourse." *Discourse Studies* 4(2): 225–252.

Wierzbicka, Anna. (2002b). "Philosophy and Discourse: The Rise of *Really* and the Fall of *Truly.*" *Cahiers de Praxématique* 38: 85–112.

Wierzbicka, Anna. (2002c). "Russian Cultural Scripts: The Theory of Cultural Scripts and Its Applications. *Ethos* 30(4): 401–432.

Wierzbicka, Anna. (2006). *English: Meaning and Culture.* New York: Oxford University Press.

Wierzbicka, Anna. (2010). *Evidence, Experience, and Sense: The Hidden Cultural Legacy of English.* New York: Oxford University Press.

Wierzbicka, Anna. (2014). *Imprisoned in English: The Hazards of English as a Default Language.* New York: Oxford University Press.

Winton, Tim. (1990). *Minimum of Two.* Ringwood, VIC: Penguin.

CHAPTER 10

Theory of Knowledge without (Comparative) Linguistics

ALLAN HAZLETT

1. INTRODUCTION

What has the theory of knowledge to do with linguistics? Here is a familiar idea: facts about how "knows" is ordinarily used provide evidence for and against particular views about the nature and scope of knowledge. This idea is presupposed by many arguments in contemporary epistemology, where, for example, evidence from ordinary language is offered against skepticism or in support of the thesis of "pragmatic encroachment."[1]

But this familiar idea is problematic.[2] "Knows" is a word in English, which is one of many human languages. Why would facts about how this word is ordinarily used have anything to do with the nature and scope of knowledge? For although "knows" is English, knowledge is not. Knowledge, whatever it is, has nothing in particular to do with England, whereas "knows" is distinctively English, having a special relationship with England that knowledge does not have. Drawing conclusions about knowledge in general on the basis of how "knows" is ordinarily used looks at least like a case of cultural chauvinism, akin to drawing conclusions about cuisine in

---

1. Cohen 1988; DeRose 1995; Hawthorne 2004; Stanley 2005.
2. Note well that the following objection does not rely on the idea that epistemological intuitions vary with gender or ethnicity (Weinberg et al. 2001; Nicols et al. 2003; cf. Nagel 2012). That idea is based on experiments conducted in English with English-speaking subjects.

general on the basis of how food is served where you live. Perhaps at the height of the British Empire there were those who thought that knowledge was a distinctively English propositional attitude, but this is hardly an adequate basis for contemporary epistemological practice.

In this chapter I will consider some ways of responding to this objection. After dismissing one kind of response (section 2), I'll briefly and nondecisively criticize two alternative responses (sections 3–4), before articulating and defending the response I favor (section 5). On my view, we should reject the familiar idea that linguistic evidence is relevant to the theory of knowledge, in favor of a picture on which theorizing about knowledge is driven by the stipulation of the value of knowledge.

2. ISSUES OF DISQUOTATION

It seems like there is a simple and straightforward way in which facts about how "knows" is ordinarily used entail facts about knowledge. Suppose we conclude that:

(1)   "Nikki knows that Abuja is the capital of Nigeria" is true.

And that we conclude this on the basis of how the sentence "Nikki knows that Abuja is the capital of Nigeria" is ordinarily used, and thus on the basis of how "knows" is ordinarily used. The objection articulated earlier (section 1), however, suggested that facts about how "knows" is ordinarily used are orthogonal to questions about knowledge. But the following seems like a trivial and necessary truth:

(2)   "Nikki knows that Abuja is the capital of Nigeria" is true iff Nikki knows that Abuja is the capital of Nigeria.

Because it seems like an instance of the principle: <P> is true iff P. In any event, (1) and (2) together entail:

(3)   Nikki knows that Abuja is the capital of Nigeria.

It seems like we have derived a conclusion about knowledge from facts about how "knows" is used. However, the situation is complicated. Consider:

(4)   "Peas are not fruit" is true.
(5)   "Peas are not fruit" is true iff peas are not fruit.
(6)   Peas are not fruit.

There is a natural interpretation of (4) on which it is true—namely, the interpretation on which "fruit" is read as having its ordinary meaning, namely, "[t]he edible product of a plant or tree, consisting of the seed and its envelope, esp. the latter when it is of a juicy pulpy nature, as in the apple, orange, plum, etc." (This is sometimes called the *culinary* meaning of "fruit.") And there is a natural interpretation of (6) on which it is false— namely, the interpretation on which "fruit" is read as having its *botanical* meaning, namely, "[t]he seed of a plant or tree, regarded as the means of reproduction, together with its envelope."[3] But the only way to get from the interpretation of (4) on which it is true to the interpretation of (6) on which it is false is via an interpretation of (5) on which it is false—one on which "fruit" is read on the left-hand side of the biconditional as having its ordinary meaning and on the right-hand side of the biconditional as having its botanical meaning.

Could something analogous happen with (2)? Could there be two different meanings of "knows"—an ordinary meaning and a disciplinary meaning? I have suggested elsewhere that "knows" is used differently in epistemology than in ordinary language: epistemologists' uses of "knows" are always factive uses, whereas non-academics often use "knows" in a non-factive way.[4] Psychologists, sociologists, and anthropologists (among others) also often use "knows" in a non-factive way.[5] It seems probable that there are other ways in which epistemological uses of "knows" differ both from nonacademic uses and from uses in other academic disciplines. The probable differences between academic disciplines are illuminating here: if philosophers and sociologists use "knows" in substantially different ways, then at most one of these two disciplinary groups is using "knows" in the ordinary way. I conclude that it is an open question whether there is an epistemological meaning of "knows" that is different from its ordinary meaning.

What is needed here is an argument that the epistemological meaning of "knows" just *is* the ordinary meaning of "knows," or an argument that these two are co-extensive. Then we could confidently infer that someone knows from the fact that she can truly be said to know, when "knows" takes its ordinary meaning. However, what this shows us is that facts about how "knows" is ordinarily used and particular views about the nature and scope of knowledge cannot be connected via any trivial and necessary truth.

3. These definitions are from the *Oxford English Dictionary*.
4. Hazlett 2010, 2013.
5. Goldman 2002, 183–185; Kusch 2009, 73.

A more substantial connection needs to be defended, if theorists of knowledge can legitimately appeal to linguistic evidence.

3. PAROCHIALISM

Above (section 1), I made fun of the idea that knowledge is distinctively English. But perhaps there is something plausible we can make of this idea. Knowledge, you might argue, is a *social construction*, whose nature and scope supervene on social practices and institutions. It is not, by way of contrast, a *natural kind*, whose nature and scope are independent of social practices and institutions. Knowledge is more like a status in a rule-governed game, like *being onside* (in association football), than it is like a chemical substance, like *gold*.[6] Particular social constructions, unlike natural kinds, are typically relative to particular societies, and this is two different ways. First, there are social constructions that are distinctive of particular societies. The Burryman's Parade is an annual event in South Queensferry, Scotland, in which a man covered in burrs is marched through the town. It would be a mistake to ask of other towns when and where their Burryman's Parade takes place. The Burryman's Parade is tied essentially to the social practices and institutions of South Queensferry. Second, when some social construction exists in two societies, it will typically be differently constructed: the nature and scope of marriage is different for different religious and cultural groups, both in terms of its basic structure (e.g., who may marry) and in terms of the customs and norms associated with marriage (e.g., marriage ceremonies). If knowledge is relative to particular societies, so the argument might continue, it makes sense for us to treat the linguistic practices of English speakers as evidence for and against particular views about the nature and scope of knowledge. For those linguistic practices are a part, perhaps a large or important part, of the social practices and institutions on which knowledge supervenes.

On the present proposal, the theory of knowledge is understood as the study of a particular social construction—namely, knowledge. On one version of this, knowledge is a distinctively anglophone social construction—perhaps because its nature and scope are essentially determined by ordinary uses of "knows." On another, although knowledge exists in non-anglophone societies, it is differently constructed in different societies—and it falls to anglophone epistemologists to study knowledge

---

6. I've borrowed this example from Michael Williams (2015).

as constructed in the anglophone world. In either case, facts about how "knows" is ordinarily used provide evidence for and against particular views about the nature and scope of knowledge.

This kind of parochialism would in many ways constitute a departure from philosophical tradition, with its emphasis on the human condition and preoccupation with things universal. There is a worry here that philosophy cannot be self-consciously parochial, that it must seek to answer questions that are broader and more general. And there is also a worry about method. The empirical and historical methods of sociology, anthropology, and psychology seem more suited to answering questions about the nature and scope of particular social constructions than do the reflective and conceptual methods of philosophy. Of course, philosophy need not be understood in this way: perhaps philosophy should focus on the particular, in its social and historical context, using suitable empirical methods. But this would raise a pressing question: what does philosophy, so understood, have to *add* to the knowledge generated by sociology, anthropology, and psychology? In any event, my principal worry about parochialism in the theory of knowledge is that it jettisons that distinctively philosophical interest in things relatively universal: the philosophical question concerns the nature and scope of knowledge, or perhaps human knowledge, but in any event not merely Anglo knowledge.

4. COSMOPOLITANISM

The idea that knowledge is a social construction (section 2) suggests a cosmopolitan, rather than a parochial, approach to the theory of knowledge. A sociologist interested in greetings would naturally study not only ordinary uses of "hello" but also ordinary uses of *bonjour, hallo,* こんに ちは (*konichiwa*), and others. Perhaps in the same way the theorist of knowledge might study, along with ordinary uses of "knows," ordinary uses of "savior," *Wissen,* 知識 (*chishiki*), and others. By broadening the target of her linguistic investigation, the cosmopolitan theorist of knowledge would straightforwardly avoid the charge of cultural chauvinism (section 1).

However, I shall argue that there is a fundamental problem with this strategy. Suppose there is some language L that includes the propositional operator "gavagai," which operator we translate with "knows." Roughly, the cosmopolitan would like to treat facts about how "gavagai" is ordinarily used as evidence for and against particular views about the nature and scope of knowledge. Suppose, for example, that we are able to conclude on the basis of how "gavagai" is ordinarily used that:

Sometimes, <S gavagai that *p*> is true and C.

For some C. The cosmopolitan would like to treat this as (perhaps nonconclusive) evidence that:

Sometimes, S knows that *p* and C.

So, for example, someone might argue that, because <S gavagai that *p*> can be true even when it is false that *p*, knowledge does not require truth.[7] Or, for another, she might argue that, because <S gavagai that *p*> can be true even when S's belief that *p* is an instance of Gettier-type luck, knowledge is compatible with Gettier-type luck.[8]

At first glance this kind of move appears chauvinistic in favor of speakers of L. But it really isn't. The argument isn't an instance of the chauvanistic form of inferring a universal generalization from a parochial regularity; it is an instance of the nonchauvanistic form of inferring the negation of a universal generalization from a parochial exception—i.e., counterexample— to that universal generalization.

The cosmopolitan argument as articulated is enthymatic; here is an amendment:

(1)   Sometimes, <S gavagai that *p*> is true and C.
(2)   <S gavagai that *p*> is true if and only if S knows that *p*.
(3)   Sometimes, S knows that *p* and C.

Now, given (2), (1) is *conclusive* evidence for (3). The cosmopolitan could get by with something weaker, but she will need something to justify drawing a conclusion about knowledge from a premise about the truth-conditions of <S gavagai that *p*>. Call this assumption, whether stronger or weaker, the *assumption of synonymy*.

The problem with the cosmopolitan strategy is that learning about the truth-conditions of <S gavagai that *p*> can easily lead to doubt about the assumption of synonymy. Recall the two examples considered above. If <S gavagai that *p*> can be true even when it is false that *p*, isn't this just as good evidence that "gavagai" does not refer to knowledge, as that

7. Cf. Baç and Irmak 2011, on the Turkish *bilgi*.
8. Cf. Machery et al., chapter 6, this volume.

knowledge does not require truth? If it seems clear to you that knowledge does require truth, the fact that <S gavagai that p> can be true even when it is false that p will appear to you simply as evidence that <S gavagai that p> can be true even when S does not know that p—i.e., as evidence against (2) (or its weaker variant). Plausibly, in such a case, "gavagai" refers to confidence, psychological certainty, belief, justified belief, socially-sanctioned belief, or some other propositional attitude that does not require truth. Alternatively, if <S gavagai that p> can be true even when S's belief that p is an instance of Gettier-type luck, isn't this just as good evidence that "gavagai" does not refer to knowledge, as that knowledge is compatible with Gettier-type luck? If it seems clear to you that knowledge is incompatible with Gettier-type luck, the fact that "S gavagai that p" can be true even when S's belief that p is an instance of Gettier-type luck will appear to you simply as evidence that <S gavagai that p> can be true even when S does not know that p—i.e., as evidence against (2) (or its weaker variant). Plausibly, in such a case, "gavagai" refers to belief, true belief, justified true belief, or some other propositional attitude that is compatible with Gettier-type luck.

This kind of problem will arise for any attempt to treat facts about how "gavagai" is ordinarily used as evidence for and against particular views about the nature and scope of knowledge. Our confidence in the assumption that justifies drawing a conclusion about knowledge from a premise about the truth-conditions of <S gavagai that p> will typically be undermined by our awareness of substantial differences between the truth-conditions for <S gavagai that p> and our existing understanding of the nature and scope of knowledge.

This problem arises because, as Quine showed, the fact that one word translates another does not mean that those two words are synonymous. Even if "knows" translates "gavagai," the truth-conditions of <S knows that p> and <S gavagai that p> might be substantially and importantly different. What makes one word the best translation of another word does not generally, if ever, require that the two words are synonymous.[9] In Spanish, our *dedos* include all those appendages divided in English into our fingers (*dedos de la mano*) and our toes (*dedos del pie*); "fingers" nevertheless translates *dedos*, but don't infer from this that you have fingers on your feet. Differences at the level of connotation and idiom are also typical, and will make a difference to the extent that we are attending to ordinary use. "Meat" translates *carne*, but in

9. Cf. Baç and Irmak 2011, 308n.

culinary contexts *carne* excludes chicken meat, and has a more specific meaning in the context of particular culinary expressions—e.g., *caldo de carne* (beef stock) or *carne adovada* (roasted marinated pork). One lesson here is that the idea of "the translation" of individual words, as opposed to expressions, sentences, and large linguistic units, is problematic. And all this merely makes it harder for the cosmopolitan to rely on the assumption of synonymy.

There is a temptation to think that every language must have a word that is synonymous with "knows." (I think this is behind our temptation to speak incoherently of the way "knows" is used in other languages.) But this temptation is based on either or both of two mistakes. First, it is a mistake to think that every language must have a word that "knows" translates. We can imagine a language having no word that "knows" translates, and into which the translation of sentences using "knows" might be extremely difficult. (The assumption that every language must have a word that "knows" translates looks itself like a piece of chauvinism.) Second, as I have been urging, it is a mistake to think that the best translation of a word is synonymous with that word. So even if every language has a word that "knows" translates, we cannot infer from this that every language must have a word that is synonymous with "knows."

The temptation to think that every language must have a word that is synonymous with "knows" may be based on an intuition that there is a universal concept of knowledge: a concept shared by all human beings that each linguistic group expresses using the words of their distinctive language. We shouldn't assume this a priori, but we should be open to the possibility of having this established empirically.[10]

In any event, my principal worry about cosmopolitanism in the theory of knowledge is a methodological worry about translation and synonymy: can we ever be sure enough that a word is synonymous with "knows" to infer any significant conclusion about knowledge from how that word is ordinarily used?

10. I have targeted here a species of cosmopolitan argument, on which conclusions about knowledge can be supported by linguistic evidence about how the "words for knowledge" in various languages are ordinarily used. It seems to me that the assumption underlying this kind of cosmopolitanism is the idea that there is one thing to which the various "words for knowledge" refer. My worries about this species of cosmopolitanism do not apply to a *pluralistic* alternative, which would pursue a project of conceptual geography, aimed at characterizing and explicating the various "concepts of knowledge" expressed in human languages. This project would naturally appeal to linguistic evidence.

5. THE EVALUATIVE APPROACH

I propose to reject the familiar idea that linguistic evidence is relevant to the theory of knowledge (section 1). Or, more precisely, I propose a project of theorizing about the nature and scope of knowledge to which linguistic evidence is irrelevant. When it comes to this project, the ordinary use of "knows" is irrelevant—but so is the ordinary use of "savior," *Wissen*, and 知識 (*chishiki*). Let me explain this.

On my proposal, knowledge is an evaluative concept. More precisely, on my proposal, it is a conceptual truth that knowledge is valuable. And I propose that this conceptual truth can be used as the primary motivation for particular views about the nature and scope of knowledge. On my proposal, when we ask after the nature and scope of knowledge, we are not asking a descriptive question about the cognitive attitude or attitudes that are picked out by our ordinary uses of "knows," but an evaluative question about the cognitive attitude or attitudes that are valuable.

To say that knowledge is an evaluative concept is akin to saying that knowledge is a normative concept. Christine Korsgaard (1996) writes that "[c]oncepts like knowledge, beauty, and meaning, as well as virtue and justice, all have a normative dimension, for they tell us what to think, what to like, what to say, what to do, and what to be" (9). The idea of normativity is articulated here in terms of prescription, and knowledge is said to be a prescriptive concept—i.e., one that tells us what to think, what to like, what to say, what to do, and what to be. Korsgaard and I are trying to articulate the same phenomenon here. I articulate this phenomenon in terms of evaluation; she articulates it in terms of prescription. It seems to me that this difference does not amount to much, as it seems to me that prescriptions imply evaluations (to say that I ought to φ implies that my φing would be good in some way) and that evaluations imply prescriptions (to say that x is good implies that x ought to be desired, promoted, preserved, pursued, respected, etc.). But, in any event, on my proposal, knowledge is an evaluative concept. If it is not thereby also a normative concept, so be it.

My proposal is based on a claim about the concept of knowledge, to the effect that it is a conceptual truth that knowledge is valuable. You might object that this conceptual claim must be supported by linguistic evidence—facts about how "knows" and other words are ordinarily used—and thus that my proposal does not offer a project of theorizing about the nature and scope of knowledge to which linguistic evidence is irrelevant. I reply that this conceptual claim is not and need not be supported by linguistic evidence. For it is not an attempt to describe the ordinary concept of knowledge, but a *stipulation* of a distinctively philosophical concept of knowledge. Thus, on my proposal, there are (section 1) two different meanings of "knows," an ordinary meaning and a disciplinary meaning, and in particular a philosophical meaning. In this respect, "knowledge" is akin to other central philosophical terms. Consider, for example, "virtue." Philosophers who study the nature and scope of virtue do not study how "virtue" is ordinarily used. Rather, they attempt to describe character traits that are valuable and to examine the extent to which people possess those traits. The philosophical theory of knowledge, on the present view, has the same structure: it attempts to describe cognitive attitudes that are valuable and to examine the extent to which people have such attitudes.

My proposal, in other words, is that we begin with a schematic characterization of knowledge as a valuable cognitive attitude, and then proceed to the work of figuring out which cognitive attitudes are valuable.[11] This implies that knowledge has both a descriptive and an evaluative aspect. On the descriptive side, knowledge is a cognitive attitude; on the evaluative side, knowledge is valuable. It seems to me that the tough work of the theory of knowledge derives from the evaluative aspect of knowledge: just what cognitive attitudes *are* valuable? This, on my view, is the fundamental hard question in the theory of knowledge.

As part of the "value turn" in contemporary epistemology, it is often assumed that the value of knowledge places a constraint on our views about the nature and scope of knowledge.[12] My proposal takes this idea one step further: the value of knowledge provides the essence of knowledge, and the primary motivation for particular views about the nature and scope of knowledge will be evaluative premises.

There is room for debate about the descriptive aspect of knowledge. We could just as easily characterize knowledge as valuable belief, or as valuable true belief, or as valuable mind-to-world fit, or as valuable representation, or as valuable accurate representation. However, it seems to me that it would be best to settle these differences by stipulation. The main of substantive debate in the theory of knowledge, then, will be about the value of various candidate cognitive attitudes, or species of true belief, or whatever we might stipulate.

It has emerged that the present proposal implies a kind of *pluralism about knowledge*. You might think, although this seems dubious to me, that there is a unique cognitive attitude picked out by our ordinary uses of "knows." But it is quite implausible that there is a unique cognitive attitude that is

---

11. Compare a Jamesian characterization of truth as "whatever proves itself to be good in the way of belief" (William James, *Pragmatism*, Lecture VI).
12. Cf. Kvanvig 2003; Riggs 2008.

valuable. Thus, I have come to speak here of the fundamental question in the theory of knowledge as the question of what cognitive attitudes are valuable.

Robert Pasnau (2013), in a paper called "Epistemology Idealized," describes a version of the evaluative approach proposed here, on which knowledge is schematically characterized as "the epistemic ideal" (989). He alternatively characterizes this as "the ideal epistemic position for a human being, given the powers we have available to us and the kind of world we live in" (989), "what human inquiry can and should ultimately aim at" (989), "the ideal limit of human inquiry" (995), and "what would count as [cognitive] perfection for beings such as us, in a world such as ours" (1005–1006). Pasnau's main point, with which I agree completely, is that epistemological inquiry into "the epistemic ideal" has little to do with, and little need for, the analysis of our ordinary concept of knowledge, which has preoccupied so many contemporary epistemologists (987–989). However, even if we choose to leave aside analysis of the ordinary concept of knowledge, "idealized epistemology" is not the only option; it is an open question whether the evaluative approach to the theory of knowledge is best prosecuted by attempting to describe the ideal (human) cognitive attitude. Compare, again, virtue ethics. Some treat the description of the ideally virtuous person as the basic task in virtue ethics, with saints and heroes taking center stage; but others reject this approach, in favor of seeking an account of ordinary, non-ideal virtue. What I am calling the evaluative approach to the theory of knowledge encompasses both Pasnau's "idealized epistemology" and the approach that seeks merely to describe cognitive attitudes that are good, even if not ideal.

Is the evaluative approach a revisionary proposal? Does it suggest a radical departure from traditional epistemology? The answer is: is some ways, Yes—but in other ways, No.

The evaluative approach is revisionary vis-à-vis contemporary epistemological practice, in as much as it proposes (i) changes to the familiar criteria for success in theory of knowledge, and (ii) a new self-understanding for theorists of knowledge. When it comes to (i), the method of counterexample is perhaps the most familiar device employed by theorists of knowledge, but, on the present proposal, this will have to go. Suppose, for example, that a case is made that any true belief meeting condition C is thereby valuable, and on this basis it is concluded that true belief meeting condition C is (a species of) knowledge. It will be no objection to this that there are cases of true belief meeting condition C that we would not ordinarily call knowledge or that there are things we would ordinarily call knowledge that are not instances of true belief meeting condition C.

When it comes to (ii), the theory of knowledge, on the present proposal, is a branch of value theory, akin to philosophical inquiries into the nature and scope of virtue, the right, the good, beauty, and justice. Theory of knowledge belongs with ethics more than it does with metaphysics (as in the familiar "M&E").

However, the evaluative approach is not revisionary vis-à-vis epistemological practice, inasmuch as there are numerous examples of the evaluative approach being employed in the history of philosophy.[13] They include:

- In Plato's articulation of the concept of knowledge as a species of true opinion in the *Meno*, the idea that knowledge is more valuable than mere true opinion is, at least in part, a motivation for thinking that knowledge and true opinion really are different. This conclusion is not based on any appeal to ordinary language.
- In the *Rules for the Direction of the Mind*, Descartes defines knowledge as certain and evident cognition. But this claim is not motivated by appeal to linguistic considerations, but by the thought that certain and evident cognition is valuable because only such cognition is immune to the fashionable skepticism threatening the authority of the Catholic Church.
- Linda Zagzebski (1996) argues that knowledge is an act of intellectual virtue. The appeal of this theory comes from the idea that intellectual virtues are valuable character traits, not from any consonance with ordinary language (since it is conceded that the theory conflicts with ordinary language).
- Richard Rorty (1989) says that knowledge is that which puts us in solidary with our community; Ernest Sosa (1987) says that knowledge is that which corresponds to objective reality. Their debate is about what matters more—solidarity or objectivity—and has nothing to do with ordinary language.

In these cases, claims about the nature of knowledge are motivated by evaluative considerations—by the idea that knowledge, understood a certain way, is a valuable cognitive attitude, something worth acquiring, something desirable or good. So the evaluative approach is not something entirely new or unfamiliar.

The evaluative approach is not the only option for those sympathetic with the idea that the theory of knowledge need not appeal to linguistic evidence. Alternatives include epistemological naturalism and a genealogical

13. See also Pasnau's (2013) discussions of Aristotle and Descartes.

approach. On the former view, knowledge is not a social construction (cf. section 2), but a natural kind.[14] Just as it would be a mistake to theorize about the chemical nature of water on the basis of how "water"—or *eau*, *Wasser*, and 水 (*mizu*), for that matter—are used, so it would be a mistake to theorize about the nature of knowledge by appeal to linguistic evidence. Our evidence, the naturalist suggests, should come from the conclusions of relevant scientific disciplines (e.g., cognitive science, evolutionary psychology), perhaps informed by philosophical reflection. Alternatively, on the genealogical approach, the nature of knowledge is illuminated by asking after the hypothetical origins of the concept of knowledge.[15] Neither of these approaches gives ordinary language pride of place in the theory of knowledge. I have nothing to say here against them. But neither is an instance of the evaluative approach. Naturalists cannot agree that knowledge is an evaluative concept—for natural kind concepts are not evaluative. She can, if she wants, offer an explanation of the value of knowledge,[16] just as a chemist might offer an explanation of the value of gold. But just as the value of gold is no part of the essence of gold, the value of knowledge is no part of the essence of knowledge, for the epistemological naturalist. And defenders of the genealogical approach do not treat the value of knowledge as a premise in their investigations. Although they may appeal to the value of the concept of knowledge, this is orthogonal to the value of knowledge itself: it is important that we have the concept of garbage, but this doesn't imply that garbage is valuable.

Let us return now to the objection considered above (section 1) and to the charge of cultural chauvinism. Would adopting the evaluative approach proposed here enable theorists of knowledge to evade the charge of cultural chauvinism?

It would not, if certain forms of cultural relativism were true. If our evaluative judgments are merely the expressions of our parochial perspectives, valid only for us, with no application outside of those perspectives, then the evaluative approach is doomed to chauvinism. But I do not think there is any reason for us to adopt these forms of cultural relativism. We can and often do engage in reasoned dialogue about evaluative matters with members of other cultures. Our evaluative judgments are not mere expressions of our parochial perspectives; they are claims that we hope to defend in a shared space of reasons, which we almost inevitably can discuss and debate with anyone who is willing. Evaluative discourse does not

14. See Kornblith 2002.
15. See Craig 1990.
16. See Kornblith 1993.

inevitably collapse into entrenchment and the concession that what is good "for me" is not good "for you." Cases in which evaluative discourse does so collapse, as when we consider conventional etiquette (e.g., whether it is correct to eat food with your hands), are exceptions that prove the rule of cases in which we can and do continue to discuss what really is good.

The case of evaluative judgment contrasts crucially with the case of linguistic convention. Linguistic conventions *are* essentially parochial. There is, in an important sense, no possibility of reasoned dialogue about linguistic conventions. Suppose, for example, that there are cases of cognition in the extension of "knows" that are not in the extension of "savior." Only a fool would attempt to resolve this would-be dispute, as there does not even appear to be a genuine disagreement between the English and the French about the relevant cases of cognition—not in virtue of the fact that certain cases are in the extension of "knows" but not in the extension of "savior."[17] This would be a verbal dispute par excellence. Compare the question of the value of the relevant cases of cognition—the ones that are instances of knowledge but not instances of *savior*. That is a question worthy of philosophical attention, where there is the possibility of reasoned dialogue.

Consider, for another example, the question of Gettier cases. If subjects' cognitions in Gettier cases fall outside the extension of "knows," but inside the extension of some word in some other language, it would be foolish to try to resolve that would-be dispute, which is merely verbal. However, it would be most fruitful to consider the question of the value of the relevant cases of cognition. The cognitive state that Gettier subjects are in: is that a valuable state, or does it perhaps fall short of some value possessed in other cases? (For my part, this kind of question has been lurking in the background all along, motivating the Gettier problem. It was not that the tripartite theory of knowledge was untrue to ordinary language – it was that the tripartite theory didn't describe what we really cared about: true belief virtuously acquired, or safe true belief, or non-lucky true belief, or whatever.)

Consider, finally, the question of factivity. If the English word "knows" is factive and some word is some other language isn't, there is no real disagreement between speakers of English and speakers of said other language. The fruitful question to consider is an evaluative one: is a factive state more valuable than a non-factive state? This is just the question of the value of true belief, which in my view is a deep question, and about which I am confident reasoned dialogue, without cultural chauvinism, is possible.

17. Cf. Ernie Sosa's (2007, 63–69) discussion of cultural differences in epistemic intuitions.

ACKNOWLEDGMENTS

I presented this paper at the Epistemology for the Rest of the World conference, in Tokyo, hosted by the Japan Advanced Institute of Science and Technology, in August 2013. Thanks to my audience on that occasion for their feedback; thanks also to Anne Baril and Tyler Hildebrand.

REFERENCES

Baç, M., and N. Irmak. (2011). "Knowing Wrongly: An Obvious Oxymoron, or a Threat for the Alleged Universality of Epistemological Analyses?" *Croatian Journal of Philosophy* 11(33): 305–321.

Cohen, S. (1988). "How to Be a Fallibilist." *Philosophical Perspectives* 2: 91–123.

Craig, E. (1990). *Knowledge and the State of Nature: An Essay in Conceptual Synthesis* Oxford: Oxford University Press.

DeRose, K. (1995). "Solving the Skeptical Problem." *Philosophical Review* 104(1): 1–52.

Fantl, J., and M. McGrath. (2011). *Knowledge in an Uncertain World*. Oxford: Oxford University Press.

Fantl, J., and M. McGrath. (2012). "Arguing for Shifty Epistemology." In *Knowledge Ascriptions*, ed. J. Brown and M. Gerken, 55–74. Oxford: Oxford University Press.

Goldman, A. (2002). *Pathways to Knowledge: Private and Public*. Oxford: Oxford University Press.

Hawthorne, J. (2004). *Knowledge and Lotteries*. Oxford: Oxford University Press.

Hazlett, A. (2010). "The Myth of Factive Verbs." *Philosophy and Phenomenological Research* 80(3): 497–522.

Hazlett, A. (2013). "Factive Presupposition and the Truth Condition on Knowledge." *Acta Analytica* 27(4): 461–478.

Kornblith, H. (1993). "Epistemic Normativity." *Synthese* 94(3): 357–376.

Kornblith, H. (2002). *Knowledge and Its Place in Nature*. Oxford : Oxford University Press.

Korsgaard, K. (1996). *The Sources of Normativity*. Cambridge: Harvard University Press.

Kusch, M. (2009). "Testimony and the Value of Knowledge." In A *Epistemic Value*, ed. A. Haddock, A. Milar, and D. Pritchard, 60–94. Oxford: Oxford University Press.

Kvanvig, J. (2003). *The Value of Knowledge and the Pursuit of Understanding*. Oxford: Cambridge University Press.

Nagel, J. (2012). "Experiments and Intuitions: A Defense of the Case Method in Epistemology." *Philosophy and Phenomenological Research* 85(3): 495–527.

Nichols, S., S. Stich, and J. M. Weinberg. (2003). "Meta-Skepticism: Meditations in Ethno-Epistemology." In *The Skeptics*, ed. S. Luper, 227–247. New York: Ashgate.

Pasnau, R. (2013). "Epistemology Idealized." *Mind* 122(488): 987–1021.

Riggs, W. (2008). "The Value Turn in Epistemology." In *New Waves in Epistemology*, ed. V. F. Hendricks and D. Pritchard, 300–323. London: Palgrave Macmillan.

Rorty, R. (1989). "Solidarity or Objectivity?" In *Relativism: Interpretation and Confrontation*, ed. M. Krausz, 167–183. South Bend, IN: Notre Dame University Press.

Sosa, E. (1987). "Serious Philosophy and Freedom of Spirit." *Journal of Philosophy* 84(12): 707–726.

Sosa, E. (2007). *A Virtue Epistemology: Apt Belief and Reflective Knowledge, Volume 1.* Oxford: Oxford University Press.

Stanley, J. (2005). *Knowledge and Practical Interests.* Oxford: Oxford University Press.

Weinberg, J. M., S. Nichols, and S. Stich. (2001). "Normativity and Epistemic Intuitions." *Philosophical Topics* 29(1/2): 429–460.

Williams, M. (2015). "What's So Special About Human Knowledge?" *Episteme* 12(2): 249–268.

Zagzebski, L. (1996). *Virtues of the Mind: An Inquiry into the Nature of Virtue and the Ethical Foundations of Knowledge.* Cambridge: Cambridge University Press.

CHAPTER 11

On How to Defend or Disprove the Universality Thesis

CHENG-HUNG TSAI AND CHINFA LIEN

1. THE UNIVERSALITY THESIS

According to the universality thesis,[1] the epistemic properties referred to by the English epistemic verb "know" contained in the expressions of the form "S knows that p" or "S knows how to φ" are shared by the translations of the epistemic verb in all other languages, such as Chinese, Japanese, Korean, Russian, and so on. Some doubt that there is reason to think the universality thesis is true because little or nothing is shown about the meanings and uses of the epistemic terms in languages other than English. Critics of the universality thesis not only think that the thesis lacks empirical evidence for supporting its own claim (or to put it another way, the thesis is nothing more than an assumption implicitly made by Anglo-Saxon epistemologists) but also find counterevidence to the thesis; that is, the evidence demonstrates that translations of the epistemic verb "know" are used differently in some languages from the way "know" is used in English. For example, as Stephen Stich and Masaharu Mizumoto note, "in Japanese there are two words used to translate 'know' in propositional knowledge attributions, *shitte-iru* and *wakatte-iru*, neither of which has the same extension as 'know'" (manifesto, this volume).

---

1. More accurately, the "English" universality thesis, because the thesis takes English as the model for other languages.

However, does such counterevidence really disprove the universality thesis? And if yes, in what sense? These are the questions we try to answer in this chapter. In section 2, we introduce and examine a concrete example by which the universality thesis is proposed (though implicitly), criticized (via providing cross-linguistic counterevidence), and defended. In section 3, we introduce three inquiries about the languages of the epistemic. In section 4, we use the distinctions among these inquiries to clarify the theoretical status of the cross-linguistic counterevidence. In section 5, we spell out the notion of the epistemic, which is central to constructing the genuine cross-linguistic counterevidence, if there is any.

2. ASCRIPTIONS OF KNOWLEDGE-HOW

If there is any concrete example of debating the universality thesis in the philosophical literature, Jason Stanley's intellectualism about knowledge-how naturally comes to mind (although the term "universality thesis" is not mentioned explicitly in the debate between intellectualism and anti-intellectualism). Stanley (Stanley and Williamson 2001; Stanley 2011a, 2011b; Stanley and Krakauer 2013) argues for a particular version of intellectualism about knowledge-how according to which a subject S's knowing how to do something is S's knowing that such and such is a way for S to do that thing under a practical mode of presentation. One of the controversies surrounding Stanley's intellectualism involves the methodology (or approach) relied upon by Stanley: he derives his intellectualism about the nature of practical knowledge from investigating the syntax and semantics of the embedded how-question in the English expressions of the form "S knows how to φ." Such an approach is doubly linguistic because it relies not only on language analysis but also on a particular language—that is, English. Some doubt the general approach that Stanley adopts (e.g., Devitt 2011). Some provide counterevidence to reject or limit Stanley's intellectualism (Rumfitt 2003; Wiggins 2012); that is, in investigating the syntax and semantics of the epistemic terms in languages other than English, no similar intellectualist results can be found or obtained. Assuming the credibility of the counterevidence, Stanley's intellectualism is either undermined because it does not tell us the genuine nature of knowledge-how or is limited in scope in that it applies only to attributions of knowledge-how made in English. However, even the second alternative would not be chosen by Stanley, for he thinks that his theory is universal in the sense that his "view of the nature of knowing how to do something is a view about the metaphysical nature of these states, and not a view in semantics" (2011a,

131). So, how might Stanley respond to the objection from cross-linguistic counterevidence? (The target of this objection is a version of the universality thesis on which Stanley's intellectualism implicitly relies. Stanley's intellectualism can be about the nature of practical knowledge only if he assumes that the properties referred to by the English epistemic verb "know" contained in "S knows how to φ" are shared by the translations of the epistemic verb in all other languages.)

Stanley is well aware of the objection:

> While ascriptions of knowing how appear syntactically to be embedded question constructions in English, there are a wide variety of languages in which they appear differently . . . . [P]erhaps my favored view of the nature of states of knowing how to do something cannot to be taken to be what is expressed by ascriptions of knowing how in languages in which they do not *superficially* take the form of embedded question constructions. (2011a, 132; emphasis added)

Stanley admits that there is cross-linguistic variation of ascriptions of knowing-how, but it seems that he would not treat such variation as "*counter*evidence" to his view for he hints that the variation appears only at the superficial level. That is to say, for Stanley, there is no variation in the deep structure of, for example, "John knows how to ride a bicycle" in English and 約翰知道怎麼騎腳踏車 *Yuēhàn zhīdào zěnme qí jiǎotà chē* (John know how ride foot-tread vehicle in Chinese).[2] So, with regard to the objection from the cross-linguistic variation, Stanley says,

> To show that the view of knowing how I advocate has the virtues I claim for it, I must show that it is the best account of the *uniform meaning* expressed cross-linguistically by ascriptions of practical knowledge. (2011a, 132; emphasis added)

This passage indicates not only the response strategy that Stanley adopts but also that he is a proponent of the universality thesis. Before addressing Stanley's response in more detail, it may be informative to say something about epistemic terms of practical knowledge in Chinese.[3]

---

2. Chinese here means Mandarin, whereas Taiwanese is the shortened form for Taiwanese Southern Min, a variety of Southern Min prevalent in Taiwan. Mandarin and Southern Min are two mutually unintelligible languages subsumed under the Sinitic language, which encompassed seven major subgroups like Mandarin, Wu, Yue, Min, Kejia, Xiang, and Gan.

3. In his "Knowing (How)," Stanley (2011b) says that he will discuss "knowing how" in Chinese, but it seems that in the end he did not give an analysis of Chinese "knowing how."

The case that the examples in Taiwanese exactly correspond to the construction featuring "know how" in English is quite rare and pretty hard to come by. The two unusual examples are taken from a database featuring Taiwanese folktales:

(1) Iau^2 m^7 tsai^{1}iann^2 beh^4 an^3 tsuann^2 pe^1
     猶毋知影卜安怎飛 (54.17鳳山市)
     Still not know want by.means.of how fly
     '(The bird) still doesn't know how to fly'

(2) Hit^4 e^5 hak^{8}sing^1 m^7 tsai^{1}iann^2 beh^4 an^3 tsuann^2 ioh^4
     彼个學生毋知影卜安怎猜 (12.08彰化縣七)
     That CLASSIFIER student not know want by.means.of how guess
     'The student doesn't know how to guess it' (viz., the riddle)

We cannot find any examples corresponding to "know how" in the database of earlier Southern Min playscripts dating back to the Ming dynasty in the sixteenth century. That is, the database of Ming and Qing playscripts show that the verb 知tsai^1 ("know" in Southern Min) is never followed by an embedded clause featuring the interrogative word 做乜 (literally, do.what "how").[4] Note that a sentence in Mandarin like 他知道怎麼說英語 *Tā zhīdào zěnme shuō yīngyǔ* (he know how speak English/"He knows how to speak English"), notwithstanding intelligible, sounds somewhat odd. But it remains an open question as to whether "know how" is attested in ancient Chinese texts pending an in-depth probe.

From a cross-linguistic perspective, we can see that *know* (x) and *know* (y) in English, or *shiru* (x) and *shiru* (y) in Japanese, correspond to *wissen* and *kennen* in German and *savoir* and *connaitre* in French, as well as 知影 *tsai^{1}iann^2* and 捌 *bat^4* in Taiwanese, and 知道 *zhīdào* and 認識 *rènshì* in Chinese, respectively. Thus, unlike English and Japanese, there is no common word for factual knowledge and experiential knowledge in German, French, and the Sinitic languages such as Taiwanese and Mandarin. Rather, the two types of knowledge are realized by disparate lexical items. So a fine-grained view of knowledge may not lump different kinds of knowledge together under a single, all-encompassing category or label. Although *know1 that* and *know2 how* may not wholly correspond to *know* (x) and *know*

---

4. 做物 *tsue^{3}mih^4* as the early precursor of modern 怎麼 *zěnme* is ambiguous, hovering between two interpretations: (1) how (manner) and (2) why (reason). "How" in "know how" in English denotes the first sense. 做物 as a why/how question word is also attested in the early modern Chinese vernacular texts no later than the ninth century. Note that 乜 in 做乜 is a demotic character of 物.

(y) in every respect, there seems to be some measure of tangible affinity between *know2* and *know* (y) if we take *know1* as knowledge based on rational thinking or inference, and *know2* as knowledge based on experience or practice. If we explore epistemology beyond the bounds of knowledge based on truth and venture into the realm of practice, there are skills that cannot fully be explained solely in terms of propositional knowledge. For example, a sommelier or wine steward is supposed to know how to taste wine. Despite the importance of factual knowledge, his expertise hinges no less crucially on the cultivation or fine-tuning of his gustatory sense.

Related to these issues is the question concerning the relationship between skill and ability. As shown in the example, we use the dynamic modal denoting ability to express the skill that one acquires by means of persistent practice. So we should be clear about what kind of ability has to do with skill. There are many kinds of ability. There is the innate ability as exemplified by birds' ability to fly. There is also the kind of ability that is a manifestation of acquired skill. Taiwanese happens to be a language that shows a difference between ability as an acquired skill and innate ability, as in 伊解曉騎骹踏車 *I^1 e^{7}hiau^2 khia^5 kha^{1}tah^8 tshia$'$* (he know/can ride foot.tread vehicle/"He can ride bikes/He knows how to ride bikes") versus 鳥仔解飛 *Tsiau^2-a^2 e^7 pe^1* (bird.SUFFIX can fly "birds can fly"). It seems to be safer and less hazardous to draw conclusions about the validity of intellectualism or anti-intellectualism concerning the debate about "know that" and "know how" by taking a comparative perspective.

Let us return to Stanley's response to the objection from the counterevidence. Stanley tries to undermine the linguistic "counterevidence" from a linguistic approach. Although Stanley admits that there is cross-linguistic variation in ascriptions of knowledge-how, he says that "it is hopeless to base an argument on such variation against either the methodology I have employed, or the view of knowing how I have defended" (2011a, 133). Why? In examining practical knowledge ascriptions in languages such as Afrikaans, French, Russian, German, Defaka, Finnish, and Hungarian (cf. Stanley 2011a, 135–137), it is easy to find a language such as French, in which:

> there is no overt question word in the sentence "Pierre sait nager." So it appears that the complement of "savoir" in "Pierre sait nager" cannot be an embedded question, since it contains no question words. So either "Pierre sait nager" (implausibly) does not provide a translation of "Pierre knows how to swim," or the complement of "know" in "Pierre knows how to swim" does not after all denote the semantic value of an embedded question. (Stanley 2011a, 138)

For Stanley, however, "this argument is not sound. Even if there is no question word in constructions such as 'Pierre sait nager,' *it is simple to give a compositional semantics that takes the complement of 'savoir' to be an embedded question denotation*" (2011a, 138; emphasis added). We will not go into detail at this time. Instead, we formulate Stanley's response strategy as an argument as follows:

(P1)   A language expresses practical knowledge either in a way that involves an embedded question or not.

(P2)   If a language expresses practical knowledge in a way that involves an embedded question, then Stanley's intellectualism about practical knowledge holds.

(P3)   If a language expresses practical knowledge in a way that does not involve an embedded question, it is simple to construct a semantics that involves an embedded question for that language.

(P4)   If it is simple to construct a semantics of an embedded question for a language, then Stanley's intellectualism about practical knowledge holds.

(C)   Thus, either way, Stanley's intellectualism about practical knowledge holds.

The key to this argument lies in (P3). If (P3) is true, then the cross-linguistic variation in ascriptions of knowledge-how fails to be the "counterevidence" to the universality thesis upon which Stanley's intellectualism relies.

So far, we have shown how the universality thesis is used, criticized, and defended by examining Stanley's intellectualism about the nature of practical knowledge. In our view, both the aforementioned critics and the defenders (Stanley as a representative) presuppose a nonepistemic construal of the universality thesis (and accordingly the nonepistemic construal of counterevidence). Such a construal, however, needs further examination. To show this, we introduce three distinctions in section 3 and apply them in section 4.

3. DISTINCTIONS: INQUIRIES ABOUT THE LANGUAGE OF THE EPISTEMIC

The universality thesis involves the *language of the epistemic*, such as linguistic expressions of the form "S knows that p" or "S knows how to φ." We can have three distinctive inquiries about the language of the epistemic.

(We do not say that these three inquiries exhaust all the inquiries about the language of the epistemic. They are just useful for clarifying the universality thesis.)

First-level linguistic-phenomenal inquiry: A description of how an L-language speaker or a group of L-language speakers uses the epistemic terms in L.

For example, the first-level inquiry might tell us that English speakers use the epistemic term "know" to construct expressions of the form "S knows O" (where S refers to a knowing subject and O refers to an object), "S knows that P" (where P refers to a proposition), and "S knows how to φ" (where φ refers to an action or a skill). The first-level inquiry might also tell us that Chinese speakers use the epistemic term 知 (*zhī*, "know") to construct expressions such as 知人 (*zhīi rín*, "know people"), 知天 (*zhī tián*, "know heaven"), 知善 (*zhī shàn*, "know good"), and 知惡 (*zhī è*, "know evil"). Further, the first-level inquiry might tell us to which property or a set of properties the epistemic term "know" is used to refer by English speakers. For example, the inquiry might *report* that the term "know" in "S knows that P" is used by English speakers to refer to *justified* and *true* belief.

Let us turn to the second-level inquiry about the language of the epistemic:

Second-level normative-phenomenal inquiry: A description of how an L-speaker or a group of L-speakers *evaluates* the uses of the epistemic terms in L.

English speakers not only use the epistemic term "know" in a certain way but also *evaluate* how the term is used. For example, an English speaker might say "It is correct/incorrect (or right/wrong) to use 'know' in such a situation" or "You should use 'know' in this way in this situation." A Chinese speaker might say 你在這情況下使用「知道」這字是不對 的 *Lǐ zài zhè qíngkuàng xià shǐyòng zhīdào zhè zì shì bú duì de* ("Under such circumstances the term *zhīdào* that you use is not proper"). The second-level inquiry describes or reports the phenomenon of evaluative judgments that are made about how epistemic terms in L are used.

The second-level inquiry describes the linguistic phenomenon of the evaluative judgments without further revelation and examination of the rationale for the judgments. The third-level inquiry goes deeper:

Third-level meta-normative inquiry: A revelation and examination of the rationale for the evaluative judgments made by an L-speaker or a group of L-speakers.

The third-level inquiry is concerned with the content of the because-clause of statements like "It is incorrect to use 'know' in such a case *because* ..." or "You should use 'know' in this way in this situation *because* ...." That is, the third-level inquiry focuses on the *rationale* for the evaluative judgments made by an L-speaker or a group of L-speakers. Such rationale might be of various kinds, epistemic or not. Imagine that one says "It is incorrect to use the term 'know' in this way in such a situation *because* this is not the way we use the term, period!" The rationale for this evaluative judgment is *conventional* rather than *epistemic*.

4. DISTINCTIONS APPLIED

These mentioned distinctions of inquiries about the language of the epistemic can help us identify what construals are made of the universality thesis and the counterevidence to it. When one uses a case of how an L-speaker or a group of L-speakers uses an epistemic term in L (such as how Chinese speakers use 知) as the counterevidence to the universality thesis, we must further ask about the level of inquiry to which the case belongs. In particular, it is *epistemologically* important that the rationale in the case be revealed. Let us explain a bit more.

Recall that the universality thesis asserts that the epistemic properties referred to by the English epistemic verb "know" contained in the expressions of the form "S knows that p" or "S knows how to φ" are shared by the translations of the epistemic verb in all other languages. For a special construal of the universality thesis, the thesis is true because the relation between words (and their combination) and the properties they refer to is arbitrary. Under this construal, one cannot study the meaning of an epistemic term by studying the term itself or how it is constructed with other terms into a sentence, although the term is needed for discussion. So, when a critic tries to provide the "counterevidence" in which the datum such as "It is correct to use the term 知 in this way in Chinese" is appealed to, the proponent of the universality thesis (of this construal) would determine whether the datum can be treated as legitimate "counterevidence" by considering whether the critic provides the *epistemic* rational for his datum. For example, this might be a legitimate counterevidence: "It is (epistemologically) correct to use the term 知 in this way in Chinese *because* this way of using the term represents something *epistemic* (and this epistemic aspect is not and cannot be represented by, say, the English epistemic term 'know')." (Compare: "It is (conventionally) correct to use the term 知 in this way in Chinese *because* this way of using the term is how Chinese speakers ordinarily use the term, period!")

Let us consider a passage from Edward Slingerland (森舸瀾; 2000), who tries to give a better understanding of 知 ("knowing") and 思 ("thinking") in Chinese:

> This is the import of Hall and Ames's contention that "thinking" (*si*) in the *Analects* is "not to be understood as a process of abstract reasoning, but is fundamentally *performative* in that it is an activity whose immediate consequence is the achievement of a practical result" (1987:44). This distinctive character of the Chinese model knowledge has been noted by many other scholars. For instance, Herbert Fingarette urges us to overcome our western "mentalistic" bias in approaching the teachings of Confucius and to redirect our focus from the "'interior' of the man . . . to the act of the man" (1972:54); Wu Kuang-ming speaks of Zhuangzi's ideal as a form of "body-thinking" (1992, 1997); and P. J. Thiel has described the Chinese model of knowledge as a sort of "experience of Being": "It is very noteworthy that we [in the West] lack a specific expression for this type of knowledge. . . . This type of experience of Being [*Seins-Erfahrung*] is not irrational, but is rather a deeper, entities-bound [*Wesensgebundene*] type of knowledge—one that is experienced with the entire spiritual personhood" (1969:85 n. 148). Several scholars have suggested that this form of practical, engaged knowledge be viewed as a kind of "skill-knowledge" (Fingarette 1972: esp. 49–56; Hansen 1975: esp. 64–65; Hansen 1983a; Hansen 1983b; Eno 1990: esp. 8–10; Eno 1996; Ivanhoe 1993; and Raphals). That is, they propose that the early Chinese conception of knowledge should be seen in terms of mastery of a set of practices that restructure both one's perceptions and values. As we shall see, while the skill model is not entirely apt in the Chinese context, it serves as a helpful illustration of how the early Chinese model of knowledge differs significantly from that most dominant in recent western thought. (294–295)

Slingerland's concern is not the same as ours, but we can still ask the following: Although, as Slingerland claims, the early Chinese model of knowledge *differs significantly* from the recent Western model of knowledge, is such significant difference epistemic? If a critic tries to use Slingerland's claim to disprove the universality thesis, the critic must say more about whether and how such a significant difference involves something epistemic that cannot be found in the Western thought. The third-level inquiry about the language of the epistemic helps us to determine the legitimacy of so-called counterevidence.

5. WHAT "EPISTEMIC" MEANS

In order to show how epistemic rationale functions in the third-level inquiry, we must explain what "epistemic" means. A comprehensive study of the epistemic goes beyond the scope of the present chapter; however, a possible construal of the epistemic is sufficient for our purpose.

Epistemology is the study of the epistemic. Philosophers usually do not give a specific definition of the epistemic, but there is a consensus among them on what can be counted as epistemic: knowledge, justification, evidence, reasoning, rationality, and reliability, among other things. These items are epistemic because, in a sense, they are related to truth in a significant way. Knowledge entails truth. Justification, evidence, and reliability are truth-conducive. Reasoning and rationality are also truth-conducive in the sense that good reasoning or the exercise of rationality involves using, say, valid deduction which is truth-preserving. The epistemic items, thus understood, are concerned with truth although they themselves are not truth. But why should we care about truth? There are several possible answers. For example, true belief is valuable or important for human beings for instrumental reasons (e.g., to survive or to live well) or for mere intellectual reasons (e.g., curiosity). Regardless of the reason, the epistemic is concerned with the particular relation between mind and world.[5]

Let us turn to the third-level inquiry. When we say that the rationale contained in "It is correct to use the term 知 in this way in Chinese *because* this way of using the term is how Chinese speakers ordinarily use the term, period!" is not epistemic, it is because the rationale is not about the particular relation between mind and world. And, when we say that the rationale contained in "It is correct to use the term 知 in this way in Chinese *because* this way of using the term denotes a truth-conducive factor" is epistemic, it is because the rationale is about the particular relation between mind and world.

We are not saying that the chapter's construal of the epistemic is uncontroversial, although the construal might be standard in contemporary epistemological literature. Nor are we saying that the study of cross-linguistic variation in epistemic terms is insignificant. But, if the

---

5. Cf.: "*Epistemology* is the philosophical study of knowing and other desirable ways of believing and attempting to find the truth. It is a central field of philosophy because it links the two most important objects of philosophical inquiry: ourselves and the world" (Zagzebski 2009, 1; emphasis in original).

study of cross-linguistic variation in epistemic terms intends to be significant in *epistemological* research, the study must tell us how it defines the epistemic and how cross-linguistic variation relates to the epistemic so defined.

Critics use cross-linguistic variation as counterevidence to Stanley's intellectualism about knowledge-how. However, they do not go deeper into the third-level inquiry to reveal the rationale behind the counterevidence. (And, we conjecture that the rationale that critics have in mind is conventional rather than epistemic.) Similarly, Stanley does not go deeper into the third-level inquiry; accordingly he treats the counterevidence as legitimate and tries to undermine it by constructing semantics of embedded questions for as many languages as possible. Since both Stanley and his critics understand the counterevidence to be nonepistemic, it is safe to say that they presuppose a nonepistemic construal of the universality thesis. However, such a construal distorts or neglects the crucial aspect of the universality thesis: the *epistemic* properties referred to by the English epistemic verb "know" contained in the expressions of the form "S knows that p" or "S knows how to φ" are shared by the translations of the epistemic verb in all other languages. If what initially motivates human beings to study epistemology is the desire to determine the particular relation between mind and world, then a study of the language of the epistemic, *if* it is an epistemological study, must tell us how the linguistic properties of a particular language determine the particular relation between mind and world.

6. CONCLUDING REMARKS

How can the universality thesis be legitimately and empirically disproved? If one can find, for example, an *epistemic* property referred to by Chinese epistemic verb 知 that cannot be found in English epistemic verb "know" contained in the expressions of the form "S knows that p," "S knows O," and "S knows how to φ," among others—that is, if one can find that the Chinese epistemic verb 知 can reveal something very special about the particular relation between mind and world that is not and cannot be expressed by the English epistemic verb "know," then this empirical finding can be used to disprove the universality thesis. In such a case, there is a unique epistemic property that can only be grasped by the Chinese epistemic verb. Such counterevidence to the universality thesis is at bottom concerned with the metaphysical relation between mind and world rather than a mere comparison of linguistic usages.

REFERENCES

Devitt, M. (2011). "Methodology and the Nature of Knowing How." *Journal of Philosophy* 108: 205–218.

Eno, R. (1990). *The Confucian Creation of Heaven*. Albany: State University of New York Press.

Eno, R. (1996). "Cook Ding's Dao and the Limits of Philosophy." In *Essays on Skepticism, Relvativism and Ethics in the Zhuangzi*, edited by Paul Kjellberg and P. J. Ivanhoe, 127–151. Albany: State University of New York Press.

Fingarette, H. (1972). *Confucius: Secular as Sacred*. New York: Harper Torchbooks.

Hall, D., and R. Ames (1987). *Thinking Through Confucius*. Albany: State University of New York Press.

Hansen, C. (1975). "Ancient Chinese Theories of Language." *Journal of Chinese Philosophy* 2: 245–283.

Hansen, C. (1983a). *Language and Logic in Ancient China*. Ann Arbor: University of Michigan Press.

Hansen, C. (1983b). "A Tao of Tao in Chuang-tzu." In *Experimental Essays on the Chuang-tzu*, edited by Victor Mair, 24–55. Honolulu: University of Hawaii Press.

Ivanhoe, P. J. (1993). "Zhuangzi on Skepticism, Skill and Ineffable Dao." *Journal of the American Academy of Religion* 61: 639–654.

Raphals, L. (1995). *Knowing Words*. Ithaca: Cornell University Press.

Rumfitt, I. (2003). "Savoir Faire." *Journal of Philosophy* 100: 158–166.

Slingerland, E. (2000). "Effortless Action: the Chinese Spiritual Ideal of Wu-wei." *Journal of the American Academy of Religion* 68(2): 293–328.

Stanley, J. (2011a). *Know How*. Oxford: Oxford University Press.

Stanley, J. (2011b). "Knowing (How)." *Nous* 45: 207–238.

Stanley, J., and J. K. Krakauer (2013). "Motor Skill Depends on Knowledge of Facts." *Frontiers in Human Neuroscience* 7, Article 503, 1–11.

Stanley, J., and T. Williamson. (2001). "Knowing How." *Journal of Philosophy* 98: 411–444.

Thiel, P. J. (1969). "Das Erkenntnis Problem bei Chuang-tzu." *Sinologia* 11: 1–89.

Wiggins, D. (2012). "Practical Knowledge: Knowing How To and Knowing That." *Mind* 121: 97–130.

Wu, Kuang-ming (1992). "Body Thinking in the Chuang-tzu." *Guoli Zhongzheng Daxue Xuebao* 3: 193–213.

Wu, Kuang-ming (1997). *On Chinese Body Thinking: A Cultural Hermeneutic*. Leiden: Brill.

Zagzebski, L. (2009). *On Epistemology*. Belmont, CA: Wadsworth/Broadview.

CHAPTER 12

Primate Social Cognition and the Core Human Knowledge Concept

JOHN TURRI

Some important philosophical research focuses on concepts and phenomena unfamiliar from everyday life. To take just a few examples,
some philosophers study the properties of formal languages, the metaphysical implications of quantum mechanics, or the ultimate basis of attribute agreement. It is fair game for philosophers to investigate concepts
and theories from nearly any specialized field of inquiry, including the
natural and symbolic sciences. Because these specialized fields of inquiry
investigate phenomena unfamiliar from everyday life, they inevitably introduce new concepts and categories, and they often produce surprising or
counterintuitive results, such as the relativity of simultaneity or quantum
entanglement. These fields are not beholden to commonsense: that the
results might be shocking is not a serious objection, even if it motivates
people to seek objections.

By contrast, much philosophical research aims to illuminate concepts
important to us in our everyday lives. With respect to these concepts,
philosophers have long assumed that patterns in ordinary usage and
common sense should constrain philosophical theorizing. The basic
assumption behind this approach is these patterns can be used as evidence
to define or otherwise characterize the relevant concepts, to illuminate the
fundamental principles determining membership in the concept's extension. "Ordinary-language philosophy" was an iconic twentieth-century expression of this sentiment, epitomized in the work of J. L. Austin, who

wrote that "ordinary language" should get "the first word" in philosophical theorizing (1956, 11). But the sentiment is of much older vintage. For example, John Locke claimed that a theory of knowledge should be informed by how we ordinarily act and talk about knowledge ([1690]1975, book 4.11.3–8). And Aristotle wrote that a philosophical theory of the good life should be evaluated "in the light not only of our conclusion and our premises, but also of what is commonly said about it" ([350 BCE]1941, 1098b, 9–11).

To characterize ordinary thought and talk, many contemporary philosophers often draw on their own experiences, social observations, and reflections about what we would say about certain situations (Ducasse 1941, chap. 10; Fodor 1964; Austin 1966; Craig 1990; Jackson 1998, chap. 2). However, this approach is subject to at least two concerns. First, it frequently mischaracterizes ordinary thought and talk (Naess 1938; Colaço et al. 2014; Turri 2016a). Second, it is almost always limited to the culture and native language of the philosopher in question, who frequently is also a highly privileged, highly educated male (Stich 2001; Weinberg et al. 2001; Buckwalter and Stich 2014). The solution to the first concern is straightforward: use more reliable empirical tools from cognitive and social science (Nichols 2004; Murphy 2014; Buckwalter and Turri 2016). In recent years, this solution has been applied, with increasing effectiveness, under the label of "experimental philosophy" (for reviews, see Knobe et al. 2012; Alexander 2012; Sytsma and Livengood 2015). The solution to the second concern is also straightforward: study people's judgments across different cultures or languages (e.g., Knobe and Burra 2006).

A recent study on knowledge judgments is an excellent example of philosophical research avoiding both concerns at once (Machery et al. 2015). The researchers' goal was to test whether people across different cultures distinguished between an agent *knowing* a proposition and *having a justified true belief* in that proposition. More specifically, the researchers investigated whether, across cultures, people would reliably judge that having a justified true belief did not necessarily suffice to know.

Participants from the United States, Brazil, India, and Japan were tested in their native language. Participants read a story about an agent who gets indirect, testimonial evidence that a certain proposition is true. The proposition turns out to be true, but the agent's evidence is oddly disconnected from what makes the proposition true. For example, in one scenario, Paul's wife, Mary, has been missing for several hours, so he calls the local hospital to ask whether someone by the name of "Mary Jones" was recently admitted. The hospital worker confirms that someone by that name was admitted, so Paul rushes out the door. However, the patient at the local hospital was another woman with the same name as Paul's wife. Nevertheless, Paul's wife was admitted that evening to another hospital several miles away. After reading the story, participants rated whether, as Paul rushes out the door, he knows that his wife was hospitalized. Rates of knowledge attribution differed significantly across cultures. For participants from the United States, Brazil, and Japan, the central tendency was to deny knowledge (70% to 87%). For Indian participants, the central tendency was to attribute knowledge (63%). Researchers attributed the results for Indian participants to a potential ambiguity whereby the Bengali word (*jáná*) used to translate "know" could also mean "belief."

Another recent but earlier set of studies tested participants from the United States and India and produced different results (Turri 2013). The central tendency for United States participants was to deny knowledge (89%). Similarly, the central tendency for Indian participants was to deny knowledge (85%). (Without excluding anyone based on their answer to comprehension checks, 67% of Indian participants denied knowledge.) The discrepancy between these earlier results from Indian participants and the later results could be explained by several factors. First, the two lines of research tested participants differently. The earlier set of studies tested all participants in English, whereas the later study tested participants in their native languages, including Bengali for Indian participants. Second, the two lines of research tested different storylines and used different response options. Third, the two lines of research sampled different populations in India. The population sampled in the earlier studies included few if any people reporting Bengali as a native language (44% reported English, 30% Tamil, 19% Hindi, 15% Malayalam, and 4% Marathi, with a few of these participants reporting native competence in multiple languages) (see Turri 2013, p. 10, n. 21). So it could be that Bengali speakers specifically have different intuitions from other people, including people from other ethnic groups in the same region.

Several other recent studies have investigated knowledge judgments about similar scenarios—that is, scenarios where an agent gets evidence for a true proposition, but the evidence is oddly disconnected from what makes the proposition true (Nagel et al. 2013; Seyedsayamdost 2013; Kim and Yuan 2015). Researchers looked for intrasocietal cultural variation in knowledge judgments. More specifically, they tested people in Western societies (United States, Canada, Britain) with different cultural backgrounds. None of these studies found evidence of intrasocietal cultural variation in knowledge judgments.

Overall, then, the balance of evidence currently suggests that people across a variety of cultures and languages reliably deny that knowledge is present in such cases. This has led some researchers to hypothesize that these judgments might reflect "an underlying innate and universal *core folk epistemology*" (Machery et al. 2015, 8). (The researchers caution that further work is required before accepting this hypothesis, including studies testing different scenarios, studies on additional cultures and languages, developmental studies, and studies collecting information on religion, socioeconomic status, age, and education.) The hypothesis predicts that "people in all cultures will possess epistemic concepts requiring more than justification, truth and belief, and in most cultures that concept will be expressed" by the term "commonly translated into English as 'know'" (Machery et al. 2015, 8; see also Spicer 2010). This prediction is supported by work in cross-cultural semantics suggesting that all human languages might contain an expression translatable as the English word "know" (Goddard 2001).

Some theorists have recently argued that we do not need empirical studies of the sort discussed above to conclude that there probably is a knowledge concept universal to all humans (Hannon 2015). The basic idea is that the concept of knowledge arises in all human societies because it "answers to some very general needs of human life and thought" (Craig 1990, 2). These needs are "severely practical" and found in even "primitive" human existence (Craig 1990, 4). Humans are essentially social beings dependent on information from others to consistently fulfill basic needs. This dependence creates a vulnerability to being harmed by others' incompetence or duplicity. Thus humans have an interest in identifying trustworthy informants. The knowledge concept serves this purpose. More specifically, "The concept of knowledge is used to flag approved sources of information" (Craig 1990, 11). An approved informant is someone with a true belief about the topic of interest and who is highly reliable in forming true beliefs (Craig 1990, 12, 91; also Hannon 2015, 773).

If this theory is correct, then the concept of knowledge is the "outcome of certain very general facts about the human situation" (Craig 1990, 10), and "we should expect every culture to have a word to express the concept of knowledge" (Hannon 2015, 772). But how shall we judge whether it is correct? The theory's proponents defend it based on how well it "matches our everyday practice with the concept of knowledge as actually found" (Craig 1990, 3). They claim that it well explains "the intuitive extension of 'know' ... [and] a variety of facts about the 'phenomenology' of the concept" (Craig 1990, 3–4). In other words, it explains important aspects of the way we ordinarily think and talk about knowledge—features of our "conceptual and linguistic institutions" (Craig 1990, 10). To identify these features, the theory's proponents rely on their own experiences, social observation, and reflections about what we would say about certain situations.

Alas, the theory's Achilles heel is predictable. Along with so many others in the recent tradition of "armchair philosophy," the theory's proponents have critically mischaracterized how we ordinarily think and talk about knowledge. Two mischaracterizations stand out.

First, knowledge does not require belief, as those categories are ordinarily understood. Several recent experimental studies have shown that people reliably attribute knowledge at higher rates than they attribute belief (Myers-Schulz and Schwitzgebel 2013; Murray et al. 2012). In some cases, the majority of people who attribute knowledge also deny belief. Moreover, in many perfectly ordinary contexts, people's knowledge attributions are not based on belief attributions (Turri and Buckwalter 2017; Turri et al. 2016). The explanation for this might be that belief ordinarily understood is connected with *feeling* in a way that knowledge is not (Buckwalter et al. 2013; Buckwalter and Turri, in press). As William James wrote, "In its inner nature belief . . . is a sort of feeling more allied to the emotions than to anything else" (James 1889, 21; see also Hume [1748]1993 on belief as a *feeling*).

Second, knowledge does not require reliability, nor do we ordinarily assume that it does. Many contemporary philosophers have simply assumed without argument that knowledge requires reliability. But there is good evidence that unreliably produced knowledge is not only possible but actual (Turri 2012; Turri 2015a). More importantly for present purposes, commonsense epistemology fully embraces the possibility of unreliably produced knowledge. In one recent series of studies (Turri 2016b), up to 90% of participants attributed knowledge in cases of unreliably produced true belief, while participants overwhelmingly denied knowledge in closely matched controls. Participants consistently attributed knowledge to reliable and unreliable believers at similar rates. Participants attributed knowledge to agents whom they actively classified as unreliable. More generally, participants understood and processed explicit information about (un)reliability, but they did not seem to consult this information when making knowledge judgments.

In light of these findings, I reject the armchair hypothesis about a universal human knowledge concept. It is based on critical mischaracterizations of ordinary thought and talk, resulting in its "explaining" nonexistent patterns in commonsense epistemology. To be sure, the armchair hypothesis describes a possible concept that could serve needs that humans actually have. But that possible concept is not the knowledge concept we actually have. (More precisely and humbly, it is not the concept expressed by "know" in contemporary anglophone societies.)

Of course, even if that one particular armchair hypothesis is false, it does not follow that there is not a core universal human knowledge concept. The cross-cultural findings on knowledge judgments discussed above provide some evidence for some universal features of human folk epistemology. Another approach to this issue is to blend some motivations from the armchair project and the cross-cultural empirical project. This approach looks for needs that (i) are common to animal life beyond just the human species, and (ii) would be well served by cultivating a knowledge concept. Similar to the armchair hypothesis, this approach begins with a thoroughly naturalist assumption that human behavior and institutions are "natural facts to be understood as the outcome of other natural facts" (Craig 1990, 9). However, unlike the armchair hypothesis but in keeping with the cross-cultural project, this approach relies on scientific evidence to validate hypotheses. To illustrate the approach, I will baldly state a hypothesis. Then I will review some evidence supporting it. Then I will discuss some of its implications.

The knowledge concept is not a human creation (contra Craig 1990, 3). Instead, the knowledge concept is an integral part of the primate social-cognitive system, which humans inherited. The core of the knowledge concept is *truth detection and retention*. Its origin is related to the basic need for predicting other organisms' behavior to guide decision-making.

Research on primate social cognition has advanced dramatically over the past fifteen years, beginning with a landmark study introducing a food-competition paradigm to probe for mental-state representations in chimpanzees (Hare et al. 2000). This paradigm was vastly more ecologically valid than previous studies, which studied, for instance, how chimpanzees decided to beg humans for food or whether to use a human's gaze to find hidden food items. Using the more ecologically valid approach based on food competition, researchers found that subordinate chimpanzees kept track of which food items dominant chimpanzees currently or recently saw and used this information to decide which food items to retrieve (e.g., Hare et al. 2001; Kaminski et al. 2008).

Subsequent variations on the food-competition paradigm showed that chimpanzees actively conceal visual information from others, that they conceal auditory information from others, and that many of the same findings extend to other apes and monkey species (e.g., Flombaum and Santos 2005; Santos et al. 2006; Melis et al. 2006; Marticorena et al. 2011; for reviews, see Call and Tomasello 2008; Seed and Tomasello 2010; Martin and Santos 2014). (The findings pertain primarily to simian primates [apes and monkeys]; findings for other primates are either less consistent [e.g., lemurs] or nonexistent [e.g., tarsiers]. See Sandel et al. 2011; Bray et al. 2014.) Researchers have also found that chimpanzees attribute simple, sensible inferences to others and use this information to guide decision-making (Schmelz et al. 2011). So, in addition to truth detection and retention, chimpanzees also recognize in others the *discovery* of truth through inference.

In light of this impressive body of research, the consensus among primatologists is that (simian) nonhuman primates attribute knowledge to others and thus have a concept of knowledge. This concept pertains to the detection, discovery, and retention of truths and is closely connected to predicting others' behavior and guiding decision-making. Nevertheless, primatologists contend that there is no clear evidence that nonhuman primates attribute false beliefs to others, from which many conclude that nonhuman primates lack the concept of belief. Overall, then, the current evidence leads many to conclude that whereas humans use belief-desire psychology, nonhuman primates use a comparatively simpler but still impressive "knowledge-goal" psychology (e.g., Call and Tomasello 2008).

These findings on primate social cognition have at least two important implications for recent philosophical research on the knowledge concept. First, contrary to the armchair hypothesis discussed earlier, it is a mistake to seek the knowledge concept's origin in distinctively human conditions. Its origin is not human information-sharing practices or other cooperative endeavors. Instead, we inherited the concept from our primate ancestors. This important fact cannot be learned from the armchair, but it should inform any serious investigation seeking to understand human social cognition as the "outcome of natural facts" (Craig 1990, 9). Moreover, this fact might help explain why some human knowledge attributions are not based on belief attributions. As mentioned above, although nonhuman primates attribute knowledge, they lack the concept of belief, according to leading primatologists. If that is correct, then nonhuman primates obviously do not base knowledge attributions on belief attributions. Thus when humans do not base knowledge attributions on belief attributions, it could just be a special instance of a more general fact about primate social cognition.

Second, the primatological findings provide strong evidence for a species-typical knowledge concept in humans. This can be crystallized in a simple argument: primates share a core knowledge concept; humans are primates; therefore, humans share a core knowledge concept. Again, this core concept pertains to detecting, discovering, and retaining truths and is central to predicting behavior (for a defense of a theory of knowledge along these lines, including theoretical and empirical reviews, see Turri 2012,

2015a, 2015b, 2015c, 2015d, 2016c; Turri et al. 2017; Turri, in press a, in press b). This in turn helps to settle one question motivating recent cross-cultural epistemological research—namely, whether there is an "innate and universal core folk epistemology" across human cultures (Machery et al. 2015, 8). In virtue of their primate nature, humans worldwide share this core knowledge concept.

Of course, it does not follow that all humans have the exact same knowledge concept. Consistent with everything I have said, there could still be important cultural or individual variation in how the core knowledge concept is elaborated, interpreted, or applied (compare Spicer 2010, 523ff; Machery et al. 2015, 8–9, 11). Indeed, by analogy with moral judgments, arguably we should expect cultural and individual differences for knowledge judgments. Our moral concepts and sentiments originate from more primitive instincts and mechanisms shared with primates and mammals more generally (Haidt 2007; de Waal 2006; Barnes et al. 2008; Lakshminarayanan and Santos 2008). And despite our having a suite of species-typical ethical concepts and susceptibilities (e.g., sensitivity to others' welfare, concern for reputation, punitive instincts), we nevertheless exhibit significant cultural and individual variation in moral judgments (for a review, see Young and Saxe 2011). The same is probably true for knowledge judgments.

It might be asked whether my discussion assumes that we have a reasonably clear and well-motivated theory of concept identity enabling us to decide when two different groups share a concept. In response, a general theory of concept identity is not required to judge the particular case at hand. We know from modern biology that primates share many genetic, anatomical, social, behavioral, and psychological traits because of their common evolutionary heritage (Mitani et al. 2012; Stanford et al. 2009). The human social-cognitive system is based upon a primate social-cognitive system tens of millions of years in the making. Thus we should expect many deep and important similarities. Nonhuman primates have a concept of truth detection, discovery, and retention whose key functions appear to include behavioral predictions and decision-making; primatologists consider this to be a knowledge concept. Humans have a concept with similar criteria and functions; cognitive scientists consider this to be a knowledge concept, and ordinary people use "know" to express it. In light of all this, it is reasonable to conclude that a knowledge concept is part of an ancient primate social-cognitive system. (Those who do not want to call it a "knowledge" concept can call it a "proto-knowledge" concept. Either way, it is still an important epistemological category in primate social cognition.)

In sum, those interested in the human knowledge concept should attend closely to evidence from comparative psychology and especially primate social cognition. Knowledge is a core category of primate social cognition, which implies that humans possess a species-typical knowledge concept whose essence will not be fully understood by studying humans alone.

ACKNOWLEDGMENTS

For feedback I thank Wesley Buckwalter, A. Y. Daring, Ashley Keefner, Michael Hannon, Edouard Machery, Stephen Stich, David Rose, and Angelo Turri. This research was supported by the Social Sciences and Humanities Research Council of Canada, the Ontario Ministry of Economic Development and Innovation, and the Canada Research Chairs program.

REFERENCES

Alexander, J. (2012). *Experimental Philosophy*. Cambridge: Polity.

Aristotle. ([350 BCE]1941). *Nichomachean Ethics*. Translated by Ed. R. McKeon and W. D. Ross. New York: Random House.

Austin, J. L. (1956). "A Plea for Excuses." *Proceedings of the Aristotelian Society* 57: 1–30.

Austin, J. L. (1966). "Three Ways of Spilling Ink." *Philosophical Review* 75(4): 427–440.

Barnes, J. L., T. Hill, M. Langer, M. Martinez, and L. R. Santos, L. R. (2008). "Helping Behaviour and Regard for Others in Capuchin Monkeys (*Cebus apella*)." *Biology Letters* 4(6): 638–640. http://doi.org/10.1126/science.1121448.

Bray, J., C. Krupenye, and B. Hare. (2014). "Ring-tailed Lemurs (*Lemur catta*) Exploit Information About What Others Can See But Not What They Can Hear." *Animal Cognition* 17: 735–744.

Buckwalter, W., D. Rose, and J. Turri. (2013). "Belief Through Thick and Thin." *Nous*: 1–28. http://doi.org/10.1111/nous.12048.

Buckwalter, W., and S. Stich. (2014). "Gender and Philosophical Intuition." In *Experimental philosophy*, 2nd ed., ed. J. Knobe and S. Nichols, Oxford: Oxford University Press.

Buckwalter, W., and J. Turri. (2016). "Modest Scientism in Philosophy." In *Scientism: Prospects and Problems*, ed. J. R. Ridder, R. Peels, and R. van Woudenberg, Oxford:Oxford University Press.

Buckwalter, W., and J. Turri. (in press). "In the thick of moral motivation." *Review of Philosophy and Psychology*.

Call, J., and M. Tomasello. (2008). "Does the Chimpanzee Have a Theory of Mind? 30 Years Tater." *Trends in Cognitive Sciences* 12(5): 187–192.

Colaco, D., W. Buckwalter, S. Stich, and E. Machery. (2014). "Epistemic Intuitions in Fake-barn Thought Experiments." *Episteme* 11(2): 199–212. http://doi.org/10.1017/epi.2014.7.

Craig, E. (1990). *Knowledge and the State of Nature: An Essay in Conceptual Synthesis*. Oxford: Oxford University Press.

de Waal, F. (2006). *Primates and Philosophers: How Morality Evolved*. Princeton, NJ: Princeton University Press.

Ducasse, C. J. (1941). *Philosophy as a Science: Its Matter and Its Method*. New York: Oskar Piest.

Flombaum, J. I., and L. R. Santos. (2005). "Rhesus Monkeys Attribute Perceptions to Others." *Current Biology* 15(5): 447–452. http://doi.org/10.1016/j.cub.2004.12.076.

Fodor, J. A. (1964). "On Knowing What We Would Say." *Philosophical Review* 73(2): 198–212.

Goddard, C. (2001). "Lexico-Semantic Universals: A Critical Overview." *Linguistic Typology* 5(1): 1–65.

Haidt, J. (2007). "The New Synthesis in Moral Psychology." *Science* 316(5827): 998–1002. http://doi.org/10.1126/science.1137651.

Hannon, M. (2015). "The Universal Core of Knowledge." *Synthese* : 1–18. http://doi.org/10.1007/s11229-014-0587-y.

Hare, B., J. Call, B. Agnetta, and M. Tomasello, M. (2000). Chimpanzees Know What Conspecifics Do and Do Not See." *Animal Behaviour* 59(4): 771–785. http://doi.org/10.1006/anbe.1999.1377.

Hare, B., J. Call, and M. Tomasello. (2001). "Do Chimpanzees Know What Conspecifics Know?" *Animal Behaviour* 61(1): 139–151. http://doi.org/10.1006/anbe.2000.1518.

Hume, D. ([1748]1993). *An Enquiry Concerning Human Understanding*, 2nd ed. Edited by E. Steinberg. Indianapolis, IN: Hackett.

Jackson, F. (1998). *From Metaphysics to Ethics*. Oxford: Oxford University Press.

James, W. (1889). "The Psychology of Belief." *Mind* 14(55): 321–352.

Kaminski, J., J. Call, and M. Tomasello. (2008). Chimpanzees Know What Others Know, But Not What They Believe." *Cognition* 109: 224–234.

Kim, M., and Y. Yuan. (2015). "No Cross-Cultural Differences in Gettier Car Case Intuition." *Episteme* 12(3): 355–361. http://doi.org/10.1017/epi.2015.17.

Knobe, J., W. Buckwalter, S. Nichols, P. Robbins, H. Sarkissian, and T. Sommers. (2012). "Experimental Philosophy." *Annual Review of Psychology* 63(1): 81–99. http://doi.org/10.1146/annurev-psych-120710-100350.

Knobe, J., and A. Burra. (2006). "The Folk Concepts of Intention and Intentional Action: A Cross-Cultural Study." *Journal of Cognition and Culture* 6(1–2): 113–132.

Lakshminarayanan, V. R., and L. R. Santos. (2008). "Capuchin Monkeys Are Sensitive to Others' Welfare." *Current Biology*.

Locke, J. ([1690]1975). *An Essay Concerning Human Understanding*. Edited by P. H. Nidditch. Oxford: Clarendon Press.

Machery, E., S. Stich, D. Rose, A. Chatterjee, K. Karasawa, N. Struchiner, et al. (2015). "Gettier Across Cultures. *Nous*.

Marticorena, D. C. W., A. M. Ruiz, C. Mukerji, A. Goddu, and L. R. Santos. (2011). "Monkeys Represent Others' Knowledge But Not Their Beliefs." *Developmental Science* 14(6): 1406–1416. http://doi.org/10.1111/j.1467-7687.2011.01085.x.

Martin, A. and Santos, L. R. (2014). The origins of belief representation: Monkeys fail to automatically represent others' beliefs. *Cognition*, *130*(3), 300–308. http://doi.org/10.1016/j.cognition.2013.11.016

Melis, A. P., J. Call, and M. Tomasello. (2006). "Chimpanzees Conceal Visual and Auditory Information From Others." *Journal of Comparative Psychology* 120(2): 154. http://doi.org/10.1037/0735-7036.120.2.154.

Mitani, J. C., J. Call, P. M. Kappeler, R. A. Palombit, and J. B. Silk, eds. (2012). *The Evolution of Primate Societies*. Chicago: University of Chicago Press.

Murphy, T. (2014). "Experimental Philosophy: 1935–1965." In *Oxford Studies in Experimental Philosophy*, ed. T. Lombrozo, J. Knobe, and S. Nichols, 1: 325–367). Oxford University Press.

Murray, D., J. Sytsma, and J. Livengood. (2012). "God Knows (But Does God Believe?)." *Philosophical Studies* 166(1): 83–107. http://doi.org/10.1007/s11098-012-0022-5.

Myers-Schulz, B., and E. Schwitzgebel. (2013). "Knowing That P Without Believing That P." *Nous* 47(2): 371–384.

Naess, A. (1938). "Common-sense and Truth." *Theoria* 4(1): 39–58.

Nagel, J., V. San Juan, and R. A. Mar. (2013). "Lay Denial of Knowledge for Justified True Beliefs." *Cognition*, 1–10. http://doi.org/10.1016/j.cognition.2013.02.008.

Nichols, S. (2004). "Folk Concepts and Intuitions: From Philosophy to Cognitive Science." *Trends in Cognitive Sciences* 8(11): 514–518. http://doi.org/10.1016/j.tics.2004.09.001.

Rose, D., W. Buckwalter, and J. Turri. (2014). "When Words Speak Louder Than Actions: Delusion, Belief and the Power of Assertion." *Australasian Journal of Philosophy*. http://doi.org/10.1080/00048402.2014.909859.

Sandel, A. A., E. L. MacLean, and B. Hare. (2011). "Animal Behaviour." *Animal Behaviour* 81(5): 925–931. http://doi.org/10.1016/j.anbehav.2011.01.020.

Santos, L. R., A. G. Nissen, and J. A. Ferrugia. (2006). "Rhesus Monkeys, Macaca Mulatta, Know What Others Can and Cannot Hear." *Animal Behaviour* 71(5): 1175–1181. http://doi.org/10.1016/j.anbehav.2005.10.007.

Schmelz, M., J. Call, and M. Tomasello. (2011). "Chimpanzees Know That Others Make Inferences." *Proceedings of the National Academy of Sciences* 108(7): 3077–3079. http://doi.org/10.1073/pnas.1000469108.

Seed, A. and Tomasello, M. (2010). Primate Cognition. Topics in Cognitive Science, 2(3), 407–419. http://doi.org/10.1111/j.1756-8765.2010.01099.x

Seyedsayamdost, H. (2014). "On Normativity and Epistemic Intuitions: Failure of Replication." *Episteme* 12(1): 95–116. http://doi.org/10.1017/epi.2014.27.

Spicer, F. (2010). "Cultural Variations in Folk Epistemic Intuitions." *Review of Philosophy and Psychology* 1(4): 515–529. http://doi.org/10.1007/s13164-010-0023-2.

Stanford, C., J. S. Allen, S. C. Antón, and N. C. Lovell. (2009). *Biological Anthropology: The Natural History of Humankind*. Toronto: Pearson Education Canada.

Stich, S. (2001). "Plato's Method Meets Cognitive Science." *Free Inquiry* 21(2): 36–38.

Sytsma, J., and J. Livengood. (2015). *The Theory and Practice of Experimental Philosophy*. Peterborough: Broadview Press.

Turri, J. (2012). "Review of Achieving Knowledge: A Virtue-Theoretic Account of Epistemic Normativity, by John Greco." *Mind* 121(481): 183–187. http://doi.org/10.1093/mind/fzs032.

Turri, J. (2013). "A Conspicuous Art: Putting Gettier to the Test." *Philosophers' Imprint* 13(10): 1–16.

Turri, J. (2015a). "Unreliable knowledge." *Philosophy and Phenomenological Research* 90(3): 529–545. http://doi.org/10.1111/phpr.12064.

Turri, J. (2015b). "Epistemic Situationism and Cognitive Ability." In *Epistemic Situationism*, ed. M. Alfano and A. Fairweather, Oxford: Oxford University Press.

Turri, J. (2015c). "From Virtue Epistemology to Abilism: Theoretical and Empirical Developments." In *Character: New Directions From Philosophy, Psychology, and Theology*, ed. C. B. Miller, M. R. Furr, A. Knobel, and W. Fleeson, Oxford University Press.

Turri, J. (2015d). "An Open and Shut Case: Epistemic Closure in the Manifest Image." *Philosophers' Imprint* 15(2): 1–18.

Turri, J. (2016a). "How To Do Better: Toward Normalizing Experimentation in Epistemology." In *Advances in Experimental Philosophy And Philosophical Methodology*, ed. J. Nado, Bloomsbury Academic.

Turri, J. (2016b). "A New Paradigm for Epistemology: From Reliabilism to Abilism." *Ergo* 3(8): 189–231.

Turri, J. (2016c). *Knowledge and the Norm of Assertion: An Essay in Philosophical Science.* Cambridge: Open Book Publishers.

Turri, J. (in press a). "Knowledge Attributions and Behavioral Predictions in Social Cognition." *Cognitive Science*.

Turri, J. (in press b). "Experimental, Cross-Cultural, and Classical Indian Epistemology." *Journal of Indian Council of Philosophical Research*.

Turri, J., and W. Buckwalter. (2017). "Descartes's Schism, Locke's Reunion: Completing the Pragmatic Turn in Epistemology." *American Philosophical Quarterly*, 54(1).

Turri, J., W. Buckwalter, and D. Rose. (2016). "Actionability Judgments Cause Knowledge Judgments: Evidence From Two Experiments." *Thought*.

Turri, J., O. Friedman, and A. Keefner. (2017). "Knowledge Central: A Central Role for Knowledge Attributions in Social Evaluations." *Quarterly Journal of Experimental Psychology* 70(3): 504–515. http://doi.org/10.1080/17470218.2015.1136339.

Weinberg, J. M., S. Nichols, and S. Stich. (2001). "Normativity and Epistemic Intuitions." *Philosophical Topics* 29(1–2): 429–460.

Young, L., and R. Saxe. (2011). "Moral Universals and Individual Differences." *Emotion Review* 3(3): 323–324. http://doi.org/10.1177/1754073911402383.

INDEX

Alexander, Joshua, 99 (n.29), 100, 124, 280
alphabet of human thought. *See* thought
Analects, chap. 4, *passim*, 275
aspect, aspectual: grammatical or lexical, 22, 28, 30, 33, 62, 79

bank case, 96, 102–4, 107–12, 189–90, 195, 197 (n.5), 200
belief, chap. 2, *passim*, 67, 70, 71, 74, 115 (n.44), 126–37, 140–5, 224–5
    as a dispositional state, 14–15, 32
    See also justified true belief; justified false belief
"belief," "believe" (as an English term), 23–4, 26–7, 32–4, 41, 131, 225
Bengali, 131, 133, 204 (n.9), 224, 281

case method. *See* method of cases
certainty/uncertainty, subjective, 33, 104, 104 (n.34), 110, 114, 149, 160, 166, 173, chap. 8, *passim*, 257, 262
chauvinism, 256, 258
    cultural, 251, 255, 263–4
Chinese
    language, chap.3, *passim*, 72, 77, 207, 218, 267, 269–70, 273–7
    philosophy, chap. 4, *passim*, 196, 275
    See also Mandarin
cognitive, 14, 15
    ability, 79, 108–9, 115
    attitude, 259–62
    ethology, viii
    load, 105 (n.35), 193
    performance, 15
    science, scientists, 263, 280, 286
    See also social-cognitive system

concept, 16, 216–19, 226–7, 233, 263
    core knowledge, 115, 196, 284–6
    formal/informal, 116
    of knowledge, knowing, etc., 12, 14, 22, 37, 112–19, 131, 174, 196, chap. 9, *passim*, 258–9, 261–3, chap. 12, *passim*
    species-typical knowledge, 285–7
    universal, 227, 233
    universal concept of knowledge, 114, 119, 216, 220, 223, 258, 282–4
    See also evaluative: concept
conceptual analysis, viii, xiii
conceptual truth, 12, 259
Confucius, 58, chap. 4, *passim*, 275
contextualism, contextualist, viii, 15, 84
Craig, Edward, 116 (n.45), 263 (n.15), 280, 282, 284–5
cross-cultural, xii, xiii, xiv, 13, 126, 187–8, 196, 199, 204 (n.9), 211, 225–7, 284
    agreement, 199
    universal, xii
cross-linguistic, xi, xii, 150, 152, 166, 218–19, 230, 235, 244, 270, 272, 276–7
    data, 149
    disagreement, 114–15, 119
    evidence, counterevidence, 233, 268–9
    semantics, 216
    similarity,
    stability of KNOW, 227
cultural chauvinism. *See* chauvinism
cultural opacity, 232–3
cultural-psychological, 118
cultural relativism. *See* relativism
Cuzco Quechua, 151, 156–7, 161–3

human social cognition, cognitive system, 285, 286. *See also* primate social cognition

inference, 152–4, 160, 162, 181–2, 285
intellectualism vs. anti-intellectualism, 92, 109, 268–9, 271–2, 277. *See also* knowledge how
intuition, xi, 13, 15–19, 48, 50, 80, 86, 93, 102, 113, chap. 6, *passim*, 155, 182, 187–8, 191, 193, 196, 199, 210–11, 215, 224, 251 (n.2), 258, 264 (n.17), 281
invariantism, 110
   interest-relative, 109–10, 114
   See also contextualism

Japanese, chap. 2, *passim*, 56–60, 62–4, chap. 5, *passim*, 130–1, 145, 182, 230 (n.6), 267, 270
justification, 15, 20, 68–9, 115 (n.44), 123, 127, 129, 133, chap. 7, *passim*, 276, 282
   justified, 224–5, 273
   justified false belief, 128–31, 133–5, 142–5
   justified true belief (JTB), 123, 182, 215, 224, 257, 280

Knobe, Joshua, 124, 189, 280
"know" (as an English term), manifesto, *passim*, 24–7, 32–4, 56, 59–60, 63, 79, 87, 95, 99, 106, 110–18, 129, 131, 205, 230, 251–5, 258–60, 264, 267, 269, 273–4, 277, 282, 284
know, knowing, knowledge
   analysis of, xi, 69, 110, 114, 116 (n.45), 117
   concept of knowledge (*see* concept)
   core knowledge concept (*see* concept)
   extended, 74
   how (*see* knowledge how)
   knowledge that (*see* propositional knowledge)
   practical, 268–72
   propositional, 62–3, 78–80, 87–8, 109, 119, 231, 247, 267, 271
   species-typical knowledge concept (*see* concept)
   universal concept of knowledge (*see* concept)

"know how," "knowing how" (as an English expression), 241–2, 270
knowledge how, 59, 88, 80, 92, 109, 234, 241–2, 244, 269, chap. 11, *passim*. *See also* intellectualism vs. anti-intellectualism
Kornblith, Hilary, viii, 70–2, 263
Kvanvig, Jonathan L., 70, 87, 89, 95, 106, 112, 118, 260 (n.12)

Leibniz, G. W., 216–19
lexical semantics. *See* semantics
linguistic turn, viii
   new (*see* epistemology)
linguistics, xiv, 81, 251

Machery, Edouard, 95 (n.26), 123–4, 131, 144, 182–3, 188, 199, 204 (n.9), 211, 215, 220, 223–5, 256 (n.8), 280, 282, 286
Malcolm, Norman, viii, 205
Mandarin, 197, 201, 204, 207, 269 (n.2), 270. *See also* Chinese
metaphysics, metaphysical, xiii, 83, 262, 268, 277, 279
method of cases, 124, 140–3

Nagel, Jennifer, 97 (n.28), 98, 123, 129, 182, 187, 188, 190, 191, 197, 205, 211, 251 (n.2), 281
natural semantic metalanguage, xi, 80 (n.7), 113 (n.43), 219, chap. 9, *passim*
Nivacle, 151, 156–9, 163, 181
Nɬeʔkepmxcín, 151, 154
normative, normativity, vii, 114, 210, 259, 273
   concept, 14, 259
NSM. *See* natural semantic metalanguage

order effect, 197 (n.5), chap. 6, *passim*
ordinary language, viii, 223, 251, 253, 262, 263–4, 280
ordinary language philosophy, 279

person restriction, 2, 28, 34–9. *See also* first-person
Polish, 221, 241

translatability, 223, 255–8, 282
true/truth, 13–14, 15, 18–19, 25, 32, 46,
    49, 51–3, 74, 133, 137, 142, chap. 7,
    passim, 225, 226, 243, 252–3,
    256–7, 260 (n.11), 271, 276,
    282, 285
  conceptual (*see* concept)
  truth-condition, 15, 256–7, 85–6, 91,
    113 (n.43)
  truth-conditional content, x
  truth-conductive, chap. 7, *passim*, 276
  truth detection, truth
    retention, 284–6
  truth-hitting, 14–15, 19
Truetemp case, 96–7, 100–12, 124
Turri, John, 13, 94 (n.23), 109–10, 114–15,
    117 (n.46, n.48), 123, 193 (n.3)

"understand," "understanding" (as an
    English term), 77 (n.1), 78–9, 95,
    106, 112, 118
universal (core, folk) epistemology. *See*
    epistemology

universal frame, 228–30, 244
universality thesis, manifesto, *passim*,
    20, chap. 11, *passim*. *See also*
    epistemic universalism

verb
  punctual verb, 59, 62, 63 (n.6), 79
  stative verb, 32, 34, 36, 59–62, 79, 85
verum, 164–81
  emphasis, 150, 165–8, 171, 173–80
  focus, 149–50, 169, 177
  operator, 164–6, 173
virtue, 15, chap. 4, *passim*, 109, 259,
    260, 262
  intellectual, 262
virtue epistemology. *See* epistemology
virtue ethics, 261

Warlpiri, 222, 229, 234
Wierzbicka, Anna, vii, xi–xii, chap.
    9, *passim*
Williamson, Timothy, vii, 2, 16, 92, 107,
    124, 188, 205, 268